GREEK AND ROMAN RELIGIONS

Blackwell Ancient Religions

Ancient religious practice and belief are at once fascinating and alien for twenty-first century readers. There was no Bible, no creed, and no fixed set of beliefs. Rather, ancient religion was characterized by extraordinary diversity in belief and ritual.

This distance means that modern readers need a guide to ancient religious experience. Written by experts, the books in this series provide accessible introductions to this central aspect of the ancient world.

Published

Ancient Greek Divination
Sarah Iles Johnston

Magic in the Ancient Greek World
Derek Collins

Religion in the Roman Empire
James B. Rives

Ancient Greek Religion, Second Edition
Jon D. Mikalson

Ancient Egyptian Tombs: The Culture of Life and Death
Steven Snape

Exploring Religion in Ancient Egypt
Stephen Quirke

Greek and Roman Religions
Rebecca I. Denova

Forthcoming

Religion of the Roman Republic
Lora Holland

GREEK AND ROMAN RELIGIONS

Rebecca I. Denova

WILEY Blackwell

This edition first published 2019
© 2019 John Wiley & Sons, Inc.

Registered Office(s)
John Wiley & Sons, Inc., 111 River Street, Hoboken, NJ 07030, USA

Editorial Office
101 Station Landing, Medford, MA 02155, USA

For details of our global editorial offices, customer services, and more information about Wiley products visit us at www.wiley.com.

Wiley also publishes its books in a variety of electronic formats and by print-on-demand. Some content that appears in standard print versions of this book may not be available in other formats.

Library of Congress Cataloging-in-Publication Data

Name: Denova, Rebecca I., author.
Title: Greek and Roman religions / Rebecca I. Denova.
Description: Hoboken, NJ : John Wiley & Sons, 2019. | Series: Blackwell ancient religions | Includes index. |
Identifiers: LCCN 2018025169 (print) | LCCN 2018038135 (ebook) |
  ISBN 9781118542774 (Adobe PDF) | ISBN 9781118543009 (ePub) |
  ISBN 9781118542903 (hardcover) | ISBN 9781118542958 (pbk.)
Subjects: LCSH: Greece–Religion. | Rome–Religion.
Classification: LCC BL723 (ebook) | LCC BL723 .D46 2018 (print) | DDC 292–dc23
LC record available at https://lccn.loc.gov/2018025169

Cover Design: Wiley
Cover Image: (front) © Lebrecht Music and Arts Photo Library/Alamy Stock Photo; (back) © OnstOn/iStockphoto

Set in 10.5/13pt Minion Pro by SPi Global, Pondicherry, India

10 9 8 7 6 5 4 3 2 1

For their patience: Jim, Rachael, PJ, Madi, Jack and Wyatt.

CONTENTS

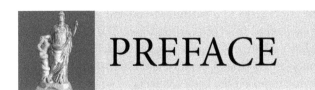

PREFACE

Standard history books on Greece and Rome often reduce religion to one or two chapters. In the ancient world, religion as a separate, conceptual category did not exist. The term was first articulated in the seventeenth century to describe systematic theology. In the ancient world, religion was not just something that involved temples and sacrifices. Religious views were integrated into all of life and helped to create ethnic identities. It was the very heart of understanding oneself as a person of status and worth, and one's place in relation to the past (the ancestral customs), to the family, the city-state, and the Empire. Ancient culture and religion were synonymous.

The Academic Discipline of Religious Studies

A relatively recent addition to the academy (within the last 70 years), Religious Studies utilizes all of the liberal arts and social science approaches to the study of human history and society. Rather than a value judgment of correct religious values or worldviews, Religious Studies scholars focus on the origins of religious authority (institutions), beliefs, rituals, sacred texts, and ethics. These phenomena have influenced human relationships, social structures, and governing powers in a given society. The emphasis is on the way in which religious worldviews *function* in society and help to provide meaning to human existence. This textbook utilizes a multidisciplinary approach in Religious Studies to the religions of Greece and Rome.

Features of this Textbook

Chapter I emphasizes the presence of divinity in all aspects of ancient life. Modern preconceptions, however, often create obstacles to understanding this integration of religion and culture. It is important to address the problem of anachronism, the bane of all historians because we are human. The use (and misuse) of descriptors such as "cult," "pagan," and the modern polarity of polytheism versus monotheism remain challenges in the construction of ancient societies.

Greece and Rome did not emerge in a vacuum; trade and war meant that cultural traditions were exchanged from the earliest times. The second half of this chapter outlines the basic features of ancient religion shared by everyone in the region, such as sacrifice, ritual, priests, prayers, and divination. This eliminates the necessity of having to repeat the basic elements as we proceed. Many terms are in bold type and are defined in the Glossary.

Chapter II provides a brief outline of the civilizations of the neighboring regions. Although we cannot always directly trace the influence of these cultures on Greco-Roman customs, both of these later societies absorbed some of the shared elements. The evolution of religious worldviews went hand in hand with remembered history. Brief histories of Greece and Rome are presented as background material. Rather than simply a standard timeline of events, I have emphasized those events that became incorporated into the ethos and religious cultures of Greece and Rome.

Chapter III begins with an explanation of the nature and function of myth in the ancient world. I have provided the basic stories of the Greek pantheon as well as a few other divinities and heroes who were also popular. Chapter IV, outlines the Roman equivalents, including Italian deities.

Chapter V highlights the temple structures and specific duties of priests and priestesses. Beginning in this chapter, the rest of the book follows a similar pattern by presenting the Greek materials first and then the Roman aspects of the same elements. This does not necessarily indicate that Greek ideas are older or prior to Roman (and Italian) concepts, but rather the fact that we have a plethora of evidence of the Roman borrowing of Greek culture.

Chapter VI follows the order of the gods presented in each pantheon and outlines the details of the calendar of religious festivals. This chapter emphasizes the communal nature and function of these rituals in ancient society. The festivals were crucial to the agricultural cycles as well as celebrating foundational myths and appealing to the protection of the gods.

Chapter VII focuses on the elements that constituted Greco-Roman culture, such as economic class, honor/shame, patron/client, and slavery. The family was the basic social unit in antiquity. This chapter highlights the religious roles of each member of the family in Greece and Rome.

Chapter VIII details the various ways in which Greeks and Romans sought to determine the will of the gods. It was important that individual, communal, and government actions be validated through divine approval. This chapter details the various methods utilized by the ancients to determine the correct balance between human activity and the gods.

The Mystery cults require a separate chapter to demonstrate the elements these cults added to the regular forms of worship. Chapter IX presents the background and evolution of the more popular Mysteries, followed by what is known of their ritual aspects.

All ancient cultures had concepts of what happens after death. Chapter X presents the evolution of these ideas and their relation to concepts of ultimate justice. The importance of funeral rites is presented in detail. Much of our evidence of Greco-Roman views on the afterlife is found in funerary inscriptions; this chapter highlights the function of the epitaphs with some examples. Students will discover that concepts of the afterlife and funeral rituals are among the most conservative elements to have survived from the ancient world.

In addition to archaeological artifacts and inscriptions, we have a font of ideas on religion from the various schools of philosophy in the ancient world. Chapter XI describes the worldview of many of these schools and includes some critiques of popular religion. The modern world considers laws and law codes as "civic" or "secular." Chapter XII demonstrates that constitutions and governance in antiquity were consistently understood to be revealed by the gods, for the communal good.

While the contributions of Greece and Rome in art, architecture, drama, philosophy, and politics are extolled in modern times, there is little analysis of the influence of Greco-Roman religious concepts on the emergence of Christianity and Western worldviews. Chapter XIII highlights the elements of ancient religions that remain important in our contemporary quest for meaning.

Boxes

An important element of Religious Studies methodology is the attempt to teach our students how to read and think critically. Religion reflects human experience. The evaluation of various artifacts of historical evidence in its own context is vital to reconstructing that experience – context explains content. Citing one of my favorite historians, Mary Beard:

> the study of ancient history is as much about *how* we know as *what* we know …
> an engagement with all the processes of selection, constructive blindness, revolutionary reinterpretation, and willful misinterpretation that together produce the "facts" … out of the messy, confusing, and contradictory evidence that survives.[1]

To that end, I have included boxes, some of which contain more detail on an ancient aspect, and some that address how we analyze ancient materials to reconstruct religious beliefs. How do scholars go about the business of piecing together the combination of archaeological remains, myth, epic poetry, literature, drama, art and architecture, poetry, and philosophical treatise?

Each chapter is followed by "Suggestions for Further Reading," with both traditional studies and more recent examinations of topical issues.

Using this Textbook

When I first created a course on Greco-Roman popular religion in our Department of Religious Studies at the University of Pittsburgh, I encountered several obstacles. Although it was an upper-division, undergraduate elective that was cross-listed with Classics, most of my students had very little background in ancient history and culture ("Western Civilization" courses are no longer required). Of necessity, most of the lectures were dedicated to supplying this background before I could get to the purpose of each unit. Secondly, students were required to buy two sets of textbooks; textbooks that provided both cultures did not exist. Third, most of the available textbooks are written by Classicists who automatically assume a certain level of knowledge, consistently referencing history and historical characters, myths, drama, and philosophical treatises without explanation. And fourth, there were very few books from the viewpoint of the discipline of Religious Studies. This textbook attempts to provide solutions to these problems in similar courses on Greco-Roman religions, history, and culture. At the same time, one combined text will help to reduce costs to the students.

For professors who teach courses on the combined Greco-Roman religions, this text can essentially serve as an outline for the syllabus. It provides an overview of ancient culture and history of the general region as well as the basic background of Greek and Roman civilizations. Many features of ancient religions and cultural elements are included in a Glossary. One of the evaluation methods that I use in the course is an assigned research paper on a particular god or goddess which traces the ancient cult from Greece to Rome through comparative analysis. This method provides students with an opportunity to understand both the similarities and the differences of these two cultures. This textbook is structured so that they can easily identify similarities and differences.

For professors who teach the ancient civilizations of Greece and Rome from a historical point of view, this textbook can serve as a supplementary resource that can provide more detailed information on the importance of religion in the life of Greeks and Romans.

Note

1. Mary Beard as cited in Jane Kramer, "The Petition: Israel, Palestine, and a tenure battle at Barnard," *New Yorker*, April 2008, 50.

LIVING WITH THE DIVINE

Greek and Roman Religions, First Edition. Rebecca I. Denova.
© 2019 John Wiley & Sons, Inc. Published 2019 by John Wiley & Sons, Inc.

Learning Objectives

After reading this chapter, you will be able to:

- Appreciate the differences between the modern field of Religious Studies and traditional methods of studying religion.
- Recognize the central role of the divine in all aspects of life in the ancient world.
- Distinguish the basic elements of religious practice shared by ancient Greece and Rome. (Terms in bold type are also described in the Glossary.)

 The ancient civilizations of Greece and Rome have had a lasting influence on Western culture. Artists and dramatists celebrated their stories in their triumphs and tragedies and architects still imitate their building designs. Greek and Roman literature (both mythology and philosophy) provided models for understanding human nature, the human psyche, and reflections on our existence. From these two cultures we inherited our alphabet, democracy, juries, tragedy, comedy, the Olympic Games, epic poetry, law codes, philosophy, the gymnasium, the republican form of government, the veto, our modern calendar, the names of our planets, a welfare system, funeral rites, the keystone arch, aqueducts, amphitheaters, stadiums, road construction, cement, apartment buildings, and last but not least, take-out fast-food.

Studying patterns of human development and behavior in the past can illuminate similar challenges as we continue to evolve. The way in which Greeks and Romans faced economic crises, natural and human-made disasters, and the never-ending challenge of war and conquest can teach us much about our own responses to similar problems. The history of ideas is equally important. The Founding Fathers did not just wake up one morning and invent a new form of governance and a new culture. Inheritors of European models, these men were well schooled in works of Greek and Roman thought and they attempted to utilize the structures of ancient Greece and Rome to create a new government and society.

While applauding this great contribution to the Western tradition from the perspective of our scientific and secular world, we often fail to recognize that many of these achievements were done within the context of a religious worldview. In the modern world, we define ourselves and our culture through categories such as nationality, political affiliation, and religious affiliation. For example, you might say that you are a citizen of the United States, a Democrat, and a Catholic. We also tend to separate secular from sacred. In the ancient world, the category of religion as a separate entity did not exist. In fact, there was no word for religion in most ancient cultures. Religion was the way humans lived each day and bound themselves to the powers in the universe; it was the glue that held culture and society together.

How did these ancient people understand their world? How did they cope with the overwhelming mysteries of life and death? The cycles of nature and the seasons provided constancy, yet, without warning, crops failed, diseases invaded the body, storms brought destruction, earthquakes toppled cities, and empires succumbed to foreign armies. At the same time, children were born, couples married, harvests were gathered, people were elected to high office, and armies won great victories. We cannot determine the precise time, but at some point people began to believe that unseen powers were responsible for everything, both good and bad. Because of this understanding, humans thought of their surroundings as existing on two planes: the physical world of everyday life, and the supernatural world of the divine. The divine was unknown and dangerous, and thus had to be separated from mundane things. In modern academic parlance, we refer to these two planes as "the sacred" and the "profane." Although separate, the two planes continually interacted.

This textbook is a survey of the way in which ancient Greece and Rome managed the relationship between the sacred and the profane, and the ways in which their religious views interacted with everyday life. Our framework will survey these cultures from 800 BCE to 400 CE. In general, each chapter will discuss the religious concepts and practices of ancient Greece, followed by those of Rome. This is not a claim that the religious traditions of Greece are chronologically older than Rome, but recognizes that Rome borrowed ideas from Greece and it will avoid having to repeat similar ideas and practices when we discuss Rome.

The study of any religious system can be interesting and rewarding, but the religious views of Greece and Rome offer a special fascination of extremes: from the epic heights of glory in battle to the lowly god of a cupboard, from philosophical meditation on the universe, to the practical negotiations for a throw of the dice. The divine realm was *always* present to people in the ancient world. It was active in people's dreams and present in all their daily activities, from plowing a field to leading an army to victory (or defeat). While we will often find common cause with ancient cultures, discovering many elements that we share as human beings, their literal belief in this multiple divine presence and interaction is one of the great differences between the modern world and the ancient one.

The Modern Study of Religion

For centuries in the Western tradition, the study of religion was largely the purview of theologians. Theology, the study of god, is actually the study of the nature of god, and the way in which humans can relate to an established system. Theologians are committed to participation in this relationship; it is an "insider's" point of view, or what we call "faith." The Enlightenment (seventeenth to eighteenth centuries) launched a new direction in the study of religion, recognizing that humans construct religious concepts, based upon their experiences. The study of religion became an important element in the emerging social sciences that considered human experience as a whole. In other words, religion was not external to human beings but something they created in order to find meaning in their existence.

The next step in a new approach to the study of religion was a revolution in the study of sacred scriptures, beginning with the Bible. No longer willing to accept the divine inspiration behind these stories, scholars joined with the new sciences of archaeology, anthropology, and sociology to begin to investigate the historical societies that produced these sacred texts. Sacred texts and literature could now be studied as evidence of the way in which ancient people understood their cultures.

In the twentieth century, the field of Religious Studies became a separate discipline, devoted to analyzing the way in which humans construct and articulate religious views, without judgment as to the truth of the claims of such views. Often simply referred to as "the academic study of religion," Religious Studies examines religious experience from a multidisciplinary approach, utilizing the disciplines in the liberal arts and social sciences: classics, history, literature, anthropology, archaeology, sociology, philosophy, and psychology. In addition to these fields, the study of religion employs analysis in economics, politics, ethnic studies, ritual, gender studies, the arts, global studies, and cross-cultural approaches. The goal of Religious Studies is to understand religious systems in their historical, social, and cultural contexts, recognizing that changes in context contribute to changes in human understanding in any given age.

All religions, including ancient ones, have formal features that are categorized as conceptual, social, and performative. The conceptual contains a set of beliefs that help to create a worldview. Worldview in this sense indicates the way in which humans conceive their relationship to each other and the universe, how the universe operates, and why things are the way they are. For example, two main functions of ancient **myth** were to demonstrate the origins of the gods, the origins of humans, and to establish the context of the duties and responsibilities of both in a partnership that would keep the universe in a harmonious balance.

Religious beliefs operate within communities with distinctive patterns of social relationships. The hierarchy among the gods and their distinctive functions reflect the hierarchy and functions of distinct social roles in society. Such beliefs validate the social order and establish the rules for social behavior.

All religions are performative in that participants *do* things; they act in specialized manners to make the sacred manifest. Ritual acts are a fundamental means of communication between humans and the divine. At the same time, ritual acts help to establish a sense of communal bonding that transcends personal involvement and concerns. Thus the modern study of religion is the study of human society in all its aspects, and this is the approach that is utilized in this text.

While not separating religion from everyday life, the ancients also did not have a word that we often render "religion." The modern term, which came into use in the seventeenth century, most likely took its meaning from the Latin root, *religio*, sometimes translated as "scrupulous observance of the cult," or those things "that tie or bind one to the gods." Nevertheless, I will apply the term "religion" to the ancient practices and beliefs as a convenient means to generalize the focus of this study.

Culture and Race

Other terms of convenience, culture and race, are also often applied to the study of ancient societies. It is important to distinguish these concepts as understood in the modern world, from their counterparts in antiquity.

In the ancient world, large nation-states based on the modern model did not exist. No one in the ancient world identified themselves by nationality in the manner one might today. People did not say "I am from Greece." Instead, people identified with a hometown, a village, or a city ("I am from Athens"). When they said, "I am Greek," or "I am Roman," they were often referring to a cultural, ethnic identity that could transcend a geographic area.

People were categorized according to a shared common ancestry, history, homeland, language, rituals, and mythology. According to Herodotus (c. 484–425 BCE), these were the traits that made someone Greek, or not. In modern nations, ethnic groups, or ethnic minorities, are those that differ from the dominant culture in some way, such as language or cultural traits. Minorities in the modern sense sometimes include the concept of race, or racial categories based on physical differences. The modern concept of racial distinction (and racial prejudice) as we understand it did not exist before the fifteenth century. Many Greeks and Romans attributed differences in skin color to climate and geography, as well as to social class (if you were darker, it might indicate that you worked in the fields out in the sun). Cultural traits created the barriers between people, not physical characteristics.

There was certainly cultural prejudice in the ancient world. For the Greeks, most other people were barbarians (particularly in the Hellenistic period) and Romans used the pejorative term "un-Roman" for everyone else. However, both Greece and Rome allowed for changes in ethnic status: once you were granted citizenship, you were "one of us." Or, at least this was the theory. Then as now, your enemies had long memories and could always recall your roots when it was politically useful. For many Romans, some cultural roots would always remain. Even if Gauls (living in what is modern France) succeeded in obtaining a seat in the Senate, Romans thought they would never learn to appreciate wine or good food!

Cults

In the modern world the term **cult**, which typically carries a negative connotation, refers to a religious group whose beliefs are radically different from the mainstream. Groups we call cults have been behind some of the more horrific headlines in America, such as the Charles Manson family (1969), the Branch Davidians at Waco, Texas (1993), and the Heaven's Gate mass suicide (1997).

The word cult was originally derived from *cultus*, with a general meaning of worship, from the Latin, *colere*, care, or cultivate. So *cultus* included everything involved in the proper care and worship of the gods: the temple or shrine, the incense shovels and burners, trumpets, wands, knives, bowls, prayers, hymns, sacrifices, and everything needed for the cleaning up process. Rather than the modern understanding of cult in relation to theological or spiritual differences, we will use the term **traditional cults** when we refer to the worship of the divinities in the ancient world.

Too Many Gods?

Historians of early Christianity have traditionally attempted to explain the various factors that contributed to the rapid rise of Christianity in the Roman Empire. A popular theory is that the sheer number of gods and goddesses populating the Mediterranean basin created anxiety: too many gods, too many myths, too many empty rituals that caused fear and anxiety in the average person. According to this consensus, insecure people could find solace in Christian monotheism and the promise of eventual salvation. Numbers do not necessarily cause anxiety. As an example, consider Hinduism. The number of Hindu deities may be as high as three million, but individual Hindus do not have to memorize all of them. Most Hindus select one or two as the object of their devotion, while also recognizing and respecting the many powers in the universe.

The large numbers of ancient divinities are a problem for *us* because we deem such a system irrational. Ancient people found nothing irrational about their system – it was just the way things were. We do find evidence of *emotional* anxiety everywhere in the ancient record. Then as now, death, disease, famine, disasters, and war heightened religious responses. However, this type of anxiety could be relieved by appealing to the gods in a variety of ways at many different sacred places. Rather than feeling confused or helpless in light of this diversity, ancient people may have found reassurance in the number of religious options available.

Polytheism and Monotheism

The modern term for belief systems that include multiple powers is **polytheism** (the belief in multiple deities), or sometimes pantheism (the belief in all powers). Polytheistic systems are often explained by contrast with **monotheism**, or the belief in the existence of a single god. Polytheism and monotheism are polarities, with many variations in-between. Scholars also use the term "henotheism" to indicate the belief in many powers, but elevating one deity to a higher position over the others. Another term, "monolatry," is the recognition of the existence of other gods but choosing to worship only one.

In the Western tradition, monotheism means not only the concept of the existence of a singular god, but specifically refers to the God of the Bible – the God of Judaism, Christianity, and Islam (always written with a capital "G"). This understanding became the standard way to compare the ancient world to the modern in terms of religious evolution; some moderns still assume that humanity developed progressively from primitive (polytheistic) to modern (monotheistic), with the God of the Bible. However, the term is used incorrectly when it refers to the ancient world, where our modern concept of monotheism did not exist. All ancient people were polytheists in the sense that they acknowledged the existence of other gods (powers), even if they proclaimed the superiority of one god over all the others.

The Jewish Scriptures demonstrate that the god of Israel acknowledged the existence of the gods of other nations. Ancient Jews conceived of hierarchies of powers in Heaven, including "sons of god" (Genesis 6), angels and archangels, cherubim, and seraphim. Late in their history they designated another power to compete with God who eventually became the Devil. Early Christians accepted these levels of powers in Heaven (and Hell), and the apostle Paul often referred to the existence of the gods of other nations in his letters. It was much later in the development of Jewish and Christian monotheism that this term came to mean the existence of only one god. What made Jews and Christians unique in the *ancient* world was their refusal to participate in the *worship* of these other gods, but they did not deny their existence. Thus, ancient Jews fit into the context of a pluralistic worldview, but differed in their exclusive worship of one god.

Toleration and Religious Pluralism

A popular way to describe religion in the Roman Empire is the claim that Rome practiced toleration of religion, a concept associated with that of **religio licta**, or the granting of legality to religious beliefs. Toleration is a misnomer because it assumes an official policy. There was *no official policy of toleration* issued by Rome, either during the Republic or the early Empire. (This would change in the latter part of the third and early fourth century, when Christianity was granted an "edict of toleration.") Both Greece and Rome simply followed the same tradition as everyone else from time immemorial – *all* the gods of different ethnic groups were acknowledged and respected. This included the gods of your enemy as well. Romans practiced **evocatio**, where gods of the enemy were invited to switch sides before a battle; Rome promised temples and worship if they did so.

While there were no official, government policies of toleration, that does not mean that we have an ancient equivalent of "freedom of religion." People could not freely and openly disrespect the gods. Particularly in ancient Greece, **impiety** (not showing respect for the gods) and **sacrilege** (damage or interference with a sacred object, sites, or rituals) carried death sentences. Such actions threatened the prosperity of everyone. One of the most famous cases in ancient Athens was the trial and conviction of the philosopher Socrates (469–399 BCE), who was charged with impiety by corrupting the youth of Athens through his teachings. Other philosophers were known to express their opinions about disbelief in the traditional gods, such as Xenophanes (sixth century BCE), who mocked the idea that the gods looked like us, but there was a very limited audience for such writing, unless the views were expressed publicly. For the most part, the average person who did not believe in the gods (an atheist) did not advertise these thoughts.

Ancient Greeks and Romans accepted religious pluralism as a fact of life, based upon tradition, and that is probably the more accurate way to describe their attitude. While this plurality was acknowledged, there were also boundaries that could not be crossed. Another term that is used for convenience when we analyze religion in the ancient world is conversion. Conversion means moving from one religious system to another. This assumes the existence of formal, codified systems of belief, which were absent in antiquity. For the most part, religion was *ethnic* – you were born into it, so it would be difficult to reject or change physical lineage. Greeks and Romans could move in and out of traditional cults without any process of conversion in the way we understand it. The closest we have to the modern concept would be found in those who joined the followers of Pythagoras or Orpheus, which required lifestyle changes. Similarly, those who left traditional cults to follow Judaism or Christianity could be said to convert in the modern sense. Recruiting people for either of those systems was highly frowned upon until the fourth century, as those systems required a denial of one's ancestral traditions, a cessation of participation in their traditional cults, and the abandoning of the very elements of one's identity.

Paganism

There were hundreds of traditional cults and religious associations in the Mediterranean basin, but there is no simple word that can represent all of them. **Pagan** became the generic term for anyone who was not Christian or Jewish, and originated around the fourth century. It derives from the Latin *paganus*, which means either rustic (not a city dweller) or civilian (and never enrolled in the army). Rustic was a term for people who lived outside of the urban centers; Christians used it as a derogatory term equivalent to "hillbillies," for those who resisted conversion. The term pagan was also associated with traditional cults that focused on nature and fertility, and became an umbrella term for anyone who refused the new faith. Later, in medieval Europe, the term was applied to people who continued to practice aspects of Celtic and Teutonic traditional cults in the same way.

In the second century a group of Christian bishops wrote treatises against the religious beliefs of non-Christians and demonized those beliefs. They claimed that the gods who resided in pagan temples were actually agents of the Devil. In their polemic against the traditional cults, they included standard charges of sexual immorality (like modern political campaigns that go viral when there is a hint of sexual scandal). The church leaders turned to the Jewish Scriptures for their ammunition against pagans, and found it in a host of sexual metaphors against the ancient Canaanites. Canaanite religion was based on fertility and the Israelites claimed that sexual immorality was at the root of this **idolatry** (worship of idols, or images). They charged that Israelite participation in such sins brought disasters to the nation.

Similarly, for early Christians, paganism became associated with sexual immorality, and the term "orgy" was interpreted as sexual excess. The Greek word *orgia* simply meant "religious ritual," but it became a popular description of some of the more ecstatic rituals of traditional and Mystery cults which required an initiation. The ancients did have a different attitude toward the body from ours and we can still be shocked by their sexual openness, although this attitude is greatly exaggerated. Hollywood has contributed to the view of ancient Greeks and Romans as sexually promiscuous. For many people, pagans remain associated with unbridled sex, drinking, violence, and every form of perversion. A more recent example of this can be found in the cable TV series *Spartacus*. For others, the term pagan also conjures up images of Satanists, or worshippers of the Devil.

There were so many traditional cults and religious associations that contained innumerable differences so a one-word description does not suffice. The other complication is that ancient peoples had the freedom to belong to several different cults at the same time. So we are stuck with the word, and until we can invent another generic term – pagan is simply easier. Throughout this text, I will attempt to avoid the term when I can, using traditional cults as a more general term. Ironically, the Western Christian tradition adopted many of the elements of pagan religious culture, as we will see in Chapter XIII.

Basic Features of Greco-Roman Religions

This section outlines the shared concepts and vocabulary in Greek and Roman religion that will be highlighted in detail throughout the following chapters. For the sources of this shared material, see the boxes "How Do We Know What Ancient Greeks and Romans Believed?" and "How Do We Know About Religion in Ancient Greece and Rome?"

Religion in the ancient world consisted of the belief in something beyond oneself, belief in the powers of nature and the unseen powers that controlled one's destiny. Modern scholars describe this as a belief in "the sacred," "the holy," or "the other," emphasizing the concept of transcendence, or something beyond the individual that is nevertheless manifest in everyday experience. For the ancients, the collective concept for that "something" was simply the divine.

The divine consisted of elements of nature personified as gods and goddesses: the sea, the winds, the earth, the sky, the sun, the moon, and the planets, as well as supernatural beings such as a **daemon**, spirit, **numen**, or the Fates. There were deities for occupations, disease, fertility and puberty rites, marriage (and the honeymoon), sailors (and pirates), war, peace, death, and the afterlife. Supernatural powers could be called upon to produce and watch over your children, keep snakes out of the house, bless the farm equipment, topple your political rivals, defeat the enemy, and take revenge against your heirs. To people in the ancient world, the divine was manifest everywhere and in everything: the person, the home, the farm, the city, the social classes, the crafts, the military, and whatever form of government was currently in charge.

The divine meant "godlike," or containing powers that were different from those of human beings. While we associate the divine with beauty or goodness, in the ancient world, the divine was a category of *all* powers that transcended humanity, including the monstrous or evil ones. There were powers of the underworld that could be summoned when necessary. The term we use for these specific divinities is **chthonic** (Greek, *chthonios*), meaning "beneath the earth." The line between the heavens and the underworld was not always defined in absolute terms. The living called upon all types of divinities.

Another element of the divine was the personification of abstractions such as peace, fear, night, sleep, death, fidelity, or virtue. We find these supernatural figures as fully functioning characters in epic poetry and art works. We can only determine if these abstractions were worshipped in the usual sense when we have archaeological or inscriptional evidence. For instance, we can confirm poetic references as well as shrines and altars to Youth, and Rome had an altar to Peace (*Ara pacis Augustae*, Augustan Altar of Peace).

Myths and Sacred Stories

All cultures in the Mediterranean basin created stories to explain the origins of both the gods and humans, or what are known generally as creation myths. Many of these myths also functioned as etiologies, or explanations of why things occur the way they do, or why a culture evolved the way it did. In this sense, a mythical etiology explains not just the remote past, but *contemporary* society. Etiologies answer questions such as: "Why are men treated as superior to women?" or "Why do we sacrifice to the gods?"

In modern usage, myth implies something that is not true. However, myth by its very nature is not subject to verification, and the ancients were not concerned about whether their stories were true or false or whether different and competing mythologies contradicted one another. There were several different myths about a particular god or goddess, arising from several different areas, but as far as we know, this did not create anxiety. Nor did most people worry about the incredible elements of these stories, any more than fans of vampire literature today are concerned that these stories describe things that are improbable.

There are multivalent meanings behind sacred stories within individual contexts of each culture, but some of the more important myths were celebrated as foundation myths, related to the founding of a city or town or a genealogy of famous ancestors. In Athens, the great Panathenaea festival in honor of Athena drew people from near and far, and celebrated Athena's gifts to the city as well as her protection. Rome had two dominant foundation myths, that of Romulus and Remus (who created the city of Rome), and the story of Aeneas, the son of Venus, who had escaped the fall of Troy and connected Roman traditions to the larger cultural and religious elements of Greek tradition (see the box "How Do We Know What Ancient Greeks and Romans Believed? Epic Poetry, Drama, History, and Philosophy").

How Do We Know What Ancient Greeks and Romans Believed? Epic Poetry, Drama, History, and Philosophy

The literary heritage of ancient Greece and Rome is quite extensive. The works of Homer (*The Iliad* and *The Odyssey*) and Hesiod (*Theogony* and *Works and Days*) provide detailed descriptions of religious practice as well as cosmology and genealogies of the gods. The Homeric Hymns were composed by anonymous bards to celebrate individual deities. The lyric poetry of Pindar (522–443 BCE) and others describes the gods as being above the moral judgment of humans. The Roman poet Horace (65–8 BCE) speculated on moral philosophy, Ovid (43 BCE to 18 CE) described religious beliefs and festivals of Rome (*Metamorphoses*, *Fasti*), and Vergil (70–19 BCE) created an epic poem of the founding of Rome by Aeneas, *The Aeneid*.

The literary world of drama sheds light on religious views, some serious, some comic. The first plays in Athens most likely arose from the Dionysus festivals in that city, which evolved into contests for the best plays. The tragedies of the three best known playwrights, Aeschylus (525–455 BCE), Sophocles (497–406 BCE), and Euripides (480–406 BCE) often dealt with the relations between humans and gods, while the comedies of Aristophanes (446–386 BCE), such as *The Clouds*, served as critiques of both religion and the political life of Athens. Very little of Roman tragedy has survived, but we have the comedies of Plautus (254–184 BCE), which presented stock characters of both gods and men.

Many ancient historians described religious or cultural practices. For Greece we have Herodotus, Thucydides (460–395 BCE), and Xenophon (430–354 BCE), and for Rome, Polybius (200–118 BCE), Strabo (63 BCE to 24 CE), Livy (59 BCE to 17 CE), and Dionysius of Halicarnassus (60–7 BCE). The study of philosophy began in the seventh century BCE in Miletus (modern Turkey), but by the fifth century BCE, many schools of philosophy were centered in Athens. Philosophy focused on reason as the way in which to understand both the cosmos and the nature of humans, but shared affinities with religious beliefs in that each school taught a way of life. Philosophers criticized and reinterpreted traditional religious beliefs, while simultaneously offering their own moral and spiritual understanding. Most philosophers in Rome were disciples of the Greek classical schools, particularly the Platonists, Stoics, and the Epicureans.

The divinities of a people are collectively known as pantheons, or the collection of officially recognized gods and goddesses. The traditional listing of the Greek and Roman pantheons are limited to the more important deities, although a complete listing would include hundreds more. In Table I.1, you will find the major deities and their titles (which also indicate their spheres of influence). It is necessary to emphasize that the Romans did not simply borrow the Greek gods, but recognized similar functions and traits with their own divinities, combining these elements with their preexisting gods. For instance, they recognized the aspects of Aphrodite in their images and concepts of Venus which also included ancient Italian beliefs of this fertility goddess.

The term "sacred," derived from the Latin *sacrum* (Greek, *hieros*), is used in the same sense as "holy." It describes anything associated with the divine, including places, people, and objects. All ancient cultures designated areas of **sacred space** as powerful vectors for communicating with the divine. Sacred space is a place, building, or landscape that is either charged with meaning or used for ritual activity. Sacred space brought together the material, social, and spiritual worlds. Altars, temples, and temple complexes were sacred, as well as some monuments and tombs. Once an area was declared sacred, it was understood as being protected by a sacred zone, as a sanctuary. In Greece, sacred lands were set off by the erection of *temenos* walls – cut-out "barriers" – while sacred buildings had *peribolos* walls, which designated a sacred court. Indicating the separation between sacred and profane, these barriers limited access to all except priests and those who had business in the sacred space.

Greek name	Roman name	Title
Aphrodite	Venus	Goddess of Love/Beauty
Apollo	Apollo	God of Light, Music, Prophecy
Ares	Mars	God of War
Artemis	Diana	Goddess of the Hunt
Athena	Minerva	Goddess of Wisdom
Cronus	Saturn	Father of the Gods
Demeter	Ceres	Goddess of Grain/Crops
Dionysus	Bacchus	God of Fertility, Wine
Enyo	Bellona	Goddess of War
Eros	Cupid	God of Love
Hades	Pluto	God of Underworld
Hephaestus	Vulcan	God of Fire/Metal-working
Hera	Juno	Queen of the Gods
Hermes	Mercury	Messenger of the Gods
Pan	Pan	God of Woods and Pastures
Poseidon	Neptune	God of the Sea
Rhea	Ops	Goddess of Plenty
Zeus	Jupiter	King of Gods

Table I.1 The pantheons of Greece and Rome

In the countryside, sacred space could be found in groves of trees, caves, mountain-tops, lakes, rivers, springs, or any landscape that appeared exceptionally beautiful. We usually don't know what originally made these areas sacred, but a common explanation was that someone had encountered the divine at a particular spot. Collectively termed **hierophanies** or **epiphanies**, these encounters were literal manifestations of the divine through sight, voice, smell, or sound (like a clap of thunder), and were also experienced in dreams. Or, someone might have encountered a nymph, a divine power associated with caves and beautiful landscapes. Often, these sites were marked with a **votive offering**, or an offering made to a deity in acknowledgment of a prayer answered, a wish fulfilled, or a visitation from a god or goddess. The erection of an **altar** or shrine would indicate that a particular landscape was sacred, with an inscription to let other travelers know what happened at this spot.

The most common sacred space was a temple, a building used to house the god or goddess, or a symbolic representation of the divine. Temples consisted of colonnades and a *cella*, or a room (Greek, *naos*, which also means temple) to house the cult statue or image (Figures I.1 and I.2). In Greece, the *cella* was often in the middle of the building, and in Rome, the *cella* was at the rear. Temples also contained tables to hold offerings and braziers, or fireproof containers for burning incense. Most Greek temples were built upon a three-step platform, while Roman temples were higher, with steps leading up to a portico. With very few exceptions, temples were not crowded with worshippers. The inside was not forbidden, but most ritual activity and sacrifices took place outdoors, under an open sky where people gathered around the outdoor altar.

Within a town or city, sacred space was most commonly located in temples and shrines near the *agora* (Greek), or the forum (Roman). Temples and shrines close to these central meeting places facilitated the divine protection and

Figure I.1   Greek temple (Temple of Neptune, 460 BCE). *Source*: iStock/Getty Images Plus.

Figure I.2   Roman temple (Maison Carrée in Nîmes, France, one of the best-preserved Roman temples, an Augustan provincial temple of the Imperial cult). *Source*: elophotos/Adobe Stock.

supervision of the community in all its facets. Urban temples and shrines were numerous and offered opportunities for people to demonstrate their respect for the gods and their beneficial contributions to the community. Much of the city of Rome itself was deemed sacred territory within the **pomerium** (the plowed line for the original city drawn by Romulus). No weapons or burials were permitted within this zone, and magistrates holding **imperium** (sacred power for certain offices) could not exercise it within the sacred precincts of the city.

Another popular site for temples was an acropolis or a fortified higher section of a town with a citadel for defensive purposes. The acropolis in Athens and the one in Corinth were famous for their large temple complexes (for Athena in Athens and Aphrodite in Corinth), and the Temple of Jupiter on the Capitoline Hill in Rome was built on the older fortifications. Temples to the sea deities were crowded along the quays and seashores. Port cities contained temples and shrines from many different traditional cults, as a convenience for sailors and commercial travelers.

Temples contained cult images (from the Greek, *eikon*, or image), usually in the form of a full-length statue of a god or goddess. (See the box "How Do We Know About Religion in Ancient Greece and Rome? Archaeology, Architecture and Art.") **Icons** could be abstract but from an early date ancient people fashioned icons with anthropomorphic features, as replications of human beings. The gods looked like us, but with either beautiful, ideal features, or grotesque features depending upon the deity's function. Although we associate ancient sculpture with white marble, the statues of the gods and goddesses were painted with lifelike features, flesh tones, and brightly colored clothing. The symbols of their areas of responsibility were held in their hand, worn on their head, or placed near the base. Far more than just wood or stone representations, these sacred images were treated with respect as a bridge that could connect humans to the divine.

The earliest cult images of ancient Greece may have been carved wooden forms. Ancient artists also crafted terra-cotta, bronze, and ivory images, although most of the ones that have survived are the small votive statues at cult sites that may replicate cult images. By the Classical period, marble and bronze were the preferred materials, although many of the bronze examples have only survived in Roman marble copies. Chryselephantine sculptures were icons that used gold and ivory for the face, eyes, hands, and other accoutrements, with the two best known examples found in the statue of Zeus at Olympia and the statue of Athena in the Parthenon in Athens, both by Phidias. Such wealth and splendor devoted to a cult image reflected the high status of the community able to produce such a luxurious item. In addition to cult images, sculpted figures depicting mythic themes were carved on the pediment and frieze, the area on top of the columns of a temple.

Male gods could be depicted either with minimal clothing or completely nude. In Greece, this conformed to an appreciation for the male body, usually with sculpted muscles and always in the highest athletic state of fitness. For centuries, female deities were always clothed, which conformed to social conventions of women not showing their bodies outside of the home. There were several later anecdotes (and jokes) over the shock and scandal of the first nude depiction of Aphrodite created by the sculptor Praxiteles (c. fourth century BCE) for the citizens of Knidos, a work that also became quite a famous tourist attraction.

How Do We Know About Religion in Ancient Greece and Rome? Archaeology, Architecture and Art

How do scholars begin to reconstruct the religions of ancient Greece and Rome? The material elements of our knowledge of ancient religious life come from the archaeological remains of houses, temples, monuments, tombs, inscriptions, and art (including pottery).

Archaeological excavations of houses have uncovered areas dedicated to household deities. The architecture of temples and sanctuaries reveals the importance of these sites in relation to their placement in urban centers, and the resources dedicated to such monumental buildings. Temple friezes, or the area above the columns, often depicted sculpted or painted scenes from mythology, while the frieze on the Parthenon in Athens depicts a religious procession before the 12 gods of Olympus. In the areas surrounding temples and shrines, archaeologists have found all of the implements necessary in the activities of worship, such as knives, incense holders, vessels, votive pits, and even buried bones of sacrificial animals. Grave pits, tombs, and catacombs reveal ancient beliefs about the afterlife shown on the walls as well as information about daily life that were included as artifacts in tombs.

Added to this plethora of material remains are the votive inscriptions, one of our best sources for ancient practices and concepts. These inscriptions demonstrate the extent of pilgrimage and travel, and illustrate the religious views and beliefs of ancient peoples. There are literally thousands of votives scattered over the lands of the Mediterranean, and oracle sites contain the inscriptions of visitors usually thanking the god of the oracle for guidance, and also list sacred laws. Similarly, inscriptions on tombstones attest to the piety and personal beliefs of individuals.

Art, in the form of statues, votive figurines, paintings, vases, and wall murals (in houses, temples, and tombs) most often incorporated elements of the gods as well as heroes. Around the eighth century BCE, potters began to draw human figures on their wares, particularly for a variety of vessels required in funeral rites. These figures are shown participating in sacrifices, prayers, and religious processions. Scenes from mythology became popular, along with the stories from Homer. The ancients used pottery for tableware, amphorae (to transport or store food, olive oil, and wine), mixing bowls, drinking cups, and small vases for perfumes and cosmetics. There was thus a constant reminder of the divine in daily use.

Acts of Worship

Rituals are those acts involved in the *cultus* of ancient religious systems, or the actions involved in the proper worship of gods, goddesses, and various powers. Rituals could be enacted in sacrifices, prayers, offerings, processions, dance, drama, and festivals. Rituals assumed heightened importance at particular times in one's life, in what are known as rites of passage (birth, maturation, marriage, death). In the areas of sacred space (usually a temple or temple complex), rituals involved the daily life of the temple area. There were **purification rituals** and rituals for the proper cleaning and storing of cult items. All ancient people practiced religious rituals in their own homes as well as in public or community ceremonies.

Rituals involve more than just ritual acts, or the repeated behavior the term usually refers to in the modern sense. Ritual, from the Latin *ritualis*, for things involved with *ritus*, or rite, was also an umbrella term for doing things the proper way they have always been done (Latin, **mos maiorum**). Thus, tradition is fundamentally important in all rituals; the ritual act must be performed meticulously and according to tradition to ensure its correctness.

Rituals include both words and actions which connect the acts to a known and embedded system of meaning for those of a shared culture. For instance, just as they do for us today, calendar or memorial rituals brought the past and the present together for the community. Rituals involved in feasting and festivals served as public acknowledgments of the shared values of a community, and could act as a solution to communal tension. The shared values always included the community's ancient ties to a god, goddess, or hero (legendary historical characters) or famous ancestors. Thus what appeared to be merely a civic festival was always rooted in the divine connections to the community. Rituals worked in this same manner in the social and political realm, validating the social order and its contemporary leadership.

Sacrifices were offerings of something of value – food, wine, and most commonly, animals – to propitiate (appease) a deity, to show piety, to atone for a violation, or to receive a benefit from the divine. The animals were slaughtered (having their throats cut) on outside altars, or stone rectangles that served as a table of sorts. Some of the blood was then collected and splashed against the altar, while the rest drained off in runnels built into the complex. Religious specialists examined the entrails to determine if the sacrifice was acceptable. Depending upon the local tradition, the fat and bones were offered to the gods, and sometimes the organs or the choicest parts were shared among the priests. The sacrifice reached the gods through the smoke of burnt offerings (which is why the altars were located outside). For the chthonic deities, dark-haired animals were chosen, and sacrificial parts were burned in what was known as a holocaust. Liquid offerings (most often wine) were called **libations** and poured on the ground.

Although modern culture considers animal sacrifices cruel, they were of fundamental importance to the welfare of the community. Certain portions of the animal were kept by the temple officials (to be shared with helpers and family), but the bulk of the slaughtered animals was distributed to the participants of the religious ceremony. In the larger temple complexes, which often saw hundreds of animals slaughtered at festival times (like the *hecatomb*, or "hundred oxen" sacrifice at Athens), most of the meat was distributed to the populace in public feasts. Communal animal sacrifices were often the only occasions when the poor had the opportunity to eat meat.

Sacrifices were vitally important rituals that served as a communal rite to help connect humans to the gods. The offerings were symbolic of this sacred connection, which included both simple offerings to the household deities, and the more elaborate offerings in public space. No major undertaking was ever done without sacrifices, be it the inauguration of elected officials or setting off to the battlefield. There were regulations that dictated the type of sacrifices, from animals (oxen, bulls and cows, sheep, rams, pigs, goats, birds) to grain, cakes, honey, oil, flowers, and wine. Sacrifices were also a measure of the state's concern for the community.

Many theories attempt to explain the origins of the concept of sacrifice, particularly the blood sacrifices of animals. We cannot pinpoint when animal sacrifice began, but many theorize that it was in the age of hunter-gatherers, with the animal as either a guilt offering to propitiate the god in return for a successful hunt, or a means of allaying community hunger which was then understood as a blessing. From very early times, blood was thought of as the source of life, and therefore sacred.

Propitiation sacrifices were offered to cure diseases, to stave off drought and famine, or to avoid other disasters. Inherent in propitiation sacrifices was an assumption that the gods were angry or that humans had violated the relationship between gods and themselves, intentionally or not. The Latin phrase *do ut des* ("I give so that you may give") is often presented as a summation of the function of sacrifices in the ancient world. Romans believed that they had a contract with their gods; if one god did not reciprocate, there was no contradiction in appealing to another one. Both the concept of *do ut des* and a contract with the divine strikes the modern mind as far too pragmatic to be accompanied by any sense of piety or spirituality. However, these ideas arose in a social context, and in this case, we have the age-old concept and ritual of **gift-exchange**, practiced at all levels of society. There were rules, even between humans and the divine – reciprocity was expected, or you took your sacrifices elsewhere. The fundamental idea behind these sacrifices was that ultimately, you were appealing to the goodwill of the gods.

Other types of offerings included offerings for one's blessings or the averting of a disaster, and votive offerings made in fulfillment of a promise or a vow. Many sacrifices involved agricultural products and gifts donated in recognition of good harvests, good vintages, and healthy flocks. Gifts in the form of material goods were also known as dedications. These were displayed, and many temples and shrines were jammed full of these offerings – vases of oil and wine, statues, paintings, war shields, and gold and silver artifacts. In this sense, many temples were actually treasuries that stockpiled the dedications of locals and visitors (with appropriate plaques to identity the donor). When temples became full, treasury houses were built nearby to accommodate the overflow. Treasuries lined the path all the way up to the temple of Apollo at Delphi, and crowded the sanctuary at Olympia.

Prayers were invocations or acts that sought communication with the gods and involved the use of words or songs. There were prayers of petitions, praise and thanksgiving and requests for guidance. Then as now, people prayed in private and in public. Prayers always accompanied sacrifices, so that the deity would know exactly what the sacrifice was for. To call upon the gods was no simple undertaking; the gods would not respond without their correct names, titles, honorifics, gender, and function. People could pray in front of cult statues, but many prayed outside at the altar, in the open air, with arms held upward.

Prayers put to music were collectively called **hymns** (Greek, *hymnos*), or songs of praise, and many hymns were extended **invocations**. Hymns of praise were a standard feature of religious festivals, with trained choirs of adults and children, some of whom would go on tour to participate in religious festivals that included competition for prizes. As such, they represented the civic pride of their hometown, as well as the deity who was the object of their praise, emphasizing the divine connection between the two. The hymns of antiquity provide us with remarkable insight into the piety and emotions of ancient religious experience.

We also have prayers of admonition, more commonly known as curses. There were many reasons to call down curses upon someone, such as revenge for an insult, jealousy of someone's success, or a perceived injustice. Through the use of formulaic language distinguished in the literature as spells, people called on deities to enact misfortune or harm to a person. The victim could attempt to reverse the spell by appealing to either the same power or a different deity. Curse tablets, usually made of tin or lead or some other long-lasting material, accompanied the dead in funeral rites. Curse tablets were not directed to the dead person. Rather, dead people would convey the request for a curse to the chthonic deities below, so the body acted as a vehicle to transport the wishes of the living against someone else.

The Priesthoods

Overseeing all of the above were the priesthoods, which included both men and women. They were responsible for the daily activities of the cult and functioned as keepers of the tradition. In general, male gods had priests, and female goddesses had priestesses (although, with a few exceptions, not in Rome). Hierarchies of religious personnel emerged. In Rome, some gods had the equivalent of a high-priest. While some of the priests and priestesses dedicated their lives to the gods, for the most part, being a priest or priestess was a part-time endeavor. When they were not working in the temple or shrine, the priests worked in various occupations and led regular lives.

Purification Rituals

Ritual purity is a complicated concept and is often misunderstood. We traditionally associate it with hygiene because most of our exposure to the concept comes from the Hebrew Scriptures, where the terms are often translated as "clean" or "unclean." However, purity was a state of being. Some common conditions that were subject to purification rites were contact with blood, semen, and corpses. In and of themselves, these items were not in any sense sinful, as they were elements of everyday life. Ancient ritual purity codes are primarily concerned with sacred space; when someone approached the sacred area of a temple or other religious site, ritual purity was required. A major element of purification rites, even among the laity, involved ritual cleansing with water (**ablutions**) to symbolically remove any contagion before entering sacred space.

Communicating with the Divine

How and why did ancient people communicate with the divine? Most attempts were intended to determine the will of the gods. These endeavors involved the art of divination and the utilization of oracles. Divination (from the Latin *divinare*, "to be inspired by a god") was practiced by **seers** (Greek, *manteis*), who had various methods to interpret **omens**, or phenomena that were perceived as signs from the gods. Many signs (known as **prodigies** in Rome) were found in abnormal phenomena in the natural world (the birth of a two-headed calf, raining blood, sweating statues). These signs were taken seriously as indicating that the gods were angry, or that humans had done something wrong in their relationship with the divine.

Another way to determine the will of the gods was **augury**, which involved reading the signs found in lightning and the flights of birds. Others were specialists in the art of **hieroskopia** (Greek), and of the **haruspices** in Etruscan and Roman tradition. These experts read the entrails of sacrificial animals to determine if the offering was favorable. Before major battles Greeks performed a ceremony, *sphagia*, to read the entrails to determine if the omens were good. Roman legions had priests who were adept at reading the behavior of sacred chickens and making sacrifices to determine favorable conditions for battle.

Oracles (from the Latin, *orare*, "to speak") were persons or agencies that could manifest or articulate the thoughts and words of the deities. This was also the term used for sites where oracular speech took place. Whereas seers and *augurs* would interpret signs, oracles were understood to convey the literal words of a god or goddess. Most often, the speech of oracles was in a hidden language which would then be translated by a priest or temple servant. At other times, oracles went into a trance-like state, or exhibited ecstatic behavior, when they were thought to be possessed by the god. The founding of new cities or colonies or the decision to go to war was undertaken after first consulting an oracle. There were also oracle sites for the chthonic divinities and heroes. Oracles could be found throughout the region, but in Classical antiquity the most famous sites were at Delphi in Greece, Dodona in Epirus, Didyma in Turkey, the island of Delos in the Aegean Sea, and the cave of the Sibyls at Cumae in Italy.

Games

Ancient civilizations had athletic competitions, or **games**. We tend to think of sports events as solely a category of entertainment, but in the ancient world athletic games were under the auspices of the gods. The circuit games of ancient Greece are probably the most famous, beginning with the games dedicated to Zeus at Olympia in 776 BCE, followed by the Pythian Games at Delphi, the games at Isthmia near Corinth, and Nemea in the northern Peloponnese. The opening day of these games was usually devoted to the god with a festival and sacrifices. Competition was not limited to athletics; dramatic contests (with prizes for the author) were part of week-long religious festivals, and choirs traveled to various cities to compete in singing contests that largely consisted of hymns to the gods. In Rome, the games (**ludi**) during the religious festivals always included plays and the ever-popular chariot races. The races opened with a parade of statues of the gods and sacrifices.

The Afterlife and Funeral Rites

Paleolithic burials may provide our earliest evidence for a belief in the **afterlife**, or a belief in some form of existence beyond death. Views on the afterlife ran the gamut from denial (or annihilation of the self at the death), to a vague form of eternal sleep, to a belief in the immortality of the soul, to very complicated systems of reward and punishment for the deeds of this life. The more elaborate the forms of reward and punishment, the more elaborate the descriptions of the geography of the place of the dead. For those who did believe in an after-life, there were oracle sites for the dead, *nekromanteia* (and thus our word, **necromancy**), where someone would attempt to contact the dead.

A great deal of our evidence of the ancient world is found in grave shafts, tombs, catacombs, and inscribed grave markers, and this evidence reveals that ancient people were very concerned about proper funeral rites. Death fractured the family and the community, so there were rituals for both the dead body and the mourners. Then as now, no one could be sure what happened to the dead, or if they even existed in some other form. In case they did exist, there was a great concern for all for them to rest in peace so that they could not harm the living. Both Greece and Rome had special days of the dead, when it was understood that spirits could roam free, with rituals designed to protect the living as well as put the departed back to sleep. At the higher end of society, in both Greece and Rome, **funeral games** could be offered by the survivors, although these were distinct from the regular games. In Greece, funeral games included a variety of the same athletic skills that were the focus of regular games. In Rome, funeral games employed trained gladiators who sometimes fought to the death (***munera***), and were separate events from the regular religious festival games of the calendar.

Summary

- The modern field of Religious Studies has emerged as an academic study of religion, focusing on the historical and social contexts of elements rather than theological faith systems. Religious Studies seeks as much as possible to eliminate anachronism from the analysis of the ancient world.
- The divine had a central role in all aspects of life in the ancient world. Individuals related themselves to this unseen universe in their daily lives as well as their position in society.
- While ethnic, traditional cults differed, there were basic concepts shared by Greece and Rome. The items in bold print will occur throughout the rest of the book and are described in the Glossary.

Suggestions for Further Reading

Eliade, M. gen. ed. 1986. *The Encyclopedia of Religion.* Macmillan. This set of reference volumes contains encyclopedia articles by scholars on the individual elements of religious concepts and ritual practices. This work is available in most libraries, with a later edition in 2005.

Mikalson, J. D. 2010. *Ancient Greek Religion*, 2nd ed. Wiley-Blackwell. An excellent overview of Greek religion which includes myths, detailed rituals, and cults of ancient Greece.

Warrior, V. M. 2006. *Roman Religion*. Cambridge University Press. This is an introductory survey of the religions of Rome, in the family, the state, and the empire.

THE ANCIENT CIVILIZATIONS OF THE MEDITERRANEAN BASIN

Mesopotamia

Egypt

The Rest of the
Neighborhood

Greece

Rome

Greek and Roman Religions, First Edition. Rebecca I. Denova.
© 2019 John Wiley & Sons, Inc. Published 2019 by John Wiley & Sons, Inc.

Learning Objectives

After reading this chapter, you will be able to:

- Recognize shared elements of the neighboring cultures with Greece and Rome.
- Identify the major events in the history of the Greek and Roman civilizations.

 Greece and Rome did not exist in a vacuum. The Mediterranean, which Romans proudly called "Our Sea," bordered the modern countries of Spain, France, Italy, Albania, Greece, Turkey, Syria, Lebanon, Israel, Egypt, Libya, Tunisia, Algeria, and Morocco. The Greeks had planted colonies in many of these lands, and Rome later established provinces in these same areas. This book focuses on the religious life of ancient Greece and Rome but it is important to recognize that trade and war provided contact with other civilizations in the region. Many religious concepts of these older cultures appeared in Greece and Rome, some borrowed directly and some adapted in light of local traditions. We will briefly examine these neighboring societies and trace some of the religious ideas that remained constant in the Mediterranean basin.

Two ancient cultures in the neighborhood of Greece and Rome, Mesopotamia and Egypt, are traditionally described as "cradles of civilization." A basic criterion for this classification is writing, which developed early in Mesopotamia and Egypt, and then spread in various forms throughout the region. Other elements include a class-based society, stratified occupational groups, and public buildings and monuments. These systems also created a hierarchy for the divine reflected in earthly society, with myths, an established priesthood, annual religious festivals, and a king at the top of the social structure in his role as mediator between Heaven and Earth.

Mesopotamia

Mesopotamia is the name for the region known as "the land between the rivers," the Tigris and Euphrates (in modern Iraq), and containing the civilizations of Sumer, Akkadia, Assyria, and Babylon (Figure II.1). Traditionally referred to as the "fertile crescent," this area's prosperity was due in great part to the improvements in irrigation systems using canals between the rivers. We also use "Mesopotamian" as a general adjective for several elements of the civilizations in this region that developed over many centuries, including various religious concepts.

Sumer was a civilization that flourished in the fourth millennium BCE at the southern end of Mesopotamia (the Persian Gulf region). Sumer is credited with the earliest form of writing and the Sumerian language survived as a form of sacred language in subsequent cultures. One of the earliest city-states of Sumer

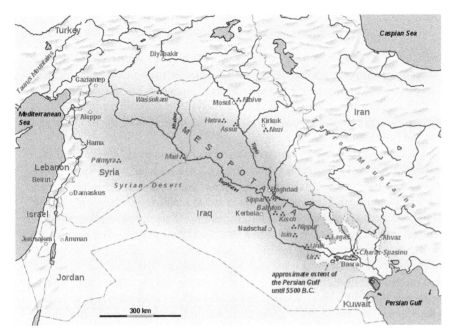

Figure II.1   Map of ancient Mesopotamia. *Source*: Goran tek-en, https://commons. wikimedia.org/wiki/ File:N-Mesopotamia_ and_Syria_english.svg. Licensed under CC BY-SA 3.0.

was Uruk, a walled city with temple complexes and a central administration headed by a king, and which was known in the ancient world as the home of the legendary King Gilgamesh (of *The Epic of Gilgamesh*). Some temple complexes were dedicated to Inanna, the Queen of Heaven, a goddess of sexual love, fertility, and war. Anu was the king of the gods who formed the head of the triad which included Enlil (god of the air) and Enki (god of water). We describe Uruk as a theocracy, where the government is understood to be ruled by divine guidance, with the king as either the representative of the gods on earth, or a living manifestation of the divine. At Uruk the king enacted a **hieros gamos**, a sacred marriage, with the goddess Inanna at the New Year festival which legitimated his rule (see the box "What Does Fertility Have to Do with the Divine?").

The Sumerian pantheon included the gods of Heaven, air, healing, the arts and craftsmanship, water, and fertility, and contained a sun god and a moon god. In the later Assyrian and Babylonian empires, the war gods Ashur and Marduk eventually emerged as supreme gods for the Assyrians and Babylonians, respectively. During the earlier Babylonian Empire (1750 BCE), King Hammurabi was the first to codify the laws of the land, which touch upon all aspects of human society. These laws originated from Shamash, the sun god, and are understood as the will of the gods. We also have early forms of the study of astrology or the relationship between the cosmos (planets and stars) and humans. Astrological divination by priests produced omens and it is in Babylon that the study of the cosmos provided some of the earliest mathematical calculations for the rotations of the planets.

What Does Fertility Have to Do with the Divine?

Long before the development of organized religious systems, early humans were concerned about fertility. Hundreds of figurines have been unearthed of fully formed women and sculpted penises, most likely used as **amulets** (good luck, protection, and symbols of prosperity). The female figurines could represent a mother goddess, as mother goddesses were always involved with fertility, creation, nurturing, and growing grain. These figurines may also represent the ideal woman; she had wide hips to facilitate childbirth and breasts full of life-giving milk.

Fertility was absolutely crucial in a world of continual natural and human-made disasters and high mortality rates, especially among infants. The earliest descriptions of male gods are paired with a female consort. Although early humans did not fully understand the process of procreation, they knew that women became pregnant after sexual intercourse. Why not assign this miraculous outcome to the gods? And why not depict these gods and goddesses as being involved in the procreation of both nature and humans?

The evidence of ancient mother goddess figures led to a traditional view that early human societies were matriarchies or societies where genealogy, leadership, authority, and morality were determined by women. Modern scholars now debate if such societies ever existed, but it is clear that patriarchal societies also honored mother goddesses in recognition of their role in fertility. The various mother goddesses shared similar functions, with one iconic figure known by various names: Inanna in Mesopotamia, Astarte in Syria, Asherah in Canaan, Hathor and Isis in Egypt, Cybele in Anatolia, Gaea, Rhea, Hera, Demeter and Aphrodite in Greece, and Ops, Juno, Venus, and Ceres in Rome.

The Greek historian Herodotus (484–425 BCE) recounted his shock at meeting women compelled to have sexual intercourse in the "houses of heaven" in Babylon, and he was even more shocked to find that they were paid (*The Histories*, 1.199). The temple of Aphrodite in Corinth was also thought to have women who performed intercourse with worshippers. Scholars in the nineteenth century labeled these practices "temple prostitution," although modern researchers continue to debate the reality of this custom. If we remove the prejudiced connotation from the word "prostitution" we can recognize that it may have been a ritual that symbolically enacted fertility. The *hieros gamos* (sacred marriage) ceremonies symbolized the potency of the king in a similar fashion. We just do not have enough information to confirm the details of these rites. We do know that fertility was of prime importance in all the cultures in the Mediterranean basin.

Two main sources for the religious beliefs of Mesopotamia are found in the *Enuma Elish* and *The Epic of Gilgamesh*. The *Enuma Elish* relates the story of how Marduk became the king of the gods when he slew Tiamat, a goddess of chaos (the oceans). It also describes how human beings were created to serve the needs of the gods and labor for them. *The Epic of Gilgamesh* tells the adventures of Gilgamesh, the legendary king of Uruk and his quest for immortality. He meets Utnapishtim (a mortal granted immortality by the gods), who tells him the story of a great flood and how he was saved at the bidding of the god Ea, who told him to build a massive boat. Many versions of a flood story circulated in the region (perhaps based upon annual river inundations), and we can see specific parallels in the story of Noah in Genesis. Gilgamesh ultimately fails to find immortality, understanding that it is a unique gift from the gods.

The Sumerians worshipped anthropomorphic images of their gods and goddesses; their deities looked like humans, only sometimes with wings or talons. Some of the earliest mud-brick temples, **ziggurats**, were built in this region. Ziggurats were stepped temple complexes that included storage rooms for offerings and courtyards with pools for purification. Although they were monumental structures, the ziggurats were not for public worship. Only the priests were permitted inside the temple on top and their duty was to take care of the gods. Priests and priesthoods developed early in Sumer, where priests were both temple custodians and mediators between humans and the divine.

Priests and temples were required in this culture as it was necessary to placate the divine, to maintain harmony between the gods and humans. Mesopotamian mythology posits an original problem of overcoming chaos by the gods and stories of gods who battled each other for supremacy. Keeping the gods happy involved music, hymns, prayers, sacrifices, and libations of beer and wine. Images of the deities were bathed, dressed, and marched around the city-states in festive parades. To find out what pleased the divine, they used divination or various readings of sacrificial organs, animal behavior, and weather patterns.

In ancient Mesopotamia we have early evidence of the belief that the dead continued to exist in some form of an afterlife. This was particularly the case with dead relatives, so that **ancestor cults** emerged as a way in which to placate dead relatives and to alleviate any harm they might cause. Initially ancestors were buried under the floors of the house, and then later it became the custom to bury people in adjacent plots of land to serve as proof of ownership for the descendants. Ancestor cults were accorded to legendary heroes and eponymous founders of ethnic groups (which influenced stories such as that of Abraham in the Hebrew Scriptures). Claiming descent from one's ancestor became vitally important in establishing the lineage of the clan or tribe and consequently was associated with fertility through procreation. A man was duty-bound to produce a son to preserve the connection between the honored dead and the next generation.

Mesopotamians believed that all the dead went to "the place of the dead," or the "land of no return." In *The Epic of Gilgamesh*, Gilgamesh conjures up his dead friend Enkidu and obtains a report about the place of the dead where people exist as ghostly shadows and suffer from continual dust and thirst. According to the *Enuma Elish*, humans were created by mixing the blood of minor deities (which gave humans intelligence) with clay. Therefore, humans return to clay and are condemned to eat clay for eternity. The only solace for the dead was the hope that their names would live on after them and that their bloodline would continue.

Egypt

Herodotus described Egypt as "the gift of the Nile," which was a reference to the annual flooding of the habitable areas by the river. Every year the land became irrigated for up to two miles on each bank, and the river deposited rich silt that provided an abundant food supply. Ancient Egypt was divided between Upper and Lower Egypt, with the Lower Delta region actually north of Upper Egypt (Figure II.2). According to tradition, these two areas were united under King Menes from Upper Egypt, c. 3150 BCE. The unification came to be symbolized by the double crown (white for Upper Egypt, red for Lower Egypt), which

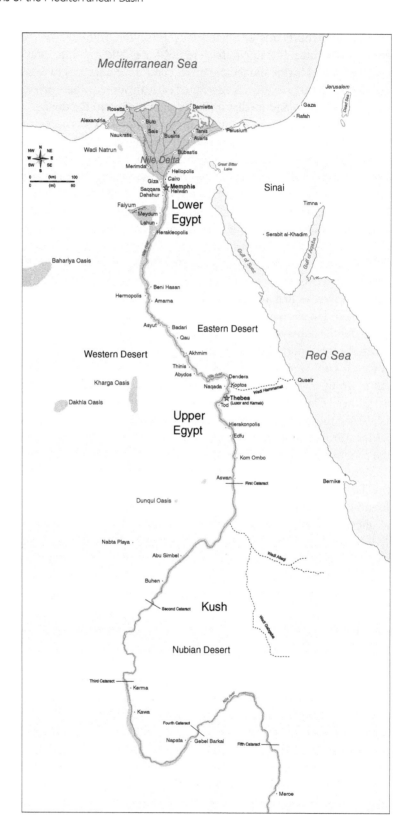

Figure II.2 Map of ancient Egypt. *Source:* Jeff Dahl, https://en.wikipedia.org/wiki/File:Ancient_Egypt_map-en.svg. Licensed under CC BY-SA 4.0.

was always worn by the reigning Pharaoh as an indication of unified and absolute rule.

Most of our evidence for the religious beliefs of ancient Egypt comes from their tombs and funeral apparatuses. The most famous tomb is that of the young King Tutankhamun (reigned c. 1332–1323 BCE), which was discovered in 1922. We also have the **hieroglyphs** (Greek, "sacred writing"). Historically the last hieroglyphs were sculpted in the temple at Philae (near Aswan) in the sixth century CE. As no one wrote hieroglyphs after that, the meaning of the symbols was lost for 1300 years. In 1799, a soldier belonging to the Napoleonic invasion of Egypt discovered a reused building stone in Rosetta, Egypt. The stone contained a message from one of the Ptolemaic kings (c. 196 BCE), written in hieroglyphs, the Demotic language, and Greek. In 1822, Jean-François Champollion announced that he had deciphered the ancient writing.

Egypt had many creation myths. Most of them emerged in conjunction with the development of major religious and administrative centers. As one example, the story in Heliopolis began with a world of darkness and endless water. A mound of earth emerged (just as land appears when the Nile recedes). The self-engendered creator god Atum ("the All") sat on the mound and emitted the deities of air and moisture (male and female). They in turn produced Geb (the earth) and Nut (the sky). Subsequent offspring were Osiris, Isis, Seth, and Nephthys, important actors in the popular cult of Osiris. Osiris was killed and dismembered by his jealous brother Seth. Their sister, and Osiris's wife, Isis, collected the body parts and resurrected him, and thus he became the Lord of the Dead. There were many additions to this story, including the miraculous birth of Horus, the son of Osiris and Isis. Pharaoh ("great house") was understood to be the manifestation of Horus on earth. Most stories of creation involved order out of chaos or the concept of Ma'at which was personified in the goddess who also stood for truth, justice, and morality.

Many visitors to Egypt were startled by the appearance of some of the gods and goddesses, with human bodies and heads of animals. The Egyptians did not worship animals per se, but they honored the animal traits of some deities. For instance, Horus was portrayed with the head of a falcon, which indicated swiftness of movement and a keen eye to watch over and protect Pharaoh. Hathor, a fertility deity and mother goddess, was portrayed as a human, but also as a nurturing cow, or as a woman with cow's ears (Figure II.3).

The gods and goddesses of Egypt were worshipped in small cult temples and in large temples in royal centers (Abydos, Memphis, Karnak, Luxor). Public assemblies took place in the outer courts of temples and in designated chapels. For the most part, average Egyptians did not enter the inner spaces, unless they were required in their capacity as food porters, craftsmen, and workers. Only the priests and temple attendants were involved with daily worship. The high-priest (standing in for Pharaoh) entered the innermost shrine where the cult statue was housed, took care of the daily ablutions, and fed the god with offerings. This was done three times a day, at all the temples throughout Egypt.

It was at public festivals that the rest of the Egyptians participated directly in religious rites, such as the Ophet festival at Karnak/Luxor. Amon-Ra (an older

Figure II.3 Some Egyptian gods. *Source:* iStock/Getty Images Plus.

deity combined with the sun god, Ra) was taken out of the temple at Karnak and placed in a barque (a wooden boat) and carried in procession to the temple at Luxor. The purpose was to reunite him with his wife Mut and their child Khonsu, who both lived at the Luxor temple. People handed over written pleas and petitions, and the answers or oracles would be indicated by the movement of the barque and interpreted by priests. Festivals like the Ophet took place all over Egypt, particularly in the worship of Osiris, Hathor, Isis, and Bes. The Beautiful Festival of the Valley on the west bank opposite Luxor was a special celebration when people visited the dead. It involved roast meats, incense, drinking, and family reunions, and had a celebratory air much like Mardi Gras in modern New Orleans.

The Egyptian Afterlife

The popular view is that ancient Egyptians were obsessed with death. The opposite was true; Egyptians were obsessed with life. Egyptians loved life and celebrated it in various festivals. They understood death as another phase of life. Just as the Nile overflowed and then retreated, Egyptians believed in a constant cycle of creation, death, and re-creation. To the Egyptians all human beings had a physical body, a name, a shadow, and a *ba*, or personality. The *ka* was the life force. Both *ba* and *ka* are often translated as soul and equated with the modern idea that the soul is the incorporeal essence of a person. Upon death, the *ba* and *ka* were released but they had to be reunited with a physical body, which was why the Egyptians mummified or preserved the dead. Once the *ba* and *ka* rejoined the body, one could become an *akh*, or one with the stars.

The Middle Kingdom period of ancient Egypt (2050–1800 BCE) saw an innovation in the concept of societal behavior in relation to existence in the afterlife. In their wisdom literature and admonition texts we have some of the earliest writings addressed to morality and social justice (which may not be attainable in this life). In other words, one's behavior and treatment of fellow humans determined one's successful existence after death. Admonition texts were often written from a Pharaoh to his successor or from a father to a son, warning that evil deeds in this life will have repercussions for eternity. For more details on the Egyptian afterlife, see Chapter X.

The Rest of the Neighborhood

Mesopotamia and Egypt were two of the largest and longest lasting of the ancient civilizations, but there were other cultures in the area that were just as old, although we only know about some of them from later periods.

Anatolia (part of modern Turkey) contains the remains of some of the world's oldest settlements, including one of the oldest monumental structures at Göbekli Tepe. This center was apparently built by hunter-gatherers a thousand years before the development of agriculture. Indo-European language groups were present, which indicates interaction with migrant groups from north of the Black Sea. Later cultures in this area include the Hattians, Hurrians, Mittani, and the Hittites, and were ancient when the Greeks began to colonize western Turkey. We have evidence of multiple fertility deities and oracle sites in ancient Anatolia.

The Minoan civilization on the island of Crete is dated from the twenty-seventh to the fifteenth centuries BCE. As an island in the eastern Mediterranean, it was strategically located to benefit from trade with the surrounding cultures, and Crete exported its crafts and ideas. Minoan artifacts have been uncovered in Egypt, Canaan, and on mainland Greece, particularly during the Mycenaean period (c. 1600–1100 BCE). Crete was famous in ancient legend as the home of the Minotaur and the Labyrinth. We have evidence of a dominant fertility goddess cult, bull-leaping rituals, and at least three hundred caves and mountain-top shrines. Because of Crete's influence in the larger Aegean area, the Minoan Age is included in standard histories of Greek civilization.

The Phoenicians emerged from earlier Semitic Canaanite tribes, largely along the eastern Mediterranean coast, with major city-states at Tyre and Sidon (modern Lebanon). From 1550 to 300 BCE, they traded throughout the Mediterranean basin, and adapted oared ships (galleys) into two-layered biremes. Through such trade contacts, they spread an alphabet that was the basis for phonetic alphabets in the region. Their main deities were the powers of nature and war, with Baal and Astarte as leading divinities. They also absorbed many religious elements from Mesopotamian culture, particularly in their burial technology and funeral rites. Their early colonies in North Africa (Carthage) and Spain would later interact with the settlers of Greek colonies and Roman provinces.

Italy itself was populated with various cultures, labeled "Italics," or indigenous peoples. From the Bronze Age to the Roman period and beyond, we have archaeological evidence for these cultures, but very little in a written record before the sixth century BCE. The tribal groups would later have names such as the Oscans, the Marsi, the Sabines, and the Latins, but almost all of our information comes from later Roman sources. Nevertheless, we will see that Roman religion included some of the indigenous Italian divinities, as well as ancient oracle sites in Italy. The Etruscan culture (800–c. 100 BCE) in northern and central Italy was a dominant influence on cultural and religious practices in ancient Rome.

Cyrus the Great (576–530 BCE) overthrew the Babylonians and became the founder of the Achaemenid Empire, commonly known as Persia. His son, Cambyses II, conquered Egypt in 525 BCE. The rest of the successors created the largest empire prior to Roman hegemony and this culture was noted in antiquity for incorporating a huge number of different ethnic groups from the Mediterranean to India (Figure II.4).

The older religions of Persia became centralized under a philosopher/holy man named Zoroaster (or Zarathustra in later Western literature), whom tradition claims was born anywhere from the eleventh to the sixth century BCE. His religion became known as Zoroastrianism and was eventually the state religion of Persia. Ahura Mazda was the one god who, by emitting paired *Amesha spentas* (**archons**, or powers in the universe), was responsible for creation. The opposite was represented by Angra Mainyu, or "druj," the destructive spirit of chaos which was the polar opposite of good. Zoroaster taught that all humans should practice "good thoughts, good words, and good deeds," the criteria for their judgment when they die. The souls of the dead had to cross the Chinvat Bridge over the chasm of a Hell-like area. This bridge was wide for the righteous and narrow for the wicked. The land of the dead in this system was

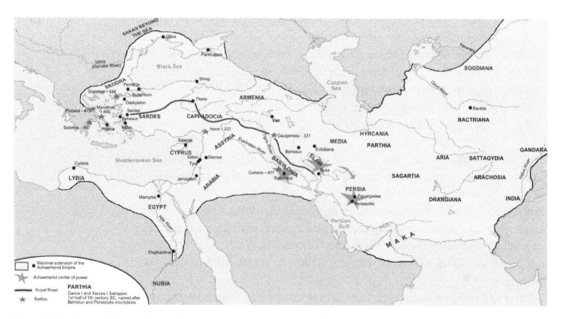

Figure II.4   Map of Persia. *Source*: Fabienkhan, https://commons.wikimedia.org/wiki/File:Map_achaemenid_empire_en.png. Licensed under CC BY-SA 2.5.

full of pollution, putrefaction, contamination, decay, thirst, torture, and fire. The good were able to reach paradise, a Persian word for garden.

According to tradition, an independent Jewish kingdom flourished in c. 1000 BCE during the reigns of King David and King Solomon. Upon the death of Solomon, the kingdom suffered a series of national disasters: the north was conquered by Assyria in 722 BCE, and the south by the Babylonians in 598 BCE. After a relatively stable period under Persia, Israel was conquered by Alexander the Great in 332 BCE. Upon Alexander's death, his generals periodically ruled Israel from the Seleucid Kingdom (Syria) and the Ptolemaic Kingdom (Egypt). A group known as the Maccabees successfully revolted against Greek rule in 167 BCE. Their kingdom lasted for roughly a hundred years until Israel was conquered by Rome in 63 BCE.

The Jews were well known in antiquity for their unique worship of one god. Although they recognized the existence of many powers in the universe, they refused to participate in their worship (literally, sacrifices). Unlike a majority of their neighbors, Jews practiced circumcision, had special dietary laws, and ceased all work on every seventh day (Sabbath). The various disasters which plagued their homeland led to Jewish migration in all the lands around the Mediterranean basin. There were large Jewish communities in Persia, Egypt, Asia Province (western Anatolia), Syria, Greece, and Rome. Their religious views and practices traveled with them, as their religion was not limited to a geographic area, and they welcomed anyone in their synagogues (places of assembly). Both the literary and archaeological evidence indicates that many Greeks and Romans were well informed about Jewish practices and beliefs.

The influence of all the neighboring ancient civilizations on Greek and Roman culture is difficult to determine as we lack direct literary evidence for many of the elements. Archaeological data are not often proof that a particular idea or element was borrowed, as it is difficult to precisely date religious artifacts even when found *in situ* (found in their original location). Nevertheless, trade and conquest in the region provided a two-way street of cultural exchange. (See the box "Interaction and Influence.")

Interaction and Influence

With their experience of thousands of years of the evolution of religious ideas, did neighboring cultures influence the religious beliefs of ancient Greece and Rome? This remains a very, very difficult question to answer. A simple "yes" or "no" is not sufficient without demonstrating the direct means of cultural influence and borrowing. We have evidence of extensive trade contacts from the Bronze Age down through the Roman Empire, but we lack literary sources that trace the history of ideas in many of these periods.

Complicating our ancient evidence is the practice known as *interpretatio graeca* and *interpretatio romana*. This was a process by which Greek and Roman gods and goddesses, religious rituals and myths were used to explain the myths and religious practices of other cultures. For example, Herodotus described the religion of Egypt using analogies in Greek religion (and claimed that Greece borrowed religious ideas from Egypt), and Dionysius of Halicarnassus (60–7 BCE) described Roman practices by using Greek examples.

This method made sense to the ancients because so many cultures had deities who shared similar traits and functions. As Pliny the Elder (23–79 CE) explained, deities were easy to translate, with just "different names for different peoples" (*Natural History*, 2.5.15). In other words, the gods were universal, but different people interpreted them in light of their own culture and language. At the same time antiquity was highly valued – the older an idea or practice was, the better. When writers described religious rituals, they always claimed that they were the same rituals laid down in olden times by the ancestors, and took pride in the claim that nothing had changed.

Cultural borrowing, whether the adoption of foreign gods, the transmission of cults to other ethnic communities, or the assimilation of transmitted practices, took place throughout the ancient world (and is equally pervasive in the modern world). Scholars of religion refer to this phenomenon as **syncretism**, variously defined as merging two or more religious beliefs or the imposition of a new belief system on an older one. When an area was conquered, the older gods were never thrown out; they just moved over to make room for new ones, or the old and new were combined into a divinity that resembled both. This system provided the advantage of flexibility when it came to the many divinities in the ancient world.

While interacting with their neighbors through trade and military conquests, Greece and Rome nevertheless developed unique elements of their own civilizations. Space does not permit a full history of these civilizations, but a brief survey of major historical events is necessary because such events contributed to the collective memories and traditions that were incorporated into the religious practices of both Greece and Rome.

Greece

The history of ancient Greece is divided into set periods, using both archaeological evidence and later literary descriptions (see Table II.1).

The Bronze Age in Greece saw the beginning of agriculture, pottery, a writing system, a form of centralized government, law codes, organized warfare, international trade, taxation, and social hierarchies that included slavery. As the name implies, the Bronze Age is noted for the development of the bronze alloy (a mixture of copper and tin), which required organized mining and produced improved weapons and tools. The nature of Greek geography dictated that hills became fortified city-states, with agricultural communities in the valleys.

Table II.1   The historical periods of ancient Greece

Early Bronze Age:	2900–2000 BCE
Minoan Age:	2000–1600 BCE
Mycenaean Age:	1600–1100 BCE
Dark Ages:	1100–800 BCE
Archaic Age:	800–500 BCE
Classical Age:	500–323 BCE
Hellenistic Age:	323–146 BCE

Port sites were initially colonized as extensions of more powerful city-states in this period, although many of them became independent.

The Minoans, based on Crete, dominated the islands of the Aegean and the coastal areas of the eastern Mediterranean as well as parts of mainland Greece. However, c. 1600 BCE the Minoans suffered a collapse (from famine, dissolution of trade or the volcanic eruption on the island of Thera) and the region was then conquered and dominated by the Mycenaean civilization.

The Mycenaean Age (1600–1100 BCE) is named after the city of Mycenae in the Peloponnese in southern Greece. During this period, society became more hierarchical, with a king and his councilors at the top controlling most of the wealth. The majority of the lower classes supported a central administrative structure through their work as artisans and farmers. Stone palace complexes and citadels were vital to this warrior culture and the structures also emphasized the status of the king and his circle. Mycenaeans took pride in warfare and this period is often referred to as "the age of the heroes." Many of the later legends and myths of ancient Greece were based in this older culture. According to Homer, the Mycenaean King Agamemnon led the coalition of Greek city-states against Troy.

The Mycenaeans invented a written form of script known as Linear B (a derivative of the Minoan language known as Linear A), although surviving artifacts are few. We do not have a body of literature from this period and little is known about religion during this age. A few texts mention the names of gods, with Poseidon being a popular deity. Some of the major Olympians are mentioned (Zeus, Hera, Ares, Athena, Artemis, Dionysus). The few remains of temples do not provide enough information about the worship of these deities.

An older theory about the end of the Mycenaean civilization posited an invasion by the Dorians, tribal peoples originally from the north. However, there is a growing body of evidence that the Dorians were already settled in Greece at this time. Another theory is that an internal social uprising took place, motivated by the impoverished lower classes. In either case, by the end of this period Mycenae and other city-states had been destroyed.

Extensive and long-time damage at all the major Mycenaean sites resulted in the period known in Greek history as the Dark Ages. It was labeled this way because it appears that the Greeks adopted previous lifestyles of pastoral and livestock grazing (understood as regressive), and we have no literature from this period. However, by 800 BCE, writing was either rediscovered or relearned, although instead of Linear B, the Greeks adopted the alphabet of the Phoenicians (who had inserted vowels), the forerunner of the English alphabet. In this later period, the Olympic Games were established, and we have the earliest sources for Homer's epics, *The Iliad* and *The Odyssey*. *The Iliad* recounts a few weeks in the final year of the Trojan War, while *The Odyssey* relates the adventures of Odysseus as he tries to make his way from Troy to his home in Ithaca.

Hesiod, a native of Boeotia in central Greece, produced two poems, *Works and Days* and *Theogony* (c. 700 BCE). *Works and Days* includes a farming manual and *Theogony* describes the creation of the gods and the ages of mankind (Golden, Silver, Bronze, Heroic, and Iron). Hesiod placed himself in this last age, with pessimistic descriptions of the fallen state of humans and society because the older virtuous traditions were no longer practiced. The works of both Homer and Hesiod became standard literature for all Greeks (and Greek colonies) for centuries.

The Archaic Age (800–500 BCE) experienced population increases and the political organization of what would become the classic city-state (*polis*), which included citizens, *metics* (resident aliens), and slaves. The rights and duties of these classes in Athens were codified through constitutional reforms by Solon (638–558 BCE) and Cleisthenes (570–508 BCE). The end of this period saw the rise of democracy in Athens, or "rule of the people," to check any attempt at tyranny. During this period Greek colonization extended to Anatolia and Phoenicia, the Black Sea area, northern Africa (Libya), southern Italy, Sicily, southern France, and Spain.

Classical Greece (500–323 BCE) is recognized as the height of Greek literature, philosophy, art, drama, the sciences, architecture, and politics, with the city-state of Athens providing most of our information. The Parthenon, the temple dedicated to Athena, the patron goddess of Athens, was constructed on the acropolis between 447 and 438 BCE. Philosophy originated in Miletus (Anatolia) in the seventh century BCE, but many of the different schools of philosophy came to fruition in Classical Greece.

One of the lasting legacies of Classical Greece in the Western tradition is the art of politics or those elements involved in governance. Derived from Aristotle, good government included the art of rhetoric (persuasion) and social control for the good of the community. Athenian democracy was limited to free, adult citizen males who completed their military training as **ephebes** (adolescents). The democratic voters most likely constituted less than a third of the population of ancient Athens.

The Greco-Persian Wars

Cyrus the Great established the Achaemenid Empire of Persia in what had been the Neo-Babylonian Empire and in 547 BCE conquered Ionia, a region in western Anatolia long settled by Greeks. In following his usual policy, he appointed tyrants in the cities to collect tribute and to keep the peace. In 499 BCE, the Ionians rebelled against Persian rule, convincing most of their neighbors to do so as well. Athens and other Greek city-states supported the rebellion and this began the wars between Persia and Greece that would last until 449 BCE. Darius the Great (the next Persian ruler) effectively put down the rebellion, but decided to punish Athens and her allies by invading the Greek mainland.

In 490 BCE, the first Persian invasion took place and resulted in the conquest of Thrace and Macedonia. However, the Athenians decisively beat back the Persians at the Battle of Marathon, which temporarily put a halt to Persian plans. (The modern athletic races, called marathons, take this name from the legendary story of the messenger who ran from the battlefield to Athens to announce the victory, a distance of 26 miles.) The second invasion was in 480 BCE under Darius's son, Xerxes I, with the largest armies ever assembled. He was only temporarily held up at the Battle of Thermopylae with the famous last-ditch effort of the 300 Spartans and 700 Thespians. After winning that battle he went on to sack and burn Athens. The Persians then suffered a devastating loss to the Greeks in the naval Battle of Salamis.

In 478 BCE the Delian League (based on the island of Delos) was formed as a naval alliance to stem future Persian incursions. However, the Delian League also served as the maritime monopoly for Athens in eastern Mediterranean trade, provided naval support for colonies in the western Mediterranean, and contributed to the spread of Greek culture. In the following decades, alliances arose and fell, battles were won and lost, and the Greco-Persian wars were essentially over by 449 BCE. The tribute from these overseas endeavors and the profits from trade helped to rebuild Athens and contributed to her golden age.

The city of Sparta led the Peloponnesian League, an alliance of states mostly from the Peloponnese (the southern Greek peninsula) which feared the dominance of Athens. This mistrust led to the Peloponnesian War in 431 BCE, with most of the other city-states choosing sides. Sparta had stronger armies, but Athens had a larger navy and these two factors served to balance each power so that the war lasted until 404 BCE. After suffering a devastating plague, Athens finally surrendered to Sparta.

Although militarily victorious, Sparta did not have the leadership experience of Athens. This problem was solved when Philip II of Macedonia conquered Athens and the other city-states in 338 BCE. Macedonia was located north of Greece, but shared many cultural elements with that nation. Philip's ambition was to unite all of Greece and then invade Persia in revenge for the Persian wars. Upon his assassination in 336 BCE, the Macedonian throne passed to his son, Alexander the Great.

The Hellenistic Age

Alexander was as ambitious as his father, although he was more charismatic, militarily skillful and was greatly admired by his soldiers because he placed himself in the forefront of battle. He conquered Anatolia, Syria, the Persian Empire, Israel, Egypt, Afghanistan, and made it all the way to India. It was the largest empire to date and his conquests resulted in the Hellenization of all these lands. Hellenization, and **Hellenistic**, is a descriptor which refers to Alexander's alterations of local customs and cultures to include Greek concepts and practices (Hellen was the mythological founder of Greece). Alexander introduced Greek religion, philosophy, science, medicine, art, literature, governance, and education to all the areas he conquered. The Greek language became the lingua franca of the entire eastern Mediterranean, or the language that became shared by the diverse ethnic groups of the conquered territories.

In 323 BCE, Alexander died of a fever at the age of 32. He had no legal heir and this created a situation where his generals fought over the remnants of his empire for the next several decades. Ultimately, Antigonus ruled Macedonia, Thrace, and parts of northern Anatolia, Seleucus ruled Syria and parts of the Persian Empire, and Ptolemy ruled Egypt from the city of Alexandria. Alexander himself created this city and it quickly rose to prominence under Ptolemy as both a commercial center and intellectual hub. Ptolemy dedicated a center of learning to the Muses (the deities who inspired learning and the arts), and thus created the "museum" and library at Alexandria which welcomed all scholars and schools of philosophy. Alexandria also boasted one of the later wonders of the ancient world, the Pharos lighthouse.

Rome conquered Greece in 146 BCE and eventually most of the lands previously conquered by Alexander (with the exception of Persia). Athens and a coalition of city-states under the influence of King Mithridates VI of Pontus rebelled against Roman rule but they were crushed by the dictator Sulla in 88 BCE. Rome had always admired Greek culture and with the conquest of Greece, thousands of statues and artifacts were taken to Rome and graced public buildings, temples, and private homes. Greece became the province of Achaea in 27 BCE under the rule of the first Roman emperor, Augustus.

Rome

While the history of Greece is measured in Ages, the history of Rome is traditionally remembered through major events (see Table II.2).

The city of Rome began as a small village on the Tiber River in central Italy where the river reaches its last stage of safe navigation. The center of this village was a swamp which eventually was drained and became the Roman forum. Surrounding this swamp were several hills (tradition claims seven, although there are more), and the plain surrounding this site was known as Latium. The first inhabitants consisted of some Latin tribes who may have emigrated from the Alban Hills in the south and who were later joined by the Sabine tribes and polyglot others. From that small village, Rome conquered its neighbors and every country that bordered the Mediterranean and some beyond (Britain, parts of Germany, the Balkans).

The Etruscans

By their own admission, many elements of Roman customs were borrowed from the Etruscans. The Etruscans flourished from c. 800 to 100 BCE in the areas of Tuscany, Umbria, the Po River valley of the eastern Alps, Latium, and parts of Campania. They often dominated the area of Rome itself; many of the early kings of Rome were Etruscan. Through trade and the hiring of Greek artisans from Magna Graecia, or Greek colonies established in southern Italy (from 800 BCE), Etruscans absorbed Hellenic culture and art. The Etruscan language has not survived in a body of texts; we only have a few inscriptions from items found in

753 BCE	According to legend the city of Rome is established by Romulus and Remus.
715–673	The reign of King Numa Pompilius, legendary founder of Roman religion.
509 BCE	Overthrow of the kings and the creation of the Roman Republic.
390 BCE	The Gauls invade Rome and sack the city.
264–146 BCE	The Three Punic Wars against Carthage.
204–202 BCE	Scipio Africanus defeats the Carthaginian general Hannibal at the Battle of Zama in North Africa.
146 BCE	Carthage destroyed; Greece conquered.
110 BCE	The first of several invasions by German tribes, which were eventually defeated by Gaius Marius who reformed the army.
98–SS BCE	Social War, the last rebellion of the Italian peoples against Rome.
88–66 BCE	Wars against King Mithridates VI of Pontus (northern Anatolia): Rome conquers Asia Province (Anatolia), Syria, Israel, and Armenia.
60–54 BCE	The First Triumvirate of Caesar, Pompey. and Crassus.
58–50 BCE	Caesar's Gallic Wars.
49 BCE	Caesar crosses the Rubicon: civil war against Pompey and the Republicans.
48–45 BCE	Pompey defeated at Pharsalus and assassinated in Egypt; Republican forces defeated in North Africa.
44 BCE	Caesar assassinated; Octavian, Anthony, and Lepidus form the Second Triumvirate.
31 BCE	Octavian defeats Anthony and Cleopatra at the Battle of Actium.
27 BCE	Octavian declared Augustus; end of the Republic and beginning of the Roman Empire.
14–68 CE	Julio-Claudian emperors: Tiberius, Caligula, Claudius, Nero
69–9 CE	Flavian emperors: Vespasian, Titus, Domitian
98–117 CE	Trajan (101–107, Dacian Wars)
117–138 CE	Hadrian; the building of Hadrian's wall in Britain
161–180 CE	Marcus Aurelius
212 CE	The Emperor Caracalla offers Roman citizeuship to all free men and women in the Empire
250–300 CE	The Empire suffers from foreign invasions, plague, inflation and military coups
284–306 CE	The Emperor Diocletian restores the Empire; divides the Empire into East and West with a hierarchy of Augusti and Caesars
312/313 CE	Constantine, the first Christian emperor; the Edict of Milan proclaims Christianity as a recognized religion in the Roman Empire.
330 CE	The center of the Roman Empire is moved from Rome to Constantinople.
381 CE	Theodosius I forbids all forms of paganism; Christianity become the sole religion of the Empire.
410 CE	Alaric and the Goths sack Rome.
476 CE	The last Roman emperor is defeated by the Germanic leader Odoacer: the Roman Empire ceases to exist in the West, but continues for the next thousand years at Constantinople/Byzantium.

Table II.2 Historical events in the history of Rome

tombs (Figure II.5). The history of Etruscan culture was written by later Roman writers so that we do have many loan words that have survived in Latin.

The way to know the will of the gods was revealed to the Etruscans by Tages, a childlike figure who arose from the tilled land. His teachings were written down,

Figure II.5   Etruscan tomb painting. *Source:* perseomedusa/© 123RF.com.

kept in sacred books, and passed on to each generation of priests. All natural phenomena (lightning, organs of sacrificial animals, flight patterns of birds) were an indication of the immanence of the divine will, which could be interpreted by specialists known as *haruspices* and *augurs*. The Romans would later refer to this lore as the *disciplina etrusca*, and trained their own priests in its fundamentals.

Etruscan influence on ancient Rome is found in art, architecture, engineering (domes, arches, sewers, city planning), the hierarchical structure that became the model for the Roman Republic (including the Senate), the toga, and the symbol of power and authority, the *fasces* (bundles of rods surrounding an ax, carried by lictors or bodyguards). Etruscans contributed the idea of the tripartite Capitoline Temple (Jupiter, Juno, Minerva, from the Etruscan Tinia, Uni, and Menrva). The gladiator games in Rome may have originated in Etruscan funeral rites, where the slaves of the dead fought to the death at the grave.

The City of Rome

According to legend, the city of Rome was established in 753 BCE by the twins Romulus and Remus. Using a plow, Romulus outlined the area around seven hills, with a valley in the middle that was originally the city's market. This demarcation line was the *pomerium* or the sacred zone of the city. The sacred zone related to imperium, or the power to command, and certain magisterial offices were thus imbued with a sacred duty. Romulus killed his brother and became the first king of Rome. Romans also claimed that their ancestors were descended from Aeneas, a son of Venus and a refugee from Troy, who had settled at the foot of Mount Alba, at Alba Longa, from where many ancient religious

Figure II.6   Statue of Romulus and Remus. *Source*: Leemage/Corbis via Getty Images.

concepts came to Rome. The two stories were reconciled by having Aeneas as the ancestor of Romulus and Remus (Figure II.6).

Numa Pompilius, of the tribe of Sabines, was the legendary second king of Rome (reigned 715–673 BCE), and according to tradition, established the institutions of Roman religion and ritual. His inspiration allegedly came from the nymph Egeria. He authored sacred books of divine teachings which established the hierarchy and function of priesthoods. He also brought the cult of the **Vestal Virgins** to Rome from Mount Alba (and some traditions claimed that his daughters were the first Vestals).

Early Romans held the concept of *numen*, a Latin term for divinity or divine presence, understood in a similar vein to the Etruscan belief in divine immanence. This was an invisible power found everywhere. The **Lares** and **Penates** were guardian *numina* that protected all that happened within the boundaries of their location, beginning with the household. The Roman writer Plutarch (46–120 CE) claimed that King Numa forbade Romans to represent any of these powers in the form of humans or beasts. This lasted for about 170 years until Greek influence dominated Roman religious representations.

In 509 BCE the Romans ousted the last of the Etruscan kings and established the Roman Republic. The republican system relied upon the election of individuals to represent the interests of the general population. There was a Senate of the nobles (the **patricians**) and assemblies where free-born citizens voted for various magistrates each year. Over the next two centuries, the non-noble class of citizens (**plebeians**) successfully campaigned for a share of political power and noble status. They also gained access to the priesthoods in Rome. A position as a magistrate and in a priesthood ennobled their families and their descendants.

In 390 BCE the Cisalpine Gauls under the leadership of Brennus attacked and occupied Rome. The only holdout in the city was the Capitoline Hill, where the defenders were alerted by the sacred geese of Juno. The Gauls demanded a ransom but while negotiations were going on, the Romans had time to regroup and eventually expelled the enemy. This event created tremendous damage to the Roman psyche and fears of another invasion from the north lasted for centuries. It was the first and last time a foreign army would conquer the city of Rome until 410 CE.

From the beginning of the Republic to the third century BCE, Rome concentrated on conquering various Italian tribes and the Greek settlements of Magna Graecia. By 290 BCE, Rome controlled most of the peninsula. In doing so Rome absorbed the indigenous Italian deities, as well as the Greek influences now attached to them, and included these elements in the traditional religious festivals of the city.

The Punic Wars (264–146 BCE)

The major rival to Rome in the western Mediterranean was the Carthaginian Empire, which was based in the North African city of Carthage (modern Tunisia). Rome referred to these people as *Punicus* because they were Phoenicians who had migrated to the western Mediterranean in the ninth century BCE. Carthaginians had settled throughout North Africa and Spain and controlled most of the commerce in the region. The Punic Wars consisted of three wars from 264 to 146 BCE, and began over the fact that Carthage controlled most of the island of Sicily. Rome was determined to include Sicily as part of the Italian peninsula because Rome needed control of the large grain fields located there.

Carthage was the dominant naval power, although this changed after Rome realized it had to build ships and create a navy. The first war ended in a draw but the Second Punic War, 218–201 BCE, almost destroyed Roman ambitions. The Carthaginian general Hannibal led his troops from Spain across the Pyrenees and the Alps and descended upon the Italian plains. He successfully defeated the Roman legions at the Battle of Lake Trasimene and the Battle of Cannae where Rome lost 80 000 men.

Rome was able to conscript and recruit more men for the legions, although they adopted Fabian tactics (named after Fabius Maximus Verrucosus who refused a pitched battle with Hannibal in favor of a war of attrition). Hannibal became less threatening because he failed to receive supplies and reinforcements from Carthage, where the ruling Council did not favor Hannibal's family. In the last stages of the war, Rome attacked the settlements in North Africa, forcing Hannibal to return to Carthage and mount a defense. He was defeated by Scipio Africanus at the Battle of Zama in 201 BCE.

In 149 BCE, Numidia, a Roman ally in North Africa, claimed to be under attack by Carthage and Rome went to her defense. By 146 BCE, Carthage was totally destroyed. Throughout the Punic Wars, Rome simultaneously waged war in Spain, Macedonia, Greece, and Syria. With victories in these areas, and the destruction of Carthage, Rome became the ruling power in both the western and eastern areas of the Mediterranean.

The Social War (90–88 BCE)

When Rome conquered the Italian tribes, most were granted the status of allies or client states, but without the privilege of Roman citizenship. Rome jealously guarded this privilege and the Senate refused to compromise. However, all of the Italian states were required to fulfill the duties of citizens, such as taxes and conscription in Roman armies. Impatient with this discrimination, almost all of the Italian states declared their independence from Rome and declared war on the Republic in 90 BCE. After two years of slaughter and exhaustion on both sides, with the Italians defeated, the Senate capitulated and granted citizenship rights.

The Social War also contributed to a growing resentment by the lower classes against the rich and powerful, who claimed that nobility of birth entitled them to rule over the majority. Many of the assemblies (made up of citizens, including plebeians) devolved into riots, and factions appealed to powerful individuals to champion their demands. A peace of sorts was established when Sulla marched on Rome with his legions (an unprecedented event), and assumed the office of Dictator in 88 BCE. He restructured the constitution in favor of the nobility while eliminating almost all of the power of the lower classes. However, after his death, many of his changes were annulled and the plebeians gained back their rights.

The End of the Republic

Most historians agree that the very size and nature of Rome and her provinces could no longer be sustained by the Republican system that limited magistrates' offices to one year, and put them at the whim of the voters. Between 60 and 54 BCE, three powerful and ambitious men in Rome believed that they could solve all the problems by combining their wealth, resources, and power. This is known as the First Triumvirate of Julius Caesar, Pompeius Magnus (Pompey the Great), and Marcus Crassus. Caesar contributed the common people's support for him and his status (even though he was a patrician), Pompey controlled many of the legions, and Crassus was believed to be the richest man in Rome.

Although Caesar was popular with the masses, one did not succeed in Rome without a military reputation. Between 58 and 50 BCE, Caesar waged his Gallic Wars (in France and Belgium), ultimately defeating all of the combined tribes. The Senate, however, refused to renew his *imperium* (magisterial power), and in 49 BCE, he invaded Italy (crossing the Rubicon River, the northern border of Italy proper). Caesar and Pompey had fallen out, and Pompey convinced the Senate to flee Italy for Greece, where he could rally more troops. Pompey and the Republicans were defeated in 48 BCE at the Battle of Pharsalus (central

Greece), and Pompey was later assassinated in Egypt. Eventually Caesar defeated the remnants of Pompey's army in North Africa in 45 BCE, essentially eliminating the old Republic.

Caesar, who had been voted by the Senate as dictator for life, was assassinated in 44 BCE by a coalition of disgruntled senators. The Second Triumvirate was formed shortly after this by Octavian, Antony and Lepidus to handle the crisis of a power vacuum. Octavian was Caesar's great-nephew and adopted heir, Antony had been Caesar's Master of the Horse (second in command), and Lepidus controlled the armies in North Africa. They hunted down and executed the assassins, finally defeating the last two, Brutus and Cassius, at the Battle of Philippi (northern Greece) in 42 BCE.

Not long after this, Octavian and Antony fell out and Antony attempted to build his own empire in the east with the help of Queen Cleopatra of Egypt. The navies of Rome defeated the navies of Antony and Cleopatra at the Battle of Actium in 31 BCE and Antony and Cleopatra committed suicide. Earlier Lepidus had been outmaneuvered and eliminated by being sent to North Africa, where he was eventually convicted of treason. This left Octavian as the sole ruler of the Roman world.

In 27 BCE, the Senate honored Octavian with the title of Augustus (venerable or esteemed) and he instituted a new form of governance, the Roman Empire. He said that he was merely the *princeps civitatis* (First Citizen), but he controlled the Senate, the armies, the treasury and soon took over the highest religious authority in Rome, that of **pontifex maximus** (13 BCE). Augustus claimed that he at last brought peace, or the **pax romana**. Because Augustus had been legally adopted as Julius Caesar's son, he added the name to his own. Hence, the name Caesar came to be associated with the highest imperial power in the term "emperor." All the successors to Augustus would use the name as their official title. (We find the same use of this title in Germany (Kaiser) and in Russia (Tsar).)

Augustus promoted Roman benefices to the empire through his religious reforms. He rehabilitated many neglected temples and revived older religious festivals, including those of foreign cults. He believed that a revival of traditional religion would promote the traditional values and morals of contemporary Romans. He instituted marriage and divorce laws, encouraging marriage (and the procreation of children), and punished those who did not comply. He made divorce harder to obtain, made adultery a civil crime, and taxed men over the age of 38 who had not yet married. Augustus presented himself as the ideal **paterfamilias** ("head of the family") but in this case, a father figure of the entire Roman Empire.

Subsequent Centuries

Imperial Rome, under the guidelines of Augustus, maintained some success through the second century CE. The successors of Augustus were often adopted (as no living sons had survived) and were drawn from the Julio-Claudian lines of Augustus and Livia. While some of his successors often ruled in the style of dictators (particularly Caligula and Nero), nevertheless the Imperial system became the norm. In the third century, a series of disasters (inflation, plague, barbarian invasions) began to expose the weaknesses of the system. Between 250 and 300 CE, there were approximately 25 emperors, most of whom died in battle or were assassinated. In 284, Diocletian took the throne (reigned 284–305) and divided the empire between the East and the West, with *Augusti* ruling each area. Nevertheless, individuals remained ambitious for complete control, which was achieved when Constantine defeated his challengers in 312 in the West, and in 324 in the East. Constantine became a Christian in 312, which eliminated the persecution of Christians in the empire. His grandson, Theodosius I, declared that Christianity was the only legal religion and outlawed all forms of native worship.

In 410 Rome was sacked by the Goths and in 476 the Roman Empire in the West fell to invading Germanic tribes. However, Roman rule continued in the East in the city of Constantinople (later known as Byzantium), until it was conquered in 1453 by the Ottoman Turks and renamed Istanbul.

--- Summary

- This chapter has provided a brief historical overview of the older civilizations of the Mediterranean basin and identified some elements of their religious concepts and practices that were shared by ancient Greece and Rome. While the means of the transformation of particular elements is often not known, nevertheless trade and conquest provided the opportunity to learn from other cultures.
- The brief history of the civilizations of Greece and Rome identified factors in their cultural traditions that were incorporated into religious beliefs and practices. As we will see in the following chapters, Greece and Rome continued to memorialize historical events in their religious festivals.

--- Suggestions for Further Reading

Boardman, J., J. Griffin and O. Murray. eds. 2001. *The Oxford Illustrated History of the Roman World*. Oxford University Press. This comprehensive volume includes art and literature, as well as the basic elements of the history of Rome.

David, R. 2003. *Religion and Magic in Ancient Egypt*. Penguin Books. This text provides both a chronological history of Egypt as well as the evolution of religious ideas.

Johnson, S. I. ed. 2004. *Religions of the Ancient World: A Guide*. Belknap Press of Harvard University Press. The details of concepts and practices of all religions in the Mediterranean basin are comprehensively outlined in this text.

Parker, V. 2014. *A History of Greece: 1300 to 30 Bc*. Wiley Blackwell. A good introductory text on the evolution and history of ancient Greece.

MYTHS, GODS, AND HEROES: GREECE

III

Greek and Roman Religions, First Edition. Rebecca I. Denova.
© 2019 John Wiley & Sons, Inc. Published 2019 by John Wiley & Sons, Inc.

Learning Objectives

After reading this chapter, you will be able to:

- Understand the popularity and function of myths in the ancient world.
- Become familiar with some of the basic myths and characteristics of the more popular gods of Greece.
- Recognize the similar function of heroes and hero cults.

 The myths of ancient Greece and Rome have provided the inspiration for literature, drama, poetry, and art throughout the centuries of Western tradition. The exploration of the human psyche as reflected in the stories continues to motivate the questions of philosophers, psychologists, and social scientists.

We do not have an ancient equivalent of sacred scripture for the gods of Greece and Rome, nor was there an authoritative institution like the Vatican that was responsible for putting together such a collection. Rather, we have stories of the gods that were recited and passed down for millennia. However, the stories come to us in various forms and through different vehicles. Homer and Hesiod presented archaic views of the gods that were collected in their day as epic poetry. Bards and lyric poets popularized hymns to various deities, priests included some details in their prayers, educated men related their own interpretations, and dramatists added different versions. Individual aspects of the divine were included in domestic cults, religious rituals, and religious festivals, while art and architecture visualized popular images and actions of the gods.

Modern students are often confused that the gods and goddesses have so many different versions of their tales. One reason for this is that local towns and cities contributed their own versions of the lives and functions of divine actors. This was particularly true in stories of the foundation of a town or city; all ancient people wanted to claim ancestry from one of the gods or the golden age of heroes. Scholars attempt to sort the older stories from the later ones, and sometimes archaeology helps, but it remains a difficult task. Contradictory stories about the same god or hero did not appear to be a problem for the ancients.

This chapter will discuss the basic elements of ancient mythology. We will then present the more popular gods, goddesses, and heroes of Greece, followed by the same treatment for Rome in Chapter IV. The myths of the gods in both chapters will of necessity be brief, as we cannot include all the stories concerning the gods. We have included the ones that highlight their background and responsibilities. We will examine the relationship of myths to some specific cult centers in Chapter VI.

Mythology

In the modern world, we separate sacred myths from secular myths (such as George Washington and the cherry tree), but in the ancient world *all* myths were sacred. Those that contained mundane or civic details were always related in the context of the involvement of the gods.

In the field of Religious Studies, myths are ways to articulate and understand experiences of the holy, expressed through a collection of stories, metaphors, and images. Myths are multivalent or subject to many different interpretations and analyses on many different levels. Most often, ancient myths arose not as a systematic or historical relating of facts, but as attempts to explain the meaning of events. In simpler terms, and for our purposes, a myth is a traditional story that explains origins, practices, and beliefs and creates a worldview for a people. In addition to teaching about the gods, myths were used to promote and validate the ideals and institutions of society and to ensure that social codes were in conformity with the will of the divine.

Origin myths contain stories of the primordial beginnings of things such as the cosmos, the gods, animals, and human beings, or relate the foundation of an ancestral lineage, a sacred site and the foundation of a town or city. Myths contain etiologies or explanations of how and why things came into existence, such as agriculture. Etiologies are always updated – they reflect the group's contemporary world and explain many elements of the social order. Scholars use the term alienation myths to classify those stories that explain how and why evil exists, or to explain the fallen state of humans from an original utopian existence. Some of these stories also explain sexual alienation, such as the story of Eve in Genesis or Pandora's box (see below).

Fables have traditionally been regarded as distinctly different from myths as a separate literary genre. Fables contain fabulous elements such as mythical monsters and animals with anthropomorphic features, including speech. There is some confusion between myth and fable as many ancient myths contain fabulous and unrealistic features, but fables always ended with a specific moral lesson. The other difference is that fables rarely discuss the divine; they deal with mundane elements of everyday life. Many fables are paradoxical by reversing expectations, as in the story of "The Tortoise and the Hare." The most widely known collection of fables was attributed to Aesop, a Greek writer from Athens in the fourth century BCE, and entitled *The Aesopica*. Nevertheless, the myths of the ancient world often included the same elements of fable: fabulous characters and events, a moral lesson, and irony.

Scholars often separate the categories of myth, legend, and folklore as a means to analyze both the content and the contextual setting of the stories. A convenient way to do this is to categorize myth as a story about a god, while legend is a story about a hero or historical figure. For instance, the stories of Heracles before he became immortal would be considered legends. However, at this distance, it is difficult to ascertain if ancient people categorized stories in the same way. Ancient historians and philosophers did discuss myths and legends but usually when describing those of another ethnic group or culture. In that case, those stories were usually derided as being false as compared to one's own cultural heritage.

Modern theorists are embroiled in the "myth vs. ritual" debate. Did people begin performing rituals for some unknown reason and then justify them with a story, or are rituals reenactments of preexisting myths? In the former situation, people have forgotten exactly why they do the ritual and try to rationalize the meaning behind it. In the latter case, ritual reenactments attempt to connect contemporary time with mythic time in order to validate the current social and religious codes of conduct. Anthropologists and sociologists continue to study contemporary primal societies that utilize oral traditions in many parts of the world to arrive at an answer.

Myth as **allegory** was a favorite topic of ancient schools of philosophy. In this interpretation, while most people continued to understand myth literally, educated men claimed that myths contain symbols that go beyond the literal to encompass ideals or universals. For example, at one level there are stories of Aphrodite involved in love affairs, but on a higher level, one can interpret such stories as essentially being about *Eros* or the life force of physical, human desires. In Plato's "Allegory of the Cave," people are chained in a cave where things pass in front of a fire behind them. What the people see are shadows or forms of reality and not the essence of reality itself. This method of explaining myths was adopted by many educated men. In the first century CE, Philo, a Jewish philosopher in Alexandria, explained the elements in the stories of the Hebrew Scriptures through allegory.

There are many more theories of myth that we could explore, but for our purposes, we can conclude with the way in which myth functions in our context. There is no doubt that many of the events related in the myths of Greece and Rome served the purpose of sheer entertainment and escapism, just as superheroes in modern action films serve that purpose today. At the same time, these myths established models of behavior and validated the social order. Set in mythic time, the stories created an aura of mystery and sacredness and provided an age-old tradition that could be rationalized as mandatory for subsequent generations. An individual was integrated into the larger group through sharing these common stories. Contrary to popular belief, myths were not always set in stone. Details changed over time, place, and circumstance and were often manipulated for social and political purposes.

In any discussion of myth we need to emphasize that myths can be divided into two sources: literary and cultic. The epics of Homer (once they were written down), Hesiod, the poets, the playwrights, the historians, and philosophers provide the most well-known stories of the gods. However, local cult centers created different myths, most of which were not written down. These myths served the purpose of their particular rituals and worship and may have had little to do with the literary traditions that coexisted. It is most likely that the early spread of epic poetry provided the images of gods, but it remains difficult to determine the local integration of the traditional, literary stories, if any. The many different cults to the same god provide the various combinations of names for both function and place, such as Zeus Ctesius (protector of the household) or Zeus Agoreus (protector of the marketplace).

In the myths of the ancient world, the gods were always described as looking like humans, but much more beautiful, stronger, and taller. They married and had children, experienced adventures and enjoyed the good life, which included music, poetry, and entertainment. The divine food was ambrosia, they drank nectar, and a fluid called ichor flowed through their veins instead of blood.

The gods also had the human emotions of jealousy, anger, fear, love, and petty revenge. They appeared to humans in dreams, in the flesh, as animals and sometimes in disguise. There are numerous occasions when the male gods had intercourse with human women (particularly Zeus), producing a child who usually grew up to be a hero or demigod. But the great difference between humans and the gods was their immortality. Even though some gods were wounded in the stories, and temporarily died, they were always restored to eternal life.

In the Beginning: Greece

Utilizing a shared concept in the ancient world in creation myths, Hesiod began with chaos, or a formless mass which produced the cosmos and the gods. From the eighth or seventh century BCE, we have two major works of Hesiod, *Theogony* and *Works and Days*. They provide accounts of the beginning of the cosmos, the succession of the gods, the origin of sacrifice, and the evolution of the stages of man (see the box "The Five Ages of Man"). It was important to establish the succession and the means by which Zeus became the head of the gods, along with the mated pairs of personified powers that established the fertility of the cosmos and the earth. Subsequently, poets, dramatists, and other writers added more details over time.

The Five Ages of Man

An evolutionary development of humankind became a popular supplement to stories of the gods. Hesiod was most likely the first to describe the ages of man in this way, in his *Works and Days*. He began with the Golden Age, the most perfect of all the ages, which had that ambience of "once upon a time." Cronus still ruled and he instructed Prometheus to mold humans out of clay. Humans and gods freely mingled together in harmony just as all men lived in harmony. There was no labor and everything they needed was taken from the earth. Humans lived long lives and eventually grew old and simply fell asleep to their deaths. Their spirits became beneficial demons and guardians of other humans.

The Silver Age followed, now under the dominion of Zeus. Humans lived to be one hundred, but only very few years as an adult. Once they reached adulthood, they fought one another and refused to worship the gods. Zeus destroyed them for this stubbornness, but their spirits became benevolent in the underworld. The men of the Bronze Age were even worse, as they were created by Zeus out of ash trees and hardened to constant warfare. Zeus brought about the end of this age with his flood. The spirits of the dead eternally roamed the land of Hades.

The Heroic Age does not follow the same negative progression as the Silver and Bronze and appears to be a nostalgic one for Hesiod. These were the humans who arose after the flood and held a special status of hero or demigod, although they dwelt with regular humans. These heroes were the characters of legend at Mycenae, Thebes, and Troy, and when they died they were rewarded with an eternity in either Elysium or the Isles of the Blessed.

The Iron Age was contemporary for Hesiod and he viewed his world in the poorest light, particularly when compared to the Golden or Heroic Age. He claimed that it was an age full of toil, misery, and evil.

There was no longer any respect for the family, the practice of hospitality was forgotten or abused, and armed might took precedence over justice. It was so bad that the gods had given up on humans and no longer intervened on their behalf. We cannot measure how much of Hesiod's view was shared by his contemporaries. However, in much of the later literature and rhetoric that has survived, we see a constant reference to what we would term "the good old days" and how the past was more perfect than the present. It was to hold onto that past that Greeks evoked ancient traditions and Romans evoked the *mos maiorum*, or ancestral custom, as the rationale for their beliefs and actions in their contemporary world.

Chaos, a formless mass, produced Nyx (night), Erebus (darkness), Tartarus (abyss), Eros (sexual desire), and Gaea (earth). Nyx and Erebus produced Aether (upper air) and Hemera (day). Alone, Nyx produced Thanatos (death), Hypnos (sleep), Moros (doom), Nemesis (divine retribution), and the Fates. Gaea alone gave birth to Uranus (sky), Ourea (mountains), and Pontus (sea). She then mated with her son Pontus and produced various sea gods and sea serpents. Gaea married her son Uranus, who became the ruler of the universe, and they produced the Titans and the Cyclops. The Titans were immortal giants and the Cyclops were giants with a single eye who were craftsmen and shepherds. Some of the more well-known Titans were Oceanus, Cronus, Helios, Selene, Eos, Atlas, and Prometheus.

Uranus disliked some of the Titans and Cyclops and imprisoned them in Tartarus, a lower area of Hades. He feared that one of his children would usurp his rule of the sky. Gaea turned to her children to get rid of him, but only Cronus volunteered for the job. He castrated his father with a sickle (cutting off his testicles), and thus eliminated his power. The testicles landed in the sea near Cyprus and the semen produced sea foam to create Aphrodite. The blood that fell on the ground produced the *Erinyes* (Furies).

Cronus was now ruler of the universe and he married his sister Rhea. Against his mother's wishes, he did not release all of the Titans and the Cyclops from Tartarus. In what became a common theme in mythology, Gaea predicted that, like his father, a son of Cronus would usurp his throne. Cronus eliminated the problem by swallowing the children he shared with Rhea (Demeter, Hestia, Hera, Hades, and Poseidon). The youngest and last child, Zeus, was hidden and Rhea gave Cronus a stone wrapped in a blanket as a substitute, which he promptly ate.

As an adult Zeus tricked Cronus into drinking a drug that made him vomit out his siblings. Led by Zeus, these siblings helped him wage war against the Titans, who supported Cronus, and this lasted for 10 years. Zeus and his allies defeated the remaining Titans, who were again chained in Tartarus (as told in the *Titanomachy*). One Titan, Atlas, was uniquely punished with having to hold up the world on his shoulders (near the Atlas Mountains in Morocco).

Again, Gaea was unhappy that all her children were not free, and so with Tartarus she produced the monster Typhon. Later embellishments describe Typhon as part man, part beast, taller than any mountain, and with dragon heads in his armpits and coils of snakes under his thighs. Typhon sired several monstrous or hybrid beings: Cerberus, the Chimera, the Hydra, the Nemean lion, and the Sphinx. Zeus eventually defeated this monster and caged him under Mount Etna in Sicily. The dragon fire of Typhon was one explanation for the volcanic eruptions on the island.

To finish out with some of the myths that explain origins, we have conflicting stories of the creation of humans. In one, Cronus created humans because he thought they might be interesting and amusing. Another version claimed that the Titan Prometheus created humans out of the clay of the earth and then Athena breathed life into them. Zeus ordered Prometheus and his brother Epimetheus to provide gifts to created beings. Epimetheus wanted to begin first, and gave gifts to the animals of the earth – beauty, agility, strength, and speed. Relative to animals, humans were defenseless so Prometheus gave them reason, fire, and his own knowledge. Zeus was particularly angry about the gift of fire to humans (this could make humans more like gods) and he punished Prometheus. Prometheus was chained to a rock and an eagle ate his liver every day (at the end of which it grew back). After several years, the hero Heracles rescued Prometheus from his chains.

Zeus remained angry and wanted to eliminate the human race, so Prometheus taught men how to sacrifice to Zeus. However, Prometheus had the offerings divided into two types, the good meat (disguised) and the skin and bones with the fat, and told Zeus to choose. Zeus chose the fat and bones, which infuriated him, but became the tradition in ritual sacrifices. This was a myth to explain why offerings to the gods contain the least desirable portions while humans were permitted to eat the meat.

Zeus ordered his son Hephaestus to mold a woman out of clay, to which all the gods and goddesses contributed some traits, and named her Pandora ("all gifts"). This creation was meant to punish and weaken men. Pandora was given to Prometheus's brother Epimetheus. Prometheus warned his brother about gifts from Zeus, but Epimetheus was charmed by her. Pandora had a box, an urn, or a jar, depending upon the version and the translation. Hesiod claimed that Zeus had two jars, one filled with all good things, and one filled with all evil things. Allegedly the latter was the one given to Pandora. Unable to resist her curiosity, Pandora opened the box, and released evil; only hope remained.

Men now acted upon evil. An Arcadian leader, Lycaon, sacrificed a baby and gave it to Zeus to eat (who happened to be disguised as a workman). In his rage, Zeus sent a flood to wipe out the human race and Poseidon helped with his waves. Again, Prometheus saved humans. His son Deucalion and his brother's daughter Pyrrha were married and were considered a pious couple. Prometheus warned them of the coming disaster and they built a boat (or chest in other versions). The rain and flooding wiped out all the rest of humanity, but the couple survived and landed on Mount Parnassus (or various other mountains).

Realizing they were alone in the world, they first sacrificed to Zeus in appreciation of their survival, and then prayed to Thetis, the sea nymph, for advice on how to repopulate the world. She instructed them to throw the bones of their mother over their shoulders. Perplexed at first, they finally realized that stones were the bones of mother earth and proceeded accordingly. From Deucalion's efforts came men, and from Pyrrha the women. The couple then produced their own children, including Hellen, the eponymous founder of the Hellenes, or Greeks.

The Myths of the Olympians

The Olympians comprised the traditional gods and goddesses who dwelled on Mount Olympus (believed at the time to be the highest mountain on earth). There were 12 Olympians, although individual lists could vary at times: Zeus, Hera, Poseidon, Demeter, Athena, Aphrodite, Ares, Apollo, Artemis, Hermes, Hephaestus, and Dionysus. Some lists have Hestia instead of Dionysus, and others include Hades and Persephone, Eros, and the hero gods, Heracles and Asclepios. The Olympians are first mentioned collectively in the Homeric Hymns (beginning in the seventh and sixth centuries BCE), and the first reference to a cult of "the twelve" was in Athens in the Classical Age (fifth century BCE). The Olympians had dominion over areas of life on earth and were portrayed with individual characteristics and symbols. While many of the myths have the Olympians in paired relationships, some of the women were known as virgin goddesses in the sense that they never married (see the box "Virgin Goddesses"). What follows are the more popular tales of the Olympians.

Virgin Goddesses

Virgin goddesses were well established in the Greek pantheon: Athena, Artemis, and Hestia. This appears to be a paradox, as these goddesses function as earth-mothers or fertility goddesses and are responsible for marriage, the birth of children, and women's work in the household. The virgin epithet indicated that these goddesses were not formally married to a male god. Virginity symbolized youth and purity and the protection that society provided for young girls until they married.

The virgin goddesses were protectors and we see this in detail in Athena's importance for the city of Athens, where she is the divine protector against the enemies of the polis. Her impregnable status as virgin is symbolic of the impregnable status of the Athenians, and socially this was upheld in the unviolated status of their virgin daughters. A later version of this same concept was the epithet attached to Queen Elizabeth I of England (1533–1603), as "the Virgin Queen." This did not refer to her intact sexual status (she had many affairs) but to the fact that ultimately she decided never to marry and to rule alone.

Zeus

Zeus was primarily a sky god, ruling over the gods and humans. He was married to his sister Hera but he also had many sexual affairs with other goddesses and human women that resulted in a number of gods, semidivine humans, and heroes. The list of his offspring included Ares, Athena, Apollo and Artemis, Dionysus, Hephaestus (in some versions), Heracles, Hermes, Persephone, Perseus, Helen of Troy, Minos, and the Muses. He also had male lovers and abducted the young boy Ganymede to serve the gods in Olympus because of his beauty. By tradition, the domains and attributes of the gods and goddesses were assigned by Zeus.

The symbols of Zeus included the eagle, bull, and the oak, and a favorite depiction of statues of Zeus was one of him with an upraised arm, ready to let loose his thunderbolt. Many myths related his sexual escapades. The cult centers of Zeus added more details and localized connections and he held sway over elements of the home, gateways, and oracle centers at various sites around the Mediterranean. An ancient and popular oracle was at Dodona in Epirus (northwestern Greece).

Hera

If anyone could be entitled, "queen of the gods," it would be Hera in her capacity as wife and sister of Zeus. She was the daughter of Rhea and Cronus and her responsibilities included women and marriage. As a protector of marriage, Hera was most famous for her jealousy concerning the affairs of her husband and her vengeful attacks upon the offspring from such liaisons. Hera was often shown with a cuckoo (later replaced by peacocks after Persian influence in the Hellenistic era) and a cow. Homer referred to her as *boopis*, translated as "cow-eyed" (Figure III.1).

Figure III.1   Statue of Hera. *Source:* MARKA/Alamy Stock Photo.

Together, Hera and Zeus produced Ares (war), Hebe (youth), Eris (discord), and Eileithyia (childbirth). In one tradition, Hephaestus (metallurgy) was a son produced by Hera alone because Zeus gave birth to Athena without her. Hephaestus was not beautiful like the other gods and so Hera threw him down from Mount Olympus. Hera was famous for her relentless revenge against Heracles, a son of Zeus and Alcmene. She sent snakes into the crib of Heracles when he was a baby. Hera then put obstacles in the way of every labor of Heracles, but they were ultimately reconciled when Heracles died and was exalted to Olympus.

Another myth involving Hera was the story known as "The Judgment of Paris." Zeus invited all the gods except Eris (discord) to a wedding feast for Peleus and Thetis. True to her name, Eris crashed the wedding and brought a golden apple inscribed with "for the fairest one." Hera, Athena, and Aphrodite all claimed it and asked Zeus to judge who was the most beautiful. Being wise enough not to get involved, Zeus assigned the judgment to Paris, a prince of Troy. Aphrodite bribed him with the promised gift of the most beautiful woman, Helen, the wife of Menelaus of Sparta (Helen of Troy). Choosing Aphrodite, Paris thus initiated the Trojan War. Hera found her revenge in supporting the Greeks over the Trojans.

Poseidon

After the battle between the old gods and the next generation, the division of spoils gave Poseidon the rule of the seas. Tradition claims that, like Zeus, he was hidden at birth by his mother Rhea when she produced a colt and gave it to Cronus instead. Thus Poseidon was also associated with horses (with a favorite epithet of Poseidon Hippios). In some ancient texts another horse association arose from a myth in which Poseidon unsuccessfully wooed Demeter, who turned herself into a mare to escape his advances. He captured her, and she gave birth to Arion, a horse who could speak. Another epithet was that of "earth-shaker." Earthquakes produced tsunamis and hence an association with the seas. Poseidon's major symbol was the trident and he was often shown being drawn by horses (and seahorses) over the waves. He was a dominant god of port cities and all sailors were encouraged to sacrifice to Poseidon for a safe voyage.

Poseidon competed with Athena for dominance in the city of Athens (see below). Although he lost the race, the Athenians continued to honor him, particularly for his help with both trade and colonization. Like Zeus, Poseidon had many lovers of both sexes, although his main consort was the sea nymph Amphitrite. In Homer's *Odyssey*, Poseidon is the enemy of Odysseus, placing obstacles to his journey home because Odysseus had blinded Poseidon's son, a Cyclops.

Demeter

Long before the categorization of the Olympians as a group, Demeter was worshipped as a fertility and harvest goddess. Her importance was recognized in the fact that grain (cereals, corn, wheat) was the basic food staple of the Mediterranean.

Because of her involvement in the harvest she was responsible for the sacred laws of nature related to the laws of agriculture. The symbolic concepts of the cycles of life and death in agriculture were manifest in both the regular cults and the Eleusinian Mysteries; her story symbolized the changing seasons.

Demeter was the daughter of Cronus and Rhea, and her brother Zeus was the father of her daughter Persephone. The most famous myth concerning Demeter was the tragedy of Persephone's abduction by Hades, who ruled the underworld. Demeter became obsessed with the search for her daughter and so the seasons failed (so that it was always winter, with no growing season) and crops died. She appealed to Zeus, who sent Hermes to the underworld to bring Persephone back and restore her to her mother. However, Hades tricked Persephone into eating the seeds of the pomegranate, which meant that she was forced to return to Hades for several months of the year. The time spent with her mother became the growing season, while her time in Hades symbolized the winter months. The story of the adventures of Demeter while searching for her daughter and their eventual joyous reconciliation became the focus of the Eleusinian Mysteries. (For more details on the Eleusis cult and others, see Chapter IX.)

Athena

Athena had an unusual birth. A second wife of Zeus, Metis (the daughter of Oceanus), had great wisdom and feared that Zeus would kill the child to keep it from usurping his position. That is exactly what Zeus thought, and on the advice of Gaea and Uranus he swallowed Metis whole. Zeus suffered a horrendous headache one day. Hephaestus split his head with an ax and Athena sprang from Zeus's head fully grown.

The city of Athens was named in honor of Athena because she won the contest against Poseidon to provide the most beneficial element to the city. According to the story, Poseidon and Athena raced their chariots and Athena was the first to arrive. She then planted an olive tree. Poseidon, arriving second, took his trident and created a salt spring. Olive oil was a major industry in Greece and so the prize was awarded to Athena. Nevertheless, she shared her position with Poseidon in the coupling of their benefits and titles (Poseidon Hippios and Athena Hippia), and Poseidon's trident marks became a sacred spot housed in one of the temples of Athena on the Acropolis.

A second foundational story connected Athena with the original inhabitants of the city. The Athenians claimed to be autochthonous, "born from the earth." Unlike the inhabitants of other cities, they had not originally migrated from foreign lands. As such, they claimed descent from an ancient king, Erechtheus. According to the story, Hephaestus fell in love with Athena and chased her to fulfill his desires. As she fought him, his semen spilled on the ground and produced Erechtheus. Athena became his foster-mother, and thus Athenians could claim that their genealogy derived from the "earth-born" Erechtheus as well as the nurturing from a divine parent.

Athena is often depicted in a helmet and armor, carrying a spear and shield. Many statues and paintings also include an owl, the symbol of wisdom (see Figure III.2, where the snake also represented wisdom). Her title of Pallas Athena remains clouded in various ancient versions. Pallas is either the father or the foster-sister of Athena. In one version, Athena killed Pallas by accident, and then took her name in order to honor her. In Homer's *Iliad*, Athena has the titles "Daughter of Zeus whose shield is thunder" and "Guard of the armies of Zeus." She directly supported individual soldiers, as well as the Greek cause against the Trojans. In the *Odyssey*, she is called "Hope of soldiers" and is the main divine support for the successful adventures and ultimate victory of Odysseus. She and Odysseus appear to share the traits of cleverness and deception.

Athena was the founder of the cultural, political, and judicial contributions of Athens to civilization. Her connection to women was found in the textile industry, which began in the home. Although active in male activities (war and peace), she did not promote similar roles for women, but rather upheld the ideal position of patriarchal rule in marriage.

Figure III.2 Statue of Athena. *Source:* Werner Forman Archive/Heritage Images/Getty Images.

Aphrodite

The goddess Aphrodite had numerous epithets and functions and we find parallels with her throughout the ancient world (especially in Egypt, Mesopotamia, and Phoenicia). She had an abnormal birth, springing from the semen of the castrated Uranus. Always associated with beauty, her sacred animals were doves, horses, and swans. With various gods and lovers, she was the mother of Eros (Ares), Hermaphroditus (Hermes), Priapus (Dionysus), Tyche (Zeus), and Aeneas (Anchises).

Either in an attempt to keep the gods from fighting over her or as the consequence of the release of Hera from a magic throne (see below), Zeus married Aphrodite to Hephaestus, the unattractive god of smiths and metallurgy. She was not faithful to Hephaestus and when she slept with Ares, he created a golden net to trap the two and publicly shame them. Another famous lover of Aphrodite was Adonis, the son of Myrrha of Cyprus. Myrrha had bragged that she was more beautiful than the goddess, so Aphrodite caused her to have a sexual desire for her father. Before being turned into a myrrh tree, she gave birth to Adonis and Aphrodite placed him in the care of Persephone in Hades. When Adonis was an adult, Aphrodite journeyed to Hades to claim him, but Persephone wanted to keep him there. Zeus judged that Adonis should spend a third of the year with Persephone, a third with Aphrodite, and a third wherever he wanted to go. When he was killed while hunting a wild boar, Aphrodite created anemones out of the drops of his blood.

Eros was the son of Aphrodite, either from Ares or as the result of the semen of Uranus present at her birth. However, Eros as a power was present at the beginning of creation, according to Hesiod, which included the principle of sexual desire. The physical manifestation of Eros later portrayed him with wings and a bow and arrow (targeted at lovers). Philosophers often allegorized Aphrodite as the motivation for sexual intercourse, the life force, and love (Figure III.3).

Ares

"Battle" was the appropriate meaning of the name of Ares, the god of war. He was the son of Zeus and Hera, and his own sons Phobos (fear) and Deimos (terror), and his sister Eris (discord) often rode in his war chariot, serving as the physical motivations necessary to successfully wage war. The valor and courage of soldiers was assigned to Ares, but the victory was usually the responsibility of his half-sister, Athena. While recognizing the necessity of aggression in war, nevertheless, in Homer, Zeus calls him the "most hateful of all gods."

There are few myths with Ares as the central character; he is most often referred to in passing in war stories. However, there were many stories about his relationships with women, beginning with the story of Aphrodite and her husband Hephaestus. With Aphrodite he fathered Eros, Anteros, Phobos,

Figure III.3 Statue of Aphrodite and Eros, 100 BCE. *Source*: Artokoloro Quint Lox Limited/Alamy Stock Photo.

Deimos, and Harmonia, from which descended the Amazons. But he also had liaisons with dozens of mortal women and deities. Ares was a main character in the founding myth of Thebes. He had sired the water-dragon that was killed by Cadmus. The dragon's teeth were planted in the ground and they sprouted warriors. To appease Ares, Cadmus married his daughter Harmonia to bring about peace. In another foundation myth, Ares killed a son of Poseidon, Halirrhothius, because he raped his daughter Alcippe. Poseidon called Ares to appear before a tribunal of the gods on a hill in Athens, where Ares was acquitted. The site became known as Areopagus, or "hill of Ares," the area that contained the law courts of Athens.

Apollo

Apollo was one of the more complicated gods of Olympus, with multiple geographic origins and multiple responsibilities that often appear contradictory. He was the god of the sun, music, prophecy, healing, medicine, herds and flocks, and poetry, but he was also responsible for plagues and destruction. His origins may have been Minoan, Mycenaean, Anatolian, Lydian, or Dorian, and he had similar traits to sun deities in Mesopotamia, which also connected him with the reading of omens in that culture and thus divination. He had oracular shrines most famously at Delphi, Claros, and Didyma.

Zeus disguised himself as a swan and seduced Leto, a daughter of the Titans Coeus and Phoebe. Hera discovered the affair and forbade Leto to give birth on earth. Leto went to the island of Delos, which was considered to be a "floating island" and therefore not under the ban. She gave birth to the twins Apollo and Artemis. As a youth, Apollo killed the dragon Python at Delphi, established the Pythian Games that were held every four years, and became the inspirational deity behind the oracle. Apollo was most often shown with the lyre, bow and arrows, the palm tree, wolves, dolphins, and laurel leaves.

Apollo had numerous lovers, although he wasn't always successful. Daphne, a nymph daughter of the river god Peneus, rejected Apollo's overtures. When he chased her she appealed to her father for help and he turned her into a laurel tree. Apollo honored her by making the laurel sacred in his cult. Apollo and Hecuba, the wife of King Priam of Troy, had a son named Troilus. According to an oracle, Troy would never fall if Troilus reached the age of 20, but he was killed. His sister Cassandra rejected Apollo's love when he offered her the gift of prophecy. Her punishment was that she received the gift, but no one would ever believe her. In revenge for the killing of the priests of Apollo at Troy by Achilles, he guided Paris's arrow that pierced Achilles' heel.

When Apollo brought Hippolytus back to life (a victim of a jealous Aphrodite), Zeus punished him by assigning him to work for King Admetus. He helped Admetus in many ways, one of which was to convince the Fates to let a volunteer die in Admetus's place. The only volunteer was his wife Alcestis. For this courageous act Heracles went to Hades and brought her back. Apollo's most famous son was Asclepios, the god of medicine (see below).

Artemis

Artemis, the twin sister of Apollo, was the goddess of the hunt, wild beasts (particularly the bear), untamed nature (groves, forests, untilled countryside), childbirth, and virginity. Scholars agree that her cult is archaic and most probably originated in an earth-mother or fertility concept (and hence her association with women and childbirth). Her attributes were a bow and arrow, a short dress (appropriate for running), and she was often depicted with a stag at her side (Figure III.4).

Tradition claims that Artemis was born first and helped her mother with her brother's birth. The young Artemis asked Zeus to grant her several wishes, which included perpetual virginity. When Agamemnon collected the Greek fleet to sail to Troy, the winds were withheld because someone killed one of Artemis's stags. He sacrificed his daughter Iphigenia to resolve the problem. In another version, Artemis intervened and substituted a deer for Iphigenia.

The hunter Actaeon came across Artemis bathing in the woods and stared at her. For this violation, Artemis ordered him not to speak. When he heard his

Figure III.4 Statue of Artemis with deer, 350 BCE. *Source:* Peter Horree/Alamy Stock Photo.

hunting party approach he cried out to warn them. Artemis turned him into a stag and he was torn apart by his hunting dogs. When Niobe, the daughter of Tantalus, boasted that she had 14 children (seven sons and seven daughters) compared to Leto, who only had two, Apollo killed the boys with his arrows and Artemis killed the girls with hers. Two men from Athens killed a bear sacred to Artemis and she sent a plague to the city. It only ceased when the Athenians promised to commit their virgin daughters to the care of the goddess every five years.

Hermes

Hermes was known as a "trickster god" who cunningly outwitted the other gods, helped thieves, and was the patron of athletes, poets, inventors, traders, and travelers. As such, he protected all boundaries and was the intermediary between humans and the gods. Zeus used him as a messenger and the most popular depictions show him with a winged helmet, winged sandals, and a herald's staff entwined with snakes. In his role as messenger of the gods, he delivered dreams to humans. As Hermes Psychopompos, he was the guide of souls to Hades because he could cross between life and death. The rooster and the tortoise were his sacred animals. When Zeus created Pandora, Hermes's contribution to her gifts included the art of seduction.

While still a baby, Hermes stole a herd of cattle that belonged to Apollo. He reversed the hooves of the cattle as well as his own shoes so that the footprints could not be traced to his cave. He snuck back to his crib and was sound sleep when an angry Apollo accused him. However, when the truth was learned, Apollo eventually forgave him because Hermes offered Apollo his invention, a lyre made from a tortoise shell.

Popular representations of Hermes were the **hermai**, stylized pillars with a bust of the god at the top and an erect phallus below (Figure III.5). The fertility symbol of the phallus reflected his patronage of herds and flocks and his sons Pan and Priapus, woodland fertility deities associated with shepherds. Herms were located at crossroads, boundaries of fields, and outside houses as amulets of good luck. During the Peloponnesian War (415 BCE), all of the herms in Athens were vandalized the night before the Athenian fleet set sail for Syracuse (Sicily). Athenians believed that this was the reason their fleet was destroyed.

Figure III.5   Statue of Herm, 280 BCE. *Source*: PRISMA ARCHIVO/Alamy Stock Photo.

Hephaestus

Hephaestus was the son of Zeus and Hera, or of Hera alone. He was the god of blacksmiths, craftsmen, metals, metallurgy, fire, and volcanos. He forged the weapons and implements of the gods and taught humans this art. He invented tripod tables that moved on their own for the banquets on Olympus, and created Pandora, the first woman. His symbols were the hammer, anvil, and tongs.

The story of the fall of Hephaestus began with his birth and Hera's rejection of him because of a shriveled or deformed foot. She threw him down from Olympus and he landed on the island of Lemnos, which became one of his earliest cult centers. (In one version of the story, he was crippled in this fall.) To punish his mother, Hephaestus created a magic throne for her from which she could never get up. Dionysus brought Hephaestus back to Olympus, made him drunk, and convinced him to undo his trick. Eventually Hera and Hephaestus were reconciled.

The Greek colonists in southern Italy and Sicily associated him with the volcano on Mount Etna. In addition to the workshop on Mount Olympus, it was believed that Etna was the location of one of his master forges. By tradition, he created the chariot of the sun god Helios, Hermes's winged helmet and sandals, Eros's bows and arrows and Achilles's armor. He was also responsible for creating the Aegis breastplate, variously assigned to either Zeus or Athena, which depicted the head of a **gorgon**.

Dionysus

The son of Zeus and Semele, Dionysus was a god of fertility and taught humans the art of making wine. The release that was experienced in wine drinking also led to divine ecstasy, or the suspension of one's self and the idea of possession by the god. This concept may have been behind the early development of acting and drama and Dionysus was the patron of yearly drama festivals in Athens. Many geographical regions make up theoretical theories for his origins (including Thrace, Anatolia, and Libya) and his many stories associate him with foreigners or foreign rituals. We can speculate that this foreign element contributed to his association with unconventional social elements as well. Beyond his regular cults, the Dionysus Mysteries were concerned with life, death, and rebirth. (For more details on the Mystery cult of Dionysus see Chapter IX.)

Zeus used to visit Semele nightly in an invisible form so that she did not know which god was visiting her. Hera, being jealous, appeared to her as an old woman and convinced Semele that she should insist on seeing her lover. Zeus was reluctant to show himself, but finally agreed. When he appeared in all his glory as a lightning bolt, poor Semele was fried to a crisp. Zeus rescued the fetus of Dionysus and sewed him into his thigh until he was born. Hera appealed to the Titans to destroy him and they tore him apart. Rhea restored him to life. Zeus then gave him to the mountain nymphs to be raised in secret out of the sight of Hera.

Dionysus's symbols were a fennel staff topped with a pinecone (known as a *thyrsus*), bulls, serpents, ivy, and wine. He was portrayed riding a chariot pulled by panthers, and sometimes he was dressed in a leopard skin. Popular art depicted his processions with followers of **maenads** and **satyrs**. Maenads were wild women who belonged to his cult. Satyrs were fertility creatures. They were shown as half-man, half animal (horse ears and tails in Greek art and goats' ears, tail, legs, and horns in Roman art). The fertility aspect was demonstrated with oversized, erect penises. The processions were always joyous, with dancing and singing, and Dionysus was celebrated as the god with the power to periodically release the tension caused by social conventions by allowing people to "break loose," in the experience of **catharsis**.

Dionysus had many adventures and once, when he sailed from Icaria to Naxos, the sailors decided to sell him into slavery. He turned the mast and oars into snakes and produced flutes to drive the sailors mad. They leapt into the sea and became dolphins. In another story, Dionysus's mentor Silenus went missing. He had been drinking and in his drunken state wandered to the court of King Midas, who offered him hospitality. As a reward, Dionysus offered Midas any wish he wanted, and Midas asked that everything he touched turn to gold. This "Midas touch" turned out to be a disaster as the king realized he could not eat and mistakenly turned his daughter into gold. Appealing to Dionysus, he was told to wash in the river Pactolus, which became a source for gold prospectors.

One of the more popular stories of Dionysus was found in the play *The Bacchae* by Euripides (405 BCE). Dionysus went to Thebes to establish his cult. Many in the city, including many of the women, as well as King Pentheus, did not believe that his mother Semele had been impregnated by Zeus and therefore thought Dionysus not worthy of worship. He convinced Pentheus to spy on the women of Thebes (who had been turned into maenads by Dionysus). Possessed by the god, in their frenzied behavior they tore apart animals. Pentheus was caught and ripped apart by his mother, who did not recognize him in her madness. The women were banished from Thebes but the cult of Dionysus was established.

Other Important Deities

Hestia

The hearth, the center of the home, was protected by Hestia, who was the daughter of Cronus and Rhea, a virgin goddess and protector of the family and the state. From Mycenaean times, Greek public buildings had a *megaron* or great hall, with a central hearth dedicated to Hestia. Wine libations were poured out to her at feasts and one of her symbols was the pig, a main staple of meat in the ancient Mediterranean. Another favorite symbol was the cow. The hearth fire was essential for the prosperity of the home and state, and Greek colonies were often blessed with fires lit from shrines to Hestia.

With the hearth at the center of the household, all newborn children and slaves were ritually made part of the family at the hearth. New brides were welcomed to the family of their husbands at the hearth, and the procreation of children was emphasized as the bride's function in the male household. As a protector of women, Hestia ensured sacredness of the wife's person and validated her role in Greek society.

In the traditional myths, after Hestia rejected marriage proposals from Poseidon and Apollo, Zeus designated Hestia to oversee the hearth of Olympus and put her in charge of the Olympian household. The fatty portions of animals were assigned to her and thus Hestia was always included in all religious sacrifices. There are few myths about Hestia, although she was often credited with kindness. She allegedly gave up her space in the list of Olympians to Dionysus to avoid a conflict, and she was also credited with creating the concept of sanctuary in temples.

Asclepios

Asclepios became the god of medicine and the healing arts, fathering Hygieia (hygiene, health, and cleanliness), Iaso (recuperation from illness), and Panacea (universal remedy). He was the son of Apollo and a mortal woman, Coronis, who was killed because of her unfaithfulness. Apollo rescued the unborn baby (and perhaps the source of his name, "to cut open?") and gave him to the centaur Chiron, who provided him with an education in medicine. After Asclepios showed kindness toward a snake, it licked his ears and imparted secret knowledge of the healing arts. The symbol of snakes entwined around his staff (the caduceus) became and remains the symbol of the medical profession (Figure III.6).

Asclepios became so proficient at healing and bringing people back from the dead that Zeus was afraid of an imbalance and Hades was afraid that his population would diminish. Another version claimed that Asclepios helped his father Apollo in the raising of Hippolytus. The result was that Zeus killed Asclepios with a thunderbolt. He was later exalted to the heavens and became one of the gods. The healing temples of Asclepios (*asclepions*) became the object of popular **pilgrimage** by people seeking cures for every known malady.

Tyche

The daughter of Aphrodite and Hermes or Aphrodite and Zeus, Tyche was the goddess of fortune or luck, mainly in relation to cities. The vagaries of war, plague, and other natural disasters were sometimes subsumed into the idea that there was a force in the universe that arbitrarily decided the fate of the community. Tyche was appealed to as an attempt to avert such disasters.

Figure III.6   The caduceus. *Source*: iStock/Getty Imges Plus.

The Fates

The Fates (*Moirai*) were the daughters of Zeus and the Titaness Themis in some sources, or the daughters of *ananke* (necessity). The three sisters were understood to be responsible for the length of one's life. Clotho spun the thread of life, Lachesis measured its length, and Atropos made the final cut. Not usually subject to official cults, the Fates were understood to be present in the home at the birth of each child.

The Muses

The nine Muses were the daughters of Zeus and Mnemosyne (memory) and were responsible for individual inspiration in literature, the arts, and sciences: Calliope (epic poetry), Clio (history), Euterpe (lyric poetry), Erato (love poetry), Melpomene (tragedy), Polyhymnia (sacred poetry, hymns), Terpsichore (dance), Thalia (comedy and pastoral poetry), and Urania (astronomy). Although attested early in Hesiod and Homer, their areas of expertise were not fully codified until the late Hellenistic period. Apollo was often recognized as their leader.

The Muses were visualized in paintings and sculpture with their specific symbols that matched their areas of inspiration: poets, historians, dramatists, and philosophers traditionally began their works by calling upon one of the Muses for both inspiration and as an acknowledgment of their favors.

Local shrines to the Muses were usually built at the site of a spring or fountain, and caves and popular sites were located at Parnassos, in Boeotia, and Delphi. Shrines to individual Muses were also found in combination with a shrine at the tomb of a successful writer. One of the more famous of the temples to the Muses was located in the Hellenistic city of Alexandria, Egypt. One of the successors of Alexander, Ptolemy Soter, built a learning complex that included the famous Library of Alexandria. All poets, scholars, historians, scientists, physicians, and inventors were encouraged to study here, where the temple of the Muses was located in the center. This "museum" became the inspiration for similar complexes in the modern world.

Heroes

While there were thousands of Greek heroes in Greek history, some were venerated after their death because of their great deeds and because of the belief that they could still help (or harm) the living. There were shrines dedicated to various heroes, but most often the focus of worship and ritual was at the tomb or *heroon*. These tombs were marked off with a fence or wall and were designated sacred space. Almost all cities claimed one of the heroes, especially those with stories that included either the founding of the city or some great deed that took place there. An example of this is the worship of Theseus in Athens and Cadmus in Thebes. There were multiple levels of divinity involved. Only Heracles and Asclepios became fully divinized as gods but the majority were either embedded in the gradients of the heavens or became beneficial chthonic deities of the underworld.

Stories of heroes can be traced to the Mycenaean Age but were probably older. Such heroes became known through the epic stories of the bards and Homer, but the majority of hero cult names have not survived. Heroes could be worshipped in conjunction with the regular cults of the divine. However, heroes received chthonic rites where black animals were used and libations were poured into the ground. They were called upon to alleviate harm or bring benefits to individuals or to the community. The section of Hades reserved for dead heroes was either the Elysian Fields or the Isles of the Blessed, depending upon the source.

Hero cults could be localized or Panhellenic, such as those of Heracles and Asclepios, whose shrines were located throughout the Mediterranean world. There were Panhellenic heroes who only had local shrines, such as Pelops at Olympia, Erichthonios in Athens, and Odysseus in Ithaca. Heroine shrines for such women as Semele, Penelope, and Iphigenia existed, but we know less about their cults. The literary focus on these women always emphasized their moral goodness or chastity rather than heroic deeds.

Individuals who died in battle did not receive hero cults. Due to the nature of war, many soldiers were cremated on site (although sometimes the urns were shipped home). A famous hero cult for a large number of the war dead was the burial mound erected for those who died at the Battle of Marathon (490 BCE). Even in ancient times, people made a pilgrimage to the site and it was always on the lists of tourist destinations. Scholars have long noted the connection between hero cults and politics. In Classical Athens, Cleisthenes divided the Athenians into voting clusters based upon their ancestral heroes (he was told to do this after consulting the oracle at Delphi).

Perhaps one of the most famous of the heroes and hero cults was that of Heracles, the son of Zeus and Alcmene, a mortal woman. Hera in her jealousy set out to ruin Heracles's life, beginning in infancy. When he was grown, she afflicted him with madness and he killed his wife Megara and their children. Heracles consulted the Delphic Oracle for his penance, and (directed by Hera), the oracle told him to put himself in the service of King Eurystheus and do any task that was asked of him. The "Twelve Labors of Heracles" were famous not only for his courage and strength, but for his cunning and wit in carrying them out. At his death, he was welcomed as one of the gods on Olympus. The cult of Heracles was spread throughout the Mediterranean basin, including the Carthaginian colonies in North Africa and Spain. Heracles (as Hercules) was included in one of the foundational myths of the city of Rome (Figure III.7).

The Greeks also honored various chthonic gods such as Hades, which are highlighted in Chapter X.

Figure III.7   Heracles.
Source: akg-images/
André Held.

Summary

- The Greek myths of the gods explained the origins of the world, details of the lives of the gods, and founding elements of their towns and cities. Myths also explained and validated the social structures and individual responsibilities.
- Stories of heroes and the establishment of their cults were connected to familiar stories of the myths of the gods. Sacred sites connected with hero cults were the pride of communities and were important elements of local religious festivals.

Suggestions for Further Reading

Clark, M. 2012. *Exploring Greek Myth*. Wiley-Blackwell. In addition to an analytical discussion of myth, Clark incorporates local customs and ritual practices in some of the lesser known stories that were important to the ancient Greeks.

Hamilton, E. 2011. *Mythology: Timeless Tales of Gods and Heroes*. Grand Central Publishing. This is an updated version of the myths that became part of the Western tradition.

Morford, M. P. O., R. J. Lenardon and M. Sham. 2013. *Classical Mythology*, 10th ed. Oxford University Press. This is a massive anthology of all the sources for each god and goddess. It contains commentaries on most of the myths and includes traditional Western art that was inspired by the stories.

Powell, B. B. 2015. *Classical Myth*, 8th ed. Pearson Education. Powell's book remains one of the most popular texts on classical mythology, where his long career in research and teaching has created expertise on ancient Greece.

MYTHS, GODS, AND HEROES: ROME

IV

Greek and Roman Religions, First Edition. Rebecca I. Denova.
© 2019 John Wiley & Sons, Inc. Published 2019 by John Wiley & Sons, Inc.

Learning Objectives

After reading this chapter, you will be able to:

• Understand the shared traditions of the myths and gods between Greece and Rome.
• Appreciate the traditions of Etruscan and Italian divinities that were incorporated into Roman culture.

 At least to the modern critical eye, Roman mythology suffers by comparison with the Greeks, bolstered by a centuries-old critique that Rome prioritized cult over literary aspirations. An older Roman conceptualization of the divine was quite different from that of the Greeks. Whereas Greek concepts of the gods reflected human characteristics, the older Italian, Etruscan, and Roman traditions understood that *numina*, or the invisible forces of power in the universe, existed without form, faces, or human aspects. *Numina* were understood as divine presence and divine will.

Each of these powers had very specific functions and responsibilities which reflected the daily functions and responsibilities of human activity. Balance and order in both the world of the divine as well as the world of the living had to be maintained. This balance was the responsibility of the Roman magistrates in their combined role as priests. The traditional way in which the priests addressed some gods reflected this older concept in the phrase "Siue deus siue dea" ("whether god or goddess"), in the sense that the gender of the deity remained unknown but that all caution had to be applied so as not to offend the specific power by an incorrect address. Jupiter Optimus Maximus (Jupiter Best and Greatest) brought all of the forces together but even here an additional line was included: "or if you would like to be called by any other name."

According to tradition, when King Numa established the religious rituals he forbade the creation of images for the powers. It was only after the influence of Greek culture in southern Italy and the Hellenization of the wider Mediterranean world that Rome began to adopt anthropomorphic images of the gods. Greek culture was admired everywhere and Rome wanted to appear just as sophisticated. Rome absorbed the stories and characteristics of the Olympians (which became part of the educational curriculum), adding their own indigenous layers. Roman mythology reflected their priority of promoting both the history of their culture as well as the history of their religious rites. While adopting the basic Greek myths of the gods, Rome nevertheless related the events to Italian locales and promoted Roman values.

Romans accepted the creation stories of Hesiod and Homer, which were collected by Ovid (*Metamorphoses*) with some editing (see the box "The Four Ages of Man in the Roman Tradition"). Rome was far more interested in the divine elements of her own accomplishments. Romans honored their own historical personages and usually treated the traditional narratives as historical even when these had miraculous or supernatural elements. The stories are often concerned with politics and morality and how an individual's personal integrity relates to his or her responsibility to the community or Roman state.

Heroism is an important theme. When the stories illuminate Roman religious practices, they are more concerned with ritual, augury, and institutions than with the formation of the cosmos.

A problem in the study of Roman mythology is that so much of the literature was relatively late and was thoroughly syncretized when it was finally written down. Writers applied the principle of *interpretatio romana*, or interpreting religious traditions in light of Rome's preexisting concepts. In the late third century BCE, the poet Ennius (c. 239–c. 169 BCE) listed the *dii consentes*, or the Roman equivalent of the Greek Olympic pantheon, and Livy (64 BCE to 17 CE) arranged them in male–female pairs: Jupiter–Juno, Neptune–Minerva, Mars–Venus, Apollo–Diana, Vulcan–Vesta, and Mercury–Ceres. Only fragments of indigenous Italian or Etruscan mythology have survived independently of the Roman writers.

The Four Ages of Man in the Roman Tradition

The Roman poet Ovid (43 BCE to 18 CE) related Hesiod's "Ages of Man" in his *Metamorphoses*, but he omitted the Heroic Age. He repeated similar traits of the Golden Age, where the land automatically produced bounty without any work from humans. In that age, men had not yet learned to navigate the seas and did not explore any of the other cultures. The Silver Age brought about the seasons and this motivated men to learn the arts of both agriculture and architecture, as the seasons gave reason to build houses. Men participated in warfare in the Bronze Age. He paralleled Hesiod in his description of the Iron Age (the current age) as the worst age of all. Men now violently opposed one another, neglected the gods through sacrilege, were immodest, and their only concern was with economic greed.

This last description appears surprising, as Ovid had patronage from the Emperor Augustus, who brought the *pax romana* or a new, peaceful age in Roman history. However, the reign of Augustus culminated in the end of the Republic and Ovid may have had some pessimistic ideas about the change. Augustus legislated against immorality and it should be noted that Ovid ended his days in exile after Augustus charged him with depravity. Appearing as scandalous now as at the time, his *Ars amatoria*, the "Art of Love," taught the arts of seduction and infidelity in what may have been intended as satire on Roman society.

In the Beginning: Rome

Romulus and Remus were twin brothers in the founding myth of Rome. They were the children of Mars and Rhea Silvia, the daughter of King Numitor of Alba Longa. This was an ancient sacred mountain area south of Rome. King Numitor's brother, Amulius, seized the throne and ordered the twins to be killed, but a servant consigned them to the protection of the Tiber River, where they floated until miraculous intervention. The most common depiction of them was being suckled by a she-wolf (an earlier, Etruscan image). A shepherd found them and raised them as shepherds. When they discovered their origins, they killed Amulius and restored Numitor. The twins then migrated north to found the city of Rome.

According to the most common legend, the brothers disagreed about which hill to choose to begin urban development at Rome. Romulus wanted the Palatine, while Remus wanted the Aventine. Romulus took a plow and drew a circle around the hills, with the Palatine in the middle of designated walls. This line was the *pomerium* and everything inside the circle was sacred territory. Remus aggressively "jumped the wall" as an insult, and Romulus killed him. The story may simply explain why the name of the city was "Roma." Later embellishments reconciled this story with that of the traditions concerning Aeneas, making the twins descendants of Aeneas and so eliminating a rival tradition (see below). The sources posit the founding date for Rome as between 756 and 728 BCE.

The center of the city was a mosquito-infested swamp and thinly populated. The swamp was drained (applying the sewer engineering skills of the Etruscans), but Rome needed a population. Romulus invited exiles, refugees, criminals, and runaway slaves to move to the city. However, he also needed women, so he created a religious festival and invited the Sabine and Latin tribes to attend. Their virgin daughters were abducted and forced to marry the Romans. (This became famous in art and literature as "The Rape of the Sabine Women.") In reaction, the Sabines declared war, but were soundly beaten by Romulus. The women helped to make peace by accepting their fate and their new homes. The defeat of the Sabines was the occasion for the first Roman victory parade (see "The Roman Triumph" in Chapter VI). In addition to being the eponymous founder, Romulus is credited with originating most of the cultural and religious traditions of the city. He organized soldiers into legions, and gathered the most noble and wealthy men to become his councilors. This patrician class became the first members of the Senate. The population was organized by tribes with concomitant voting rights and civic duties.

There are two contradictory versions of the death of Romulus. In one, he disappeared during a storm while offering sacrifices near the Quirinal Hill. The second version claimed that the Senate was angry at his tyrannical dictates and so they killed him. Nevertheless, the understanding was that he had undergone **apotheosis,** or exaltation to divinity. Romans worshipped him in the form of the god Quirinus (after the name of the hill) and Romans often referred to themselves as **Quirites** in recognition of their ancestral founder.

Aeneas

A second founding myth of Rome involved the adventures of Aeneas, a son of Venus and the mortal Anchises of Troy. During the rule of Augustus, earlier versions of the myth were brought together to become one of Rome's founding and ancestral masterpieces, the *Aeneid*, by the poet Vergil (70–19 BCE). Although mentioned briefly in Homer's *Odyssey*, it is from the *Aeneid* that we have the fullest version of the "Trojan Horse" story, with Vergil's famous line, *Timeo Danaos et dona ferentes* ("I fear Greeks, even those bearing gifts").

In the myth, Aeneas escaped from Troy with his son and his father. The palladium, an ancient, sacred wooden image (either of Athena or an unknown talisman), was stolen by Odysseus in one version, but ended up in the hands of Aeneas so that ultimately he could bring it to Rome, where it was housed with the Vestal Virgins. In parallel with the adventures of Odysseus, Aeneas is confronted with ill-winds, bad omens, and a series of adventures before he can achieve the will of the gods, which was to bring him to Italy. When he landed in Carthage, Queen Dido fell in love with Aeneas and convinced him to dwell with her for several years. However, Aeneas remembered his destiny and abandoned her. Dido cursed him (a rationale for the later Punic Wars between Rome and Carthage) and then committed suicide.

In Vergil's version, after finally landing in Italy, Aeneas was unsure of himself and decided to consult his father, who was now dead. With the help of the Sybil at Cumae, he descended to Hades to obtain Anchises's advice. (Vergil's descriptions of the various sections of Hades became the prevailing images in the Western tradition and served as the basis for art and literature through the Renaissance (Dante's *Inferno*) and up to the modern period.) Anchises presented him with an array of the future depicting all of the famous Romans and Roman achievements that would flow from Aeneas. Heartened, Aeneas settled in Lanuvium near Alba Longa, married the king's daughter and established the beginning of Rome. Julius Caesar and the first five emperors after him claimed direct descent from the line of Aeneas and thus from Venus.

Jupiter

The Roman equivalent of the "king of the gods" was Jupiter (often called Jove), who was the dominant god of Rome throughout its history and who shared the attributes of Zeus (Figure IV.1). He also held a thunderbolt, and the symbol of his eagle was placed on coins and later adopted by the Roman army. The Roman Jupiter incorporated elements of the earlier Etruscan sky-god Tinia. According to tradition, Jupiter helped provide the divine inspiration for King Numa to establish Roman religious ritual. All Romans swore their oaths to Jupiter as "best and greatest." The higher levels of magistrates in Rome held all-night vigils in the temple of Jupiter, followed by banquets in his name, after their inauguration ceremonies.

According to Roman myth, Jupiter was the son of the ancient Italian deities Ops and Saturn (see below). Like Cronus, Saturn devoured all his children so that no one would usurp him. Ops hid Jupiter and gave Saturn a stone to eat which did not agree with him and so he disgorged all of his children. Jupiter overthrew him and forced him to leave Italy for a while, although Romans would retain Saturn in their pantheon and festivals. There were many stories of Jupiter's love affairs and the stories paralleled those of the Greeks. He was the father of Venus, Mercury, Proserpina, Apollo, Diana, and Minerva.

Figure IV.1   Statue of Roman Jupiter. *Source*: Peter Horree/ Alamy Stock Photo.

Jupiter's responsibilities were identified by his epithets, pairing his name with particular functions: Jupiter Terminalis (defender of boundaries), Jupiter Victor (helping armies to victory), and Jupiter Feretrius (in charge of the spoils of war). There were dozens of these combinations, including those powers connected with agriculture and vine-growing. Some of the oldest *ludi* or games in Rome were dedicated to Jupiter (the *ludi Romani* in September) and certain days of the calendar were devoted to him as well (the Ides and Nundinae).

The dominant temple for Jupiter was located on the Capitoline Hill above the forum. Originally housing Jupiter, Mars, and Quirinus, during the Republic it became the home of the state triad of Jupiter, Juno, and Minerva. The temple contained a colossal statue of Jupiter which according to tradition was sculpted by the Etruscan artist Vulca of Veii. The top of the temple had a statue of Jupiter driving a *quadriga* or four-horse chariot. Other temples and shrines to Jupiter were located throughout the city. An important temple was dedicated to Jupiter Stator, attributed to Romulus. This was the function of Jupiter as the "stayer of the armies of Rome." There were several legends which related crises when soldiers needed encouragement and a morale boost so that they wouldn't flee the field; Jupiter stayed their urge to desert.

Juno

Juno was an ancient Italian deity, the daughter of Saturn and Rhea and the wife and twin sister of Jupiter. She was responsible for women as well as the Roman state. With Jupiter, Juno was the mother of Mars and Vulcan, and she was honored in the Capitoline Triad along with Jupiter and Minerva. Her symbolic animal was the peacock, and in Rome she had sacred geese. Juno is the source of the name for the month of June, which was by tradition, the luckiest month to marry.

The roles and functions of Juno were multiple and complex and were reflected in her many epithets. In marriage she was present at the loosening of the bride's girdle (Juno Cinxia), was in charge of the Roman mint (Juno Moneta), fertility (Juno Mater), childbirth (Juno Lucina), calendar days (Juno Kalends), and the protector of Rome (Juno Sospita). A late tradition equates the *genius*, the generative force and guiding spirit of men, with a parallel concept for women, *juno*.

In keeping with the nature of Roman mythology, most of the stories of Juno parallel those of Hera. This is particularly true in the many stories of Juno's revenge against her husband's victims of love. The pinnacle of Roman literature about Juno was achieved in Vergil's epic poem, *The Aeneid*. In this story, her revenge against the Trojans is extended to the survivor Aeneas, where she functions in the same role as Poseidon in *The Odyssey*, acting as a constant obstacle to the character's destiny of founding Rome.

Juno's incorporation into the Capitoline Triad most likely arises from Etruscan tradition where all Etruscan towns had triple temples to Tinia (Jupiter), Uni (Juno), and Menrva (Minerva). According to a popular story, Juno was called upon by a Roman commander (through evocation) after a 10-year siege of the Etruscan city of Veii. She was invited to leave Veii and take her place in Rome where she was promised a temple and devotion.

Tradition assigned Juno as a savior of Rome when the Gauls stormed the city in 390 BCE. The attack came in the middle of the night, but the dogs of the city failed to bark and alert the sentries. The geese of Juno quacked loudly enough to rally the Romans. The Gauls did take the city, but ultimate destruction was avoided by the timely intervention of Juno's geese. From that time onward, gaggles of geese were housed on the *Arx* of the Capitoline (separated from the northern part by a depression in the hillside) near the temple of Juno Moneta. This story was the source for what may have been one of the strangest Roman religious festivals. Allegedly, once a year the historical events were remembered by rounding up many stray dogs in the city. They were led in procession by magistrates carrying the geese on cushions. Afterward, the dogs were crucified or impaled as their punishment. (The authenticity of this religious festival remains subject to debate by scholars.)

Neptune

The Roman god of the seas was Neptune, the son of Saturn and Ops, brother of Jupiter and Pluto. Like the Greek Poseidon, he was also a god of horses (Neptunus Equester) and the patron god of horse-racing and chariot-racing (along with the ancient fertility god Consus). Older Etruscan traditions (where he was known as Nethuns) associated him with the rivers, lakes, and springs. With his sea nymph wife Salacia (related to salt water), he had a son named Triton who was half-man, half-fish. Neptune was associated with another nymph, Venilia, who represented both the destructive as well as the beneficial powers of water. Thus Neptune was connected to more ancient concepts of a fertility god and was a benefactor who brought the rains.

A contest was held among Vulcan, Minerva, and Neptune as to who had the greatest skill. Vulcan made a man, Minerva a horse, and Neptune a bull, which probably explained why the bull was a proper sacrificial animal for his cult. In the story of Aeneas, Neptune was not as destructive as Juno and at one point rescued the Trojan fleet from her vengeance, mainly because she dared to work up the seas against them and the seas were his domain.

Minerva

Derived from the Etruscan name of a similar goddess, Menrva, Minerva was associated with wisdom, music, the arts, weaving, poetry, medicine, trade, soldiers, and war strategy (FigureIV.2). She was also a virgin goddess who ruled without a male equivalent. Like Athena she was born from the head of Jupiter and she shared other traits with the Greek goddess. The Etruscan Menrva's sphere of influence may have originally been the moon and with *mens*, or "mind," found Roman associations. The Roman Minerva was portrayed with a helmet, shield, spear, owl, a snake, and an olive tree.

Minerva had temples all over Italy (later in the provinces) and a large temple on the Aventine Hill. She was also known as Minerva Medica at a temple on the Quirinal Hill in her role as patron of medicine and doctors. There is no body of independent Roman literature that relays the myths of Minerva that has survived. What remains is found in Ovid's *Metamorphoses* VI and *Fasti* III. Minerva is the "goddess of a thousand works," and the poet encourages all poets, artisans, craftsmen, musicians, and laborers to honor her.

Ovid relayed the story of Arachne and Minerva. Arachne rivaled the goddess in the art of weaving and boasted that her work was superior. Minerva visited Arachne disguised as an old woman and advised her to ask forgiveness from the goddess. When Arachne refused, a contest began. Minerva's tapestry glorified the Olympians, while Arachne's only showed scenes of rape and violence. Minerva humiliated her rival to the extent that Arachne hung herself. In a move of pity, Minerva then turned Arachne into a spider. This myth not only explained the origins of spiders and their webs but it also taught respect and fear of the gods.

Figure IV.2   Statue of Minerva. *Source:* iStock/Getty Images Plus.

Mars

Mars, the Roman god of war, was highly celebrated and an integral part of the Roman identity. He was combined with elements of agriculture and had an important role in the founding of Rome as the father of Romulus and Remus. The month of March (*Martius*) was named after him and was originally the time of the New Year for the beginning of war campaigns and spring planting. He had a place in the earlier Roman triad with Jupiter and Quirinus, but his eventual removal from that triad did not diminish his importance. As Rome expanded throughout Italy and beyond, Mars was central to successful Roman conquest and was also worshipped as a personal god of the legionaries. Roman youth began their military training on the Campus Martius, which had an altar to Mars originally dedicated by King Numa.

In Roman mythology, Mars was the son of Juno alone, conceived with a magic flower. His main consort was Nerio (valor), who was the feminine vital life force in conjunction with the masculine traits of Mars. The Romans included the Greek story of the love affair between Ares and Aphrodite (now Mars and Venus) and they were a favorite depiction as a couple in Roman art as well as funeral inscriptions. The wolf and the bear were sacred to Mars and his favorite bird was the woodpecker (*Picus Martius*), whose beak was strong enough to break through the bark of trees. Mars wore a helmet and carried a shield and spear.

According to legend, a shield (*ancile*) fell from Heaven during a plague. On the advice of the nymph Egeria, King Numa had 11 copies made to guard against thieves. At the time, a voice from Heaven proclaimed that Rome would be mistress of the world as long as the shield was protected. The shields were in the keeping of the *salii*, the special priests of Mars.

Mars was also associated with an ancient Italian goddess, Anna Perenna, who was responsible for the New Year. According to the story, Mars fell in love with Minerva but she rejected him. He appealed to Anna Perenna for help but she herself was in love with the god of war. She disguised herself as Minerva and tricked Mars into marriage. Her cult was celebrated on March 15 (the Ides of March) by young girls who wore garlands of fruit and flowers, sang bawdy songs, and were released from the usual behavior dictated by social conventions.

In recognition of his final victory over the assassins of Julius Caesar, Augustus built a temple to Mars Ultor (the "avenger"). It became a place for the Senate to meet and decide on wars, and it became a central place for young men to don their adult toga in recognition that they were also ready to do their military duty for Rome.

Venus

Romans borrowed the basic myths and functions of the Greek Aphrodite in their understanding of Venus as the goddess responsible for beauty, love, desire, sexuality, and prosperity, but she also retained ancient elements from the indigenous tribes of Italy (Figure IV.3). Venus was considered the foundress of the Roman people through her son Aeneas, whom she guided to Latium in her manifestation as the morning star. Roman "luck" was evident in the mundane dice games, where the highest number of points was achieved in "the Venus throw" (adding the highest numbers from the six die).

Venus had multiple and varied epithets which combined her traits with ancient deities, Roman history, and local elements: Venus Cloacina (as a purification deity of Rome's main sewer, the Cloaca Maxima); Venus Erycina (initiated by Fabius Maximus after the battle of Trasimeno in 217 BCE, and representing

Figure IV.3 Venus arising from the sea, Pompeii. *Source:* iStock / Getty Images Plus.

the conventions of both proper Roman matrons and prostitutes); Venus Felix ("lucky" Venus); Venus Libitina (linked to the other polarity of life, funerals and funeral rites); Venus Genetrix (Venus the Mother, as the source of the Roman people); and Venus Victrix (Venus the victorious over both hearts and enemies of Rome).

The sacred symbols of Venus were roses and myrtle, which was known for its medical properties as well as the belief in its powers as an aphrodisiac. Most statues and portraits of Venus had wreaths of roses and myrtle covering her hair and brides carried roses in their bouquets (a custom still in use today). The most famous artistic renderings of her in Roman art were copies and variations of the famous statue sculpted by Praxiteles for the city of Knidus, the first nude statue of feminine beauty.

Apollo

Apollo was one of the Greek gods who was the object of Roman worship without change, most likely due to the fact that temples to Apollo were located throughout southern Italy in the cities of the Greek colonists as well as the areas of Etruscan dominance. One of the last kings of Rome, Tarquinius Superbus, allegedly consulted the oracle at Delphi and he was told to worship Apollo in Rome. In 431 BCE a temple was built to Apollo to honor his help in the cessation of a plague. In the Second Punic War in 212 BCE, the *ludi Apollinares* (Apollonian Games) were established. Apollo was an important god in the Imperial period, as Augustus claimed his personal protection and promoted the cult by building a temple to him next to his residence on the Palatine Hill.

Often referred to as Phoebus Apollo, Apollo was the son of Jupiter and Latona (one of the original Titans) and the brother of Diana. He was responsible for light, medicine and healing, oratory, music, poetry, archery, and prophecy. Statues of Apollo included a lyre, a bow and arrow or a sword, and he was traditionally portrayed as representing the most ideal beautiful youthful body. His sacred animals were wolves, crows, ravens, swans, and roosters which announced the rising of the sun. In Heaven he ruled as the sun, drawn in a chariot by four horses, but on Earth he was associated with Liber Pater and the harmony of civilized life. The Romans absorbed the traditional myths about Apollo, including his love interests, and a temple was built to his son Asclepius (the Roman version of Asclepios) on an island in the middle of the Tiber River.

Diana

Diana shared the same responsibilities as Artemis as a divinity of the hunt, the moon, pregnancy and childbirth, and was always associated with wild animals. However, Diana also incorporated ancient indigenous aspects of the religious beliefs and rituals of Italy. One of her sacred symbols was the oak (reflecting her divine parentage from Jupiter perhaps). Her mother was Latona, who gave birth to her twin brother, Apollo. The Roman Diana was often portrayed as a triple complex that merged her with Luna (moon goddess) and Hecate (goddess of boundaries).

Diana had one of the earliest temples on the Aventine Hill. This area was outside the *pomerium*, which meant that her cult was sometimes treated the same as a foreign deity. However, Diana had a special relationship with the plebeians and slaves of Rome. Any slave could find asylum at the temples of Diana. She was shown wearing a short tunic and boots, holding a bow, and accompanied by deer and hunting dogs. The crescent moon often appeared as a crown upon her head. The Romans incorporated most of the Greek myths concerning the stories of Artemis into the Roman versions.

Ancient Italian origins for Diana are most likely the explanation for one of her oldest cults in Italy, at Aricia near Lake Nemi in the Alban Hills south of Rome. The sources are contradictory and confusing, but may relay an old conflict among the Latin tribes and the settlers in the region of Cumae and Etruscan areas. At Lake Nemi, Diana's sacred priest, the *rex Nemorensis*, was a slave who held this position until another slave challenged him to a duel and killed him. The winner became the new *rex Nemorensis*. The Temple of Diana at Lake Nemi was a popular site for infertile women and those who sought an easy delivery in childbirth.

Vulcan

Like the Greek Hephaestus, Vulcan was the god of fire, volcanos, and metalworking. The Etruscan name was Sethlans. His temple at the foot of the Capitoline Hill was one of the oldest shrines in Rome and his festival, the Vulcanalia, was established in the time of the kings. Tradition claimed that his shrine was built by Romulus in thanksgiving for a victory.

Vulcan was the son of Jupiter and Juno and the husband of Maia (a Titan) and Venus. His smithy or workshop was under the volcano on Mount Etna in Sicily. The constructive power of fire was honored, but additionally Vulcan had to be appeased in light of the destructive power, as fire was greatly feared in the tightly packed cities of Italy. Vulcan was a dominate god of Ostia, the port city for Rome, and had temples in the towns located around the rim of Mount Vesuvius (always affected by earthquakes and sulfurous fumes).

The Romans absorbed the story of Vulcan's fall from Olympus, with the variation that the baby was found and raised by the sea nymph Thetis. He was fascinated with fire as a child and forged a beautiful necklace for his mother, who wore it to a banquet on Mount Olympus. Through this clue, Juno discovered the identity of the child and ordered him home. He came with the gift of the magic throne. After Juno was trapped in the throne, Vulcan released her when Jupiter offered him Venus in marriage. Vulcan's discovery of his unfaithful wife with Mars was the source of the volcanic eruptions on Mount Etna.

Some ancient towns of Italy claimed Vulcan as their ancestral founder (e.g. Praeneste). In this capacity he was the progenitor of kings, while in one ancient version he was the father of Jupiter as well. The more famous tale was his impregnation of virgins, one of whom received his divine spark and gave birth to the monster Cacus, who was later destroyed by Hercules (see below). On the local level, Vulcan was the protector of the trades associated with fire: brickmakers, potters, cooks, and bakers.

Vesta

Vesta, the Roman equivalent to Hestia, was also a virgin goddess in charge of the hearth, the home, the family, and the state religion (FigureIV.4). Vesta represented the sacred earth itself as the font of life. As goddess of the hearth, she was the focus of women's rituals in the home, together with the preparation of food and was invoked before meals. The Vestal Virgins were one of the few priesthoods that were a full-time job. These were six women devoted to the care and maintenance of Vesta's hearth fire in the heart of the Roman forum.

Roman mythology repeats the story that, like Hestia, Vesta asked Jupiter if she could permanently maintain her chastity and receive the first portions of all the sacrifices. Her favorite animal was the donkey because the braying of a donkey alerted the sleeping Vesta to a rape attempt by the fertility god Priapus.

Figure IV.4   Statue of Vesta. *Source*: akg-images/Interfoto.

For this reason, Romans honored the beast at her festival. Romans were committed to the belief that if the hearth fire of Vesta failed or if one of her servants was violated, Rome would lose her prosperity and well-being.

Tradition assigns the creation of the Vestal Virgins to King Numa, who organized all the institutions and priesthoods of Rome. As the supreme authority over all religious elements, King Numa held the office of *pontifex maximus* (chief priest) and had direct supervision over the Vestals. In some versions, Rhea Silvia was not permitted to remarry and may have been acknowledged as the first Vestal (an older temple to Vesta was located in the Alban Hills). As the mother (eventually) of Romulus, in this way Vesta was connected to the founding myth of Rome. A sacred spring used by the Vestals was located near the temple and was associated with the stories of Numa's inspiration from the nymph Egeria.

Mercury

The *dei lucrii* were ancient deities of profit who became syncretized into the Roman god Mercury, along with the traditional aspects and responsibilities of the Greek Hermes: commerce, oratory, divination, travelers, boundaries, luck, thieves, music, and as a guide to Hades. He was the son of Jupiter and Maia. As a patron of the grain trade he is associated with fertility. According to tradition, the nymph Larunda (or Mater Lara) was punished by Jupiter with the inability to speak because she revealed his affairs to Juno. Mercury accompanied Larunda to the underworld but fell in love with her. They became the parents of the Lares or household and crossroads gods. Mercury was depicted with the winged helmet, winged sandals and the caduceus, or a herald's staff with intertwined snakes. His animals were the rooster, a ram or goat, and the tortoise as a symbol of the lyre.

When Mercury's temple was built in Rome in 495 BCE (between the Aventine and Palatine hills), there was a dispute between the two ruling consuls at the time as to which one should dedicate it. The Plebeian Assembly, to spite the Senate and the patrician consuls, gave the job to a military commander instead. Mercury therefore had associations with plebeian interests, and the plebeian **aedile**s were charged with regulating commerce (weights and scales, licensing fees, etc.) with Mercury as their patron.

Ceres

Crescere, "to grow" (create, increase), was the appropriate root for the name of Ceres, the Roman goddess of agriculture, grain, fertility, and mothers. She was called upon for lustrations (blessings) of the fields, of harvests, and during marriage and funeral rites, and the *ludi Ceriales* celebrated the prosperity of Rome. In addition to her similar traits to Demeter, Ceres had ancient traditions in the indigenous Italian tribes. Her symbols were sheaves of wheat, sows, snakes, and a torch (in the search for her daughter).

Ceres discovered wheat, invented the yoking of oxen and plowing, and guided all aspects of the cycle of agriculture. These innovations contributed to men settling down (and thus adhering to laws). Another element of her connection with laws was a focus of an ancient temple to Ceres located on the Aventine Hill, where she was the protector of the plebeians and their rights. The records of the plebeian aediles were housed in the basement of the temple along with Senate records. The physical bodies of the Tribunes of the Plebs were sacred to Ceres and thus inviolable. Those who broke the civic and licensing laws were fined in her name and the dues collected to fund her games and festivals. In the countryside, similar laws were applied against those who let their herds violate public lands.

The story of Ceres and the search for her daughter Proserpina was incorporated into Roman tradition and associated with Liber and Libera (older agricultural deities, see below). The story of life and rebirth was behind the concept that both Ceres and Proserpina helped the shades of the dead make the transition to the underworld. This idea related to older traditions concerning the *mundus Cerialis*, "the world of Ceres," which was an underground vault or pit that was opened three days a year to offer sacrifices for fertility and to temporarily release the spirits of the dead. Upper-class Romans made pilgrimages to Eleusis to take part in the Demeter/Ceres Mysteries.

Other Important Deities

Penates

The *di penates* were domestic and household deities who were an important element of the Roman family. The *penus* ("household provision") stood for the storeroom which contained supplies of food, wine, and oil, and by extension barns or silos where wheat and other grains were stored. Often described as **tutelary gods** ("guardian spirits"), the Penates served as protectors and may have originated as ancestor cults. They were associated with the Lares (see below), Vesta at the hearth, and the prosperity of the family. There were hundreds of Penates which protected every nook and cranny of the household, farm buildings and at family rituals such as the wedding night.

There were public Penates that served the community of Rome, with one of the earliest cult sites located at Lavinium and thus connected to the story of Aeneas. According to some traditions, the Penates were the objects rescued by Aeneas and carried to Italy from Troy, which were then kept by the Vestal Virgins at their temple in the forum.

Lares

The origin of the Lares remains unknown. Etruscans had ancestor and family cults which may have influenced the Roman concept. The main function of the Lares was tutelary in relation to the hearth, doorways, fields, crossroads, and all objects and events enclosed within boundaries. Statues of the family Lares were kept in a **lararium** and were placed on the table at family meals. They were included in all family events such as births and marriages. The Lares were invoked at the start and end of journeys. Statues and paintings of Lares most often showed them in pairs, as dancing male youths, sometimes raising a drinking horn and carrying a libation dish.

The *Lares praestites* were the public Lares of the city of Rome and housed in the Regia in the Roman forum (near the temple of Vesta and *domus publica*, the house of the p*ontifex maximus*). As part of his religious reforms Augustus revived and promoted *Lares praestites*, which he related to his own hearth and family, extending this protection to all throughout the Empire. *Compitales* (crossroad shrines) were located in towns and cities for public Lares because crossroads were dangerous places (banditry, ambush). **Collegia** (fraternal organizations) at these shrines were charged with maintenance of the shrine and were open to **freedmen** and slaves.

Saturn

Most often compared to the Greek god Cronus, Saturn was an ancient Italian deity responsible for agricultural fertility, prosperity, wealth, regeneration, revelry, and time. Romans placed him in the "Golden Age," where, along with Janus, he was one of the first to rule the city of Rome. In the mythic role of Cronus, he was the father of Jupiter. His temple in the Roman forum housed the treasury of Rome. Saturn's main consort was Ops.

The understanding of Saturn in Roman religion is complex because fragments of earlier material have been syncretized with later Hellenistic concepts. Although he was a god of fertility, he was also responsible for lightning strikes (along with Jupiter), which may reflect the destructive side of him (Cronus). The benevolent side was most popularly seen in his main religious festival, the Saturnalia, held at the winter solstice, a time understood to be dangerous with the ending of one season and the anticipated rebirth of the next.

Ops

Serving in the same capacity as Rhea (the sister-wife of Cronus), Ops was an ancient Italian deity who was the consort of Saturn (and sometimes Consus, another fertility deity). Ops had a temple on the Capitoline Hill, but her antiquity was reflected in the Roman tradition that originally she had no image and could be understood as either male or female. After the Hellenistic period, she was often shown seated (as a chthonic deity related to the earth) with a bundle of corn and a scepter. She was responsible for riches, prosperity, and the abundance of the earth. Her cult originated with one of the Sabine kings of Rome. In some stories, she was the mother of Jupiter, Neptune, Pluto, Juno, Ceres, and Vesta.

Bellona

From the Latin *bellum*, "war," Bellona was the sister (and sometimes wife) of Mars, usually shown with a military helmet, shield, armor, and sword. Bellona had her own temple outside the *pomerium*, recognizing that most wars were conducted against foreigners. A square of earth with a column (the *columna bellica*, "war column") in front of the temple symbolized foreign soil and it was here that the Roman Senate formally met with ambassadors and delegations of foreign states. It was also here that a symbolic spear was thrown by one of the *fetiales* (priests of Jupiter) into the soil to officially declare war against another nation.

Bellona had special priests, the *bellonarii*, who danced in warlike frenzy and slashed themselves as a symbol of the fury of war. After his conquests in Asia Province (Anatolia), the dictator Sulla brought similar rites of the goddess Ma to Rome and these were absorbed into the festivals of Bellona. She provided the necessary motivation for courage and boldness in war.

Fortuna

The goddess of both community and individual fortune, Fortuna and "luck" were used synonymously. Early temples were attributed to the Etruscan kings, where she carried the epithet *copia* ("bountiful"). Luck could be good or bad, and as a symbol of Fate (like the Greek goddess Tyche) she was often depicted as blind or veiled, representing the capriciousness of life.

Although Fortuna could be capricious, she was bound to the Roman ideal of *virtus* or strength of character. Romans often remarked that a man could "make his own luck," meaning not through chance but by living and demonstrating the ideal virtues of Roman traditions and behavior. By doing so, he would invite the auspices of Fortuna, but by ignoring the ideals he would invite her dismissal. This was particularly true when a man's pride reached the level of hubris. Both the dictators Sulla (ruled 82–79 BCE) and Julius Caesar (ruled 48–44 BCE) claimed to be favored by Fortuna.

Liber/Libera

Liber (often called Father Liber) and Libera were the male and female powers of fertility, vines and winemaking, and freedom (as the names imply). They were embedded in the fertility cults and associated with Ceres and Proserpina, and stood for freedom and the rights of individuals (especially free speech). In this capacity, they were the patrons of the plebeians, and an early triad of Ceres, Liber, and Libera was worshipped on Rome's Aventine Hill. This triad was understood as the plebeian opposition to the triad of the Capitoline Hill of the patricians. Liber's aspects were eventually understood to have affinities with Dionysus, and thus the Roman Bacchus.

As god of the vine, Liber was offered the first pressing during the grape harvest, when it was undiluted with water (unlike regular wine-drinking) and set aside for temple and ritual use. The procreative life force of semen was attributed to Liber, and his temples had images of a phallus which would be paraded in towns at his festivals. Ovid equated the donning of the *toga virilis* (the "manly toga") by a young man as the symbol of freedom personified through Liber Pater, as the young man was now free to vote, free to marry, and free to take up his tasks as a citizen.

Bacchus

Bacchus was the Roman god of fertility, vines, and winemaking, the equivalent of the Greek Dionysus. Like Dionysus, Bacchus had both public cults and Mysteries. In later Roman art at least, he was portrayed as a rather plump youth, naked with an ivy wreath, and usually in a hilarious mode, as Romans viewed him as a god of hilarity and the unleashing of social conventions with the forgetfulness that drinking brings (Figure IV.5).

In addition to the same Greek stories of the birth, youth, and adventures of Dionysus, the most famous story concerning Bacchus involved the scandal of

Figure IV.5   A more youthful depiction of Dionysus/Bacchus. *Source:* Werner Forman Archive/ Heritage Images/ Getty Images.

his cult and the Senate legislation of 186 BCE. (The fullest account of the story was written by the Roman historian Livy.) Allegedly Paculla Annia, a priestess of the Bacchus cult (which was originally a daytime festivity for women), created a night ritual with wine and feasting which included men and women of all ages and all social classes. The screams of subsequent moral and sexual violence were drowned out by the drums and flutes and anyone who betrayed the activities was murdered. An ex-initiate and prostitute revealed the actions to one of the consuls, who called the Senate into emergency session. The Senate took over control of the cult throughout Italy; meetings were permitted but only on approval by the Senate and limited to four or five persons at a time. The real threat to the state may have been found in the leadership of the cult at the time.

Scholars have long debated the historical details of Livy's account and point out that for Livy the real scandal may have been the mixing of gender and class, making it more socially than religiously unacceptable. It could have been a reaction to what may have been perceived at the time as too much "Greekness" working its way into Roman customs. Nevertheless, the images provided by Livy have had a long legacy in the association of wild, unbridled sexual orgies in the cult of Bacchus (and other Mysteries).

Janus

Janus was the god of beginnings, endings, and transitions, which made him responsible for gates, doors, and passages. He was portrayed with two faces, looking to the future and the past. We have the month of January as part of his legacy, and it eventually became the beginning of the New Year, replacing March. As all journeys had a beginning and end, he was also in charge of travelers and trade and the beginning and end of wars. He was appealed to at the beginning and end of the harvests, the change from youth to adulthood, marriage, and death, and so symbolized the passing of time itself. He was always invoked at the beginning of all prayers regardless of which god was the object of the prayer. In this sense, he controlled access (or the "door") to the gods.

Janus had an altar on the Janiculum Hill (across the Tiber) and an altar that marked the terminus of the road that once ran from Veii to Rome, distinguishing between Etruscan and Roman territory. The doors of his temple in the city (Janus Geminus), front and back, were constantly open in times of war and closed when there was peace. It should be noted that, especially in the latter days of the Republic and early Empire, the doors were rarely closed. According to Ovid, Saturn welcomed Janus as a guest and rewarded him for teaching the art of agriculture to a local nymph named Crane, who became the goddess of door hinges.

Pluto

Ancient Greek mythology held a concept of *Ploutos*, a god of mineral wealth (tin, copper, silver, gold, gems) and the seeds of the earth, which were often associated with the underworld. In this sense, Ploutos expanded the traditional aspects of Hades. Latinized as Pluto, this was the name most often used by Romans for the god of earthly prosperity as well as lord of the Underworld. Pluto was often portrayed holding a cornucopia and demonstrated a positive future.

Pluto was associated with Orcus, a rural ruler of the underworld who was often depicted as a hairy giant or demon in Etruscan art. (This figure survived into the Middle Ages as "ogre" and may have been the source for Tolkien's "orcs" in *The Lord of the Rings* trilogy). Another god associated with Pluto was Dis Pater ("rich father?"), whose name, along with Orcus, was utilized as a symbol for death. Both Orcus and Dis Pater were gods who were the subject of sworn oaths. Romans simply assumed that Pluto was the Roman form of the attributes of both of these ancient gods.

In Roman mythology, Pluto has no love affairs, although there are some confusing traditions about children, with Pluto as a chthonic form of Zeus (e.g. as the father of the Eumenides, "the Furies" or "friendly ones"). Pluto was portrayed in a sympathetic light, especially for lovers and spouses who were parted in death, such as Alcestis and Orpheus.

Hecate

Romans absorbed the Greek Hecate, who had all the similar responsibilities: boundaries, crossroads, and interaction with the chthonic deities in Hades. She guided souls to Hades with her torch, which was an image probably derived from the Etruscan concept of the *vanth*, a chthonic deity with wings and a torch. There was a temple dedicated to Hecate near Cumae that was believed to be an entrance to the river Styx. Indigenous Italian culture contained various categories of female herbalists and witches, and Hecate was called upon in their ritual formulas.

Tellus

Tellus (Terra Mater) was an early mother-earth goddess who was also associated with Ceres for agricultural fertility and considered a state goddess. She was shown with a cornucopia and bunches of flowers or fruits. She had an early temple within the *pomerium* on the Oppian Hill. An object stored in that temple was called the *magmentarium* and was understood to be a symbol of Italy on a wall, perhaps as a map. Her name could be used as a form of "earth," just as Jupiter could be "sky." Tellus shared aspects with another numen, Dea Dia, who was celebrated by the Arval Brotherhood and connected with fertility and the earth. At the yearly festival of Tellus, a pregnant cow was sacrificed, symbolizing the potential seed within the earth.

Sol Indiges

Sol Indiges (the "native sun?") was one of the oldest Roman gods, honored by the Sabines and Latin tribes, and in some way was distinguished from Apollo, Helios, and the later Sol Invictus (unconquered). In the *Aeneid*, Vergil claimed that Aeneas's marriage to Lavinia connected Rome's ancestors to the sun, as Lavinia was the daughter of Circe who was the daughter of the sun. Sol Indiges had a shrine on the Quirinal Hill and in the Circus Maximus and was the favored god of an early dominant family, the Aurelii. Under Emperor Aurelian (reigned 270–275), the worship of Sol Indiges became a dominant religion of the state and most likely merged with Sol Invictus at this period.

Castor and Pollux

Known as the *Dioscuri*, Castor and Pollux (Polydeuces) were twin brothers but with different fathers. Castor, a mortal, was the son of Tyndareus, a king of Sparta, and Pollux, divine, was the son of Zeus. In some versions, they were born from the same egg that hatched Helen of Troy and Clytemnestra (the wife of King Agamemnon). A Latin term for the twins was *Gemini* (which later became the constellation). Upon the death of Castor, Pollux asked Zeus to let Castor share Pollux's immortality so that they could always be together. They were the patrons of sailors, travelers, boxers, athletic games, and horsemen and were usually portrayed in statues with horses (Figure IV.6).

Rome absorbed the Etruscan traditions (as Kastur and Pultuce, sons of Tinia) and the Greek traditions of Castor and Pollux from southern Italy, but

Figure IV.6 The *Dioscuri. Source:* Lanmas/Alamy Stock Photo.

also had its own unique involvement with the twin brothers. The Battle of Lake Regillus in 493 BCE was fought against the Latin League and the last kings of Rome. According to legend, the twins appeared on the battlefield on the side of the Romans and assured the victory. To honor them, a temple to Castor and Pollux was built in the Roman forum next to a fountain where they watered their horses.

Their association with horses meant that they were considered patrons of the *equites* (the second class of knights in Rome). On July 15, a day held sacred to Castor and Pollux, the equestrians paraded through the city with full panoply, including armor and decorations for their public horse (a horse provided by the state in recognition of class and service). Comedic Roman plays traditionally had women swear by Castor (*ecastor!*) and men by Pollux (*edepol!*). These were not binding or contract oaths, but expressions of amazement or frustration, analogous to common swearing today.

Heroes

Hercules (the Etruscan form for Heracles) was one of the hero cults that Rome adopted from the Greek influence of Magna Graecia as well as North Africa and Spain where the cult was established by the Phoenicians (Carthaginians). Hercules may have been evoked to turn his back on the Carthaginians and support the Romans and thus may have been considered responsible for the ultimate victory of Rome over the Carthaginians in the Punic Wars (Figure IV.7).

According to tradition, the first inhabitants of Rome had been terrorized by the fire-breathing giant Cacus, a son of Vulcan. He stole everyone's cattle, ate humans, and lived in a cave at the foot of the Palatine Hill. In one of his adventures, Hercules stole the cattle of Geryon and stopped to pasture them near Cacus's cave. While Hercules slept, Cacus promptly stole some of the cattle. After a fierce battle between the two, Hercules triumphed over the monster.

Hercules built an altar to mark his victory at the Forum Boarium, which became the cattle market of Rome (along with all other animals sold for meat and sacrifices). A temple to Hercules at this site was the focus of those who merited a triumph. On the day of the triumph, the statue of Hercules was dressed in the clothes and accessories of the triumphing general, including the red-painted face. Hercules was connected with children and childbirth (perhaps because of his great deeds as a child?) and brides wore belts with a "Herculean knot" (difficult to untie). With a few exceptions, Romans did not generally adopt the Greek (and Eastern) concept of *apotheosis*. The legendary heroes of Greece were respected of course, but only Hercules and Asclepius were worshipped. Eventually, however, the concept was applied to Roman emperors, but not until the early Empire. (See Chapter XII for details of the Imperial Cult.) Instead, Rome elevated historical figures in its history and

Figure IV.7   Hercules.
Source: DEA PICTURE LIBRARY/De Agostini/ Getty Images.

promoted them as models of exemplary behavior, loyalty to the state, and ultimately the bearers (and conveyors) of the fullest understanding of the *mos maiorum*, or the traditions laid down by the gods and the ancestors of Rome. Every schoolchild was expected to learn these stories and apply them in his or her life.

Later writers and poets related many myths of earlier Roman history which emphasized moral codes (both positive and negative) and idealized behavior. Many of these stories took place in the context of the last wars with the kings of Rome that resulted in the founding of the Republic. Examples include Horatius Cocles ("one-eyed") defending the Sublicius bridge against the army of Lars Porsena (509 BCE), Mucius Scaevola, a Roman spy who was caught by Lars and held his hand in the fire to show his defiance (506 BCE), and the dictator Cincinnatus who showed modest ambition and returned to his farm after leading Rome through a crisis (439 BCE). Women were also upheld as models of virtue and integrity: Lucretia, who preferred death over dishonor (d. 510 BCE), and Cornelia, mother of the Brothers Gracchi (d. 100 BCE). The closest Rome came to "hero cults" were the continued visits to some tombs of famous heroes such as Scipio Africanus, the hero of the Second Punic War against Hannibal. His tomb remained covered with offerings of flowers, wreaths, and small votives. Similarly, the site of the assassination of Julius Caesar became (and remains) a pilgrimage site.

Like the Greeks, Romans honored chthonic deities, which are highlighted in Chapter X.

Summary

- The basic stories of the gods of Greece were incorporated into myths that emphasized their characteristics and attributes important for Roman culture. Rather than simply just changing the name of a god or goddess, Romans recognized their own concepts in the stories of the Olympians.
- Rome also added characteristics of similar elements found in the traditions of the Etruscans and indigenous Italian cultures.

Suggestions for Further Reading

Beard, M., J. North and S. Price. 1998. *Religions of Rome*, 2 vols. Cambridge University Press. A compendium of the basic elements.

Morford, M. P. O., R. J. Lenardon and M. Sham. 2013. *Classical Mythology*, 10th ed. Oxford University Press. In addition to the Greek myths, the stories are also told with the Roman variations.

Scheid, J. 2003. *An Introduction to Roman Religion*, trans. J. Lloyd. Indiana University Press. This book surveys the elements of Roman religion through aspects of daily life and also includes the background information on the Roman gods.

Turcan, R. 2001. *The Gods of Ancient Rome: Religion in Everyday Life from Archaic to Imperial Times*, trans. A. Nevill. Routledge. In the section on rituals and worship, the author provides background material but the bibliography has mostly French sources.

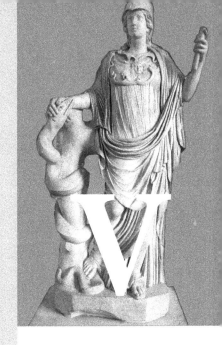

TEMPLES AND PRIESTS

Greek and Roman Religions, First Edition. Rebecca I. Denova.
© 2019 John Wiley & Sons, Inc. Published 2019 by John Wiley & Sons, Inc.

Learning Objectives

After reading this chapter, you will be able to:

- Understand the function of temples in ancient Greece and Rome.
- Distinguish the roles of priests and priestesses in traditional cults.

 We have seen that any area associated with the divine was considered sacred space, which could be a place, a building, or a landscape. Sacred space was protected by a sacred zone as a sanctuary. The more common sacred space was the temple, which served as the center to maintain the relationship between the gods and the community. Modern churches, synagogues and mosques are understood as gathering places for "assemblies" (Greek *synagogues* for Jews, *ekklesia* for Christians, and *masjid*, "a place of prayer," or *sajada*, for Muslims). In the ancient world, large congregations of people did not crowd into the temples but instead gathered outside in front of the outdoor altars.

When we think of congregations now, we assume that a fundamental purpose of priests, rabbis, and imams is to ensure the care and well-being of members of the community. In ancient Greece and Rome, the primary function of the priest or priestess was ensuring the care and well-being of the god or goddess. Ultimately, this did contribute to the well-being of the larger community, but there was not an equivalent concern for what we consider the care of individual souls.

Temples

Sacredness belonged to an area inside a *temenos* wall, with the temple (*naos*) and temple complex in the middle of what became a sanctuary. The oldest Greek and Roman temples were made of wood and mud bricks, but over time became monumental buildings of stone and marble. Greek temples developed between 900 and 600 BCE with distinct floor plans in relation to the columns. There were three column types which differed mainly in the architectural pattern at the top of the column: Doric, Ionic, and Corinthian (see Figure V.1).

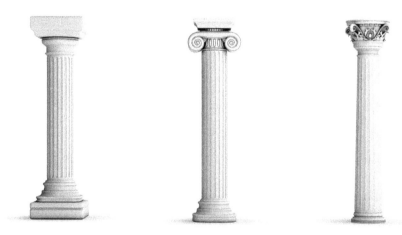

Figure V.1 Types of Greek columns. *Source*: iStock/Getty Images Plus.

Greek temples were built on a three-stepped platform. What began as a porch (*pronaos*) at the entrance to a temple evolved into a row of columns forming the *peristasis*. The portico provided shelter during inclement weather or simply a place to stand for visitors. The cult statue was in the center of the temple, the *cella*.

In Rome, temple architecture derived from both Etruscan and Greek models. The Etruscan influence was found in an emphasis on the front of the building, with a row of columns rather than being able to see the inner part from all sides. Romans also elevated their temples, with staircases leading up to the entrance or portico. The *cella* was located at the back of the temple rather than in the middle. The English word, temple, is derived from *templum*, which was not just the building but the entire sacred complex. The more common word for a shrine itself was *aedes*.

What appears to us now as brown or white rubble remains does not do justice to the colorful elements of ancient temples. The columns of Greek and Roman temples were painted, using white, blue, red, and black. The spaces above the columns (the frieze and metopes, the decorated plaques above the columns) contained sculpted reliefs and paintings. Rather than just another image of the god, the art usually included a story or myth and sometimes depicted battles. The pediment triangles in the upper structure (on the front and back sides of the temple) could also contain freestanding sculptures (see Figure V.2). The tiled roofs of temples contained *acroteria*, or sculpted figures on the top and corners of the building, most often of mythical animals and deities. Most temples were oriented to the east and utilized the rising sun for morning rituals.

The location of temples depended upon several factors, which included environment, myth, function, and divine experience. Mountain-tops were popular locations for the temples of Zeus and Apollo, with the understanding that these areas touched the sky, the domain of these gods. Caves and grottos were associated with birth stories and were also openings for chthonic deities. Springs and lakes provided a practical element for purification purposes. Temples were also built as an important element of citadels and on the borders of territory for divine protection against enemies. Temples to Poseidon and Neptune were popular in port cities.

The majority of temples were built on a site associated with myth, most often a place where a god or goddess either performed some feat or founded a town or city. In this sense it was believed that the deity was present or manifest at that location, or at the very least, this was a site where contact with the divine offered

Figure V.2   West pediment of the Parthenon. *Source*: akg-images/jh-Lightbox_Ltd./John Hios.

the best circumstances. In Rome, many of the temples were associated with events in Roman history, often in thanksgiving for a military victory. Urban temples were dedicated to the founding deity and at the same time served a civic and social function. Temples and shrines validated the structures of governance and class and provided the opportunity for individual benefactions.

The various donations of votives and gifts to the gods became the treasuries of the temple complexes. The larger temple served in the function of the first banks, which were eventually regulated by state officials. The basement of the Temple of Saturn in Rome held the state treasury and treasury offices.

Altars were located in front of the temple and were the center of cult activity. They were originally raised mounds of earth or piled field stones, but evolved into stone structures that were sometimes decorated with sculptures of a particular facet of the deity or an event from myth. The altar was usually square with a flat top and sometimes lined with a metal pan for the burnt offerings. The flat top was necessary for *ouranic* deities, or deities "of the sky," to receive the sacrifices. For chthonic deities, low-lying pits were used, with openings in the earth to receive liquid libations of animal sacrifices, milk, honey, and wine.

Priests and the Priesthood: Greece

Priests and priestesses functioned as mediators between humans and the divine through the proper rituals of sacrifices, prayers, incantations, hymns, prophecy, and purification. We can collectively refer to all these activities as "worship." The priest or priestess was responsible for all aspects of the sacred elements of a god or goddess. However, all worship was not the exclusive domain of the priests; kings, magistrates, and heads of households also offered prayers and sacrifices on behalf of the community and family.

Priests were not required to be experts on all the gods or all things divine. There were no training schools for the priesthood such as we find today in modern seminaries. Their expertise was learned through the passing on of knowledge from other priests and through on-the-job training. They were not theologians in the sense understood today. In other words, they were not necessarily experts on the intellectual aspect of religion which results in systematic theology. If you had a theological question, you could consult an *exegete*, a state official who was knowledgeable on that subject.

For most of the priests and priestesses, the priesthood was a part-time job and their time was served in rotation. This meant a full integration of religious duties with civic duties and social obligations. In a world where women were relegated to the household, priesthoods provided opportunities for women to emerge as important civic leaders. The highest priestly official for Athena in Athens was a woman, who could advise and address the assembly. There were many priestesses in Greece as servants of the many Greek goddesses.

Selection

Though there was no professional guild of priests, there were certain qualifications that had to be met. The first criterion was that of citizenship of the city-state or town in which the individual resided. In Athens, no *metic* or foreigner could serve as priest. The second criterion was membership in a **phratry** (clan), ensuring that a priest should have a proper birth record. Women could not qualify under the criterion of citizenship in Greece, but family background was applied to women candidates as priestesses. Some of the clans claimed long generations of ancestors so that priesthoods became hereditary in some cases. In Athens, the Eumolpidae clan held the office for the Eleusinian Mysteries, and the Eteobutadae were the hereditary clan who served Athena Polias.

A third criterion was purity of both mind and body. Priests and priestesses had to be "of sound mind" and they had to have a clear conscience. There could be no scandal in their background or breach of the proper social conventions. Bodily purification was equally important, particularly during the time of service in the temple. Service to the gods required purification rites that were related to the sacred nature of these tasks. Ritual purity was associated with hygiene in one sense, as it involved ritual washings, but it was actually a state of being. Contact with blood, semen, and corpses caused impurity as well as sexual immorality, corruption, and murder. Purity codes were unrelated to social rank, economic class, or gender. The impurity involved related to sacred space. Priests and priestesses were often required to follow purity codes for their time of service, and a few temples required virgins or eunuchs (castrated men), but this was rare. Bowls of water were readily available at temples for ritual washing (ablutions) before proceeding with the rites.

There is little evidence that priests and priestesses were selected by voting, although voting may have taken place for the initial slate of candidates. A more common method of selection was by **sortition**, or casting "lots." We have few details as to how this was actually done but it could have been the same process that was used in civic voting for offices. A number of tiles or balls were placed in a drum or jar and then selected. This method was probably preferred because it indicated that the choice was the will of the gods.

Duties

The duties of the priesthood were both religious and administrative. Priests were responsible for calculating and maintaining the list of sacred days (see the box "Calendars: Sacred Time"). Over time, some of the administrative duties were taken over by the state, especially the finances and revenues. The ritualistic care and maintenance of the statue and the temple was vitally important, as the temple was understood to be the home of the deity. The priests had to keep it clean and ritually pure. In some temples, the statue was bathed regularly and given a new set of clothing during particular religious holidays.

Calendars: Sacred Time

One of the duties of priests in ancient Greece and Rome was to keep track of sacred time and to alert the public to religious festival days. Such days were so important to the prosperity of the entire community that work ceased (even in banks and law courts) so that everyone could devote their time to the gods. Greek calendars appear quite confusing to us because people lived under a number of simultaneous calendars depending upon the purposes. At the same time, different city-states operated under different calendars.

Athens had a festival calendar of 12 months established on the cycle of the moon. In the Classical period a state calendar was created, incorporating civic purposes and memorials of historical events. Underpinning both of these was an agricultural calendar of the seasons (to regulate planting and harvesting) based upon astronomical data.

In ancient Rome, according to tradition, King Numa established a calendar based upon the new moon cycle and applied a numbered system for different days of the month. The Kalends was the first day of the month, the Nones (or the "half-moon") were eight days before the middle of the month and the Ides were either the thirteenth or the fifteenth day of the month. With a lunar calendar, this meant that there were often extra days each year which would accumulate over time, eventually forcing the calendar out of sync with the seasons. It was the duty of the *pontifex maximus* to keep the calendar aligned by the intercalation of extra days in the month of February.

The calendar system was published by carving the dates in stone for the public, marking religious festivals, days the courts were open, market days, and divisions of the month. The markers of *fastus* (F, permitted) and *nefastus* (N, not permitted) indicated religious holidays when work ceased. It has been estimated that the number of religious and civic holidays in Rome left a total of 104 working days remaining in the calendar.

The most important function of the priest or priestess was to offer sacrifices to the deity. The sacrifice was a gift of something valuable and became sacred through the ritual. These gifts consisted of food and drink: animals, cakes, fruit, grain, vegetables, milk, honey, olive oil, and wine. Such gifts held the expectation of a return in the realm of fertility, prosperity, health, and victory. (For the probability of human sacrifice, see the box "Human Sacrifice in Ancient Greece and Rome?")

Human Sacrifice in Ancient Greece and Rome?

The traditional sacrificial victim in ancient Greece and Rome was an animal. However, some questions do remain as to whether Greece and Rome originally practiced human sacrifice at an earlier time. Although still debated, the resolution to the question has to include the various ways in which the ancients would have defined the concept.

There is evidence that the neighboring cultures of Mesopotamia, Egypt, and Phoenicia practiced human sacrifice. In Mesopotamia and Egypt slaves or royal retainers have been uncovered in very early burial excavations. The results of examinations of these bones remain inconclusive as to whether these deaths were mandated or voluntary. Phoenicians were known for the sacrifice of babies and young children (particularly in the *tofets* – altars of ritual sacrifice – of North Africa), although the evidence is still subject to critical debate.

The Bible contains stories of human sacrifice: Abraham's near-sacrifice of his son Isaac (Genesis), Jepthah's sacrifice of his daughter (Judges), and the king of Moab sacrificing his son in hopes of a victory over Israel (1 Kings). Although it relates the story of one evil king of Israel imitating the practice, the Bible is quick to condemn such behavior. In this as in other matters, Israel is never to imitate the rituals of its neighbors.

In ancient Greece, we find human sacrifice in mythology and drama. Agamemnon sacrificed his daughter Iphigenia to Artemis to obtain the winds for his fleet to sail to Troy. There was an ancient festival for young men with games to Zeus Lykaios which incorporated a myth of human sacrifice and cannibalism. The festival of the Thargelia to Apollo allegedly sacrificed two ugly men by stoning them, but scholars debate if the men actually died. Greek tradition ultimately condemned human sacrifice as something the barbarians did and as an improper offering to the gods. During the funeral games for Patroclus in *The Iliad*, Achilles sacrificed Trojan prisoners of war. However, Greeks would not see this as human sacrifice; it was simply the destruction of the enemy and part of the spoils of victory that belonged to the gods.

There were remnants of human sacrifice in ancient Rome. In the ritual of the Argei every spring, straw figures of humans were thrown into the Tiber River as a ritual purification of the city. This may reflect an ancient rite when actual humans were sacrificed in this way. When the Romans were defeated by Carthage at Cannae during the Second Punic War, two Gaul and Greek couples were buried under the Forum Boarium. A law in 97 BCE banned human sacrifice, but by then it was so rare that the law was more symbolic than having administrative clout.

The ritual killing of enemies in a Roman triumph could be viewed as human sacrifice. Defeated enemies were held under "house arrest" (and treated well) in various towns until the date of the triumph. Paraded through the city, the enemies were then taken to the Tullianum prison and ritually strangled. Romans did not consider this human sacrifice in the same sense that they viewed the barbaric practices. The defeated enemies were part of the spoils of a victory and thus were offered to Jupiter along with the other spoils.

Depending upon the occasion or the limitations of cost, the sacrificial animals were cattle (usually bulls), oxen, pigs, sheep, goats, or birds. These were domesticated animals rather than wild (unless a wild animal was associated with a particular god or goddess). The animals also had to be perfect specimens or the god would be offended. They were specially bred for sacrificial purposes in the countryside. The animal was cleaned and dressed with ribbons, painted, and with gilded horns and wreaths of flowers was then led in a procession to the temple. The victim was sprinkled with grain, flour, or seeds, and water was poured on the head. This would make the animal nod, or put his head down, indicating that it agreed to be sacrificed. In no sense was an animal sacrifice associated with violence; an unwilling animal or one slaughtered through violence was deemed unacceptable (Figure V.3).

The animal's throat was then slit and the blood was caught in a special receptacle. Seers examined the entrails of the animal, especially the liver, and declared it acceptable or unacceptable. The animal was slaughtered with portions of the fat and bones burned upon the altar. Depending on the occasion, choice pieces of the organs and meat could also be offered. The bulk of the animal was

Figure V.3   Greek ritual sacrifice. *Source:* De Agostini/Getty Images.

distributed among the priests and the public for consumption. It was believed that the god also participated in his community meal.

Priests and priestesses were highly honored members of the community. The evidence from Athens demonstrates that priests and priestesses held the same honor as magistrates, and they participated in processions and were privileged with reserved seats at the drama festivals. We usually find their service highlighted on their tombstones. In small towns and cities they may have enjoyed a house next to the temple. An advantage of the priesthood was the receipt of the skins or hides of sacrificial animals, which could be sold for profit. Everyday perishable offerings such as cakes, milk, and fruits were supplements to the priest's household.

There is no evidence of distinctive dress for the priesthood; most of the art shows them in a standard Greek *chiton* (tunics made from large pieces of cloth that were pinned or sewn on the shoulders). There is no written mention of an initiation rite for priests and priestesses, aside from the Mysteries, but we often read that the priest or priestess became the property of the god or goddess, in service to the deity.

Priests and the Priesthood: Rome

The common inclusion of *do ut des*, "I give so that you may give," by Roman priests is usually described as a contract between humans and the divine. This was an exchange offered in conjunction with vows. The petitioner offered a vow to carry out certain things (such as more specific offerings, building a temple, funding a priesthood) if a prayer was answered. All of this was based on *fides*, or a relationship of mutual trust and respect. Roman priests and priestesses were the ritual experts in this relationship; the ritual was crucial for the balance between humans and the divine.

This concept may have been introduced through Etruscan religion and the earliest references to Roman religion cite the *disciplina etrusca* as the source for understanding how to regulate the human relationship with the gods. Etruscans believed that human destiny was determined by the gods and that their will could be seen in natural phenomena such as lightning, the organs of sacrificial animals, and the flight patterns of birds. The experts who interpreted these signs were the *augurs* and *haruspices*.

In the period of the Roman monarchy, the king was solely responsible for the religious rites. Tradition claims that the unmarried daughters of the king became the Vestals, while the sons acted as *flamens* for the important state gods. With the institution of the Republic, these rites were handed over to various colleges of priests, who may have originally been advisers to the king. Nevertheless, the ancient office of **rex sacrorum** ("king of rites") was maintained in the Republic in order to not offend the gods. There were four major colleges of priests (where a college meant that the members were legally authorized under the Twelve Tables, the law codes of Rome): the **pontifices**, the *augurs* (specialists trained to read omens), the *duoviri sacris faciundis* (at first two, and then 15 men, *quindecimviri*, who "carry out rites"); and the **epulones** (men who set up feasts at festivals).

The College of *Pontifices*

The College of *Pontifices* (*Collegium Pontificum*) made up the highest ranking priests in ancient Rome. In the beginning of the Republic, *pontifices* were drawn solely from the patrician class of old and wealthy families who had political influence. Around 300 BCE the plebeians were also included in the College. Vacancies were filled through co-option, which meant that the group selected one from the membership of the College. Under the jurisdiction of the *pontifices* were the *rex sacrorum*, the major and minor *flamens* and the Vestal Virgins. The appointments were for life (with the exception of the Vestals). *Pontifex* meant "bridge builder," and could originally have had associations with Tiberinus, the god of the river, but could also be understood metaphorically as bridging the distance between humans and the divine.

The College was supervised by the *pontifex maximus*, who was originally co-opted from within the membership. In the late Republic, however, the office of *pontifex maximus* was elected by the various assemblies. Although open to election, the slate of candidates was chosen by the College. During the Imperial period, following the precedent set by Augustus, the office was automatically given to the reigning emperor. The *pontifex maximus* was the highest authority on religious matters in Rome, and along with the rest of the College, acted as an advisor to the Roman Senate.

Pontifices combined politics and religion in the sense that originally they were experts on Roman law, which included the proper formulas for litigation in the law courts, the legalese for adoptions, and supervised wills. They were formally in charge of public *ludi* and religious festivals. The College of *Pontifices* was in charge of the *libri pontificales* (pontifical books). These included the ritual manuals, commentaries, sacred days, yearly records of magistrates, and the list of the correct names of the gods. Only the *pontifices* had access to this material, which was consulted during times of crises or when there was disagreement on some ritual. The College was particularly important for interpreting prodigies. *Pontifices* were assisted in their work by a scribe, who was referred to as a *pontifex minor* in the Imperial period.

The official base of the College of *Pontifices* was the Regia, a small building that tradition claimed was the original home of Roman kings along the Via Sacra in the forum. This building held the archives of the *pontifices*, formulas, and instructions for sacrifice, the sacred calendar, and the *Annales* or the events of each year. It also contained the *sacrarium Martis* ("the shrine of Mars") where the *ancilia* (shields) of Mars were kept along with the sacred lances dedicated to Mars.

Rex Sacrorum

The *rex sacrorum* ("king of the sacred rites") was a position left over from the time of the kings, when kings alone were responsible for public rituals. The base for the *rex sacrorum* was the Regia. The position may also have been influenced by Etruscan and Italian traditions. The holder could not seek political or military office and one of his distinctive attributes was an archaic ax that he carried. Some of his responsibilities included sacrificing on certain days of the month (the Kalends and the Nones).

The individual for this position was selected from a slate of candidates from the patrician class whose parents had been married by *confarreatio* (the strictest form of Roman marriage). He had to be married to his wife by the same ceremony. She then became the *regina sacrorum* ("queen of the sacred rites"). This was a joint priesthood as they were both responsible for special duties. If the *regina sacrorum* died, the *rex sacrorum* had to resign his position. Over time, the *regina sacrorum* could be accepted if she was a plebeian married to a patrician.

Flamens

The *flamens* were the priests who were assigned to the maintenance of the cult of a specific deity. In this sense they could be equated with being the "high-priest" of the god. There were 15 major *flamens* (*flamines maiores*) and 12 minor ones (*flamines minores*). The three major *flamens* were the *flamen dialis* (Jupiter), the *flamen martialis* (Mars) and the *flamen quirinalis* (Quirinus). Tradition assigned the appointment of the *flamens* to King Numa.

The three major *flamens* were always patricians and were provided with state houses on the Via Sacra in the Roman forum. *Flamens* were known by their distinctive dress: a *laena*, which was a heavy woolen cloak (sometimes with colored stripes), and an *apex*, a leather skull-cap with a chin strap. The *apex* had a pointed olive wood top (resembling a spindle) with a lock of wool that formed the base of the pointed wood (Figure V.4). The major *flamens* were treated with high honor and respect, and the *flamen dialis* was automatically a member of the Senate. If a criminal bound in chains happened to pass the *flamen dialis*, his chains were immediately struck off and he was freed.

Although they were privileged with such honors, the *flamens* were also subject to severe restrictions. They could not touch metal, ride a horse, or come near a corpse. The restrictions for the *flamen dialis* as the high-priest of Jupiter were even more severe. He could not leave the city for even one night (and therefore could never govern a province), run for the consulship, go near an army outside the *pomerium*, or swear an oath. His clothing, including shoes, could not have knots, he could not walk under vines, and could not eat any yeast or leaven (removing regular bread from his diet). Only a free man could cut the *flamen*'s hair and nails and the clippings had to be buried under a tree. The legs of his bed were covered in clay. The wife of the *flamen dialis*, the *flaminica dialis*,

Figure V.4 *Flamens* with distinctive hats. *Source*: akg-images/ Album/Prisma.

had her own duties to the god and they performed the rites jointly as a couple. If the *flaminica dialis* died, the *flamen dialis* had to resign his position.

The Vestal Virgins

The Vestals served the goddess Vesta and were responsible for the eternal flame of her hearth fire in the Roman forum. The well-being of Vesta was literally understood as the well-being of Rome itself. According to later traditions, the Vestals were created by King Numa at Alba Longa and then brought to Rome. There were six Vestal Virgins at any one time, with the *Virgo Vestalis Maxima* (the chief Vestal) acting as their supervisor and holding a seat in the College of *Pontifices*.

The Vestals were Rome's only official college of female priestesses. They were selected by lot from a slate of candidates of girls aged six to ten years old from patrician and plebeian families. These girls had to be free of physical defects and have both parents living. If selected, the child was literally handed over from the hand of her father to the hand of the state. The *pontifex maximus* stood in loco parentis to the Vestals and had direct supervision over all of them, including the *Virgo Vestalis Maxima*. Near the temple of Vesta in the forum was the *domus publica*, the closest thing Rome had to a state palace. The house was divided in half, with a temple in the middle. The *pontifex maximus* lived on one side and the Vestal Virgins on the other.

The length of service to Vesta was 30 years, during which a girl devoted her chastity to the goddess. In the first 10 years a Vestal learned the rituals, and the next 10 years were devoted to carrying out the rituals. The last 10 years were spent teaching and supervising the new youngsters. At the end of 30 years, Vestals received a state pension and were free to marry if they chose to do so. Most did not and often remained in the house of the Vestals. Vestals dressed distinctively in white, with an elaborate headdress of seven rolls of wool (the same as was worn by brides) and a white veil (see Figure V.5).

In addition to keeping the hearth of Vesta burning, the Vestals carried water from a nearby sacred spring and prepared food and cakes (***mola salsa***) used in various rituals in the city throughout the year. They also guarded the palladium (a secret sacred object from Troy). The Vestals organized the yearly festival of Vestalia in June. What became an ever increasing duty of the Vestals was the keeping of wills and testaments, a sacred entitlement of all citizens. Once a will was sealed and handed over to the Vestals, it was sacrosanct and could only be opened by the executors and witnesses.

The Vestals had many more privileges compared to the normal life of non-religious Roman women. When they visited or attended state events, they had a *carpentum* (a covered two-wheeled carriage) with a lictor (a state bodyguard) in front to provide them with the right of way. They also had reserved seats of honor at public games and at the theaters. Being independent of their *paterfamilias*, they were free to own property, make a will, and vote at special times in

Figure V.5 *Virgo Vestalis Maxima. Source:* DEA/V. PIROZZI/De Agostini/Getty Images.

the priestly colleges. They could provide evidence in courts of law without having to take an oath. Condemned prisoners could be freed upon encountering them, even those who were on the way to execution. The *Virgo Vestalis Maxima* shared authority with the men in the College of *Pontifices*.

On the other hand, if the sacred fire of Vesta went out, a Vestal could be scourged. The most severe punishment was reserved for the violation of a Vestal's chastity, which could offend Vesta and harm the city. If a Vestal violated her oath and had sex with a citizen, it was considered an act both of incest as well as treason. The individual man was scourged and put to death, while the guilty Vestal was paraded in a mock funeral through the city and taken to the Campus Sceleratus ("evil field") near the Colline Gate. To avoid the law that no one could be buried within the city and to avoid the guilt of murder, the Vestal was lowered into a chamber and buried alive with some bread and water. Her fate was left to Vesta. While charges against the Vestals were rare, they usually coincided with a political or military crisis.

The College of *Augurs* and *Haruspices* and the *Duoviri Sacris Faciundis*

In Rome, experts who could interpret the divine will, the *augurs*, were categorized under a college and were priests. Their activity revolved around divination. The *duoviri sacris faciundis* were priests who were charged with maintaining and interpreting the sacred books that held the Sibylline Oracles. (See Chapter VIII, for the details of *augurs* as well as *haruspices*, the experts on reading sacrificial entrails.)

Fetiales

Fetiales were priests devoted to Jupiter who also served as advisors to the Senate on foreign affairs. They made formal declarations of war and confirmed international treaties. The appointment of *fetiales* goes back to the period of the monarchy. They may have been headed by a *pater patratus* (meaning uncertain), whose traditional role was to announce Roman demands on nearby territory, beginning at the border. He was to repeat this with the first man he saw when he entered a gate, and when he arrived at the forum in front of the magistrates. If the demands were not met, he returned to Rome and within 33 days declared war. The *pater patratus* then threw a javelin into enemy territory. As Rome began to expand, this rite became impractical and was symbolically carried out in front of the temple of Bellona. The rites of the *fetiales* helped to sanctify war and peace.

Triumviri Epulones

In the second century BCE, Rome created a new college of priests, the *Triumviri Epulones*, who were charged with supervising the *epulum iovis* ("feast of Jupiter"), which was an integral part of the Jupiter and Plebeian games. Traditionally, these duties had been directly administered by the *pontifices*, but were now under this new college. They worked with the elected aediles, who were actually responsible for the games. Originally three, the *epulones* were later expanded to seven and were elected by the citizen assemblies.

Sodales

Additional organizations of priests and priesthoods were referred to as **sodales**, sodalities or "associations." These groups were established with the permission of the state; in modern language, we could say they were licensed by the state. Like colleges, they were dedicated to one particular god or goddess, although sodalities also existed for members of the same trade or craft. A reason to create a sodality of priests was when a new cult was introduced to the city of Rome. Such was the case when the cult of Magna Mater (Cybele) was set up in Rome during the Second Punic War. Her priests were licensed as a sodality which organized the *ludi Megalenses* each year.

Luperci

The **luperci** were two associations of priests, the *luperci quintilii* (of Romulus) and the *luperci fabii* (of Remus), drawn from the Equites class of Romans. These "brothers of the wolf" were responsible for the yearly festival of Lupercalia.

Fratres Arvales

The "Brothers of the fields" or the Arval Brotherhood, were devoted to Dea Dia and organized her festival held every year in May. Their rituals and hymns were so ancient that by the first century, Romans could not understand the words. Tradition claims that the association was established by Romulus, who took the place of the dead son of his nurse, Laurentia, and formed the group with her other 11 sons. The priests offered sacrifices to Dea Dia, an ancient fertility goddess, as well as to the Lares, and had propitiation rites at boundaries and fields. Their rites during the festival of Dea Dia were kept secret among the 12 priests, where the rites on the second day were held in a sacred grove outside the city walls. The membership was co-opted from within the group appointed by the pontifices and the Senate, and they wore a white ribbon around their heads that held a sheaf of grain.

Salii

The *salii* (from "to leap") were the leaping priests of Mars who were allegedly founded by King Numa to guard the *ancilia* (the shield that fell from Heaven, as well as the 11 fake ones). They were 12 young men in number and selected from the patrician class. But the Etruscans had *salii* that predated the founding of Rome and claimed that their origin began in Samothrace.

The *salii* held their festivals in relation to the opening and closing of the war season, March and October. The *salii* dressed as ancient warriors, with a tunic, a red cloak, a breastplate, a sword, and the spiked headdress, or *apex*. They paraded around the city dancing and leaping and chanting archaic hymns. The parade ended in a day of feasting.

Libitinarii

The *libitinarii* were a priesthood solely devoted to Venus Libitina, the goddess of the cessation of the life force, or death. Their main temple was on the Esquiline Hill and they were in charge of funeral rites. For more details of this priesthood, see Chapter X.

Duties

Like their Greek counterparts, many Roman priests were responsible for sacrifices, prayers, incantations, hymns, and other types of offerings. Sacrifices to the deities of the sky were done in daylight with white animals; chthonic deities required nighttime rituals and black animals. The sex of the animal was determined by the gender of the god or goddess. Depending upon the occasion (private or public), the sacrifice was followed by a meal or feast.

Figure V.6 Roman sacrifice. *Source:* De Agostini/W. Buss/ Getty Images.

Public sacrifices began with a procession through the city, with criers calling attention to the proceedings and inviting all to join in. These processions included musicians, drummers and sometimes dancers, singing hymns known as *carmina* (chants). An assistant would lead the animal, which was decorated in garlands and ribbons, and sometimes with gilded horns. A common practice was to drug the animal beforehand; a victim had to go willingly to the gods (Figure V.6).

Sacrifices had to be done with the correct epithets and prayers. If any part of the ritual, including the prayers or sacrifices, had a flaw, the process had to begin again. To avoid mistakes and having to start over, a flute player was employed to filter out sounds from the crowds or the city. The **immolatio**, or the killing of the beast, was a step-by-step procedure. The priest sprinkled wheat or flour on the head of the animal and then took some hairs and threw them on a nearby brazier. He then sipped from a cup of wine (the *libatio*) and poured the rest of it between the animal's horns. An assistant called a *popa* took a mallet and stunned the animal between the eyes. In theory the animal should fall to the right, with its head to the ground indicating its acceptance as a victim. As it fell another assistant would slit its throat, catch the blood in a vessel, and then throw the blood against the altar. A *haruspex* then read the entrails to determine if the god accepted the sacrifice.

In Rome the priesthoods were an essential part of the offices of the magistrates, at all levels of governance. Individuals held priesthoods and magistrate positions simultaneously and all elected officials were expected to have knowledge in rituals, prayers, and sacrifices. At times this meant that religious duties could often become "political." For example, if someone was against impending legislation, then the omens from *augurs* or *haruspices* could be declared unfavorable.

Summary

- Temples functioned as the centers of religious and community life in ancient Greece and Rome.
- Priests and priestesses were the caretakers of the gods and goddesses and served as mediators between the human and the divine.

Suggestions for Further Reading

Dignas, B. 2010. "A day in the life of a Greek sanctuary," in *A Companion to Greek Religion*, ed. D. Ogden, pp. 163–177. Wiley-Blackwell. Dignas provides an hour-by-hour description of the duties of a Greek priest.

Mikalson, J. D. 2010. *Ancient Greek Religion*, 2nd ed. Wiley-Blackwell. This text details the functions and rituals of the priesthood in ancient Greece.

Scheid, J. 2003. *An Introduction to Roman Religion*, trans. J. Lloyd. Indiana University Press. Scheid presents a readable history and describes the function of Roman rituals and concepts in the role of the priesthood.

WORSHIP OF THE GODS: COMMUNITY RELIGIOUS FESTIVALS

VI

Greek and Roman Religions, First Edition. Rebecca I. Denova.
© 2019 John Wiley & Sons, Inc. Published 2019 by John Wiley & Sons, Inc.

Learning Objectives

After reading this chapter, you will be able to:

- Become familiar with the details of community religious festivals;
- Appreciate the religious rituals that bound people to the divine and to the community.

 Community religious festivals were the heartbeat of the ancient world. They kept the universe in balance, regulated the seasons, and ensured that the community would prosper (or fall). In this chapter we will highlight some of the more common religious practices and the popular religious sites visited by the faithful, and the festivals that helped to ensure the goodwill of the gods. Many of the festivals were related to myth or founding stories. This chapter is organized according to the stories of the gods and goddesses that were highlighted in Chapters III and IV.

There were hundreds of opportunities for worship and religious festivals that varied between the city and countryside, but we are only highlighting some of the larger and shared festivities of the major gods and goddesses. Towns and villages continued to celebrate festivals for their own, older deities in addition to the ones noted here. At the same time, there were many festivals that marked the calendar year, especially the celebration of the New Year and the planting and harvesting cycles. The ancients also celebrated the summer and winter solstices.

Pilgrimage

Before we outline the details of worship, a brief review of the concept of pilgrimage is necessary to set the stage for the importance of religious sites and festivals all over the Greek and Roman world. A pilgrimage is a journey to a religious or holy site in the search for spiritual or moral meaning and reconciliation, or to obtain a benefit from a deity. In the modern sense, a pilgrimage also implies a metaphorical understanding of an individual's seeking a redress against alienation from God or one's beliefs. The concept of pilgrimage is very ancient and we have evidence of pilgrimages in ancient Egypt that were coordinated with annual religious festivals. In Egypt pilgrimage was facilitated by the easy and cheap access to the temples located along the Nile River. The importance of pilgrimage in other lands can be demonstrated by the distances that people were willing to travel to achieve the benefits of participating in this process.

Many of the festivals in this chapter were offered in conjunction with pilgrimage, and the sites and celebrations were the goal of both individual and group pilgrimage. Examples of individual pilgrimage sites were the oracular temples such as Delphi and the *asclepions* of the healing god Asclepios. (For the details on oracular sites, see Chapter VIII.) Group pilgrimages were also made to oracular sites, particularly when a city was in a crisis and needed advice. Greeks and Romans traveled both overland (riding or walking) and by sea to participate in these events. The various temples and sites associated with Mystery cults were a popular destination for pilgrims. Individuals as well as groups traveled to participate in the initiations and other rites at different times of the year.

The Worship of the Gods in Greece and Greek Colonies

Zeus

By tradition, the birthplace of Zeus was Crete and there were shrines at caves throughout the island to commemorate his early life. Many of these shrines were pilgrimage sites, with **incubation** (sleeping) as a common source of divination. In Athens (and other cities), the Diasia festival was one of the oldest festivals to Zeus as Zeus Meilichios (an earlier chthonic deity), which was done at night. This was celebrated as both a springtime rural and urban festival, bringing people into the *polis* and the *polis* to the countryside. Offerings of sheep, pig-shaped pastry and other sacrifices were accompanied by dances, hymn-singing, and chanting. In this aspect of Zeus, he was the appeaser and purifier. Crimes were atoned for in these rituals by offering the sacrifice as a holocaust (a whole burnt offering), where the god received everything.

The larger festivals honoring Zeus were part of the Panhellenic Games. These games were offered in rotational years, with participants who came from all over the Greek world. During the period of the Games, truces were granted among warring cities to enable all to travel safely. The four games were held at Olympia (Zeus), Delphi (the Pythian Games to Apollo), Nemea (Zeus, Heracles), and Isthmia (Poseidon). Originally only Greek citizens could participate, but after the conquest of Greece by Rome, any citizen of the Empire was eligible. The athletic events included chariot racing, wrestling, boxing, foot races, javelin throwing, and discus throwing. Some of the games include music, drama, and poetry contests.

The Olympic Games were the oldest of the Panhellenic Games, allegedly begun in 776 BCE. According to various traditions, the games originated as either a victory celebration by Heracles over the nearby city of Elis, or the funeral games that Pelops put on for his victory over his father-in-law Oenomaus. Eventually the games were dedicated to Zeus at a temple which contained his famous colossal statue. The award ceremonies took place in front of the temple, where the winners received olive wreaths. During the games a hundred oxen were sacrificed to Zeus.

The Nemean Games may have originated when the "Seven Against Thebes" slew a dragon that had killed the child of the priest of Zeus and Eurydice. Another version claimed that Heracles honored his father Zeus after he slew the Nemean lion. In addition to the standard athletic events, the Nemean Games included horse racing, running in armor in the stadium, archery, and musical contests. The prize for the victors was a wreath of celery (a symbol of fertility).

Hera

Some of the earliest Greek "house sanctuaries" were dedicated to Hera and an early public temple was built at Samos ca 800 BCE (and later known as a *heraion*). There were also early temples at Argos and Mycenae. An example of a temple to Hera remains at Agrigento, Sicily. There was a major temple to Hera at Olympia (perhaps older than the temple to Zeus). Olympia was the site of the Heraean Games, foot races for women dedicated to the goddess. The winners were given olive wreaths and meat from the sacrifices, and were permitted (like the men) to erect statues of themselves at Hera's temple.

Two major festivals to Hera in Plataea and Boeotia were the Greater Daedala (every 14 years) and the Lesser Daedala (every four years). The central element of these rituals was an oaken carved image (a *daidalon*) which was dressed as a bride and taken on a procession through the city. The accumulation of these images over the years was used in the Greater Daedala and all were burned upon a pyre. The foundation for these festivals may have been an ancient story that Hera once tricked Zeus in his philandering by having someone substitute a wooden image for his targeted lover.

Poseidon

As god of both the seas and earthquakes, Poseidon had major temples in the larger cities and seaports. He maintained an important influence in Athens, recalling his contribution in the origin myth of the city. When Athens became a major player in the maritime Delian League, Poseidon was called upon to favor the seafaring trade and adventures that were inherent in that organization. He was important at Delphi, and after consultation on establishing new colonies, he blessed the new undertaking. He was known as an "averter of disaster." In Athens and other cities, altars to Poseidon had basins of seawater next to them. There were claims that this seawater would stir into waves on its own. The temple to Poseidon at Sunium (near Athens) sat atop a cliff overlooking the seaport and included a fort for defensive purposes. At this site he was Poseidon Soter ("savior").

The Panhellenic Isthmian Games were dedicated to Poseidon and administered by Corinth (where the Isthmus was). The Games included athletics and the arts, and a highlight was chariot-racing as Poseidon was also a god of horses and horse-racing. Traditionally, the winners received a wreath of celery, and later pine wreaths. Winners had the right to erect a statue and have an ode written about them, and there were also statues of winning horses in honor of Poseidon Hippios (horse-god).

Demeter

Temples to Demeter were located throughout the Mediterranean Basin and often contained statues of her daughter Persephone (also known as Kore).

Some temples were located at sites associated with the myth of Demeter in the search for her daughter. When the first fruits of the agricultural season were offered to the gods, Demeter received the first corn and grain. A major festival for Demeter in the Greek cities was the Thesmophoria. The name derives from *thesmoi* (laws) and refers to Demeter's rule in instituting the laws of agriculture and the seasons. The Thesmophoria was one of the festivals that were restricted to married women, the spouses of citizens. Their husbands paid for the setting up of shelters, food, and drink.

Although the festival celebrated fertility there was a period of sexual abstinence and purification. In Athens, on the first day, the women processed to the Thesmophorion near the hill known as the Pnyx. The second day was spent in mourning and fasting for Demeter's grief over her lost daughter. The third day was a celebration of renewal spent in feasting and drinking. This celebration allegedly included bawdy jokes and stories, as an imitation of the stories that Demeter was told in an effort to cheer her up. An important element of this festival was the digging up of the carcasses of pigs that had been buried earlier in the year. These remains were mixed with other ingredients and were considered a good fertilizer for crops. The pigs may relate to the story that a swineherd lost his pigs when they were swallowed up in the ground when Hades abducted Persephone. The Thesmophoria was one of the festivals where social conventions were relaxed, and commentators have often claimed that this was one of the opportunities for women to escape the restrictions of the home and visit with their female relatives.

Important rituals for Demeter were enacted during the Eleusinian Mysteries (See Chapter IX).

Athena

Temples to Athena were located throughout the Greek world with some of the more noteworthy in Athens, at the port city of Piraeus, and at Corinth on the Isthmus. In Athens and elsewhere, Athena was often combined with the goddess Nike (Victory). Other cities besides Athens celebrated Athena's myths, although the largest was the Greater Panathenaea in Athens, which was held every four years, to which thousands made pilgrimage. The festival included athletic competitions, poetry, and musical contests. The Lesser Panathanea was held every year.

Between festivals, a *peplos* (a Greek dress) was woven by girls specially selected from the aristocratic families. The *peplos* was carried in a procession from the *agora* to the acropolis and other girls had baskets holding secret offerings. The *peplos* was draped on a life-size statue of Athena. A hecatomb (a hundred oxen) was sacrificed and provided a community meal. The festival included the Pyrrhic dance, performed by youths in battle gear. Tradition claimed that this was the dance that Athena performed after her victory over the giants. A frieze on the Parthenon displayed the city's procession of the Panathanea.

Aphrodite

The main festival of worship for Aphrodite was the Aphrodisia (note our modern word, aphrodisiac), which was celebrated throughout Greece, with the largest celebrations at Athens, Corinth, and the port city of Paphos on the island of Cyprus. Cyprus was her traditional birthplace, where she came out of the sea. Images of the goddess were carried and washed in the sea and some women were invited at this time to become initiates, receiving salt and sacred bread, perhaps in the form of a phallus. White he-goats were important in the ceremonies.

The festival of Adonia was celebrated only by women and was in the nature of a private rather than a public festival. The rites honored Aphrodite's lover Adonis, with both mourning for his death and celebration of his subsequent resurrection. Women gathered together on roof-tops, weeping and mourning on the first day, and rejoicing, drinking, and singing on the second day. An element of this festival was the planting of the "Gardens of Adonis," where women planted wheat, barley, lettuce, and fennel in bowls and clay vessels. The gardens were symbolic of fertility.

Ares

There were few major temples to Ares, although there were shrines and groves dedicated to him throughout the Greek world. Ares was the recipient of sacrifices before armies went to war. In Sparta, a statue of Enyalius (an older form of the war god) was chained in place to keep him from leaving. It is here that young boys sacrificed puppies to Enyalius/Ares as part of their rituals of passing to adulthood. His statues also appeared in conjunction with the other gods in various temples. There was a temple to Ares near the *agora* in Athens, the Areopagus, or "hill of Ares." This was the site of Athenian trials and meetings of the elders. Many more rituals to Ares were conducted on the battlefields.

Apollo

Apollo had temples everywhere and there were festivals to honor him, as well as festivals to honor him with his sister Artemis. The Daphnephoria was held at Thebes every nine years. The procession was led by a boy selected from the noble families who carried an olive branch hung with a bronze ball and several smaller balls (the sun, moon, and stars). He was followed by young girls singing hymns to Apollo.

The Boedromia was held in Athens to honor Apollo Boedromios (helper in distress) and thank the god for his help during wars. The Thargelia was celebrated for the Delian Apollo and Artemis and was held on their birthdays (the end of May). This was both an agricultural and expiatory festival. The early harvest was offered in thanksgiving and there were purification rites for the city. At the end of the festival, two ugly men (and perhaps a woman?) were selected to act as scapegoats (or to take on the problems of the city) and were stoned. It is debated if in later times the victims actually died or were rescued. The Delphinia had girls who processed to Apollo's temple carrying branches and was most likely based upon the tradition that Theseus originated the ceremony before he left for Crete to slay the Minotaur.

The Panhellenic Pythian Games were held every four years (in rotation before and after the Olympic Games) and dedicated to Apollo in commemoration of his slaying of the python at Delphi and his establishment of the Delphic Oracle. They included athletic games as well as competitions for music, theater, art, and dance. The music contests were for the *aulos*, a reed pipe and the *kithara*, a string instrument. The winners received a laurel wreath (see the box "Religious Origins of Dance and Drama").

Religious Origins of Dance and Drama

As with many other elements of ancient culture, we cannot pinpoint exactly when dance and drama originated, but the consensus believes that both had their origins in religious expression and practices. The evidence of apparently dancing figures in cave paintings may or may not be related, but at least from the Bronze Age the connection of dancing and drama in religious festivals is apparent. Dance may also have helped in the reenactment of myths.

In ancient Egypt, temple and tomb drawings portray dancing women and singers as an integral part of religious worship and festivals from at least the third millennium BCE. They carry sistrums, or rattle-like instruments (sacred to both Isis and Hathor), and were accompanied by drums and flute-like accoutrements. Singers helped to transmit the sacred hymns to each generation.

In Greece, festivals of the agricultural cycle included dancing and song (hymns) and were an important element of the celebration of the particular deities who oversaw planting and harvesting. This was particularly true of the Dionysus festivals, with a central focus on vines and winemaking which included the freestyle dances which were examples of both the result of drinking and possession by the god.

There is evidence of drama in ancient Egypt, where religious festivals served as the occasion for plays and mythic stories of the gods that were enacted by priests. At Abydos, a main cult center for Osiris, a "passion play" was performed that recited the story of the murder of Osiris by his brother Seth and his subsequent resurrection by his wife, Isis.

As early as the Olympic Games, the *choros* (chorus) consisted of temple servants and may have been the origin of the chorus in the evolution of dramatic festivals. In satyr plays, tragedy and comedy, a group of singers/dancers of up to 50 performers provided background or summary material of the story. The earliest formal plays were created as part of the Dionysus festivals in the city of Athens, where prizes were awarded for the best of both tragedy and comedy (in the early sixth century BCE). In the beginning one actor recited the lines of the stories, but two, three and more were later added. Only men were permitted to perform on stage and they took the roles of women.

In Rome, a further development in drama resulted in the pantomime, referring to a dancer who originally sang and enacted all parts of a myth or legend. The various roles were indicated by masks and what became stock gestures with the hands. Pantomime was extremely popular and conveyed many of the stories and myths important to the spread of Roman culture. In the realm of comedy, pantomimes incorporated exaggerated elements of class distinctions, particularly those of master and slave. They were also infamous for their exaggerated erotic content. Pantomime was influential in the later development of the art of ballet and Commedia dell'arte in Europe.

Dance and drama also had the benefit of sheer entertainment. These arts provided sound and color and exquisite demonstrations of the human experience. They portrayed both joys and sorrows and gave expression to a community's quest for meaning.

Artemis

Some Athenian girls celebrated the transition from girlhood to puberty called "playing the bear," with rites known as the Arkteia where they imitated she-bears and participated in ritual dancing, foot races, and other activities. In this aspect of Artemis (Artemis Brauronia, of Brauron, a town south of Athens), young girls participated in rituals so that they would be pure before taking up their wifely duties. This established Artemis as a protector of not only virginity but pregnancy and birth.

The Lakonians (in southeastern Peloponnese) had a ritual dedicated to Artemis Orthia that contained a wooden image of the goddess. In recognition of ancient blood spilled on the altar, men of noble birth were scourged as propitiation to the goddess, while young girls danced. Tradition indicates that originally a young man was selected to be sacrificed, but the writers in the Hellenistic period claimed that this practice had been substituted with just some drops of human blood on the altar.

The most famous temple to Artemis was in Ephesus (Anatolia), Artemis Ephesia, and it was known as one of the Seven Wonders of the ancient world. The earliest temple dated to the Bronze Age and perhaps was originally associated with the Amazons who fled there for the goddess's protection. Henceforth, the temple was associated with asylum. Over the centuries it suffered from natural disasters and was rebuilt many times. Around 550 BCE, Croesus of Lydia (the richest man at the time) funded a new structure and allegedly it was the first temple built of marble. The cult image of this Artemis was unique (breasts or testicles?) and there was a tradition that it had fallen from the sky (Figure VI.1).

The yearly Artemisia festival included a procession of young women carrying an image of the goddess through the streets, but young men participated as well. This festival may have been part of a larger one known as Haloea, a solstice celebration which was also celebrated elsewhere and which combined rites for Artemis, Demeter, Dionysus, and especially Poseidon. Social conditions were relaxed, women had the opportunity to drink wine, and the festival became an occasion for the young to seek marriage partners.

Hermes

Hermes cults were found in the countryside in his capacity as a god of nature, shepherds, boundaries, and roads. In the cities, his temples were often combined with those of Aphrodite, and every *agora* or market square contained a statue of Hermes as the god of commerce. Young men, in their phase of hunters and soldiers, often sacrificed to Hermes or had initiation rites as part of the cult of the god. His statue was a popular one in gyms and at the temple of the Twelve Gods in Athens. The *hermai*, or boundary markers sculpted with the head of Hermes and a phallus, also received offerings of wreaths of flowers and sometimes libations. Those acquitted through trial on the Areopagus (hill of Ares) in Athens laid a wreath at the foot of a statue of Hermes nearby.

Figure VI.1 Artemis at Ephesus. *Source*: akg-images/Gilles Mermet.

In Boeotia there was a tradition that Hermes alleviated a plague by carrying a ram on his shoulders around the city. The most handsome youth was selected to make a circuit round the walls with a lamb. The Hermaea was a celebration throughout Greek lands, with sacrifices, athletics, and gymnastics, restricted to young boys only. Offerings included gold, silver, the milk of sheep and honeycombs.

Hephaestus

There was a large temple to Hephaestus overlooking the *agora* in Athens. Hephaestus and Athena Ergane (in Athena's role as patroness of craftsmen) were jointly celebrated each year in a festival called Chalceia by craftsmen, bronzesmiths, and artisans. There was a main cult center on the island of Lemnos (one of the sites where tradition claims that Hephaestus fell from Mount Olympus) that involved secret rituals of the *Kabeiroi*, who claimed to be sons of the god. There was a temple on Mount Etna (Sicily) with a sacred grove, where an eternal flame was kept. Sacred hounds were also kept here to greet visitors.

Dionysus

A festival known as the Dionysia combined both rural and city components. The rural Dionysia celebrated the growing of vines (and winemaking). There was a festive procession (a *pompe*) where participants carried *phalloi* (carved phalluses) and young girls carried baskets with loaves of bread and other offerings, and jars of water and wine. This was followed by contests of dancing and singing. Some towns included dramatic contests as well.

The city Dionysia, particularly in Athens, was an ancient festival that celebrated the recognition of Dionysus and his elimination of a plague. He had cursed the genitalia of the Athenians. This was the reason that *phalloi* were carried in procession. In Athens, the procession wended its way through the city to the Theater of Dionysus on the Acropolis and included the baskets, water, and wine jars, and bulls that were sacrificed at the theater. Choruses (along with flute-players and poets) competed. This was the time when performances of the playwrights were presented. The final day saw another festival procession when the winners of the plays were announced.

The Dionysia was a time for inverted or relaxed social conventions. Slaves were permitted to participate with the family for the opening of the casks of wine. Everyone dressed in their finest clothes and visited friends and relatives. There were drinking contests as well. A second festival, the Lenaia, was a small version of the dramatic contests but emphasized comedy and included a celebration of the Maenads, or the female followers of Dionysus. For the Dionysian Mysteries, see Chapter IX.

Hestia

Rather than distinct temples, Hestia had sacred altars in the cities (in the equivalent of municipal buildings) which were maintained by civic officials who also administered priestly rites. The Theater of Dionysus on the Acropolis had a special seating section for these priests. Each home had a hearth where morning rituals began to the goddess to protect the home and the family. A bride and groom lit a candle together to reflect the creation of a new home from the hearth fires of the older generation. Newborn babies were carried around the hearth of Hestia, where they were given a name. When a new town or colony was founded, flames from the mother city-state were carried to the new one.

Hades

Temples to Hades were few and when his statue did appear it was often in the company of Demeter and Persephone. There was a temple to Hades at Elis (near Olympia), where the doors were opened once a year for one priest to enter. This may have symbolized that a man journeys to Hades once in his life. In Asia Province his temple complex included a cave where nude men released a bull and let it run loose inside until it dropped dead. Another cave site near Nysa served as an incubation place for those who wished to cure their diseases.

Given the nature of his realm, people avoided both the powers and name of Hades, often using a euphemism such as Polydegmon ("he who receives many"). He was not evil, but described as cruel because all mortals could not escape going to his realm. As the ultimate chthonic power, his sacrificial animals were black; instead of blood being poured on the altar, it was poured into pits on the ground. Hades was an integral figure in all funeral rituals and in the Mystery cult of Eleusis. He was called upon in necromancy rituals (communicating with the dead) and he had a cult center at the Oracle of the Dead at Thesprotia in western Greece and at Cumae in Italy. (For more on Hades and his realm, see Chapter X.)

Asclepios

The worship of Asclepios was slightly different in the ancient world as this cult was not related to the mandatory civic worship of the gods. In other words, his worship was undertaken voluntarily as needed, which usually meant a health problem, disease, or appeals for fertility. In Athens two community festivals, the Epidauria and the Asclepieia, included the usual processions and offerings and focused on the health and welfare of the community.

Asclepions, or the healing temples, were located throughout the Greek world with sites on the islands of Kos, Rhodes, and Crete and in Athens, Corinth, and Pergamon. The most famous complex was at Epidauros in the Peloponnese. These temple complexes, in addition to the temple itself, included clinics, dormitories, sacred groves, gymnasiums, and treasuries for the collection of votive offerings. For the details of the incubation rites for Asclepios, see Chapter VIII.

Tyche

Tyche had a temple at Itanos on Crete where she was celebrated as Tyche Protogeneia ("first-born") and connected to the myth of one of the daughters of Erechtheus in Athens. There was no specific festival dedicated to her but she was always much on the minds of Greeks since she was the originator of the good or bad fortunes of individuals and communities. In the Hellenistic period, Tyche often appeared on coins.

The Fates

The Fates (*Moirai*) controlled the destiny of gods and men, and like Tyche, were of much concern to individuals. The Fates were thought to direct the actions of the *Erinyes*, those powers in Hades who were responsible for revenge. Sacrifices offered to the Fates and *Erinyes* were the same. The Fates had sanctuaries in Corinth, Sparta, Olympia, and other cities where they were appealed to in redirecting the harassment of the *Erinyes*. Seers and diviners often appealed to them in predicting the future of an individual. Influential at birth and death, the Fates were appealed to through sacrifices to Zeus, and their portraits would often appear in the proximity of paintings and statues of Zeus.

The Muses

The Muses were honored as the source of music, the arts, the inspiration of ideas and inventions, and schools of philosophy. One of their oldest temples was in Pieria in Thrace and they were believed to dwell on mountain-tops at Helicon, Parnassus, Delphi, and Pindus. Springs on these mountains were sacred to the Muses. They were offered libations of water, milk, and honey but not wine.

The worship of the Muses was an element at the tomb of Hesiod in Boeotia. The most famous temple to the Muses in the Hellenistic period was located in Alexandria, Egypt where Ptolemy Soter built a learning complex and invited scholars and scientists from the known world to come and study. From this complex we get our term, museum.

The Worship of the Gods: Rome

Rome (and Italy) had hundreds of religious festivals throughout the year and as the Empire expanded, the festivals grew to include some of the traditional cults of the conquered territories. The combination of ancient Etruscan, Greek, and foreign cults resulted in festivals that were often dedicated to several different gods at the same time. In this section we will describe the most important festivals of the Romans and, with the exception of some older Italian deities, the list will parallel that of the Greeks.

Jupiter

As king of the gods the sky temples to Jupiter were located on the tops of hills and mountains. He had an ancient temple on the Alban Hill located south of Rome where he was worshipped as Jupiter Latiaris (for the league of Latin cities). His most important and famous temple was located on the Capitoline Hill in Rome overlooking the forum (Figure VI.2), as Jupiter Optimus Maximus ("Jupiter Best and Greatest"). He shared this temple with Juno and Minerva and together these deities were known as the Capitoline Triad. Jupiter was always worshipped with the sacrifice of white animals.

Any place that had been struck by lightning was enclosed with walls and declared a sacred space. Jupiter was responsible for oaths and oath-taking and the magistrates of Rome took their oaths of office in his temple. For the office of consul, the elected candidates held an all-night vigil here before their inauguration

RECONSTITUTION DU FORUM ROMAIN VU DE LA MAISON DES VESTALES
Dessin de J. Hoffbauer, superposant exactement les monuments à leurs ruines actuelles.

Figure VI.2
Reconstruction of the Roman forum. *Source*: DEA/G. DAGLI ORTI/De Agostini/Getty Images.

into office the next day (in consultation with the *augurs*), followed by a banquet in the temple complex. Such rituals reflected Jupiter's protection of the state. The largest festival to Jupiter was the *ludi Romani* ("Roman Games") held in mid-September. Originating in the last days of the monarchy, the games were in honor of Jupiter in gratitude for vows made to the god for military victories and conquests. They consisted of dramatic, comedic, and pantomime performances as well as chariot-racing and eventually lasted 15 days.

The most popular element of the Games was the chariot-racing held in the Circus Maximus, which could seat up to 200 000 in the wooden tiers (Figure VI.3). In the city of Rome, there were racing factions identified by colors: the Whites,

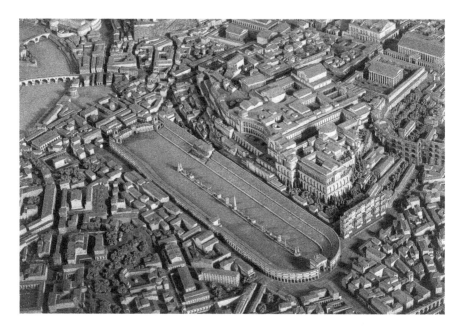

Figure VI.3
Reconstruction of
the Circus Maximus.
Source: DEA/A.
DAGLI ORTI/De
Agostini/Getty
Images.

the Greens, the Blues, and the Reds. Each faction had stables at the Circus where you could find statues of famous horses. The winning drivers had the right to have their wreath laid upon their funeral bier. The interest and enthusiasm for chariot-racing during the Jupiter Games was equivalent to our modern enthusiasm for World Cup Soccer or the National Football League.

Juno

Throughout Italy the cult of Juno featured the annual feeding of barley cakes to a sacred snake by virgin girls, who approached the snake in blindfolds. This ritual was associated with Juno's role in fertility and the welfare of the community.

Most of the temples and festivals dedicated to Juno in Rome were related to early traditions. In the old Roman calendar the variable month of February was a time of passages of the old year ending and a new one beginning. But it was also a dangerous time. Juno was called upon (as Juno Februata) along with Janus to purify the city from contamination from the underworld and also to renew her protection of the city during this month in the celebration of Juno Sospita (Juno "Savior"). After the birth of a child, a coin was deposited in the temple of Juno Sospita.

March 1 was the day of the Matronalia, attended by married women and mothers. Men and daughters gave the women gifts, and men were expected to offer prayers for their wives. This practice can be found in our modern "Mother's Day." The festival celebrated Juno's role in childbearing (Juno Lucina) and only women could participate in the rituals, many of which were kept secret. We do know that women wore their hair unbound and were forbidden to wear any belts of knots on their clothing. This may have symbolized a woman being prepared for childbirth. During the festival, women were expected to prepare a meal for their slaves and relax the usual distance between the classes. The Matronalia also celebrated Juno's help in reconciling the Sabine women in their new roles as Roman wives.

The temple to Juno Moneta was located on the *Arx* of the Capitoline Hill near the *auguraculum*, the site for *augurs*, and thus she was associated with their pronouncements. This temple housed the city mint and reflected the influence of Juno in protecting the finances of the city (and later Empire). The Nonae Caprotinae ("The Nones of Wild Figs") was another women-only festival, which included female slaves and was dedicated to joyous feasting, dancing, singing, and wine-drinking. Juno Curitis was the goddess of new brides. In preparation for the wedding, the bride's hair was parted with a spear called a *caelibataris hasta* and symbolizing Juno's protection in marriage.

Neptune

The association of Neptune with horses (following Poseidon) was reflected in the Roman temple to Neptune at the Circus Flaminius on the Campus Martius, where it merged with the earlier Italian horse and fertility god Consus (celebrated at the festival of Consualia aestiva) when the harvest was completed. This temple had an underground altar, which indicated an association with the chthonic powers of fertility as well. Horses and mules were decorated and paraded through the streets, followed by races.

The main Roman festival to Neptune was the Neptunalia, held during the hot days of summer, when springs, wells, and rivers sometimes ran dry. Romans built temporary huts or shelters (*umbrae*, "shades") out of laurel branches. In the huts, families feasted (on a bull sacrificed to Neptune if they could afford it) and there was water and wine drinking and a festive atmosphere which relaxed the social conventions. Neptune was asked to bring the rains to refill the water supplies and avoid drought.

Minerva

The Quinquatria festival in March was established either as a celebration of the birthday of Minerva, to mark the beginning of the military campaign season, or as a commemoration of the founding of her temple on the Aventine. Residents of the area claimed that the temple was older than other temples, although it was outside the *pomerium*. The Aventine became associated with plebeians and common workers, and thus Minerva was cherished as their personal protector. This temple was also a meeting site for writers and dramatists who took their inspiration from Minerva.

At the Quinquatria, women especially were involved in the rites, but they also consulted fortune-tellers and diviners on the first day, although this connection to Minerva remains vague. The emperor Domitian (ruled 83–96 CE) moved the festival to the Alban hills, which may have reflected the older, Latin, and Italian origins of Minerva, adding wild beast shows and contests for dramatists and poets. As Minerva Medica, she was responsible for doctors and healing.

Mars

Mars had his own priest, the *flamen martialis*, one of the three most important priests in the state cult. He was responsible for leading all the rituals on Mars's sacred days and festivals. Despite the association with war however, the *flamen martialis* could not leave the city and so had little to do with actual warfare.

The *salii* performed the ritual war dances at the opening and closing of the war season (March to October). While devoted to the ancient goddess Dea Dia, the priesthood of the Arval Brothers also propitiated Mars to drive away rust fungus, a problem for both crops and weapons. Mars Silanus (of the woods) kept the forests away from arable farmland and most farms had altars to Mars for this propitiation. In Rome, soldiers swore to Mars Gradivus for strength in battle at a shrine near the Capena Gate, and Mars Quirinus protected the **curiae** (citizen assemblies) when they swore an oath involving treaties. There were also rituals to Mars in the camps of the legionaries.

All of Rome turned out on October 15 for the ritual for Mars that became known as "the October Horse" (Equus October). October signified both the end of the military campaign season and of the agricultural season. The ritual originally consisted of a chariot race, which eventually evolved to a horse race. Members of the Subura (Rome's "slum") and the Via Sacra neighborhoods competed for this honor. The race was held either in the Circus Maximus or the forum. The winning horse was sacrificed to Mars by having its head and tail cut off. The tail was then immediately transferred to the Regia, where it was burned in a brazier and the ashes used by the Vestals in their ritual offerings throughout the year and in the **lustratio** (purification ritual) for the Parilia (see below). The head was tossed to the riders, who scrambled to race with it to their respective neighborhoods amid a street battle where no rules existed in the fight for supremacy. The winning faction displayed the head through the year, with subsequent bragging rights. This ritual may have had ancient traditions in a horse sacrifice to Mars, but by the late Republic most Romans could not identify the exact meaning of it; it was just something that had always been done in the past.

Venus

Throughout Italy, the Vinalia Rustica celebrated wine, crop growth, and fertility, where gardens were dedicated to Venus. The sacrificial animal was a white female lamb. In April the festival of the Veneralia (for Venus Verticordia, or Venus "the changer of hearts") was held to commemorate the disasters of the Punic Wars, which were blamed on the sexual immorality of the Romans (particularly the unchaste violations of some Vestal Virgins). It was to remind

Romans of the proper conduct of marriage and sexual behavior. The statue of Venus was taken to the men's baths and then dressed with myrtle. The Vinalia Urbana was celebrated in conjunction with Jupiter to recognize the gift of what was known as common wine for the people. The worship of Venus Genetrix ("Venus as mother") combined older concepts with a new temple built by Julius Caesar in 46 BCE not only to celebrate his victories, but to elevate a family cult to state sponsorship. For the rituals of Venus Libitina, see Chapter X.

Apollo

Apollo was worshipped throughout Italy in many temples that were originally Greek and Etruscan. As an oracular god, he had an ancient temple at Cumae in conjunction with the Sibylline oracular complex. The temple in Rome, to Apollo Sosianus, was located outside the *pomerium* in the Campus Martius because he was a foreign god. This temple was dedicated to Apollo Sosius (named after Gaius Sosius, who rebuilt an older version). The original temple was dedicated after Apollo intervened in stopping an epidemic in the 430s BCE. In this sense, Apollo also had the epithet of Apollo Medicus because of his healing abilities. Apollo had special priests, *duoviri sacris facundis*, in charge of the prophecies and who prayed in the **ritus graecus** ("the Greek rite") with their heads uncovered.

Romans celebrated the *ludi Apollinares* (Apollo's Games) in July. Tradition claims that they were instituted at the behest of one Marcius who claimed an interpretation of Apollo's prophecies that requested the Games in his honor during the Second Punic War. The Games were held in the Circus Maximus and included chariot-racing and drama. These Games lasted eight days.

Diana

Diana was an ancient goddess worshipped especially by the Latin tribes, in whose areas she had many sanctuaries. A temple dating from the period of the monarchy in Rome was allegedly dedicated by King Tullus Hostilius on the Aventine Hill (outside the *pomerium*, and thus a foreign cult). Because King Tullus was descended from a slave, Diana's temples offered sanctuaries for slaves. She was also a patron of the plebeians.

One of the oldest temples to Diana in Italy was at Lake Nemi in the Alban Hills south of Rome. This temple was a site of pilgrimage for women in quest of pregnancy and successful births. In August, the festival of Nemoralia began at Diana's temple in Rome (and in other cities at her temples) and processed to Aricia. The participants carried lighted candles and there were candlelight vigils at the lake each night for the duration of the festival. Many women offered votives of a mother and child made out of clay, as well as small statues of stags.

At times, Diana was portrayed as a triple goddess, representing the wild, the hunt, and the moon. At other times this tripartite concept was sculpted as three heads: a horse, a dog, and a boar. The statues were placed at roadside shrines where three roads met.

Vulcan

Vulcan was a particularly important god at the seaport of Ostia and in the areas around Mount Vesuvius on the Bay of Naples. His importance was connected to smiths and craftsmen in Ostia and his priest (the *pontifex Fulcani et aedium sacrarum*) was also the highest administrative office in the city. The towns in the vicinity of Mount Vesuvius connected the prominent sulfur vapors in the area with the workings of Vulcan.

The oldest shrine to Vulcan in the city of Rome, the Volcanal, was located at the foot of the Capitoline Hill and kept a perpetual flame with a *quadriga* (a war chariot) and a lotus tree dedicated by Romulus. In August, when the danger from drought was at its peak, the Vulcanalia was celebrated with festival bonfires. People hung cloths out in the sun (perhaps their clothing) and did their work by candlelight. Small animals and live fish were thrown into the fires. This was followed by games in the Campus Martius. A smaller festival was the Tubilustria, where trumpets used in ritual sacrifices were purified through the intervention of the god.

Vulcan had his own *flamen*, the *flamen volcanalis*. He was in charge of the ceremonies to the goddess Maia, an ancient fertility goddess who was a consort of Vulcan. (She was originally one of the Titans who was the mother of Hermes in some traditions.) The offerings included a pregnant sow. Fire was beneficial but it was also one of the most dangerous elements in an extremely crowded city. Vulcan was always placated after a major fire, such as the Great Fire of Rome in 64 CE.

Vesta

The most common and traditional worship of Vesta began in the home, with daily rituals centering on the hearth fire. The fire symbolized all of the good that came from the earth and protected the family and community. One of the oldest centers for the worship of Vesta was located near Bovillae in the Alban Hills south of Rome.

The public festival of Vestalia was celebrated in the last two weeks of June and was understood as a purification ritual for all of Rome. This was a public festival where women could fully participate in the rituals. It was also a special holiday for the bakers because, according to tradition, in the early days of Rome bread was baked in the sacred ashes of Vesta's hearth instead of ovens. During the festival, the Vestals would prepare the *mola salsa* or the sacred bread used in sacrifices. At this time the Temple of Vesta was ritually swept clean of all impurities and the detritus was taken to the Tiber River to symbolically purify the city.

Mercury

The major temple to Mercury in Rome was in the Circus Maximus and became a plebeian stronghold because many plebeian classes were involved in commerce and trade. A sacred well near the Porta Capena (at one end of the Circus) was used by merchants, who sprinkled their heads, their merchandise, their ships, and other accoutrements of trade on May 15, the Mercuralia festival. This water was known as the *acqua Mercurii* and was beneficial in the forgiving of past and future sins, the luck needed to turn a profit, and even for success in cheating customers.

Ceres

Ceres was extremely important in her role as the creator of spelt (wheat) and thus the source of the basic food staple (bread). In January, along with Tellus, she received offerings of spelt and a pregnant sow at the Feriae Sementivae. This was a rural festival which also called upon other deities to help with the entire process (such as Vervactor, "he who ploughs," and Insitor, "he who plants seeds"). The head priest for Ceres was the *flamen cerialis*, although most of the actual rituals were performed by women. Sacrifices to Ceres were performed in the *ritus graecus*.

The main festivals for Ceres were the Cerealia in April and the Ambarvalia in May. These were the times for planting seeds and her protection was necessary for a successful harvest. The Cerealia in Rome was under the supervision of the plebeian aediles, who also had special connections to her main temple on the Aventine Hill, where she shared space with Liber and Libera. Ceres also was the patroness of the elected Tribunes of the People and abuse of one of the Tribunes resulted in the death penalty. As the protector of laws, the official decrees of the Senate (**senatus consulta**) were archived in her temple.

The Cerealia began with the *ludi Circenses*, Ceres's Games, and included a race in the Circus Maximus. Women wore white and carried torches to reenact Ceres's search for her daughter. This was followed by the release of foxes with lighted torches tied to their tails, which perhaps served as a purification ritual. The Games concluded with a week of *ludi scaenici*, which were theatrical religious plays. The Ambarvalia was a festival in May which included the sacrifice of a bull, a sow, and a sheep, or a **suovetaurilia** sacrifice. The family rituals were led by the *paterfamilias*, with his children and slaves, processing in the villages surrounding the towns and cities and ending at boundaries where the ceremonies were conducted by *fratres arvales* (priests and leading citizens).

In everyday life, Ceres was part of weddings, and the bride carried a torch in the procession from her home to her husband's house. She was invoked in funeral rites to help transition from life to death, and she assisted in getting rid of revengeful ghosts (*lemurs*). On August 24, October 5, and November 8, the *mundus cerialis* (the opening in the ground to the underworld) was conducted to contact the ***di manes*** (the ancestral spirits) and offerings were made to Ceres. In November, this was followed by the Plebeian Games in her name.

Saturn

Saturn was understood as the Greek Cronus and so there was a mixture of ancient Italian concepts as well as Hellenistic influences. We know very little about his cult throughout Italy, although it most likely was associated with the Etruscan god Satres, a deity aligned with lightning and death. His main temple in Rome was located in the forum and also served as the treasury with his patronage of underground wealth. His statue was veiled and filled with oil (the origin of which remains unknown, although oil would keep a wooden statue moist). His feet and legs were bound. (This may reflect the tradition that after Zeus overthrew Cronus, he set up a stone at Delphi which was constantly kept covered in oil and bound with wool.)

The major religious festival for Saturn was the Saturnalia, held in mid-December at the winter solstice, a time when the agricultural world appears to die. In Rome, the statue of Saturn was unbound at this time and carried outside to preside over a banquet. The Saturnalia was a time when social conventions were relaxed and everyone participated in gift-exchanges, feasting, family visits, and revelry. The gifts included candles, with ceremonies of candlelit vigils as a symbol of the renewal of light in the dark of winter and the renewal of crops and fertility. The family celebrations included a game where a family member was selected in a type of "king for the day," creating rules for silly games. On the last day of the festival, family members served their slaves a festive meal. Many of these traditions were later incorporated in the Christian celebration of Christmas which was officially sanctioned by the emperor Constantine in 324 CE.

As a powerful deity associated with death, an ancient ritual dedicated to Saturn took place on the Ides of May at the Pons Sublicius (an ancient bridge over the Tiber River). A procession of priests carried straw effigies of men to the bridge and threw them into the river. This ritual may reflect an ancient tradition that Saturn originally demanded human sacrifice, or it may have been an Etruscan belief in the symbolic destruction of enemies. A similar idea may also lie behind the practice of offering gladiatorial *munera sine missione* ("gifts without mercy") to the god. This was especially true when gladiatorial combats were held during the Saturnalia. In a *munera*, Gladiators fought to the last man (see the section on "Funeral Games" in Chapter X).

The Lares

In addition to worship of the Lares in the home, the Compitalia was celebrated once a year for the Lares Compitales or the deities of the crossroads. Offerings included honey-cakes presented in the houses bordering the crossroads. The original establishment of the festival was said to have required *capua* ("heads"), sacrificed to the mother of the Lares, whose small statue appeared in every home. Woolen balls and heads of garlic were substituted instead. The shrines for the Lares were organized by neighborhood *collegia* and the festival always had an air of a neighborhood carnival. At times, *ludi* were added, depending upon economic conditions. In the late Republic, some of the festivities were banned by the Senate, but Augustus restored them with a focus on his own household Lares as the state Lares for the Empire, with special priests known as **augustales**.

Ops

Ops, an ancient Italian deity representing plenty, was understood to be the consort of Saturn, although she was also associated with Consus, another fertility god. The festival of Opiconsivia was held in August at the time of the harvest season and the Opalia was held in December, when it was combined with Consus's role in the storage of grain (the Consualia). Ops was worshipped while sitting, with hands on the ground because she ruled as a chthonic power. The festivals were supervised by the Vestals and the *flamen quirinus* (the priest of Romulus in his deified form) and thus associated with the early history of Rome. A chariot race was included.

Bellona

In her role as a goddess of war, Bellona motivated the courage and valor necessary for success in battle. Perhaps as a demonstration of these traits, on March 24, her special priests, the **bellonarii**, celebrated the *dies sanguinis* ("day of blood"), sometimes referred to as "Bellona's Day." Adherents danced and slashed themselves in a frenzy and offered the blood as a sacrifice.

Fortuna

At Fortuna's ancient temple in Praeneste, rituals of divination occurred in which a young boy was selected to choose one of several futures that were written on oak rods. The earliest temple in Rome to Fortuna was built in fulfillment of a promise of victory against the Etruscans and was located on the right bank of the Tiber River in the area known as Trastevere. In June, Romans took boats down the river to other temples and then rowed back. Both the people and the boats were covered with garlands and the ceremonies included much festive drinking. The temple of Fortuna Muliebris was the site of worship for married women.

Liber/Libera

Liber and his female consort, Libera, were associated with fertility, winemaking, and freedom. The wine used in sacrifices, the *sacrima*, was taken from the first pressing of the grapes for religious rituals. At the temple in Lavinium, a month-long festival was held, beginning with a procession carrying a phallus to all of the crossroads shrines, which was then crowned by a chosen matron in the forum. The Liberalia was held in March with a portable shrine that was carried through various neighborhoods, and the offerings included honey-cakes, which were then sold. Young men, during their manhood ceremony, donned the **toga virilis** or *toga libera* as a symbol of virility. Liber was also associated with rituals in honor of Bacchus.

Bacchus

The worship of Bacchus in ancient Italy was largely influenced by the myths and rituals in the worship of Dionysus, which included both public and private cults. (For the mystical nature of the worship of Bacchus, see Chapter IX.) These cults included the same Greek concepts of ecstasy and liberation, as well as the celebration of wine and fertility. After the Senate restricted the Bacchanalia in 186 BCE, worshippers were permitted to meet in small numbers with permission, or, as is most likely the case, they met in secret. The wine-drinking element of Bacchus was understood to be present at meals, especially the state banquets that became popular in the late Republic and the early Empire.

Janus

Janus was invoked for the beginning and ending of all things and was responsible for transitional areas such as gates and doorways. He was the first to be petitioned in prayers and at the beginning of each day and new month. Janus was important at the beginning of sowing and harvesting and marriages. The *rex sacrorum* was his special priest and associated with Portunus, who was a gateway and harbor god. Both were invoked at the beginning of a journey.

Janus's most important time was the beginning of the New Year. On January 1, Romans exchanged good wishes with each other and gave gifts of dates, figs, honey, and coins called *strenae*. Special cakes were burnt on the altar. A few days later, a ram was sacrificed to Janus at a rite called the *agonium*. Janus was also invoked at the beginning and end of the war season (March and October) when the *salii* (priests of Mars) officiated. In October, Romans gathered at the Sororium Tigellum, a gateway that guarded the border between Rome and Latium. By tradition, this ritual purified soldiers from the pollution of war. The boundary between Rome and Etruria was located on the hill bearing his name, the Janiculum. Immediately below this hill was the docking area for the end of the journey of boats coming up from Ostia.

Pluto

Pluto was greatly respected as a god of wealth and prosperity, but at the same time, his role as Lord of the Underworld generated fear so that there were not typical festivals held in his honor. However, Pluto was associated with older Etruscan and Italian deities, notably Orcus and Dis Pater, who both had roles in the Roman afterlife. All three were invoked in funeral rituals and during the Feralia and Lemuralia when spirits of the dead roamed through the cities and towns. (See Chapter X for details of these "days of the dead.")

Pluto was the center of the Secular Games (along with Proserpina and Dis Pater), which were held every hundred years, following an oracle from the Sibylline Books, "so that Rome should be safe as long as this festival was performed." (These games were later modified by Augustus.) A subterranean altar to Pluto on the Campus Martius was dug up at this time and received black bulls. The festival lasted for three days and herbs were burned to purify the community.

Castor and Pollux

The worship of Castor and Pollux was absorbed from Greek and Etruscan traditions in Italy. Because of their association with horses, they were patrons to the *equites* and members of the cavalry. On July 15, 1800 equestrians who were honored with the "Public Horse" (a horse and equipment provided by the state) paraded through the streets of Rome with all of their honors and military decorations.

Bona Dea

Bona Dea ("Good Goddess") was an ancient fertility goddess of Italy whose origins may have sprung from Phrygia or other sites in the east. She was worshipped by both men and women, but women also conducted Mystery rites twice a year. The winter festival put the goddess to sleep, while the spring festival reawakened her. Her temple housed snakes which were fed bowls of milk.

The winter festival was organized by the Vestal Virgins and included married matrons. The ceremonies were held in the houses of the chief magistrates and were considered an honor for the hostess. All male elements of the house were evacuated for the rituals, including slaves, and even male cats and dogs. If there were statues or busts of males in the house, they were veiled for the duration. Offerings included honey, milk, and wine with prayers, songs, and hymns. Further details of the rituals remain unknown.

One of the most famous stories concerning the rites of Bona Dea occurred during the last days of the Republic. A patrician, Clodius Pulcher, violated the rites by disguising himself as a woman and gaining access when the festival was held at the house of Julius Caesar (at the residence of the *pontifex maximus*). He was later murdered on the Appian Way, near an ancient shrine to Bona Dea.

The women of Rome were convinced that this was how Bona Dea obtained her revenge for his sacrilege.

Flora

As the ancient goddess of flowers, vegetation, and fertility, Flora had a temple near the Circus Maximus and another, Flora Rustica ("rural Flora"), on the Quirinal Hill. Flora had a special priest, the *flamen florialis*, and sacrifices were also offered in the sacred grove of the Arval Brothers, which included hares and goats. Flora was honored with the festival of Floralia in April. The festival included the *ludi Florae* consisting of chariot races and theatrical productions. Noteworthy at this festival was the participation of prostitutes, who danced naked and reveled in the streets. People were pelted with various types of beans, symbols of fertility.

Romulus

Romulus, the founder of Rome, was deified as Quirinus and was periodically invoked as the spirit behind the Roman people. In Rome, he had a special priest, the *flamen quirinalis*, who also supervised the offerings to Robigus (a god who protected plants against mildew) and Consus (the god who protected stored grain). In December, the Larentalia was held. According to one tradition, Larentia was the wet nurse for Romulus and Remus.

The Quirinalia commemorated either the apotheosis of Romulus or his murder. This was commemorated in conjunction with the Fornacalia, a festival for the *virites*, who were the female equivalent of the citizenship virtues of Romans. Another festival, the Curiae Veteres, was held twice a year to celebrate the *curiae* of tribes of ancient Rome. Members gathered in a banquet hall on the Palatine Hill. Recently, archaeological excavations have uncovered this site of assembly and worship.

The Lupercalia

The Lupercalia was a festival on the Ides of February that combined various elements and deities, including Juno in her capacity to oversee women and childbirth, Februa, a god of purification, and Pan, Priapus, and Faunus as fertility gods, and was also associated with the myth of the founding of Rome by the twins Romulus and Remus. The name of the festival was derived from Lupercus, who was associated with Pan and Faunus and was also one of the Roman gods of shepherds. The festival began at the Lupercal, the alleged cave where Romulus and Remus were nurtured by the she-wolf, located on the Palatine Hill.

At the Lupercal, goats and a dog were sacrificed and the skins made into whips. The participants (the *luperci*, or "brothers of the wolf") smeared blood over their bodies that were partially covered in goatskins or naked. The *luperci* were divided into *collegia*, the *Quinctiales* and the *Fabiani* (from two ancient *gens*, or clans). They then ran through the city while women stepped out from the crowds to be struck with the skins. It was believed that the skins would grant fertility and an easy birth. Purification and rebirth were important elements of these rituals.

Parentalia

The Ides of February was reserved for the Parentalia (*dies parentales*, "ancestral days") which commemorated the ancestors and deceased family members. Added to this was the Feralia in February and the Lemuria in May, two other festivals involving the dead. For details on all three see Chapter X.

Parilia

Pales was an ancient deity of shepherds whose festival was rural but also celebrated in towns and cities. In April, purification rites were performed at the Parilia for both the person and the flock. The rituals to Pales were eventually absorbed into the birthday of Romulus and the performance of the October Horse. Sheep pens were decorated with branches and were swept out at dawn, with the remnants added to olive branches, laurel, and sulfur, all of which were burned. The shepherd (or head of the family) then jumped over this bonfire, followed by his sheep. Offerings to Pales consisted of cakes and milk. Afterward, the shepherd washed his face, faced east and prayed for protection for both himself and his flock. After drinking milk and boiled wine, he jumped through the fire three more times. In the Imperial period, *ludi* were added to the festival in Rome.

Hercules

The traditions of Hercules/Heracles were spread by the Phoenicians and Greeks throughout the Mediterranean basin from at least the eighth century BCE. The "Labors of Hercules" became popular art on funeral urns for the Etruscans and the Greek colonists of southern Italy. In Rome, Hercules was absorbed into the founding myth of the city when he killed the monster Caucus. At his *ara maxima* ("greatest altar") located in the Forum Boarium ("cattle market") he was Hercules Invictus ("the unconquered"). There were also temples to Hercules in the Campus Martius and at the Circus Flaminius.

Sacrifices at the *ara maxima* were to be eaten by men only and finished before the end of the day. In periods of crisis (plague, famines), Hercules was always included in a **lectisternium**, or a propitiatory meal offered to the gods. Gods and goddesses were placed on dining couches for the ceremony. Several *gens* in

Rome claimed descent from Hercules (the Fabii, Potitia, Pinaria) and Hercules was thus included in their family rituals. The priests of Hercules had a Sabine name, *cupenci*. Once a year the urban praetor offered a young cow. In Rome Hercules was also associated with the Muses.

The Roman Triumph

Perhaps the most famous of all Roman rituals was the parade known as a triumph for a successful general (Figure VI.4). While heavily inlaid with military symbolism, nevertheless the triumph was first and foremost a religious event. By tradition the triumph was instituted by Romulus as the first king, although historians also find elements of Greek military rituals and the processional and festive elements of the Dionysus rites. We know some details of ancient triumphs because of the descriptions from Roman historians and the *Fasti triumphales*, or the official record of triumphs etched in stone by the Roman Senate.

There were criteria for the Senate to obtain permission for a triumph. The general had to have defeated a foreign enemy and his actions had to have

Figure VI.4   Sculpture of a Roman triumph. *Source*: DEA/G. DAGLI ORTI/De Agostini/ Getty Images.

increased the borders and the honor of Rome. A set number of the enemy had to have been killed and the general's soldiers had to have declared him *imperator* on the field. The general applied to the Senate and the Plebeian Assembly to hold a triumph, and if granted, he and his army camped on the Campus Martius until the date of the triumph. Crossing the *pomerium* into the city meant that the general gave up his *imperium*. Usually only one legion participated in the parade. For small military victories, a general could be granted an *ovation* where he rode a horse through the city and the celebrations were limited.

The general spent the night in a vigil before taking the auguries. On the day of the triumph he dressed in a purple *toga picta* ("painted toga"), which reflected his kingly status for the day. He wore a wreath of laurel and his face was painted in red *minium*, the color of the face of the statue of Jupiter in his temple on the Capitoline Hill. The general rode in a chariot. The triumphal parade began on the Campus Martius, entered the city through an ancient arched gateway and paraded through the Circus Maximus, exiting on the other side. Here began the final stretch down the Via Sacra in the Roman forum, ending at the foot of the Capitoline Hill. Allegedly (according to later historians), a slave rode with the general in his chariot, periodically reciting the line, "Remember, you are mortal."

The parade not only included the soldiers, but displays of recreated battle scenes and wagons of loot, a percentage of which was dedicated to Jupiter and to the treasury. The prisoners of war and their families of the higher classes (such as kings or chieftains) marched in the triumph as well. At the foot of the Capitoline Hill, the prisoners who were preselected for execution were led away to the Tullianum prison, an underground chamber where a state executioner strangled the prisoners. The general then climbed up to Jupiter's temple and made the requisite sacrifice of a white bull or ox.

The event of a triumph was celebrated by all the populace. Work ceased for the day, all the temples were open, and the parade was accompanied by musicians, dancers, and singers, strewing flowers and rose pedals. To all this noise was added the soldiers singing ribald songs about their general and yelling, "Io triomphe!" Either from private funds or from the loot, the general hosted a feast for the magistrates as well as the public on picnic tables throughout the city. Some triumphs were followed by *ludi* or games. This ritual was equivalent to one of our Fourth of July or other national celebrations, incorporating both the individual and the state. Beginning with Augustus in the Imperial period, triumphs were limited to rare occasions and usually only to members of the Imperial family.

Summary

- This chapter has outlined some specific details of community religious festivals and the actual worship of gods and goddesses in Greece and Rome. Many of the festivals aligned with mythic elements but local traditions were also incorporated.

- Community religious festivals bound people to individual deities and created a sense of solidarity for the respective communities. The festivals also provided entertainment and, for the poor, a source of extra food and drink.

Suggestions for Further Reading

Beard, M., J. North and S. Price. 1998. *Religions of Rome: Volume 1: A History.* Cambridge University Press. This is a compendium that provides the historical context for worship in Rome. The second volume in the set is a source book with excerpts from Roman literature.

Mikalson, J. 2010. *Ancient Greek Religion*, 2nd ed. Wiley-Blackwell. There are several chapters that contain step by step details of Greek ritual for specific cults throughout Greece and the Greek world.

Nagle, B. trans. 1995. *Ovid's Fasti: Roman Holidays.* Indiana University Press. Ovid (43 BCE–17/18 CE) provided a detailed description of Roman festivals for each month from January to July (the rest is lost). In many of his descriptions he also attempted to provide the historical background of specific rituals.

Price, S. 1999. *Religions of the Ancient Greeks.* Cambridge University Press. Price includes both mythical and historical roots for the background of Greek rituals.

Turcan, R. 2001. *The Gods of Ancient Rome: Religion in Everyday Life from the Archaic Period to Imperial Times*, trans. A. Nevill. Routledge. This volume surveys Roman rituals from the home to public festivals.

RELIGION AND SOCIETY

Greek and Roman Religions, First Edition. Rebecca I. Denova.
© 2019 John Wiley & Sons, Inc. Published 2019 by John Wiley & Sons, Inc.

Learning Objectives

After reading this chapter, you will be able to:

- Identify elements of ancient Greek and Roman society.
- Distinguish the different religious roles of family members.
- Appreciate the interaction of private and public religious roles in relation to communal well-being.

 The basic social unit in ancient Mediterranean culture was the family, which also included the parents, in-laws, slaves (and ex-slaves, freedmen), **clients**, and dead ancestors. Family was the template for understanding the way life was lived in a social context, beginning with the gods. Most pantheons, including the Olympians, had a father and a mother, numerous children, in-laws, and complicated lineages. As populations migrated from the farm to the city, the city-state included clan and tribal associations which were celebrated. When Rome evolved from a Republic to an Empire, Augustus portrayed the state as a large extended family and, by extension, himself as the father figure for millions of constituents.

The way in which the family was promoted and validated was through extrafamilial elements of society that were common to all regions of the Mediterranean basin. One's social class defined the parameters of status and rank, while **honor and shame** established the codes of ideal behavior for both individuals and the community. The **patron/client** system provided the network for relationships necessary for the common good, including relationships between humans and the gods. These extrafamilial elements became encoded in the self-perception of all classes and levels of society, both free and slave, in social morals, and in one's relationship with the divine (cult).

First we will look at the overall social structure of ancient Greece and Rome and the shared cultural elements that kept it in place. Then we will consider the individual roles of family members and how those roles supported the larger social structure and the religious well-being of the community.

Social Class

When we think of class in the modern world, we automatically think of economics: upper, middle, and lower classes. In the ancient world, economics were an important element of the social classes, but not necessarily the most important part; blood trumped wealth. The ancestors of one's family played a prominent role and validated one's class, status, and rank. A family could be reduced to poverty and yet rank high on the social scale because of the existence of these dead ancestors. In Rome, you could achieve the highest political office, the consulship, simply based upon the fact that you had an ancestor who was consul, even if it was several hundred years ago. Our image of the upper and middle classes will usually include education, just as it did in the ancient world (although levels of education differed). In ancient society, slaves also had opportunities for education.

In Greece the classes consisted of free males, foreigners (*metics*), women, freedmen, and slaves, in a descending order in relation to rights and duties. Within the class of free males there were further divisions. At the top of the social order was the aristocracy ("rule of the excellent"), where governing power resided in a small, privileged class who claimed descent from ancient, founding families. It was the bloodline that endowed nobility. In Classical Athens, rule by one powerful man (a tyrant) was replaced by democracy, or "rule of the people." However, members of first families continued to hold the highest offices and influence, based upon their wealth in land and property in and near the city-state. In democratic Athens free men who were citizens owned property, could hold public office, and voted. They were expected to have enough wealth to be able to contribute their own horses and military equipment in war and to contribute to public benefices such as religious festivals. *Metics* were a class in ancient Athens who did not share citizen rights but were taxed and expected to serve in the armies in an emergency.

Another class of males was equivalent to our middle or business class, where they engaged in manufacturing, trade, and banking. They could not claim the same kind of ancestry as the aristocracy, but they could and did accumulate wealth. The poorer free males often lived and farmed small plots of land around the city or worked as craftsmen. Most lived in villages near the city-state for protection, but often migrated to the city when their farms failed. Slavery was an essential feature of ancient society and slaves were employed in every occupational capacity. Some slaves could move to the level of ex-slave or freedman and eventually obtain some rights at that level (see below for more details on slavery). Women in ancient Greece could not vote, own land, or inherit wealth or property; the woman's role in society was to procreate and raise children. They also managed households, and the poorer women worked outside the home.

In Rome social class was also hierarchical, but included several determining factors that could fluctuate depending upon circumstances: ancestry, census rank (based upon wealth and political office), attainment of honors, and citizenship. In the beginning only the patrician class (made up of the founding families) held civic offices and priesthoods. The majority of free Romans, the plebeians, were of the non-noble class. Eventually the plebeians achieved many of the same rights as the patricians, including the right of veto against the Senate in the Plebeian Assembly and membership in the priesthoods. Once intermarriage between the two was permitted, the distinctions began to blur. Through marriage, plebeians could claim ancient ancestry.

The senatorial classes of Rome were expected to perform public service to the state through the process known as the **cursus honorum**, or the "course of honor": military tribune, quaestor (finance), aedile (maintenance of markets, temples), praetor (judge), consul (the highest civic authority), and censor (maintenance of the census rolls, public contracts). These were elected offices that ran for one year (with the exception of censor, a five-year term), and were largely held by wealthy men as elections were expensive (and everyone utilized bribery). Rarely, a *novus homo*, or new man, such as Cicero, could climb the ladder without having notable ancestors, but the upper classes often considered this an aberration of the *mos maiorum*, or the way things had always been done in the past.

The census categorized citizens according to class, wealth, property, and clout. In order to enter the Senate, you had to prove that you had at least 1 000 000 sesterces, preferably invested in land, as agriculture was considered the noblest way to make money. In fact, senators were forbidden to directly participate in business or commerce, although this was easily overcome through silent partners. The *equites* (equestrians or knights) were those who engaged in commerce and banking. Historically, those of the *equites* class had to demonstrate enough assets to properly outfit themselves for war, including a horse and armor. The classes were categorized by economic levels for voting in the **centuriate** – in addition, the Tribal Assembly was based on ancestral tribes, and the **Plebeian Assembly** consisted of Roman citizens below the aristocracy.

Foreigners who resided in Rome and Italy proper were known as *peregrini*. These foreigners could only conduct business with a sponsor from the upper citizen classes and they had a special magistrate, the *praetor peregrinus*, who was responsible for hearing lawsuits and settling their legal problems. During the early days of the Republic only the nobility and the *equites* fought in Rome's armies. Eventually the recruiting needs of an expanding Republic resulted in opening up the legions to the plebeians and the "head-count," or Rome's poor (free males). Citizen allies of the Italian colonies and foreign auxiliaries also joined the armies.

Women in Rome were citizens, but could not vote or hold public offices. Roman women could inherit property and even initiate a divorce. However, legally, women had to have male relatives or guardians to oversee their affairs. The class differences among women ran along predictable lines. Upper-class women were expected to become wives and mothers but also were responsible for household budgets, and even large villas, when their husbands were away at war or governing a province. Then, as now, being poorer, lower-class women had to work in their husbands' and their own businesses and crafts.

Despite such structural categories there was interaction among the classes and social movement was condoned, although one should always move up in status and class. One's class could be improved through government service, military prowess, an advantageous marriage, and manumission or being freed from slavery.

Honor/Shame

Cultural anthropologists use the category of honor/shame to describe cultures that promote attitudes and behaviors that accrue public honor against its opposite, public shame. In Rome, the concept helped to maintain social order and social values through group morals. The individual was then judged by those standards. Shame is the designation of being "honor-less" or accruing dishonor.

Honor was not just a private goal of an individual but a public acknowledgment of one's worth or value to the community. A person with honor was one who adhered to social codes and conventions and this trait was crucially important for one's public persona, or one's dignity and status in the community. Educated, upper-class Greeks learned through various schools of philosophy that men should always be in control, never letting the passions rule (especially anger), and claimed that both private and public behavior was the foundation of societal harmony, peace, and goodwill.

A man's public honor was built upon how well he performed his family and public duties, which included military and government service and active participation in the native cults. Any deviation from traditional and accepted practices or behavior brought shame and diminished one's dignity, while simultaneously diminishing one's standing before the gods. A man's reputation was crucially important because ultimately this was his legacy or the way in which he would be remembered. Conformity was the path to becoming an honored ancestor.

The level of one's honor was not solely up to the individual. Men were responsible for their entire families and extended families. The behavior of any one of these individuals could bring shame, or destroy the honor of the man, just as the shameful behavior of a man could reflect on the honor of his entire family. Misbehavior in the family was an indication that the man had lost control. Then, as now, people remembered gossip and scandal.

Ancient Romans referred to **dignitas** and **auctoritas** as concepts to describe individual characteristics in Roman society. *Dignitas* included a man's reputation, moral behavior, and ethical worth to the community. It also indicated the sum total of a man's achievements in life, for which he was then entitled to respect. *Auctoritas* measured a man's prestige (his clout), and in relation to politics, referred to his ability to gain supporters and to lead men in battle. But *auctoritas* was also understood as a particular gift from the goddess Fortuna.

To overcome severe shame (cowardice in battle, extreme corruption, treason), ancient Greeks and Romans had recourse to the noble death. Voluntary death or suicide was never condemned in antiquity; it was understood that a proper man would choose death over living with shame. However, suicide should never be attempted because of the normal vicissitudes of life (the death of your wife, or to avoid taxes). The noble death should be undertaken for a noble reason and the manner of your death (with dignity) contributed ultimately to your honor and reversed the shame.

In Rome, a good suicide was also measured against circumstances. The legendary Lucretia, who was faced with unwanted, forceful male attention, set the standard for women. When confronted with "a fate worse than death," all women should commit suicide. In the story of the *Aeneid*, Queen Dido of Carthage killed herself when her lover Aeneas left her. This was considered a good act as Aeneas was fated to found Rome and not dally in Carthage.

Some crimes in Rome were punished by exile, which meant that you could not receive hospitality from anyone within 500 miles of the city of Rome. In some cases, the state would confiscate your property as well, but if you committed suicide, your family would be spared and could inherit.

The Patron/Client Relationship

In Mediterranean society the way in which things got done was through the patron/client system. In contemporary slang the concept would be, "Scratch my back and I will scratch yours." As early as the Bronze Age a system of gift-exchanges evolved on several different levels in order to establish social, economic, and political relationships that were beneficial to the entire community. Such relationships then entailed obligations. *Philotimia* ("the love of honor") entailed a relationship between two parties of different status, higher and lower. It was understood that the lower-class man would receive more profit from the relationship, but the higher-status person received the honor because of his largesse.

Gift-exchanges were vitally important to the economics of a region and provided the means by which the classes could help each other. The wealthy relied upon the lower classes for food production and labor, while the lower classes relied upon the wealthy often for sheer survival. In Greece the city-state consisted of tribes (*phylae*), organized into *phratries* (brotherhoods) and *gene* (people claiming a common ancestor). It was through such associations that the business of the city-state and region got done, and both sides were honor bound to meet their obligations. Gift-exchanges took place between friends and business associates, and were a major element in hospitality to guests. If the guest was from a foreign country, reciprocity would have to wait until you traveled, but when you arrived he was obligated to play the host. Civic gift-exchanges also took place between city-states and foreign cities and colonies, and the largesse was inscribed on public buildings.

The concept of "doing good deeds" (*euergetism*) influenced religious gift-giving and donations to the building of religious and civic monuments. These voluntary gifts functioned as a legitimization of the benefactors of both genders to the city and served as a commemoration of their status long after they were dead (with their name carved on the buildings). City councils commissioned temples and statues, and especially statues to local heroes.

In ancient Rome a *patronus* and *cliens* had clearly defined legal roles. The *patronus* (from which we derive our term patronage) was ideally an upper-class noble who was the sponsor, protector, and benefactor of a lower-class individual. Quite often, class in this sense had nothing to do with wealth; some clients were richer than their patrons. But the social rank enabled the patron to have the honor and prestige of someone who had the clout and influence to grant favors. For Romans, such noble patronage was an important factor in their concept of good citizenship because it benefited society as a whole; good citizenship was a religious obligation.

A patron was obligated to help his client in business deals with either money or introductions to business contacts, defend him in the law courts and help him campaign for political office. This relationship extended to the next generation; if a client's son needed promotion in the military or a mediator in a marriage contract, the patron was expected to help. For his part, the client was expected to oblige the patron in anything required. Clients arrived at the patron's house at dawn to either hand in petitions or just be available for the needs of the patron that day. Sometimes the clients just followed the patron around the forum and the size of a patron's entourage indicated his level of *auctoritas*.

The concept of patron/client was reflected in the relationships between humans and the divine. All communities had a local god or goddess, understood as their **patron deity**, and who was committed to protecting and fostering community prosperity and pride. It was equivalent to having a friend at court, one who could intervene and mediate with the higher deities on behalf of individuals and the community when necessary. The local people, as clients, were duty-bound to respect and care for the patron deity, appeasing him or her with sacrifices and pious devotion.

Slavery

Slavery in ancient Greece and Rome was not the same institution experienced in the antebellum South in the United States. Slavery was common throughout the ancient world, but it was not confined to one ethnic group or class; it consisted of all cultures and economic classes. Some educated Greeks sold themselves into slavery to work as pedagogues or tutors, and could thereby advance themselves. The *metics* of ancient Athens included many ex-slaves, but they did not have the same rights as citizens. The Spartan *helots* were in an intermediate category, more equivalent to serfs of the Middle Ages, and some of them could be granted rights if they volunteered for Sparta's armies.

There were several categories of slaves, the earliest of which were most likely war captives, both men and women, who were taken as the spoils of war. In the early Greek period, prisoners of war were ransomed by their city-state or relatives, although we cannot confirm how often this was done. After conquering a territory, Rome made no distinction between defeated soldiers and civilians, selling all into slavery and sometimes dividing the profits as part of the legionaries' pay. The ingrained belief in fate, controlled by the goddesses Tyche (overseeing the fate of cities) and Fortuna (overseeing one's personal luck), justified enslavement of captive peoples. If the gods did not look with favor upon a city or person, then enslavement should be accepted as one's destiny. Some victors believed that defeated soldiers should resolve their status honorably by committing suicide rather than suffer the humiliation of slavery, and thus felt little sympathy for these survivors.

Slaves worked the farms (especially the large *latifundia* or Roman plantations), served as craftsmen, and worked in temples. Slaves accompanied their owners during military service, worked for the town or city, and were occupied in all domestic chores. In Greece, only citizens could participate in politics and gymnastics so these opportunities were not open to slaves By the Hellenistic period the island of Delos served as the largest slave market in the Mediterranean and was largely administered by pirates. Pirates attacked both commercial and private shipping, as well as coastal villages. Those captives of high status were ransomed, but the rest were sold at the slave markets.

The ownership of slaves was understood in relation to status. Even a poor man had one slave and this elevated him above the very poor. This one slave was often a woman, who served in the kitchen as well as the bedroom. Sexual relations with slaves was common and was not condemned. Sex with a slave was not adultery (defined as the violation of another man's property), but an owner's entitlement. Children born of such unions belonged to the owner, who could sell them, and slaves were included in the estate left to a man's heirs. The price of slaves depended on their skills, their health, and their country of origin.

Both Greece and Rome utilized slaves in the mines, quarries, and as rowers for commercial fleets. (Marines, not slaves, manned the naval fleets.) The mines, quarries and galleys were where rebellious and disobedient slaves were sent for severe punishment. The life expectation in these occupations was very low and the living conditions were deplorable. However, prime specimens of war captives were enrolled in gladiator schools, where despite their nature, life expectancy was much higher.

The worst punishment for slaves was crucifixion, which was also the punishment for rebels, on the premise that most slaves were inherently rebellious. Although rarely attested, at least in the Roman law codes if a citizen was murdered, the entire household of slaves were the first suspects and could be crucified if the real murderer was not found. Crucifixion was most prominent in the provinces (such as Judea), but the most famous case was when General Crassus crucified 6000 slaves involved in the Slave Rebellion of Spartacus (73 BCE). After the last battle, he crucified the surviving slaves on either side of the Appian Way between Naples and Rome as a lesson against future rebellion.

Under Roman law the testimony of slaves was not admissible in court unless they first underwent torture; loyalty to their master or their own self-interest would lead to perjury. On the other hand, testimony as the result of torture was viewed skeptically. A slave (or actually anyone) would say anything to make the torture stop.

The status of slaves was recognized by both free citizens and by slaves themselves. The educated slave tutors were at the top of the slave pyramid and were often treated as intimate family members. Then, as now, trained cooks were highly valued and the luckier slaves were occupied as nannies (for the younger children), hairdressers, bath attendants, masseurs, banquet servers, musicians, doorkeepers, house cleaners, and kitchen aides.

Manumission, the freeing of slaves, could occur either if the master paid over the price of the slave, or by the slave if he had saved enough money to buy his freedom. There is very little surviving literature about the manumission of slaves in Greece. In Rome, however, domestic and commercial slaves were paid a minimum wage or sometimes given the management of a piece of property (*peculium*) that could be accumulated against their eventual manumission. Many slave owners, particularly businessmen, freed slaves and then set them up in business, where the freedman still retained a client's obligation to his former master. In Greece, freedom did not include the right of citizenship, but in Rome, citizenship was conferred with manumission. Roman freedmen could not hold public office or priesthoods, but they could vote, and their children were free citizens. The possibility of manumission (and change of social status) is one of the great differences between slavery in the ancient world and the antebellum South.

Estimates for slavery in the ancient world run the gamut from 25 to 40% of the population. It is amazing, therefore, that we know so little concerning slaves' religious beliefs. Until recently, modern studies of antiquity have neglected this aspect of the ancient world, which is understandable in light of the scant evidence. Similar to the problems inherent in research on women in the ancient world, all of our literature is written by free male elites. But more recent research has focused on epigraphic remains such as funerary inscriptions, records of slave manumissions, votive offerings, oracle consultations, and prayers and hymns commissioned by slaves and freedmen.

Slaves were expected to adopt the religious beliefs of their master and his household. We see them always in the background in art and sculpture, present at the family cults, and in charge of the animal sacrifices, holding utensils, and generally involved in other cult activities. In theory, slaves could privately retain their own religious beliefs, but we just do not have enough information to determine what those were. We remain unaware of a specific god of slaves in general or even a common cult that slaves shared. It makes sense that many slaves may have privately remained loyal to their own gods in their land of origin, while simultaneously adopting the gods of the family and the state cults. Slaves could join *collegia* and Mystery cults and could claim asylum at many altars. We have evidence of intermarriage between citizens and ex-slaves; most likely the ex-slave adopted the religion of the citizen.

The Family in Ancient Greece

In ancient Greece, the household (*oikos*) was divided between the *andronitis*, where all male activity took place, and the *gynaikonitis*, or "women's gallery," where cooking, weaving, and the rearing of children were confined. This separation of the proper stations of society was ideally upheld in Greek drama and literature. For the majority of Greeks their first religious experiences began in the household.

The Father

The average Greek house was of one or two stories built around an open court-yard. However, very few of these structures have survived. We can only assume that shrines were located in various places around the house, including the hearth. The father had sole responsibility for religious matters in the household. Every morning he performed his duty to the god responsible for the property and prosperity at a shrine in the household or to the god responsible for protecting the enclosure. The most common shrines were of Zeus, not only in his capacity as Father, but as a manifestation of his role as protector (Zeus Kte-sios, Zeus Herkeios). The door of the house was most often under the auspices of Apollo or Heracles as averters of evil.

Hestia was the ancient hearth goddess and her importance was recognized when children, brides, and slaves were formally accepted as family members at the hearth. The entire family was present while the father led the ceremonies. The assumption is always made that because of the combination of "home and hearth," Hestia and the hearth fire would have been significant only to women. But it was the father's responsibility if the hearth fire was extinguished.

Depending upon his wealth and status in a village or town, the father would have religious responsibilities to the community and he was expected to con-tribute to the cost of sacrifices and festivals. This included his membership in his *phratry* (brotherhood) and if he was an aristocrat, the rituals involved with his *genos* or ancestral group. He also represented his community in the larger religious festivals in the cities. At times, he traveled with delegations to other cities for competitions and athletic events.

The father was solely responsible for the proper funeral rites of his ancestors. Without this detail, the dead ceased to exist. A grave full of weeds and litter was a public testimonial that the family responsibilities had not been filled. The other duty to the ancestors was to sire a son (see the box "Infanticide in Ancient Greece and Rome"). If there was no male heir to carry on the duties for the father's grave he would be forgotten, a Greek's direst fear. To ensure the lineage, the father arranged marriages for his children.

Mothers

The wife was handed from the domain of her father to her husband in her middle teens. Her dowry was held in trust by the husband. A dowry was compensation to the man's family for having another person to house, feed, and clothe. Wives did not have any household gods of their own that we know of, although they attended their husband's rituals. Wives kept charge of the stores, cleaned, worked in textiles and wove the clothes of the family, cooked, and raised the children. In wealthier families, slaves did all the work but the wife supervised both the slaves and the household budget.

Women may have participated in the local cults (but again, sacrifices would have been done by the men), although the more prominent role for women in religion was in the cults of Artemis, Asclepios, Athena, and Demeter. All of these deities were important for the fundamental role of women, that of procreation and fecundity. These cults were significant for the major city-states. Women from even small villages and towns would travel to take part in the religious festivals.

Despite their limited social and leadership roles, women in ancient Greece nevertheless were major priestesses in over forty state cults. Women had significant roles in both the Lesser and Greater Panathenaia festivals in Athens. We have already mentioned the all-female Thesmophoria, and both women and men participated in the rites of Demeter at Eleusis.

Infanticide in Ancient Greece and Rome

One of the most notorious aspects of ancient Greco-Roman family life involves the practice of infanticide, or the killing of unwanted children. There are references to this in the literature, but the archaeological remains are scarce. Some neighboring cultures in the Mediterranean did practice child sacrifice, which is a different category than infanticide. Child sacrifice was a propitiation ritual most often called for in a community crisis. Greeks and Romans considered the practice barbaric. Infanticide did not include rituals that we know of, but involved the exposure of infants to either the natural elements or natural starvation. Allowing it to be natural eliminated the charge of murder, which would have angered the gods.

The most famous cases of infanticide are assigned to Sparta. Later literature described a council of elders who examined all newborns to discover any deformities. Spartan culture emphasized the strength and discipline of its citizens, and those with disabilities or mentally challenged were not welcome to participate in their military culture. Elsewhere the exposure of unwanted infant girls was part of the legal code, or at least recommended. It was crucially important to have a son to carry on the family lineage, while daughters were expensive because of the required dowry. On the other hand, daughters were good collateral for political alliances through arranged marriages.

The idea that infants were exposed on barren hillsides is found mostly in myth; this was a popular theme where the baby was always rescued and went on to do great deeds. In both Greece and Rome, fathers waited a few days after the birth to see if the infant survived. Then it was formally accepted as part of the family. Unwanted infants (most likely sickly, premature infants, or infants with disabilities, and perhaps sometimes healthy girls) were placed in pots or jars and left outside the door of the house. This was an indication that the infant had been rejected as a member of the family. We know that some of these infants were rescued to become slaves or were adopted children of infertile couples. Slave names often reflected their point of origin, such as "lifted from the garbage dump."

We cannot ascertain the percentage of deaths due to infanticide. However, we have literary evidence that both sons and daughters were welcomed and loved, although conditions of poverty may have dictated other outcomes. The evidence of tomb inscriptions indicates that the death of either a son or a daughter was equally lamented and considered the direst tragedy for the parents.

Sons

Greek sons were formally admitted into the family in a ritual conducted by the father at the hearth (within 10 days). He was then presented to his father's *phratry* or brotherhood. This was an important ceremony where his father laid claim to the legitimacy of the son. As the son grew, he would learn the household rituals for when he had his own family. At 16 he was presented to the *phratry* again, in recognition that he could now be entered as a citizen on the public rolls. In Athens, the *phratry* deities were Zeus Phratrios and Athena Phratria. The son made an offering of hair and an offering of wine to Heracles at this second ceremony. His father swore again that he was legitimate and offered a sacrificial animal. If there was no challenge, the meat was shared with the members.

The son, as an *ephebe* ("young man," between 18 and 20), joined a group of his peers, all of whom were committed to community service for two years. At the same time they received their military training. This commitment began with an oath to the gods to uphold the laws and the ancestral traditions. They attended meetings of the ***ekklesia*** (assembly), where they learned the essentials of civic duties. As young recruits, they were stationed at border outposts as part of their training. Their religious education was learned through collective visits to temples and shrines all over Greece, and they participated in all the religious festivals. This peer group provided the essential contacts that would be important in their later life as community leaders.

In ancient Greece the practice of **pederasty** ("love of boys") was understood as an important element in the moral and cultural education of a young man. An adult man (not a family relation) initiated a relationship with a younger man, serving as mentor for the social skills that he would need when he became an adult citizen. The relationship could be chaste or physical. It was understood by both parties that the relationship ended when the younger man reached adulthood and marriage. Any older man who continued to court younger men outside of this relationship was scorned. Greece also had laws against child prostitution, for both males and females.

Some of the city-states also had initiation to manhood rituals, as was the case in Sparta, in a ritual known as Krypteia. Young boys were sent to the countryside in winter, armed only with daggers, and were expected to survive on their own. This ritual also included the killing of any helots they came across and was understood as the culmination of war skills that they would need later on. Another ritual only in Athens was known as the Oscophoria and involved cross-dressing. Boys processed dressed as girls, which was viewed as their transformation from the weaker to the stronger (male).

Sons learned the importance of athletic skills. They competed in the games at the larger festivals in the cities, as well as in the chorus competitions of the Dionysia festivals. Depending upon his class, a son most likely had a *pedagogus* or a tutor, an educated slave who accompanied him to school, and supplemented his education in the home. Sons were trained to become military commanders and civic leaders. Technically, sons remained under the authority of their father until the age of 30. That was the usual age for a son to participate in an arranged marriage, where the betrothal ceremony dictated his fundamental role, "for the plowing of legitimate children." His bride was taken into his father's house. The son was responsible for the care of his parents as they grew old.

Daughters

A Greek daughter spent most of her first 15 years or so learning the skills of the household from her mother. At birth she was formally accepted into the family, but there was no later equivalent of registering her as a citizen. She was present at household rituals, but she eventually transferred any loyalty to the household gods of her husband. She would also not be a participant in the *phratry* or *genos* cults, which emphasized male lineage.

Greek daughters did have significant religious participation outside the household in the state cults and those that marked the passage from youth to womanhood. Girls were a major feature of the cult of Athena Polias, although the selection was often from the high-status families. Four girls known as *arrephoroi* spent a year weaving the new *peplos* (dress) for the statue of Athena at the Panathenaea. Two other girls were selected for a secret ritual, the Arrephoria, when they spent time living near the temple of Athena. On the day of the festival, they carried baskets on their heads filled with what the priestess secretly placed there. They descended through a secret passageway and emerged with a new item in the basket. Hundreds of other girls were selected for the festivals to prepare offerings of cakes and to carry jars of oil and baskets containing grain and other items. We saw that many Greek girls participated in the Brauronia ritual of Artemis.

The daughter's marriage was arranged by her father and the betrothal ceremony set out the details. There was no priest present at the wedding, although traditional customs were observed. The bride offered her toys and childhood mementos to Artemis, symbolizing the end of her virginity. An offering of money was also made to Aphrodite. Both the bride and groom had a bath (using special, purified water). The bride was unveiled, there was a banquet, and then the couple rode in a cart to the groom's house accompanied by friends. The bride was welcomed by her mother-in-law, and a ritual at the hearth made her one of the family.

The Family in Ancient Rome

As in Greece, the Roman family was the cohesive core of society. Romans extended the concept of family by literally framing state cults and rituals on the model of family life. The city of Rome had its family Lares, Penates, and sacred hearth, and created temples and institutions to maintain these ancestral traditions. Rome had over thirty *curiae* (tribal assemblies) where descendants of a common ancestor (*gens*) would meet over family meals. Over time, some of the domestic cults of the founding families of Rome were incorporated into city-wide, annual festivals.

The Father

The term, *paterfamilias*, "father of the family," in ancient Rome included the concept of **patria potestas**, "power of the father." The father literally held the power of life or death over all family members, regardless of age or those included by adoption. He was also the technical owner of all the property and income of the extended family, which included clients and freedmen. The *paterfamilias* was the oldest male of the family. His power and position were considered sacred and only upon his death could the next generation take over his duties and responsibilities. However, the father could manumit a son upon the son's coming of age, which meant the son was freed from his father's responsibility.

The duties of the *paterfamilias* were ratified through Roman law, the Twelve Tables, for he was duty-bound to raise good citizens for the state. He was also bound to honor his clan and his ancestors by fulfilling the obligation to procreate new generations. This concept was so important in ancient Rome that the severest penalty under law was reserved for a parricide ("father-killing"). Anyone convicted of such a crime was stripped naked, publicly flogged, and then sewn into a leather sack containing a monkey, a snake, a dog, and a rooster and thrown into the Tiber. Destroying the seed that gave one life was considered the highest sacrilege and offense against the gods.

The Roman home was comparable to a temple, with the father serving in the capacity of a priest. Everything in the Roman home was touched by the divine so that there were dozens of rituals undertaken daily from the moment of waking. Overseeing domestic space were the Lares (household gods), Penates (storeroom gods), and the Gens. This latter included the *genius* or the guiding spirit of a tutelary deity that acted as a guardian or protector of a place or person. The *lectus genialis* was embodied in the marriage bed, where this guardian spirit was passed from generation to generation. (In the Augustan age, genius came to mean "inspiration.") Janus guarded the doors of the household and Vesta protected the hearth.

Every morning the father was joined by the family and slaves to offer to the Lares familiaris in the family shrine, the *lararium*. The shrine contained images of these deities, which were kept near the hearth or in the atrium as well as in the kitchen area. The statues were brought to the table when the family gathered for meals. The Lares were offered the choice parts of meat. A Lar was greeted (right foot first) before crossing the threshold of a door and upon returning home and invoked before the start of any journey.

In the countryside, outside of the home, the father was responsible for the rituals to ensure the well-being of the estate and all of its produce. There were Lares at nearby crossroads, as well as the god Terminus whose domain was the boundaries of the farm. The plow that had outlined the first furrow of the year was burned on the hearth of the Lares so that wild animals would not attack. Every element involved in farming and the grazing of herds was under the tutelage of a god, from planting the seeds to turning the first furrow to the final harvest, with everything in between. As in Greece, the father was responsible for carrying out all the duties to honor the dead ancestors and their graves.

Mothers

Like her Greek counterpart, the Roman mother's primary religious obligation was to produce offspring, preferably a son, and to raise daughters in the skills of managing a household. However, she shared in her husband's duties by making her own offerings to the numerous deities involved in domestic affairs. Many of these offerings consisted of wreaths and garlands, and she was responsible for decorating the house for family events and religious holidays. The ideal Roman mother was not only expected to raise children, but she had to raise them as good citizens. This meant that many Roman women were at least minimally literate, and for younger children she oversaw their education. With the exception of the poor, many Roman boys and girls attended schools, although the wealthier children also had access to a tutor at home.

Upper-class and wealthy wives were expected to efficiently manage not just the home, but several country villas and estates. All male citizens had to do military service to Rome and some offices required men to be in the provinces for several years. The work of running several households and managing the economy of the estates was left in the hands of trusted stewards, but the wife held overall responsibility. We have very little evidence as to how the religious obligations of the home and estate were handled during the absence of the husband, but we have to assume that an accommodation was made.

Outside the home, Roman mothers participated in religious festivals for mothers and married women. Many of these festivals were devoted to Juno, who looked after the concerns of women, especially Juno Lucina and Juno Sospita, who helped in pregnancy, childbirth, and delivery. Many aspects of Juno were derived from the ancient tribes in Italy so that there were various local cults to her. In addition to the temples, sacrifices to Juno were also offered in every home for continued blessings of the household and marital fidelity.

The festival of Mater Matuta, the goddess of Dawn, was restricted to wives who had been married once (*univerae*), and was combined with the rites of the goddess Fortuna. With the high rate of divorce among the upper classes of Rome, the woman who had been married once was elevated to an ideal, loyal concept of a true Roman wife. This designation (*univera*) was always noted on tombstones when applicable. The focus of this festival was not the woman's children, but her nieces and nephews, or, in other words, a celebration of an aunt as a protector to her sister's or brother's children.

While the Vestal Virgins of Rome remained unmarried, their festival of Vestalia held in June was open to all mothers, who participated by bringing food and grain offerings. Throughout the cities and towns of Italy, wealthier married women were expected to endow and refurbish local temples. Local communities often acknowledged their largesse and donations by erecting statues of the women, usually located in the town forum. As a parallel to the Greek Thesmophoria, Roman women had religious festivals with secret rites, most notably found in the worship of Bona Dea.

Sons

When a son was born a coin was offered to Juno Lucina for the safe delivery. The midwife presented the baby to the mother, while the grandmother or aunt rubbed saliva on the baby's forehead to ward off the evil eye. The father lifted the child and held it upright to show that he acknowledged the child as his. On the ninth day the son was purified and given a name (on the eighth day for a girl). Every stage of a son's life, and throughout childhood, was under the care of a specific deity. Boys wore a **bulla** (amulet) that held a talisman or a sacred image. A son also wore a *toga praetexta* with a purple band that was also worn on the togas of priests and magistrates.

By age 17 or so, the son underwent a religious ritual that provided the transition from boyhood to manhood. This was when he shed his *toga praetexta* for the *toga virilis*, or the toga of manhood. He also surrendered his childhood *bulla* and hung it upon the family Lares. If he lived in Rome, he would go to the Temple of Jupiter on the Capitoline Hill with family and friends, and after the sacrifices, return home for a family party (the original "toga-party"). In conjunction with this ritual, and depending upon the timing, he participated in the Barbatoria, under the auspices of the Fortuna Barbata, who was responsible for the growth of the beard. This was the first time a young man was barbered or shaved, and was followed by another family feast. Roman culture did not share an interest in pederasty for young boys and often derided this custom as "the Greek practice," a negative description. This does not mean that same-sex relationships were absent in Rome, but that such relationships were never ennobled.

After reaching manhood, young men were expected to do their military training. For the upper classes, this was done through the office of Military Tribune based upon election or appointment. As tribunes, young men were assigned to work under the tutelage of a commander in the field and they had to complete 10 campaigns. At this time, many young men could be legally manumitted from the hand of their father, although it was a ritual undertaken by choice. The middle classes arranged for their sons' training in the countryside and they eventually served in the field through the patronage contacts of the father. The lower classes served their time only when they were recruited or called up in a military crisis. Young men were expected to marry and begin raising families in their mid-twenties. The upper-class sons were educated in rhetoric so that they could act as advocates in the law courts and obtain some initial experience in civic administration.

Daughters

Daughters spent their early years learning the domestic duties of their mothers. We know that girls attended schools with boys and played the same games in childhood. There were no specific religious rituals or festivities for young girls, with the exception of participating in choirs at certain times. However, young girls were included in the domestic rites of the household and always accompanied their mothers in some of those rituals shared by women throughout the calendar year. The true importance of a daughter's life did not begin until her marriage.

The father arranged a marriage for his daughter, where she passed from the *manus* (hand) of her father to that of her husband. In the early Republic, most patricians married by *confarreatio* (sharing food), which was understood to be for life, while plebeians and most others married by *manus*. In a *confarreatio* marriage the *flamen dialis* (the priest of Jupiter) and the *pontifex maximus* officiated. If a divorce was necessary (either through adultery or infertility) a special sacrifice was required to properly undo the relationship.

The *manus* marriage meant that the daughter's dowry or other property was automatically given to the husband. By the first century BCE, however, many people opted for a "free marriage" so that the wife technically stayed under the hand of her father and her husband had no access to the dowry or other property. This change was a practical consideration at a time of high divorce rates, or if the husband died. In such a case, the dowry would be returned and applied against the daughter's second marriage. It also permitted a degree of independence for Roman women, which ran against the conventions of other contemporary cultures. A divorced woman with a father no longer living could be declared legally independent (*sui iuris*), but nevertheless would have a male guardian appointed to handle her financial and legal affairs.

Daughters were betrothed and married between the ages of 15 and 18, although some betrothals among the aristocracy were organized much earlier. The betrothal ceremony was an occasion of gifts between the bride and groom. The auspices were consulted for the best date for the marriage, as it could not take place on unlucky days. On the wedding day the bride would offer her childhood toys and clothes to the household Lares. She then dressed in a white tunic as women prepared her hair in special tresses. The tunic was belted with a girdle known as a "Hercules knot," that could only be undone by the groom. The bride wore a *flammeum* or veil, which traditionally has been understood as a red color, but contemporary literature actually describes it as saffron, or yellow-toned.

A traditional verbal exchange between the couple was, "Where you are Gaius, I am Gaia," followed by the joining of hands and the sacrifice of a pig. The *augur* was usually the best man and had the job of making sure that the marriage contract was legitimate. The witnesses signed the contract, thus making the marriage official. The wedding party went in a procession to the groom's house, where the groom carried the bride over the threshold. She then offered her new husband fire and water, offered prayers at the family hearth, and took her place in the family. The Roman wedding night was an extremely crowded event, as multiple deities were called upon for every single movement, from help in undressing the bride to a successful performance by the groom. The next time that the bride would be surrounded by so many deities would be at the birth of her children.

The Ideal Family and the Ideal Society

You will notice that the prescribed religious roles of the various family members in both Greece and Rome were designed to ultimately prepare everyone for their larger role in the community. Hence, the framework of family as the metaphor for the city-state or the Empire was fully integrated into a system where everyone was trained from infancy to contribute to the greater good. Deviation from conventional roles would anger the gods.

Of course, what has been presented here was the ideal family for the ideal society. In reality, then as now, not everyone followed the rules, resulting in upheavals in both individual families and society at large. All these family members had their own personalities, and the father's control may not have been as rigorous as portrayed. Wives did not always obey their husbands, and children often rebelled (just like city-states and provinces). Nevertheless, the ideal was consistently upheld in literature and drama, always beginning and ending with the social conventions that were laid down by the gods and the ancestors.

Our information about religious roles for family members is very one-sided because almost everything we know about family life was written by upper-class men. With the exception of the works of women poets such as Sappho and a few letters and philosophical treatises, we remain uninformed about what most women (or children) actually thought. Particularly when it comes to women, we have inherited two polarized views from antiquity: the goddess or heroine and the seductress. Mythology presents a number of strong-willed women who wield power in their own right and who act on their own authority. Several women were presented as legendary heroines, even spurring men into battle. On the other hand, there were also stories of women who used their sexuality to seduce men or who enchanted men for evil purposes (Circe and Medea).

Summary

- The concept of honor/shame delegated the rules for social conduct, while the patron/client relationship provided the network to serve the community good. Class structures existed in a pyramid form, with the wealthiest classes at the top and the mass of the poorer classes below. Slavery was a widespread institution, although slaves could be manumitted over time.
- All members of the family had defined religious roles that were established in ancient tradition. Different deities supervised the various stages of life.
- The religious roles of the family were designed to prepare all members for their roles in the community.

Suggestions for Further Reading

Lefkowitz, M. R. and M. B. Fant. 2016. *Women's Life in Greece and Rome: A Source Book in Translation*, 4th ed. Johns Hopkins University Press. Original material for the lives of women, while also revealing their roles in religion and the family.

Mikalson, J. 2010. *Ancient Greek Religion*, 2nd ed. Wiley-Blackwell. This book details many of the community religious festivals and explains the religious role of family members.

Pomeroy, S. 1995. *Goddesses, Whores, Wives, and Slaves: Women in Classical Antiquity*. Schocken. This is another anthology of primary sources, but includes more on women than the Lefkowitz book.

Turcan, R. 2001. *The Gods of Ancient Rome: Religion in Everyday Life from the Archaic Period to Imperial Times*, trans. A. Nevill. Routledge. This volume surveys Roman rituals from the home to public festivals.

COMMUNICATING WITH THE DIVINE

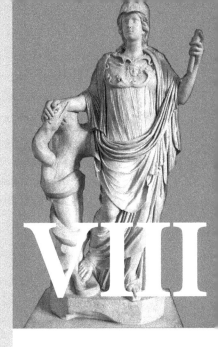

VIII

Greek and Roman Religions, First Edition. Rebecca I. Denova.
© 2019 John Wiley & Sons, Inc. Published 2019 by John Wiley & Sons, Inc.

Learning Objectives

After reading this chapter, you will be able to:

- Distinguish the various ways in which Greeks and Romans communicated with the gods.
- Understand the important role of divination in maintaining the balance between individuals, the community, and the divine

 Ancient Greeks and Romans believed that humans and gods could communicate with each other and develop a relationship that was mutually advantageous. In a world where chaos and disasters threatened destruction of the individual and the community, it was crucial to maintain open channels between the parties. From the human side there were prayers and hymns, and various methods of divination; from the divine side there were visitations, possessions, and revelations. Despite the diversity of the methods of communication, all the forms combined to produce a system where both benefited. Conceptually and in practice, Greece and Rome shared the basic elements of this system, differing only in the individual circumstances behind the methods.

Prayers and Hymns

Prayers were invocations and acts that involved the use of words or songs. From the Latin *precatio*, prayer was the formal and proper way to address a deity and to gain the attention of the god or goddess (Figure VIII.1). It was believed that

Figure VIII.1 Praying man from the Catacombs in Rome. *Source*: De Agostini/ Getty Images.

prayers would attract the presence of the deity as a partner in the various rituals. While prayers could stand alone, the sacrifices were ineffectual without the proper words. There were prayers to petition the gods for favors, praise and thanksgiving, requests for guidance, lamentations, and confession of sins. In ancient Greece and Rome, sins were immoral actions that violated the human/divine relationship and not necessarily bad thoughts (as in the later Christian concept).

Prayers provided the correct format for success. It was believed that the gods would not respond without their correct names, titles, honorifics, gender, and function and so prayers were the standard way in which to include all of these items. In addition, the prayers had to mention exactly what was being prayed for so that there would be no confusion on the part of the gods. Because the gods controlled nature and all events in the universe, it was believed that prayer and sacrifices could demonstrate thankfulness for benefits as well as appeasement for any actions that angered the gods. (See the box "Socrates' Prayer to Pan.")

The exactness of a specific request was indicated in the combined epithets of the gods. For instance, if you were praying for the welfare of the city of Athens, you addressed the goddess as Athena Polias. If you were praying for financial success in Rome, you addressed Juno Moneta (in her role as patron of the Roman mint). People prayed in front of cult statues in the temples, but most prayers were performed in front of outdoor altars with hands raised to the sky. Then, as now, people also prayed privately throughout the day and when occasion arose.

Socrates' Prayer to Pan

While we associate most prayers to the gods with being for material objects or beneficial events and circumstances, prayers also had higher motives. Some philosophers prayed for the ideals of the philosophical life, or how to live the best life. Plato (428–348 BCE) relates a prayer of Socrates as he strolled along:

> Beloved Pan, and all you other gods who haunt this place, give me the beauty of the inward soul, and may the outward man be joined in perfect harmony. May I reckon the wise to be wealthy, and may I have such a quantity of gold as none but the temperate can carry. Anything more? – That prayer, I think, is enough for me.

> (*Phaedrus*)

The Roman concept of the importance of prayer (and sacrifice) was known as the ***pax deorum***, or "the peace of the gods." The concept was based upon reciprocity or the exchange of services. The phrase, "do et des," "I give that you may give," summarized this exchange with humans and the gods as partners in a sense. Keeping the benevolence of the gods entailed prayers that glorified and honored them for both their past protection as well as future patronage. Upon reciting the correct prayers and sacrifices, it was understood that the gods were honor-bound to respond positively to any request. (See the box "Cato's Prayer to Mars at His Farm" for an example of a prayer that covered all contingencies.)

Cato's Prayer to Mars at His Farm

Cato the Elder (234–149 BCE) was a plebeian statesman who achieved fame for his service to the state, his oratory and his writings, most of which promoted the traditional ideals of Roman virtues. One of his favorite themes was the degeneration of Roman life by the import of Hellenistic concepts and religious changes. In his manual *De agricultura* ("On Agriculture") he detailed the proper methods of farming and harvesting, which were all in accord with the proper prayers and sacrifices at the proper time. The following prayer to Mars was offered in conjunction with a *suovetaurilia*, which was a sacrifice of a pig, a sheep, and a bull and was done in the hope that Mars would bless his farm through a *lustratio* or a purification of the land.

Father Mars, I pray and beseech you to be gracious and merciful to me, my house, and my household; to which intent I have bidden this *suovetaurilia* to be led around my land, my ground, my farm; that you keep away, ward off and remove sickness, seen and unseen, barrenness and destruction, ruin and unseasonable influence; and that you permit my harvests, my grain, my vineyards and my plantations to flourish and to come to good issue, preserve in health my shepherds and my flocks, and give good health and strength to me, my house and my household. To this intent, to the intent of purifying my farm, my land and my ground, and of making an expiation, as I have said, deign to accept the offering of these suckling victims; Father Mars.

There were also prayers of admonition, more commonly known as curses. Some of the reasons to call down curses upon someone included revenge for an insult, jealousy of someone's success, or to influence a lawsuit or a perceived injustice. Through the use of formulaic language that distinguishes them from the modern term "spells," people called on deities to enact misfortune or harm to a person. (Spells were essentially the same as prayers, although the intent was directed to a different outcome.) The victim could attempt to reverse the spell by appealing either to the same power or a different deity.

Particularly malevolent curses required propitiation sacrifices, or sacrifices that atoned for an offense created by a curse. One of the most famous cases of a public curse occurred in the city of Rome in 55 BCE. A Tribune of the Plebs, Gaius Ateius Capito, opposed Marcus Crassus's war against the Parthians. He stood at the gate and cursed not only Crassus but the entire undertaking. Along with the curses (which included ancient Italian and Etruscan formulas) he uttered the secret name of Rome, forbidden to be spoken aloud. (Some traditions claim that the secret name was simply *Roma* pronounced backwards, "Amor.") The city panicked and the colleges of the *pontifices* and priests met to decide what to do. They carried out a propitiation ritual in which a white ox, a boar, and a ram were carried around the city seven times on the shoulders of the senators. Crassus subsequently lost his life, his son, and three Roman eagles as well as most of his legions at the Battle of Carrhae in Parthia in 53 BCE.

Prayers put to music were collectively called hymns, or songs of praise, and many hymns were extended invocations. Hymns of praise were a standard feature of religious festivals, performed by trained choirs of adults and children. These choirs went on tour and participated in religious festivals that included competition for prizes. They represented the civic pride of their hometown as well as the deity who was the object of their praise, emphasizing the divine connection between the two. Such choruses would be accompanied by drums, cymbals, a flute and/or a *kithara* (a lyre). The hymns of antiquity provide us with remarkable insight into the piety and emotions of ancient religious experience.

Some of the most ancient hymns are known as the Homeric Hymns, credited to the poet Homer but which were in fact anonymous. Many of the epithets and functions of the gods mentioned in *The Iliad* and *The Odyssey* are similar and may date from the same period when the Homeric narratives were written down. Most of these hymns originated in religious festivals and were passed down by itinerant bards. (See the box "Homeric Hymn to Artemis.")

The Homeric Hymns vary in length, from a few lines to over five hundred, where the longer hymns include mythic elements of a particular god or goddess and were the basis for oral epic. In addition to narrative-type hymns, there were paeans (hymns that expressed more enthusiastic praise or triumph), which could be propitiatory or hymns of thanksgiving. Hymns were often expressed in ritual dance, which was an important part of the festivals. The combination of prayers, hymns, sacrifices, and dance formed the basis of the liturgy, which was a term that referred to the public duties and services of wealthy citizens to the gods. The price of the offerings, the musicians, and the dancers required for liturgies elevated the personal and public status of rich citizens.

Homeric Hymn to Artemis

I sing of Artemis, whose shafts are of gold, who cheers on the hounds, the pure maiden, shooter of stags, who delights in archery, own sister to Apollo with the golden sword. Over the shadowy hills and windy peaks she draws her golden bow, rejoicing in the chase, and sends out grievous shafts ... But the goddess with a bold heart turns every way destroying the race of wild beasts: and when she is satisfied and has cheered her heart, this huntress ... goes to the great house of her dear brother Phoebus Apollo, to the rich land of Delphi, there to order the lovely dance of the Muses and Graces.

In Rome a musical hymn was known as *carmen* (song, plural, *carmina*). Festivals included dancing in a *pantomimus*, which was an early version of ballet with a story. In addition to the common Greek musical instruments, Romans had woodwinds (*tibia*, or double-reed pipes) and brass instruments similar to trumpets and tubas. The larger ones were *cornu* ("horn") which wound around the player's body. For events in the circuses, they also had early versions of organs, some of which were hydraulic or operated by water pressure. (See the box "The *Saeculare* of Horace.")

The Saeculare *of Horace*

The Roman poet Horace (65–8 BCE) was commissioned by the emperor Augustus to write several odes (put to music as hymns) for the *ludi saeculares* (Secular Games) in 17 BCE. The Secular Games did not refer to a non-religious celebration, but celebrated the *saeculum* (100–110 years) of passing from one age to another. The reference of Diana to her brother Phoebus (Apollo) was in recognition of the inauguration of a temple to Apollo on the Palatine Hill at the time of the Secular Games.

O Phoebus, Diana queen of the woodlands, bright heavenly glories, both worshipped forever and cherished forever, now grant what we pray for at this sacred time, when Sibylline verses have issued their warning to innocent boys, and the virgins we've chosen, to sing out their song to the gods, who have shown their love for the Seven Hills. O kindly Sun, in your shining chariot, who herald the day, then hide it, to be born again new yet the same, you will never know anything mightier than Rome! ... May Phoebus, the *augur*, decked with the shining bow, Phoebus who's dear to the Nine Muses, that Phoebus who can offer relief to a weary body with his healing art, may he, if he favors the Palatine altars, extend Rome's power, and Latium's good-fortune ...

Divination

Divination (from Latin *divinare*, "to be inspired by a god") was a crucially important method of communication between humans and the divine. It was also one of the most ancient forms of communication, with evidence of divination practices in Mesopotamia, Egypt, Babylonia, Israel, and Persia. While prayers and hymns were human appeals to the gods, divination was the way in which the gods communicated their will to humans.

It was important to know the will of the gods, to discover if they were happy or angry. If angry, necessary steps had to be taken to rectify any breach in the human/divine relationship. Divination methods were utilized by **prophets**, seers, *augurs*, *haruspices*, oracles, dream interpreters, healers, interpreters of portents and prodigies (omens), astrologers, and necromancers. All of these categories and titles were not independent of each other; the ancients often applied the same names and terms to the several different methods of divination.

Scholars classify divination as inductive and inspired. Inductive divination focused on human observation: of flights of birds, of omens in nature, entrails of sacrificial animals, and prodigies (omens of unnatural phenomena). Inspired divination originated with the gods and possessed a person or object, or directed individuals to interpret their divine words and signs. What follows is a general description of the actors and actions involved in determining the will of the gods.

Prophets

Prophets, from the Greek *profetes*, functioned as "advocates" or "speakers." Prophets were individuals who were open and receptive to the gods and who could speak for them. Although present in ancient Mesopotamia, Egypt, Babylon, and Persia, the term is perhaps best known in the Western tradition through the Jewish Scriptures, where the prophets of Israel had their sayings written down and collected in books (e.g. Isaiah and Jeremiah). As intermediaries between humans and the divine, prophets were usually seized by the deity and, while they were in an ecstatic state, the words of the deity were channeled through them; they were the spokespersons for the gods.

This possession by the gods resulted in speech that either predicted future events or clarified a question or problem between the god and the petitioner. Because it was speech of the gods, it remained unknown and had to be interpreted by a priest. Both Greece and Rome recognized that non-priestly individuals could also be inspired to prophesize. The spiritual possession by a god led to a general characterization of the person as charismatic, from the Greek *charis*, which relates to "gifts" (and hence our word, charity). In this sense, someone possessed by a god had received a divine gift.

Seers

Seers in ancient Greece and Rome were experts skilled in divination, particularly in the reading of the flights of birds and the entrails of sacrificial animals. Interpreting the state of entrails usually involved the liver of the animal, with an examination of the lobes. One difference between prophets and seers was that prophets required interpreters but seers made their own declarations. Seers could also function as priests and were selected from the educated, aristocratic citizens of the cities. Their interpretations were crucial for political and military decisions. (For famous seers in Greek literature, see the box "Classical Seers.")

Greek armies had their own seers who performed two types of interpretation, the *hiera* and the *sphagia*. The *hiera* was performed in the camp with a sheep whose liver was then read to determine if conditions were favorable for the upcoming battle. The *sphagia* was a sacrifice performed at the line of battle. The seer sacrificed a she-goat by slitting her throat and then watched which way the blood flowed. Seers in the army were utilized not only for the outcome of battles, but as consultants for military strategy.

Classical Seers

In mythic literature and drama, some famous Greek seers were Tiresias, Calchas, and Cassandra. What they had in common was that they were all in the service of Apollo, who was the patron god of seers and oracles.

Tiresias was a seer in ancient Thebes. According to one tradition, he was blinded by Athena for coming upon her bathing in the nude. Nevertheless he received visions, interpreted the song of birds, and interpreted the smoke of sacrifices. In *The Odyssey*, Odysseus traveled to the entrance of Hades to consult the dead shade of Tiresias. In *Oedipus the King* by Sophocles, Tiresias revealed the fact that when Oedipus killed King Laius, he actually killed his father. In *The Bacchae* by Euripides, Tiresias warned King Pentheus of Thebes not to reject the worship of Dionysus. Ignoring this advice, Pentheus was later torn apart by the Maenads of Dionysus in their frenzy.

The seer Calchas was connected with the war against Troy, which he predicted would last 10 years. He told King Agamemnon that in order to receive favorable winds for the fleet to sail to Troy he would have to sacrifice his daughter, Iphigenia, to the goddess Artemis. When the Greeks first attacked Troy, they slew the priests of Apollo and took the priestess Chryseis captive. Apollo then sent a plague on the Greek armies as a punishment. Calchas claimed that Chryseis should be returned to stop the plague. The argument over what to do with Chryseis established the plot device in *The Iliad*, the quarrel between Achilles and Agamemnon, who both claimed her as the spoils of war.

The daughter of King Priam of Troy, Cassandra was a seeress, or prophetess. However, she received this gift of prophecy from Apollo because he wanted to seduce her. When she rejected him, the gift remained, but with a curse. Apollo determined that no one would ever believe her prophecies. She foresaw that Paris's abduction of Helen would bring about the Trojan War, the trick of the Trojan horse, the murder of Agamemnon by his wife, and her own murder at the same time. The frustration of not being believed drove her to madness.

Independent seers operated beyond the validation of the state or outside of the authority possessed by elected or appointed priests. Sometimes referred to as "soothsayers" (from Shakespeare's *Julius Caesar*), they could be found on the perimeters of temples or near the public squares of towns and cities. Offering their services freely, there was nevertheless an expectation of a handout (such as modern beggars or musicians expect on our own streets). Plato discussed "seer beggars" who went from door to door (in his *Symposium*). According to the Roman biographer Suetonius, a forum seer named Spurinna warned Caesar to "beware the Ides of March."

Augurs and *Haruspices*

More often known from Roman literature, *augurs* were the seers who observed the skies (for comets, lightning, and thunder) and the flights and sounds of birds. Unlike prophets, *augurs* did not predict the future, but determined if decisions already agreed upon had the favor of the gods. Rome incorporated both Etruscan and Greek rituals, and the art was referred to as *ius augurium* or *auspicium*. Public *augurs* in Rome had distinctive dress and paraphernalia: a cloak with a purple border (*trabea*) and a **lituus**, or *augur*'s wand for pointing to sectors of the sky.

Augurs were called upon for both private and public auspices, and all state legislation was subject to augury. *Augurs* were high-ranking magistrates who had been commissioned by law to make pronouncements on their observations and were organized into priestly *collegia*. The rules for augury were secret and inherited from Etruscan *augurs*. However, many of their pronouncements were codified in the *Commentarii augurales*, a collection of past interpretations. The success of augury could only be judged in retrospect.

In order to "take the auspices," *augurs* first determined the *templum* or the sacred space in the sky that was the focus of observation: right, left, before, and behind. A rectangle was then drawn on the sky. The positions were relative to the *augur* facing north or south, and even in antiquity there was some debate over which way the *augur* should face. Greek *augurs* looked north while Roman *augurs* looked south.

The important birds to watch were owls, ravens, woodpeckers, and eagles (which trumped all other birds in Rome) and it was also important to observe where the birds landed. Another practice involved sacred chickens, which in Rome were kept in an area of the *Arx* on the Capitoline Hill. The *augur* threw down corn and watched the chickens' reaction. If the chickens immediately ate the corn, it was a good omen; if they ignored it, it was considered bad. *Augurs* and their chickens accompanied the armies of Rome and they took the auspices before each battle.

An important way to determine the will of the gods was by seers who were experts in the art of haruspicy, the reading of entrails of sacrificial animals, particularly the lobes of the liver (Figure VIII.2). The liver was understood as a

Figure VIII.2 Roman *haruspices. Source:* Christophel Fine Art/ UIG via Getty Images.

source of blood, and therefore of life. We have an Etruscan model that may have been used for training purposes where various lobes were designated zones of particular deities. After the conquest of Etruria, Etruscan priests were brought to Rome as *haruspices*. Both *augurs* and *haruspices* had the power to cancel or change official business if the omens were bad. Elections were canceled several times as a result of their readings.

Portents and Prodigies

The terms portent and **prodigy** were used interchangeably to describe natural and unnatural phenomena. They were understood as omens or signs from the gods and required a seer, a *haruspex*, a pontiff, or an *augur* to interpret them. There were probably as many good as bad portents, but the bad ones made it into the literature. In Rome, a portent that was giving the usual interpreters problems could be referred to the *duoviri sacris faciundis*, who would consult the Sibylline Oracles (see also below).

Events that were understood as portents were lightning strikes, earthquakes, unseasonal rains and floods, eclipses, plagues, and military disasters. In Rome unnatural phenomena known as prodigies were collected and reported to the Senate to determine their meaning. Prodigies indicated an imbalance in the cosmos created by the anger of the gods. We have lists of unusual animal births (two-headed cows and goats), astral phenomena (two suns in the sky, fiery hail), bleeding and sweating statues, and statues that moved. In such cases greater and lesser expiation or propitiatory rituals were required. While the modern United States Senate applies a filibuster to defeat or delay the passage of a bill (a concept that originated in the Roman Senate), individual senators in Rome often cited the appearance of prodigies to delay legislation that they opposed.

Pilgrims and tourists often reported such events when they were traveling through Greek lands and Italy, and scribes of the Senate collected lists of all reported abnormalities. Many of these were ignored as merely interesting events unless there was a political or military crisis at hand. However, the interpretations often differed. For Greeks a comet could indicate the signal of an important birth or era, but for Romans a comet was sometimes dire. A notable exception was the series of comets that appeared after the death of Julius Caesar which the common people claimed was an indication of his apotheosis, or becoming a god.

Oracles

An oracle was the term used to designate the individual seer, prophet or priest as well as the site where oracular activity took place. The word indicated the nature of the activity involved, which was that of a question asked and the god's response. Some of the more ancient oracles appear random to us, when questions were

Figure VIII.3 Ruins of ancient Delphi. *Source*: iStock/Getty Images Plus.

answered by lot (sortation) or tossing objects into a sacred spring. The larger oracles had priests or prophets who acted as vehicles for the words of the gods. There was a popular oracle of Zeus at Dodona in Epirus. At this site, barefooted priests lay under an ancient oak and observed the rustling of the leaves. The most popular god associated with oracular sites was Apollo, whose largest oracles were at Delphi, Didyma, and Claros (Figure VIII.3).

The oracle at Delphi had a prophetess known as the Pythia, named after the monster Python slain by Apollo. The belief was that the Python fell into a fissure and its rotting body produced fumes. After drinking from a sacred spring and chewing bay leaves (or another substance), the Pythia sat on a tripod over the fumes and then went into a trance. (Modern archaeologists, excavating the fissures and cracks in the ruins of Delphi, still debate this tradition.) Her ecstatic speech had to be translated by priests, who then presented it in hexameters. These translations were sometimes famously ambiguous and it was up to the questioner(s) to interpret them (see the box "The Ambiguity of a Delphic Oracle"). If the oracle turned out to be wrong, the blame was placed on the interpreters and not the god Apollo.

Individuals as well as delegations from city-states made pilgrimages to Delphi for consultation on all important matters. The Pythia was consulted before military adventures and the establishment of new colonies. She was not available in the winter months and only on certain days. The responses were recorded and pilgrims often had stone votives inscribed with the questions and answers, displaying them either at the shrine complex or in their hometown. In gratitude, statues were erected at the site and valuable offerings were donated to the treasuries.

We must allow for the possibility that oracles were collected and validated *post eventum*, or after the fact. To validate a decision already made, oracles

The Ambiguity of a Delphic Oracle

Many of the prophecies at Delphi were ambiguous and therefore subject to human interpretation (and error). A few remain open to various meanings even today. Two of the most famous mottos inscribed at Delphi were "Know thyself" and "Nothing in excess," which could be applicable to individuals as well as city-states (e g. "Know thyself" in what sense? physically? mentally? emotionally?)

When there was disagreement over an interpretation, a second and sometimes a third question was presented. Questioners also had to be aware of omens that could interfere, such as an owl landing nearby. If insight remained elusive, a competing oracle was sought, although Delphi remained first in faith as the truest of the oracles.

One of the more famous ambiguous oracles involved Croesus, the king of Lydia. Croesus was known as one of the richest men in antiquity and the first to introduce coins as money. Around 560 BCE, with a Persian invasion pending, Croesus asked the Delphic Oracle if he should go to war or form an alliance with the Persians. He was told that if he went to war he would destroy a kingdom. Croesus of course interpreted this to mean that he would destroy the empire of the Persians and so went to war, only to be defeated. The kingdom that was destroyed was his own. He not only lost the battle but was captured by his enemy. According to tradition, however, he was redeemed at the eleventh hour. When King Cyrus ordered him burned on a funeral pyre, the god Apollo spirited him away.

Perhaps the shortest and least ambiguous of the prophecies was in response to a friend of Socrates who asked if there was anyone wiser than the great philosopher. The reported answer was simply, "None."

offered credibility and sanction. But there was also room for skepticism, sometimes about Delphi, but particularly about individual, itinerant oracles. These men and women were suspected of providing what people wanted to hear for money. However, even though Xenophon in his *Anabasis* criticized and dismissed some itinerant oracles, he nevertheless kept oracles in his army and consulted them regularly.

The Sibylline Oracles

Sibyls, female prophetesses, were located throughout the Mediterranean basin, with a famous site at Cumae, Italy, near a temple of Apollo on the Bay of Naples (which can still be visited today). It was a sibyl from Cumae who served as the guide for Aeneas during his journey to the underworld. Tradition claims that one day a sibyl approached one of the last kings of Rome, Tarquinius Superbus, and offered him nine books of prophecies concerning the fate of Rome. After he refused her steep price, three comets appeared in the night sky, symbolizing three burned books. The next day she offered him six for the same price and he refused again, with the same comets appearing. On the final day, with the books reduced to three but still at the original price, he accepted and received what became the Sibylline Books that were stored in the temple of Jupiter in Rome.

A special group of priests who were 10 leading citizens, the *quindecimviri sacris faciundis*, consulted the books only in times of crisis. But the temple of

Jupiter burned in 83 BCE, resulting in the loss of the prophecies. Delegates from the Senate searched throughout the Empire for other Sibyline prophecies and brought them back to Rome. This was done each time a catastrophe destroyed the books, including a major search when Augustus was emperor. The oracles were written in Greek hexameter and any consultation utilized Greek interpreters. Several times, upon consultation in a crisis, the interpretation resulted in propitiation rituals, the dedication of new temples in Rome, or the introduction of a new cult.

According to Ovid's *Metamorphoses*, the original sibyl was a thousand years old, a gift of longevity from Apollo. Seekers made a sacrifice at the temple in order to petition Apollo to inspire and possess the sibyl, who then went into an ecstatic trance. The responses were written on oak leaves.

Incubation/Healers/Dream Interpretation

Incubation was the process of going to sleep, usually to effect a cure for a disease, as a healing process, to learn information or to cure infertility. All of the temples and oracle sites that offered this service either had prophets, seers, or priests and they all required some basic ritual elements, including sacrifices and prayers. It was believed that the gods often revealed information through dreams, which then required dream interpretation.

Epidaurus

One of the most famous incubation temple complexes was located at Epidaurus in Greece, which was dedicated to the healing god Asclepios, where one tradition claimed this city as his place of birth. This *asclepion* contained a temple, an *enkoimeterion* or sleeping hall (what we would now call a dormitory), gymnasiums, mineral springs and a huge theater and racetrack for the games that were celebrated every four years at the Panhellenic Asclepieia. One of the buildings had an underground labyrinth which housed snakes. Snakes were symbols of rebirth and regeneration and a favorite symbol of Asclepios.

After undergoing purification rituals, patients went to sleep in the dormitories, hoping that the god would appear in their dreams and offer cures. The priests kept vigil through the night (and perhaps listened as people talked in their sleep?). The next morning healing priests would administer the cures or recommend medical procedures. Part of the medical prescription included the proper prayers to be recited when undergoing the regimen. Greeks and Romans would never drink a medical potion or carry out a doctor's orders without the benefit of prayers at the same time.

In gratitude most patients left a votive offering, usually in some form that symbolized their problems such as carvings of ears, eyes, limbs, and even genitals if the complaint had involved fertility. Depending upon the complication of the cure, patients could utilize the gymnasium and the services of the priests, who also studied medicine at this site. There were major *asclepions* at Athens, Pergamum, and on the island of Kos (where the *asclepion* also served as a temple bank). According to tradition, the Romans took a snake from Epidaurus to the island in the middle of the Tiber River to alleviate a plague. The island became the center for the worship of Asclepios and a hospital in Rome.

Dreams

Beyond the incubation and healing centers, dreams were believed to be one of the ways in which the gods communicated with humans, and as such were therefore vitally important. People were concerned to literally carry out any instructions they received from the gods in their dreams. The ancients understood that most dreams were caused by everyday activities and events, especially eating, and many dreams were ascribed to bad digestion. For the dreams that contained a visit from a god, or dreams that contained bizarre or unfamiliar images and ghosts, dream interpretation was sought to understand these messages.

It was dangerous to view a god or goddess in all their glory, so deities often appeared in disguise in a dream, usually in the form of a known friend, a servant, or an old woman. Many ancients dreamed of ghosts, who also could deliver an important message. In the *Iliad*, Achilles dreamed of his dead companion Patroclus, who urged him to perform his proper burial rites. Vengeful ghosts required the services of a necromancer (see below).

An aid to dream interpretation took the form of books and catalogues, some of the oldest stemming from ancient Egypt, Mesopotamia, and Persia. Perhaps influenced by these writings, Greeks compiled books of their own. In the fourth century BCE, Antiphon differed from most dream interpreters in creating a catalogue that emphasized natural conditions that gave rise to dreams, such as fears, anxiety, and certain foods. Various philosophers promoted such scientific aspects of dreams, including Aristotle, who claimed that dreams were extensions of reality intruding into the imagination.

In Rome in the second century CE a Greek physician named Artemidorus catalogued dreams according to visions, oracles, fantasies, and apparitions. *Somnium* dreams predicted the future, while *insomnium* ones dealt with everyday life. He included a dream dictionary to elucidate objects and symbols. For the majority of the uneducated, however, individual dream interpreters provided a service to those who sought an understanding of their nightly adventures.

Sortition

Sortition, also known as cleromancy, was a system used throughout the ancient world as a means of selecting individuals for both religious offices and government leadership. The familiar term "casting lots" was often used to identity the best person for a job, but we often lack any particular details as to how this was done. Although this system would appear completely random to us, the assumption was that casting lots was an indication of the will of the gods.

In Athens the system *may* have been adopted from the myth that Zeus, Poseidon, and Hades divided the universe through sortition. With the concept of Athenian democracy, it was believed that this system was fairer and resulted in less corruption. The system was particularly utilized for the section of juries (which could number up to 500 citizens). Allotment machines (*kleroteria*) were filled with balls or tiles with names inscribed upon them. Sortition was most likely applied throughout Italy for many of the local priesthoods, but we only have evidence for its use in the selection of some magistrates and priesthoods in the city of Rome.

Manipulating the Divine

A final group of practitioners is generally catalogued under "magic," and with our added bias of "superstition." The majority of textbooks usually have a separate chapter or section on magic, although this remains a modern distinction that would not have been understood in the ancient world. Magic was essentially just one more tool in the toolbox that people utilized in their religious endeavors. Our bias is demonstrated when we describe the prayers used in this category as incantations and spells. Yet all the incantations and spells followed the same format as prayer in an attempt to either communicate with a specific power or plead for a special benefit. In this sense of divination, the activities included prayers and rituals to various deities who were called upon to help enact the petitions and to reveal special knowledge to the practitioner.

The word magic itself is derived from **magoi** (*magus* in Latin), the Greek word for the Zoroastrian court astrologers and fire-priests of the Persian Empire. The term implied esoteric knowledge and the ability to manipulate cosmic and natural forces. However, it is important to understand that *most* people in the ancient world would not have recognized a distinction between magic and religion the same way we do; these different rites were simply several methods utilized to communicate with and to manipulate the will of the gods.

Unlike seers, prophets or *augurs* who uttered divine revelations or interpreted signs, these diviners performed additional tasks by attempting to manipulate the forces of nature. They utilized special tools such as wands, crystal lenses, potions, and special plants. Greeks and Romans did not make distinctions when it came to the source of some of these activities, and the legacy of these rituals as superstition comes from negative literature. Much criticism was leveled against rituals that were practiced by foreigners and therefore not part of the local cult. Cicero applied the term "superstition" to those ethnic cults that did not conform to Roman concepts and practices. The traditions of one's ancestors were protected and revered, and new and foreign practices threatened those traditions.

In addition to Cicero, other critics such as Ovid and Pliny set the tone for the Christian adoption of the same attitudes toward these ethnic practices. The church leaders associated all these elements of divination with an evil source, the Devil. Thus began the continuing legacy of the negative connotations attached to this element of ancient religion, and the continuing practice of separating "magic" from religion. Because these rituals attempted to manipulate the divine, we use "magic," "superstition," and "sorcery" interchangeably.

The most severe criticism in the ancient world was directed not so much against the process as against the individual practitioner. Their rituals reached beyond the traditional cults, so that many of these individuals were accused of impiety and of angering the gods.

The charge of impiety was especially serious when a practitioner was perceived as having hubris or excessive overconfidence and pride in their achievements. When one of these diviners came to believe that their own power was equal to or superior to the gods, they were accused of impiety and an absence of fear of the gods, which all humans should have. Remuneration (being paid for one's services) was also a problem and many of these people were accused of fraud. When that happened they were deemed *goetes*, a word which meant "swindler" or "imposter," and placed into the equivalent of being called a "pirate."

Perhaps the most important aid in understanding the nuance between religion and this type of divination was the element of intent. Traditional rituals had good or beneficial goals for individuals and the community, whereas rituals that caused harm were crimes often punishable by death. Our modern categories of white and black magic derive from this similar distinction in antiquity. Some forms of unrequited love (compelling the desire of an inappropriate partner), murder (of family members and political rivals), manipulation in gambling, unjustified revenge, interfering with the courts (causing muteness or lapses in a lawyer's speech), and promoting bad luck against a prominent citizen fell under the category of what we term "the black arts."

Many of these practitioners utilized a modern anthropological classification known as **apotropaic magic** ("to turn away") as a means of directing and diverting malignant forces. In ancient Greece a popular visual symbol was the head of a gorgon, a chthonic deity with fangs, snakes for hair, and a protruding tongue (A gorgon's head was displayed on Athena's shield at her colossal statue in the Parthenon.) What appears frightening to us nevertheless would be classified as white magic because of its intent. Gorgon heads were used to forestall and deter foreign enemies as well as bad luck.

To turn away "the evil eye," eyes were literally painted on bowls and cups as well as ships. Phalluses were also believed to avert evil, which is why

Figure VIII.4   Phallus above a doorway at Pompeii.

the ithyphallic herms were placed at crossroads. Romans painted and sculpted phalluses above their homes and over the doorways of their businesses. Not only did the phallus represent fertility and prosperity, but it may have been a way to diffuse the envy and ill-will of others through humor (Figure VIII.4).

One final area of confusion involves the divine players in these practices. What may appear simple in terms of black and white was more complicated in relation to the deities called upon by the experts. They appealed to *both* heavenly and chthonic deities in their rituals. It was not a simple case of calling upon the heavenly deities for good spells and the chthonic deities for harmful intent or curses. Chthonic deities were labeled as such because of their associations with Hades, the underworld of the dead, but that did not necessarily make them evil powers.

For example, in Western culture Hecate eventually became the patron of witches and witchcraft. Originally she was an ancient goddess who was responsible for crossroads, doorways, knowledge of special plants, and as a guide for souls into Hades. It was in this relation to the underworld, as a chthonic deity, that certain diviners called upon her for assistance. She thus became associated with necromancy (see below). Hecate, however, was not inherently evil; her guidance to Hades and her advice were beneficial to all.

It was only through witches calling upon her for help that she became the later "queen of witches" in the Middle Ages (see below).

Astrologers and Herbalists

Astrology encompasses the observation of the elements in the sky. At least as early as Neolithic times, humans began studying the sun, moon, stars, and planets to determine seasonal changes and agricultural cycles. Such observations also contributed to the formation of calendars, both lunar and solar. The Sumerians, Egyptians, and Babylonians noted the position of the planets and the stars in relation to seasonal flooding, but also began to consult the heavens in planning major events such as temple-building and festivals.

The compilation of astrological omens in Mesopotamia began c. 1800 BCE. The omens were utilized to predict weather at first and then extended to major events. As the planets and stars appeared to move, the powers of individual gods were understood to lie behind such activity. The particular characteristics of the deities evolved into a set zodiac or division of the year which emerged into the portrayal of gods and animals in the Greek and Roman zodiacs which we still use today.

Greeks and Romans consulted astrologers for the reading of horoscopes, which were astrological charts showing the position of the sun, moon, and planets at the time of an event to determine which power was the most influential. This was most often done at the birth of a son to help predict a future career and military success. We have several references in Roman literature deriding such practices (known as "Chaldean wisdom"). Under Imperial Rome some astrologers became famous for their work with the royal family (such as the empress Livia and her son Tiberius). The death penalty was assigned to anyone else found consulting an astrologer for the horoscope of the emperor. Such action indicated a potential treasonous plot.

Theurgy (divine-working) was a concept that described many methods of communication mostly associated with good intentions. Theurgists were prevalent in ancient Greece but most of our literature comes from later periods when neo-Platonism was popular (during the latter half of the Roman Empire). Theurgy became the practice of rituals and prayers that attempted to either unite one's soul with a particular god or power or draw the presence of the divine near.

Philosophical speculation included not only the ways and means by which to unite oneself with the deity, but how to manifest the knowledge and peace of mind in one's daily life that resulted from such unification. One of the methods of the theurgist was an out-of-body experience in which the heavens as well as the underworld could be traversed in search of meaning and power.

Wonder-workers, *magoi*, were believed to have special relationships with the divine. They were approached most often for medical cures or infertility. There were both local and itinerant wonder-workers; the latter traveled through the various districts working their miracles for the public. Competitors to healing gods such as Asclepios, wonder-workers offered a benefit to those too poor to travel to the larger *asclepions*. One of the more famous wonder-workers of the first century CE, Apollonius of Tyana, offered his followers both medical miracles and hints of immortality because he raised people from the dead. His disciples claimed that he was resurrected after he was put to death by a Roman magistrate. (Apollonius and Jesus of Nazareth, contemporaries, are often compared.)

These wonder-workers provided prayers against major diseases and some offered to relieve old age and even death. Plato discussed those who went door-to-door as "begging seers," and other writers discussed their tricks of illusion. Like our modern stage magicians, wonder-workers performed illusionary tricks to demonstrate their power and control over nature. Many of these illusions involved talking and moving statues, making it rain, attempts to control the moon and sun, and particularly cures for epilepsy, considered a disease sent by the gods. Wonder-workers performed at private parties, at crossroads, and even in the theaters.

In the Homeric period, we have little information on the exact way in which wonder-workers actually achieved their manifestations of divine powers. By the Hellenistic period a belief in demons became more widespread. The universe was understood to contain various powers, including *daemons*, which could be harnessed for good or evil. Demons were not originally evil in and of themselves. Over time demons were believed to be the agents that wonder-workers and other experts utilized in order to perform their cures and illusions. Demons were only considered evil if the intent was malicious. The word became fully associated with evil under later Christian teaching.

Herbalists were men and women who were experts in folk wisdom and folk medicines, and most often they were associated with the indigenous tribes and peasants of the countryside. They traveled to towns and cities on market days and set up stalls and booths in the center of town to offer their wares. In addition to the various medicines and substances, the herbalists provided the proper prayers and rituals that were an equally important part of their prescriptions, and thus they had many elements in common with other magical practitioners. Herbalists claimed that their special knowledge and skills were passed down through the ancestors in conjunction with the gods.

Herbalists were a source of ancient fertility cures and popular love potions (traditionally called love-philters). Love potions were sought for both unrequited love as well as a cure for a marriage partner who "had fallen out of love." For the most part, the purchase of a love potion was benign, but it was not considered proper or even legal to buy a love potion if the object of one's desires was beyond one's social class. Greece and Rome had regulations for marriages between the classes. And of course it was forbidden to purchase a love potion for someone who was married, as this violated the adultery laws.

Many of the herbalists sold amulets, whose effectiveness depended upon individual needs. An amulet was endowed with power to protect its owner from harm. Amulets consisted of small statues, engraved gems, coins, rings, and sometimes a ritual prayer that was stuffed into another object. Young Roman boys at the age of nine days old were given a *bulla* to wear on a chain around their necks. These were made from cloth, lead, or gold, depending upon the family's circumstances. They were often in the form of a phallus. The *bulla* was removed upon the boy reaching manhood at the toga ceremony and dedicated to the gods. Young girls had their own amulets, and these would also be given up along with their toys when they married. In both cases, the amulets staved off evil and diverted the jealousy of others.

Necromancy

Necromancy was a form of divination that involved communication with the dead and was related to other forms of divination when necromancers called upon chthonic deities for help in their work. Necromancers were consulted to foretell future events, to seek knowledge from the dead, or to keep the dead from harming the living. They were especially useful in obtaining the assistance of chthonic deities and the dead for revenge or retribution. Earlier evidence of necromancy is found in Egypt, Mesopotamia, Babylon, Phoenicia, Persia, and Etruria.

Necromancy originated in the belief that the dead continued to exist in some form, especially the ancestors, who could either help or harm their descendants. One of the earliest Greek accounts of using necromancy rituals is recounted in *The Odyssey*, when Odysseus seeks a dead seer at the gates of Hades.

The *nekromanteion* was a shrine at Epirus in Greece dedicated to Hades and Persephone and was believed to be an entrance to the underworld. The term *nekromanteion* translates to "oracle of death" and was popular as a site for people to contact their dead relatives. Other oracles of the dead were located throughout the Mediterranean basin. Some of the rituals required a meal of special food and drink (sometimes a narcotic) and many of the temples had underground passages, labyrinths, and rivers that replicated the various parts of Hades.

Another oracle of the dead was located in Boeotia and was dedicated to Trophonius, who along with his brother built the temple to Apollo at Delphi. According to one story, the Delphic Oracle told the brothers to do whatever they wished for six days and on the seventh their wish would be granted. On the seventh day, they were dead. The oracle of Trophonius at Boeotia was a man-made, dome-like cave which was entered after a seeker purified himself and made the proper sacrifices. This experience inside the cave left him shaken and sometimes in a stupor for days. It was an ancient equivalent to our modern Halloween fun houses and, like those, most likely was designed to frighten as part of a therapeutic spiritual experience. Descending into this cave became a euphemism for being "sacred to death."

A Greco-Italian oracle of the dead was located at Cumae near Lake Avernus, which was also believed to be an entrance to Hades. This oracle was combined

Figure VIII.5
The Oracle at
Cumae. *Source:* akg/
Bildarchiv Steffens.

with a temple to Hecate, important in her role as guide and solace to the souls of the dead. Seekers descended through a passage where there was an underground river (the Styx), and where they would often see ghostly figures.

Necromancers were useful in both bringing up the dead as well as forcing them back to Hades. The classic "ghost story" is very ancient (we have examples from Egypt and Mesopotamia as well as Greece and Rome), and necromancers were useful in both types of ghost stories. If you wanted to avenge an injustice against someone you could call up the dead to haunt him or her, and at the same time, if you believed you were haunted, you could call upon a necromancer to appease the spirit.

Sorceresses and Witches

The distinction involving intent, beneficial, or malicious, separated traditional female seers from those who were entitled sorceresses. A **sorceress** called upon powers to aid in malicious and harmful deeds. Another difference between sorceresses and more common witches was that sorceresses usually had divine as well as aristocratic lineages. In classical literature, two of the most famous sorceresses were Circe and Medea.

Depending upon the source, Circe was the daughter of either Helios or Hecate, and was famous for her knowledge of herbs and potions. By using a special wand she turned her enemies into animals. In *The Odyssey* she invited members of Odysseus's crew to a dinner, where they drank wine with one of her special potions and were turned into pigs. Warned by Hermes, who gave him a special antidote, Odysseus was able to remain immune to her potions and her charms and eventually freed his men. In later Latin tradition, armed with this story, Aeneas avoided Circe's island on his journey to Rome.

Medea was the daughter of the king of Colchis, a niece of Circe, and a priestess of the goddess Hecate. She married Jason (of the Argonauts fame, *Argonautica*). After she helped her husband through many adventures by using her special skills, one tradition (and a later play by Euripides) claimed that Jason betrayed her with Glauce, the daughter of the king of Corinth. Medea sent Glauce a poisoned dress and crown, and then murdered her own children by Jason as the ultimate revenge.

In Virgil's *Aeneid*, when Dido, the queen of Carthage, was abandoned by Aeneas, she consulted a priestess, who commanded nature and put obstacles in Aeneas's journey to Italy. Dido became identified as a sorceress when she cursed Aeneas and all his descendants, calling upon Juno, Hecate, and the Furies to try and change the fate of Rome. In the second century CE Latin novel by Apuleius, *The Metamorphoses*, the writer traveled to Thessaly to indulge his curiosity about witches. He stayed at the home of a local sorceress, Pamphile. He was turned into an ass when he drank one of her potions. After many adventures as an animal, he was eventually restored by the goddess Isis.

Rome had categories of witches, usually determined by intent and function. Herbalists were often called witches, but were perceived as relatively harmless. A malicious witch was called a *strega*. This was an herbalist who crossed the line from providing beneficial herbs to far more dangerous services. Some of these practitioners were alleged experts in poisons. It was against Roman law to patronize these women because of the assumption that a client (usually female) would be in pursuit of an elixir for an abortion or help in eliminating a husband.

The work of some witches required special items and ingredients to be effective. Objects such as hair, fingernails or clothing were transformed into elements that were utilized in conjunction with special prayers and rituals. Waxen figures, reminiscent of Voodoo rituals, were custom-made and were sold with special instructions. These figures were either pierced or burned to produce pain and destruction.

Horace set the tone in Latin and subsequent medieval literature for witches when he described them dressed in black, with long nails and wild hair consisting of snakes. He claimed that they inhabited cemeteries at night to select their herbs at the full moon and conjured up ghosts after sprinkling the tombs with the blood of sacrificial animals. They were also sometimes accused of abducting and sacrificing small children, a misconception that became associated with witches in the Middle Ages.

-- Summary

- Greeks and Romans communicated with the gods through prayers, hymns, and various forms of divination. Oracles were always consulted for important decisions and were located throughout the Mediterranean world.
- Divination in the form of seers, *augurs*, *haruspices*, oracles, wonder-workers, and necromancers maintained the balance between the community and the divine by determining the will of the gods and attempting to manipulate the divine will for the good of the individual and the community.

-- Suggestions for Further Reading

Bonnechere, P. 2010. "Divination," in *A Companion to Greek Religion*, ed. D. Ogden. pp. 145–159. Wiley-Blackwell. This chapter outlines the various types of divination in the Greek world and includes some literary references in both the early and later periods. The oracles are also covered in depth.

Dickie, M. 2010. "Magic in Classical and Hellenistic Greece," in *A Companion to Greek Religion*, ed. D. Ogden. pp. 357–370. Wiley-Blackwell. This is a good article for distinguishing the nuances of religion vs. magic and includes contemporary views on magic.

North, J. 1990. "Diviners and divination at Rome," in *Pagan Priests*, ed. M. Beard and J. North. pp. 49–71. Duckworth. This chapter details both divination and the various roles of priests in the divination process in Rome.

Scheid, J. 2003. *An Introduction to Roman Religion*, trans. J. Lloyd. Indiana University Press. In addition to the basics of Roman religion, divination aspects are detailed in the role of seers, *augurs*, *pontifices*, and *haruspices*.

THE MYSTERIES

Greek and Roman Religions, First Edition. Rebecca I. Denova.
© 2019 John Wiley & Sons, Inc. Published 2019 by John Wiley & Sons, Inc.

Learning Objectives

After reading this chapter, you will be able to:

- Trace ancient elements of native and fertility cults that developed into distinct concepts and rituals known as the Mysteries.
- Distinguish the differences and similarities between native cults and the Mystery religions.

 "The Mysteries" are a collective term applied by scholars for various native cults that both resembled and differed from the traditional cults of Greece and Rome. The word "mystery" is taken from the Greek **mysterion** and the Latin **mysterium** and indicated that the cults taught secret rites or doctrines that were not available to the general public. The term is also significant in the fact that participants took an oath of secrecy never to reveal the higher rituals of the cult, and with few exceptions, many of the details remain a mystery to this day.

During the past century scholars speculated that the Mysteries were a popular element of the Hellenistic period, focusing on some of the concepts and rites that appealed to individuals rather than the community as a whole. Many theorists saw this as evidence of historical and social changes in the traditional religions that were connected to the spread of Greek ideas after the conquests of Alexander (c. 330 BCE). However, such theories were also combined with reconstructions of the rise of Christianity, which also focused upon the individual. In this sense, it was theorized that studies of the Mysteries were the way in which to explain the attraction of Christianity. Describing Christianity as transformational, it was believed that people were more interested in the Mysteries in this era because they were searching for something missing in the traditional cults.

It is important to recognize that almost all of the various Mystery cults originated in the archaic period, if not earlier, and thus were very ancient by the time of Alexander. Therefore, Mystery cults contained the same elements of traditional cults such as sacrifices, purifications, sacred meals, etc. This does not rule out religious innovations of the Hellenistic period, particularly the infusion of Greek ideas into preexistent local customs. However, we have far more literature that has survived from the later period, which could also account for what appears to be a rise in the popularity of Mystery religions at this time. It is best to treat the Mysteries as both old and new; the Mysteries were part of a continuum of religious concepts that were ancient and yet fluid enough to accept new ideas.

The Mysteries all shared the principle of **initiation**, which was not required in the traditional cults. The initiates (*mystai*) had to undergo a period of training or education concerning the Mystery cult, learning things or being exposed to things in a gradual system of hierarchy or rankings. Such initiations were not exclusive in relation to traditional practices; a person could routinely participate in the traditional cults while simultaneously belonging to a Mystery cult. One did not have to choose between such cults to be a full member. The Mysteries were not competition to the traditional cults but were to be understood as a supplement to one's religious experience.

We explore some of the Mysteries, first the Greek ones and then the Roman ones. There were many more than those that we cite, but these are also the ones for which we have some basic information.

The Eleusinian Mysteries

Perhaps the most famous and well known of the Mysteries, the story of Demeter and Persephone, included the elements of the origins and miracle of agriculture. The Eleusinian Mysteries lasted for thousands of years, with details of the rituals appearing in *The Hymn to Demeter* (c. 600 BCE, if not earlier). The Eleusinian Mysteries were open to all Greeks and eventually to other ethnic groups and Roman citizens. The city of Eleusis was important in the story of Demeter and her search for Persephone. In the disguise of an old woman, Demeter arrived at the well in Eleusis, where the women took pity upon her and tried to amuse her with bawdy stories and jokes. They also suggested that she become a nurse for the children of the local king, Celeus, who took her in.

In gratitude, Demeter decided to make his son Demophon immortal by holding him in the flames of the hearth each night. His mother, Metanira, discovered this and took the child away, horrified that he was being harmed. Demeter then taught the second son, Triptolemus, the secret of the art of agriculture. The rebirth of seeds was symbolic of the rebirth of Persephone when she returned part of the year to be with her mother. Traditional native cults of Demeter were held throughout the year, with the Lesser Mysteries held once a year at spring, and the Greater Mysteries held yearly but more lavishly every four years.

King Celeus was the first participant in the Mysteries and under Peisistratos of Athens the rites became pan-Hellenic and under state control, with pilgrims traveling from across the Mediterranean to participate. Two ancient families of Eleusis, the Eumolpidae and the Kerykes supervised the overall rituals and organization. Two requirements of participation were no blood guilt or not having committed a murder, and initially, not being a barbarian or foreigner (who could not speak Greek). The rites were open to men, women, and slaves. Having taken a vow of secrecy, the participants were categorized as priests, priestesses, initiates, and those were who already members.

The Greater Mysteries began with a proclamation of a truce between all warring parties, and an admonition to protect pilgrims on their way to Eleusis. A procession was led from Athens to Eleusis (where sacred objects from Eleusis had been brought earlier to the city), with everyone walking along "the sacred way." The initiates carried piglets washed in seawater. Everyone participated in an all-night vigil. The sacrifices and all of the rituals were conducted by male priests, allegedly the descendants of the first families of Eleusis.

At the Telesterion, the initiates' hall, the new members went through certain rituals, the details of which remain obscure other than the knowledge that they "had things done," "were shown things," and "heard things said." One source comes from a Christian, Clement of Alexandria, who reports the initiates' ritual formula: "I have fasted; I have drunk the *kykeon*; I have taken from the chest (*kiste*); having done the work, I have placed in the basket (*kalathos*), and from the basket into the chest" (*Exhortation to the Greeks*, 2.21). Initiates carried chests and baskets, although we are not sure what they contained. Again, the source from Clement claims that the baskets contained anything from sacred cakes, a serpent, pomegranates, to perhaps models of male and female genitalia. The special drink, the **kykeon**, remains a subject of debate among scholars, with some suggesting a type of psychedelic drug that would result in opening the subject to ecstatic experiences.

Following the initiation, all-night dancing and feasting celebrated the completion of the rituals, perhaps as a rebirth of the individual. New members honored the dead by pouring libations into the ground. In theory, the punishment for revealing any of the rituals was death. This was taken seriously and hence our limited information about the Eleusinian Mysteries. These Mysteries had an honored and esteemed reputation, not only throughout Greece, but throughout the Roman Empire. (See the box "Cicero's Acclamation of the Benefits of the Eleusinian Mysteries.")

Cicero's Acclamation of the Benefits of the Eleusinian Mysteries

The Roman advocate Cicero (106–43 BCE) was famous for his rhetorical style in several of Rome's most famous trials, and rose up through the ranks to become consul. But he also wrote treatises on many subjects, and this included Roman traditional religion as well as the various cults in Rome during the period of the late Republic. While traveling in Greece, he took advantage of the opportunity to become an initiate of the Eleusinian Mysteries:

For among the many excellent and indeed divine institutions which your Athens has brought forth and contributed to human life, none, in my opinion, is better than those mysteries. For by their means we have been brought out of our barbarous and savage mode of life and educated and refined to a state of civilization; and as the rites are called "initiations," so in very truth we have learned from them the beginnings of life, and have gained the power not only to live happily, but also to die with a better hope.

(*Laws* II, xiv, 36)

Bona Dea

A cult in Italy that involved similar elements of the Mysteries of Demeter was that of Bona Dea, "the Good Goddess." She was associated with female fertility, modesty, healing, and was a protector of the Roman state. According to tradition, she was brought to Rome from Magna Graecia in the early

Republic and presented with a temple on the Aventine Hill. Various stories claim that she was the wife, sister, or daughter of Faunus and thus associated with Fauna, the female counterpart, who was known for her prophetic ability. Bona Dea also had aspects of Ops, Magna Mater, and Ceres. Bona Dea's temple on the Aventine was unique in Rome for being surrounded by a wall. The temple precincts were also a home for snakes, and there were rooms for the storage and use of healing herbs and medicines that were dispensed by her female priests.

The goddess was often portrayed with a cornucopia, a sign of plenty, in one hand, and a snake feeding from a bowl in the other. The snake always represented healing and regenerative powers. Like Demeter, the worship of Bona Dea was open to all men and women, all classes, freedmen and freedwomen, and slaves. However, her true or secret name was only revealed to women. She was a patroness of the plebeians in Rome, where her cult was supervised by the Vestal Virgins. In the other cities and provinces, matron priestesses served in her temples and shrines. There were two major festivals to Bona Dea in Rome. The public festival was held on the Aventine on May 1, which connected it with other mother-goddess festivals.

The private festival was the one that involved Mysteries. Nocturnal rituals were conducted by female initiates and female priestesses. There was a sacrifice of a sow, music, dancing, feasting, and wine-drinking. The wine was euphemistically referred to as "milk," and served from "honey pots." A second festival was held in winter, when the image of the goddess and a snake was honored with offerings of all the growing plants, a sacrificed sow, and libations of wine, to officially put the goddess to sleep. Some scholars have claimed that the euphemisms of milk and honey refer to transformative experiences involved in the rituals, but we do not have enough information about the sacred rites. Bona Dea became part of Imperial ideology during the reign of Augustus when his wife Livia became a major patron for the festivals.

The Mysteries of Dionysus

The worship of Dionysus, like Demeter, was an ancient traditional cult. His worship contained elements that evolved into one of the Mysteries. In one of his myths, Dionysus came to Athens and taught Icarus the art of making wine, so that he was also known as Dionysus Eleuthereus, the "one who sets free." The association with wine (and its resulting behavior) remained a constant in his Mysteries, as it also remained a source of inspiration for the drama festivals in Athens. Worshippers reached a state of ecstasy (**ekstasis**), or "standing outside of oneself." This state could also be reached through dance and song, major elements of the Dionysian Mysteries. An additional element of the Dionysus rituals was that of catharsis, or a cleansing of the emotions. An analogy is found at the relief one feels after "a good cry."

The origins of the Mysteries remain obscure, with Thrace, Phrygia, and even Libya suggested as the homeland for the rituals. The idea that Dionysus was a late, foreign god was derived from the stories that described him moving into established city-states and demanding worship. Dionysus wasn't originally listed in some of the lists of the Olympians, and so some scholars claimed that this reflects his lateness as well as his coming from outside. However, his name appears on a Mycenaean tablet, which dates his cult to early Greece. Dionysus's rites became associated with ancient wine cults and festivals. The effects of wine consumption were often explained as possession by the god. This possession was a characteristic of the cult and understood as just "letting go." Because all classes and sexes participated, it was often understood as a psychological outlet for the social and class restrictions of Greek and Roman culture, as well as a return to nature.

An element of the Mysteries of Dionysus was that of **katabasis** (descent). This referred to a descent to Hades. Returns were rare as mortals never escaped death, but some gods did travel there and return. There were several stories of the descent and return of Dionysus. He was restored to life after he was ripped to shreds by the Titans on Hera's orders, and he also descended to Hades to rescue Hephaestus, Ariadne, and Semele, his mother. Such stories promoted the idea of death and rebirth for the participants of the cult. What happened individually to the initiates in their descent remains undocumented.

In Greece the Dionysian rituals for men often took place in caves and may have involved stories of hidden things sought and returned (at least symbolically), drinking of sacred wine, being shown secret things (in a **liknon** or sacred basket), and receiving their **thyrsos**. In the rituals for women, the initiate was sometimes dressed and prepared as Dionysus's bride, Ariadne. According to some information, the earliest of the "things shown" in the liknon was a goat's penis, which later became a wooden phallus. In the city of Pompeii, there is a house known as the "Villa of the Mysteries," which depicts the Romanized form of the cult (Figure IX.1). In one of the panels, the initiate is being whipped by Eros, and so flagellation may have been a standard part of the initiation, whose purpose, again, remains unknown.

A special festival known as the Tristeria was held on Mount Parnassus and celebrated Dionysus's return from Hades. The rituals were led by the Maenads in an ecstatic state in which they hunted and tore apart and ate wild animals. (According to some men, they hunted humans, but this cannot be verified.) Nymphs, known as *Thyiades* ("ravers") celebrated with the satyrs. This combination gave the Dionysus cult an infamous reputation, in the ancient world as well as the modern.

Orpheus and the Orphic Mysteries

Associated with the Mysteries of Dionysus were the Mysteries of the cult of Orpheus. Orpheus was a musician and poet who had the ability to charm all with

Figure IX.1 Panel from the Villa of the Mysteries, Pompeii. *Source:* Alinari/Alinari Archives, Florence. Reproduced with the permission of Ministero per i Beni e le Attività Culturali/ Alinari via Getty Images.

his wonderful music (even stones). He was credited with the Orphic Hymns, and some of his shrines were oracle sites. He was allegedly the son of a Thracian king and the Muse Calliope. According to one tradition, he accompanied Jason and the Argonauts on their quest for the Golden Fleece. The basic myth relates the story of his attempt to rescue his dead bride, Eurydice, from Hades.

According to the later story by Virgil, on the wedding day of Orpheus and Eurydice, Eurydice was attacked by a satyr as she walked through some reeds. Running away, she stepped into a nest of snakes and was fatally bitten. On the advice of the gods, Orpheus traveled to Hades in an effort to use his music to soften the hearts of Hades and Persephone. They permitted Orpheus to take Eurydice with him back to the land of the living on the condition that he not look back at her until they had reached the sunlight. However, in his anticipation, the moment that he saw the doorway, he looked back and she returned forever to Hades. Later traditions claimed that Orpheus scorned women, resulting in some maenads tearing him apart in their rituals. His lyre was placed in the heavens by the Muses. His soul was reunited with Eurydice in Hades.

The Orphic Mysteries were for the philosophically inclined and are described as ascetic and mystical. ***Askesis***, or "discipline," meant being committed to a lifestyle that usually shunned the normal social conventions and behavior, and was known as "the Orphic way of life." This asceticism included giving up material possessions, refusing to eat meat, eggs, and beans, not drinking wine, and abstaining from sexual intercourse. There was a hierarchy of priests (often referred to as "beggar-priests"), with such titles as "leader of the sacrifices," "leader of prayers," "the hymn singer," and a "cowherd."

Mysticism is the term applied to those who seek both higher knowledge of the divine and ultimate spiritual union with a particular god. All religions have mystical elements and this idea for ancient Greece was said to have been introduced by the school of Pythagoras, who also may have participated in Orphic rites. Mystics were always ascetic, dismissing material possessions and social conventions in their belief that these were obstacles to contemplation by the believer and a self-surrender to the divine.

The discovery of inscribed gold tablets from tombs in Thurii, Crete, and Thessaly contain elements important to the Orphic Mysteries as well as those of Dionysus and perhaps some Egyptian cults. These tablets were inscribed and then rolled or placed in a capsule and either placed around the neck of the dead person, or in the coffin/sarcophagus. They contain instructions on how to navigate the transition to the afterlife, as well as the appropriate responses when standing before judges in the underworld and before Persephone.

Bacchus

The Roman equivalent of Dionysus, Bacchus had both public cults and Mysteries. What little we know of the Bacchus Mysteries comes from the story of the scandal reported by Livy that took place in 186 BCE. Bacchus rituals were included in the Liberalia, but we do not know if there were elements of any Mystery concepts of Liber that were adopted. The private Mystery cult most likely was very similar to the Mysteries of Dionysus.

The Mysteries of Cybele, the Great Mother

Cybele was a very ancient mother goddess, who most likely originated in ancient Anatolia in the region of Phrygia. The cult of Cybele is one of the oldest attested religions in the Mediterranean area, with Stone Age sculptures of her found at the ancient site of Catal Huyuk, which is over six thousand years old. Her cult was absorbed by Greek colonists in the region and spread to the islands of the Aegean, Magna Graecia in southern Italy, and other areas of the Mediterranean in the sixth century BCE. She shared features with Rhea, Minoan goddesses, and

Figure IX.2 Statue of Cybele. *Source:* FOR ALAN/Alamy Stock Photo.

Demeter. Her areas of protection included mountains, town and city walls, nature, and wild animals. Her favorite animal was the lion and she was most often portrayed with lions at her feet (Figure IX.2).

The main shrine at Pessinos had an image of Cybele in the form of a piece of black stone which was most likely a small meteor. Pessinos was ruled by priest-kings in dynastic succession through adoption, and they had reputations as international diplomats. In 189 BCE, the high-priest predicted a victory for Rome over the Galatians, and in 103 BCE one of their priests traveled to Rome to address the Senate. The attributes placed Cybele in a position of mediator between the wilds of nature and civilization. Her image in funeral art was perhaps as a mediator between the boundary of the living and the dead.

At the end of the fifth century BCE, a *metroon* (a temple to a mother goddess) was dedicated to Cybele in the city of Athens. According to the story, one of her priests had been killed and Cybele punished the city with a plague. To appease her, the cult was introduced with an appropriate temple, which also became the location of the Athenian archives (and thus under her protection). A statue of Cybele was also placed in the *agora*.

Cybele's public cult was similar to that of Dionysus (and often combined with his festivals). They both were portrayed driving chariots, followed by ecstatic followers with music and frenetic "Phrygian dancing" (named after this central province in Anatolia). Cybele's images included the *tympanon* or a hand drum, similar to a tambourine.

The private cult of the Mysteries of Cybele was most likely derived from the only major myths associated with her that have survived. These involved the story of Attis, who, according to different versions, was sometimes the son or sometimes the lover of Cybele. Attis may also have been an ancient independent god of vegetation. The myths are not only complicated but they contain contradictions and most of our sources are very late, including some from later Christians.

According to one of the traditions, Cybele rejected the advances of Zeus, so he spilled his semen on her while she slept. Cybele then gave birth to Agdistis, a hermaphroditic (both sexes) demon whom the gods feared. Because of this fear, they castrated him (removed his testicles), and when the blood from this attack fell to the ground, an almond tree sprang up. The almond tree then produced a daughter, Nana, who ate the fruit of the tree. She became pregnant and delivered a son, Attis, whom she immediately exposed on a hillside. Shepherds rescued and raised him and he was so beautiful that Cybele fell in love with him.

When Attis grew older he fell in love with the daughter of the king of Pessinos. In her jealousy Cybele drove Attis crazy, which resulted in his self-castration and bleeding to death. Another story had Zeus sending a wild boar to kill Attis in his jealousy. In either case, both regretted Attis's death and Zeus helped Cybele to resurrect him. This death and resurrection became a theme of the death and rebirth aspect of Cybele's Mysteries.

The story also explains the unique priesthood of Cybele, that of eunuchs, known as **galli** in Rome (see below). According to tradition, once a year in remembrance of Attis, her priests and devotees performed purification rituals that included self-castration. After mourning for three days, Attis's resurrection was celebrated with wild dancing and feasting. While the cult of Cybele spread throughout the Mediterranean, it always maintained an element of foreignness and there was a negative attitude toward its rituals. Castration went completely against the concepts of male virility and the religious duty to produce offspring.

An iconic symbol associated with Cybele and Attis was the "Phrygian cap," a soft conical cap with the top pulled forward. It was native to some Anatolian cultures, including Phrygia. Because it resembled the *pileus*, or the felt cap worn by manumitted slaves in Rome, the two became synonymous as a symbol of freedom. In vase paintings and sculpture, Attis is commonly shown wearing the cap, and it became adopted by Rome's plebeians as a symbol of liberty. It was also a symbol for the cult of Mithras (see below).

The Mysteries of Magna Mater

Most of our surviving information for Cybele in Italy and Rome comes from Roman sources on the cult of Magna Mater or "great mother," as she was known there. Rome officially adopted her cult during a crisis in the Second Punic War (218–201 BCE). According to the story, several major defeats by the Carthaginian general Hannibal (Lake Trasimene in 217 BCE and Cannae in 216 BCE) had left Rome dangerously short of men when Hannibal laid siege to Rome itself. Rome then experienced prodigies that included a failed harvest and a meteor shower. The priests of Rome consulted the Sibylline Books. Their interpretation of the oracles claimed that the Great Goddess of Pessinos should be invited to take up residence (and cult) in the city, where she would protect the residents from both famine and the scourge of Hannibal.

On the way to obtain the black stone, the delegation from Rome stopped at the Oracle of Delphi, which confirmed the Oracle of the Sibyls. But as the ship bearing the stone sailed up the Tiber, it appeared to be on the brink of sinking. Claudia Quinta (of the ancient family of the Claudians), whose chastity had been suspect up to this point, reached out and grabbed the mooring rope, stabilizing the ship, saving the cult object, and restoring her reputation. Meanwhile, the oracles were fulfilled in that Hannibal gave up the siege. The temple to Magna Mater was built on the Palatine Hill next to the cave that sheltered Romulus and Remus.

For many Romans the establishment of the cult of Magna Mater in their city may have been a mixed blessing. On the one hand, her presence meant the salvation of the city (and something that would last until the year 410 CE when Alaric the Goth conquered Rome). As she was considered the dominant goddess of Ilium or Troy, many patricians welcomed her to the city that was founded by a descendant of Troy, Aeneas. On the other hand, Rome had imported what many considered a very un-Roman form of worship. The cult had foreign rituals that included possession, but the *galli* (her priests) dressed in women's clothes, wigs, and makeup and participated in "Gallic rites" of castration. As such, any Roman citizen was forbidden to become a *gallus*, as something inherently effeminizing and against the traditional role of Roman males. Augustus later permitted it in the early Empire.

As with other Mysteries, there was both a public side and a private side to the worship of Magna Mater. The entire city of Rome participated each April in the annual Megalesian Games, dedicated to Magna Mater by the Plebeian Aediles. This was the only time that the Roman public had any contact with the *galli*. They could be heard on the Palatine Hill, loudly bewailing their grief for Attis during the days of mourning. This was followed by *galli*-led adherents processing through the streets in hilarity at the restoration of Attis, with loud singing, flutes, banging of drums, and Phrygian dancing. There were week-long religious plays and chariot races in the Circus Maximus. The *spina*, the central structure of the racetrack, held a statue of Magna Mater seated on a lion. On the "day of blood," the priests of Magna Mater slashed themselves in frenzy and initiates performed the rite of self-castration. In the Imperial period, the sacred stone and ritual implements were carried in procession and washed in the Tiber, followed by rejoicing at the resurrection of Attis.

Because of the restrictions on self-castration, the number of initiates was limited to non-citizens. However, believers could participate through the ceremony known as the ***taurobolium*** (a bull sacrifice) and the *criobolium* (a ram sacrifice). The *taurobolium* had been practiced in other areas of the eastern Mediterranean, where the blood of the bull (an ancient symbol of fertility) brought rain and gave life to grain, and held other regenerative powers. *Tauroboliums* were performed for the Senate, the people of Rome, and the Imperial family.

We have very little information on the transformational nature of the experiences of the initiates in the cult of Magna Mater. We can assume that initiates experienced some of the same religious insights found in the other Mysteries, and where the focus on Attis would have identified them as being "reborn."

The Cult of Mithras

Sometimes referred to as Mithraism by modern scholars, the cult of Mithras, or "the Mithraic Mysteries," became a popular cult in the Roman Empire, particularly for the legions of Rome. The cult is widely attested in hundreds of archaeological sites throughout the Western Empire. Mithras was a divinity in the state cult of Persia, Zoroastrianism. He was a god of contracts and oaths, a protector of truth, a guardian of cattle, harvests, and water. He was also one of the three judges at the Bridge that all souls had to cross after death. Persian sources for Mithras stem from "The Hymn to Mithras" in the *Avesta*, or sacred scriptures of Zoroaster. But we have very little information on a cult of Mithras in Persia itself.

The Roman writer Plutarch (46–127 CE) claimed that the cult was practiced by the Cilician pirates of the eastern Mediterranean, where they participated in secret mysteries. Dio Cassius (c. 155–235 CE) credited the introduction of the rites to Rome with a visit by a king of Armenia, Tiridates I, during the reign of Nero in the first century CE. While scholars continue to debate the origins of the cult, nevertheless most agree that it was a late addition to Roman religion.

It is mainly from the visual remains of the temples (**mithraea**), monuments, and artifacts that we can attempt to reconstruct the complex ideas of the worship of Mithras, as there are no sacred texts that have survived, and initiates swore an oath of secrecy.

The *mithraea* were either constructed as an underground cavern or from a natural cave, although basements of buildings were also utilized. The *mithraeum* underneath the Basilica of San Clemente in Rome was attached to an *insula*, or apartment building. Each *mithraeum* contained a sculpted image of Mithras slaughtering a bull, known as the **tauroctony**. Sometimes he was portrayed in images of his birth from a rock, or banqueting. The most common image had Mithras wearing the Phrygian cap and looking over his shoulder at the sun god, Sol, as he slaughtered the bull. The pictures include a raven, a dog, a snake, and a scorpion. Two other characters, Cautes and Cautopates, bear torches and are sometimes shown as shepherds and stand at either side. One holds a torch up, while the other holds it down, perhaps symbolizing the rising and setting sun.

These images were the central focus, while altars dedicated by initiates are found in niches. The *mithraea* contained benches for communal feasting, mirroring a banquet scene of Mithras and Sol.

As far as we know, there were no public rituals associated with Mithras as it was specifically limited to initiates and members. According to some traditions the celebration of the New Year and the birthday of Mithras took place on December 25. But other celebrations took place on that day as well, including the Natalis Invicti (the birthday of the invincible sun), a later Imperial celebration. We do know that prayers were offered to the sun three times a day and Sunday was sacred.

Initiates had grades, or levels of initiation. (These are often compared to degrees in modern Freemasonry.) There were seven grades, each with symbols, and under the protection of a tutelary deity (see Table IX.1). Some *mithraea* contained plaques listing the grades of the initiates. At these different levels, initiates had to undergo tests, both physical and mental. The physical ordeals (perhaps in an "ordeal pit") may have involved exposure to heat and cold, or threats of physical harm. We have very little information on the nature or content of the questions asked or the successful answers.

Once an initiate reached the level of *Pater*, he was welcomed with a handshake from the senior officers (like the one between Mithras and Sol) and more information was conveyed to him. This was followed by a banquet. The cult of Mithras was popular with the military, but also merchants and bureaucrats. During the revival of native cults under the emperor Julian in the mid-fourth century, many aristocrats became initiated. The philosopher Porphyry mentioned female initiates, but many scholars debate if that was realistic.

There is information that ethical standards had to be met by the initiates, with ritual purity concerns and behavior that did not bring harm. Late literature refers to "commandments of Mithras," and a second-century Church Father, Tertullian, stated that members of the cult were excused from wearing celebratory headgear, because initiates of Mithras were taught to refuse an offered crown, as only Mithras ruled. Over the centuries, the *taurobolium* of Magna Mater and the *tauroctony* of the Mithras Cult may have become confused with the similarities of a bull sacrifice. This is why many claim that Mithras initiates

Degrees	Symbols	Deity
Corax (raven)	Beaker, caduceus	Mercury
Nymphus (bridesman)	Lamp, bell, diadem	Venus
Miles (soldier)	Helmet, lance, breastplate	Mars
Leo (lion)	Sistrum, thunderbolts	Jupiter
Perses (Persian)	Phrygian cap, sickle	Luna
Heliodromus (sun-runner)	Torch, Helios whip	Sol
Pater (father)	Miter, shepherd's staff, ring, cape, jeweled robe	Saturn

Table IX.1 Degrees of initiation in the cult of Mithras

underwent the *taurobolium* ritual. However, evidence has not been discovered of *taurobolium* pits in the excavations of Mithras temples or meeting places, and in fact, there hardly appears to be room for one in their small caverns.

Because of the complete absence of narratives, mythology, or liturgy, much of the cult of Mithras remains unknown. As with other Mysteries, we can only speculate on the transformative nature of the experience of the initiate. At the same time, we remain in the dark about the nature of the concepts of birth and rebirth and the afterlife, usually associated with Mysteries, although on the theoretical level, the role of the sun (rising and dying and rising again) was most likely symbolic of hope in the afterlife.

The Mysteries of Isis, Osiris, and Serapis

The Egyptian cults of Isis and Osiris arose in ancient Egypt and spread dramatically in the Hellenistic Age after the conquests of Alexander the Great (330 BCE). For thousands of years the Egyptians participated in the combined worship of Isis and her husband, Osiris, in what became standard Egyptian religious worship as well as the sanctification of concepts of the afterlife. Sometimes Isis was worshipped in her own right and sometimes in combination with Osiris.

The story of Osiris and Isis has come down as one of the most ancient and endearing love stories of the ancient world. Osiris was credited with being the first pharaoh of Egypt. He was married to his sister Isis (a traditional social convention for the rulers of Egypt). His brother Seth was jealous and devised a way to take over power. He held a party where he presented a beautiful box (a coffin) and challenged all to try and lie down in it; the one who fit would get the box as a prize. Of course, only Osiris fit (it was designed for him) and as soon as he lay down, Seth nailed the coffin shut and sent it down the Nile to the sea. It landed in Byblos (modern Lebanon), where the local king had it set in the base of a giant tree.

Osiris's wife Isis then began a long journey to seek out the coffin, finding it at Byblos and talking the king into letting her return with it. As she opened the box, Seth saw her and managed to take the body again and cut it into 14 pieces, which he distributed throughout Egypt (in the 14 Nomes, or districts of the country). Isis began another journey, this time finding the pieces and restoring them through magic. This became the resurrection of Osiris, who then took his honored place as the king of the dead. Isis also reconstructed the penis (the only body part still missing) and was able to impregnate herself with their son, Horus. Seth, in his anger, began attacking Horus and their battles became the substance of several different myths. At last the gods settled the dispute, elevating Horus as the successor to Osiris on earth. Thereafter, every pharaoh was the manifestation of Horus while he ruled, and then became identified with Osiris upon his death.

For centuries, Egyptians made pilgrimages to the sites associated with the buried parts of Osiris, especially at the city of Abydos where periodic "passion plays" were performed, recreating the story of Osiris and Isis. Perhaps even earlier than the emergence of these stories, Osiris was also a god of fertility. He was most often portrayed in mummy wrappings, with his face either green or black (the black land of the fertile Nile valley). He also served as the judge of the dead when all had to review their lives and confess their shortcomings.

Isis was a goddess of fertility, women, motherhood, children, nature, and magic. As the mother of Horus, she was also a protector of the house of the ruling pharaoh. She was a friend to all, rich and poor, aristocrats, and artisans. In her role in the story of the resurrection of her husband, she was also essential for protection in the afterlife. As the mother of Horus, she was the source of the four sons of Horus, the deities who protected the canopic jars that contained the mummified organs of the dead. Her cult was centered in an Iseum, such as the one at Philae, where she received the standard offerings. Her priests became known for healing and prophecy.

Greek ideas concerning Isis coincided with the description by Herodotus (fifth century BCE), who compared her to Demeter and referred to the worship of Isis as the "Egyptian Mysteries." After the Hellenization of Egypt by Alexander the Great, his successors, the Ptolemies, granted her the title of Queen of Heaven and she absorbed the attributes of Astarte (Mesopotamian) and Aphrodite. Isis was worshipped on Delos, at Delphi, Eleusis, Athens, and the harbor cities, where she was invoked by sailors for safe voyages. The festival in her honor was the Navigium Isidis ("vessel of Isis"). The story of Isis and Osiris was made popular by the Greco-Roman writer Plutarch (46–120 CE), who ironically left us the most complete and detailed story that far surpasses any of the ancient Egyptian versions discovered so far.

There were many temples to Isis in Rome and throughout Italy, although worship was temporarily suspended during Octavian's war with Anthony, when Cleopatra identified herself with the goddess. Her worship was restored and enhanced by Octavian at the conclusion of that war, and her cult spread as far away as Britain. A common portrayal of Isis had her seated, with the child Horus on her lap (Figure IX.3). This icon was later absorbed into Christianity as the Madonna, or Mary with the baby Jesus.

In the second century, the Roman writer Apuleius created an adventure novel that contained religious themes and experiences. In *The Golden Ass* (also known as *Metamorphoses*), the hero of the story is magically turned into an ass, but finds salvation and redemption through Isis, who answers his prayers when he undergoes initiation into her Mysteries (see the box "Isis Responds to Prayer").

According to the novel (as well as the description of her rites by the writer Pausanias), initiates were chosen by the goddess when she appeared to them in a dream. The details of the rituals were read to initiates from a book with unknown letters (hieroglyphics?). Initiates confessed their sins, were ritually purified with water, and had to abstain from meat and wine for 10 days. Gifts were given by other members of the cult and then the initiate descended into

Figure IX.3   Statue of Isis and Horus. *Source*: Ivy Close Images/Alamy Stock Photo.

an underground part of the temple. What happened next was an experience of journeying through the underworld as well as the heavens and meeting the gods of each. However, Apuleius reminds his readers that he can never reveal the details. When the initiate emerged, he was dressed in an elaborate cloak and presented to his fellow believers. This was followed by a banquet. He underwent more initiations in Rome, including one to Osiris, who appeared to him in a vision. He mentions several times the fees that were required for each initiation.

What actually happened to Apuleius (or the hero in the story)

Isis Responds to Prayer

"You see me here, Lucius, in answer to your prayer. I am nature, the universal Mother, mistress of all the elements, primordial child of time, sovereign of all things spiritual, queen of the dead, queen of the ocean, queen also of the immortals, the single manifestation of all gods and goddesses that are, my nod governs the shining heights of Heavens, the wholesome sea breezes. Though I am worshipped in many aspects, known by countless names … the Egyptians who excel in ancient learning and worship call me by my true name … Queen Isis" (*The Golden Ass*).

remains open to speculation. The symbolism of descent and the experience of both the underworld and the heavens and meeting the gods would have brought the believer into an event that placed him or her beyond the physical world, to that of the divine. His third initiation to the cult of Osiris in Rome shows the continued connection between Isis and Osiris. The fact that Osiris came to dominate the last experience emphasizes the belief that the initiate would be better prepared for the afterlife when it came.

Serapis

After the conquest of Egypt by Alexander, his successors, beginning with Ptolemy I Soter, created a new form of a god that they thought would help to reconcile Egyptians with Macedonian (Greek) rule. However, by tradition, people did not just create brand new gods. Ptolemy claimed that the god Serapis already existed in Anatolia and that he was instructed in a dream to bring a statue of the god to Alexandria. Other sources claim that he was a local god in the original fishing village of Rhakotis, now part of the new city of Alexandria.

Be that as it may, the name Serapis included the ancient Egyptian cult of the Apis bulls, combined with a god of the underworld who was a combination of Osiris and Hades (or Pluto in the Roman terminology). His statue was of a seated god with long hair and beard, with a basket on his head (a *modius*, used to measure grain). He held a scepter to demonstrate his rule, and at his feet was the dog Cerberus, the guardian to the entrance of Hades. A snake at his feet symbolized the *uraeus*, the traditional protective sign of rule in Egypt.

The main cult temples, **serapeums**, became the traditional centers for the worship of Serapis (Osiris + Apis or Aser-hapy), and one of the largest ones was built in Alexandria. This temple was famous for its flying chariots and doors that mysteriously flew open. Many of these items were most likely invented at the museum complex in Alexandria. The *serapeum* sites continued the older Apis bull traditions of ancient Egypt, with catacombs that contained mummified bulls, cats, birds, dogs, and baboons. These were popular votive offerings left by pilgrims and numbered in the thousands.

A large and popular cult center was also located at Canopus in the Nile delta. Here Isis was also worshipped as the consort of Serapis, along with their son, now associated with Anubis, and Hermes. This combination contributed to the interest in Hermes Trismegistus (Thoth and Hermes), as the source of esoteric knowledge. These two deities were associated with writing and wisdom. Temples to Serapis were also built in Pergamon, Ephesus, and Miletus.

In Rome a section of the city was named Isis et Serapis because of the dominance of their temple there, built in the first century BCE. The emperor Caligula (37–41 CE) built another temple on the Campus Martius. Vespasian (69–81 CE) credited Isis (and her consort) with his victory on becoming emperor. The emperor Hadrian (117–138 CE) built one at his villa near Tiber and he also portrayed Serapis with himself on his coinage. Caracalla (196–217 CE) built another one on the Quirinal Hill. *Serapeums* were located throughout the Roman Empire. However, we have very little information on the Mystery aspects of the Serapis cult in relation to initiates.

The Mysteries and the Afterlife

The nature of the gods and goddesses who were worshipped in some of the various Mystery cults shared the elements of dying and rising deities. These aspects either arose from their original myths or were part of the age-old rituals of their traditional worship. Thus the Mysteries included the benefit of an easier transition from death to the afterlife, or even a guarantee of a blessed afterlife. While most Greeks and Romans believed in some form of existence after death, no one could be absolutely sure. This may be one explanation for the popularity of Mysteries. With the rise of the Christian teaching on resurrection and a blessed afterlife, participants of the Mysteries may have found an affinity in this element of the new religion.

However, too strong an emphasis on the afterlife as the main focus of the Mysteries may be exaggerated. From the little concerning the initiations and the beliefs that have survived, we find an equal emphasis on appeals to benefits in the here and now. People prayed for good health, business success, healthy children, and success in war. The two purposes could exist simultaneously. Overall, the various Mystery cults can be understood as both ancient and innovative. They never replaced the traditional cults, as one could be an initiate without having to cease activity in the regular cults.

Summary

- While containing many basic elements of traditional cults, the Mysteries served as supplements to these practices and provided flexibility and choice among the cults. Many individuals enjoyed an expanded experience with the divine through these practices.
- The differences and the similarities between the ancient cults and the Mysteries indicate continuity of tradition as well as innovative ideas in the expansion of Mystery cults in the Hellenistic period.

Suggestions for Further Reading

Bowden, H. 2010. *Mystery Cults of the Ancient World*. Princeton University Press. This book presents both archaeological as well as textual evidence of the Mysteries and particularly focuses on the goddesses.

Burkert, W. 1989. *Ancient Mystery Cults*. Harvard University Press. Burkert is one of the foremost experts on ancient religion and in this text he also includes scholarly theory of the role of the Mysteries.

Meyer, M. ed. 1987. *The Ancient Mysteries: A Sourcebook of Sacred Texts*. University of Pennsylvania Press. This book includes short summaries of the various Mysteries and excerpts from the ancient sources.

Pomeroy, S. B. 1975. *Goddesses, Whores, Wives, and Slaves: Women in Classical Antiquity*. Schocken. Focusing on the different classes of the ancient world, this book provides the sources for women's culture and religious beliefs, with prayers to some of the goddesses of the Mysteries.

DEATH AND THE AFTERLIFE: FUNERAL RITES AND FUNERAL GAMES

Greek and Roman Religions, First Edition. Rebecca I. Denova.
© 2019 John Wiley & Sons, Inc. Published 2019 by John Wiley & Sons, Inc.

Learning Objectives

After reading this chapter, you will be able to:

- Identify the various historical, cultural, and religious origins of beliefs in the afterlife, disposal of the dead, and funeral rituals in ancient Mediterranean culture.
- Analyze the social context and function of specific beliefs in the afterlife and funeral rites as a reflection of social values, economic class, and projections of delayed social justice.

 Approximately 100 000 years ago, people began burying the dead together with tools, weapons, decorated artifacts, and jars of food. Most scholars agree that these practices demonstrated a belief that there was another form of existence after death; the grave items would be useful. Generally, a belief in an afterlife refers to specific beliefs that a person continues to exist in some form, either in a disembodied personal essence (soul), or a combination of soul with a new or reconstituted physical body. A belief in an afterlife also assumes a location for this existence outside the realm of earthly life. In connecting the ancient world to the modern, we find belief in an afterlife and funeral rituals to be one of the most conservative elements in history, changing very little over the centuries.

Ancient Concepts of the Afterlife

Ancient civilizations perceived a tripartite universe, with the heavens above, the earth in the middle, and the underworld below. With very few exceptions, Heaven remained the realm of the gods. The one common element shared by all cultures was the realization that death for humans was inevitable. It became difficult to believe that the human person (and personality) could simply be annihilated. In dreams, the dead appeared alive. The idea began to emerge that the dead still existed in some form, and that the dead resided in a separate place. Often deemed the netherworld or the underworld, this place was located under the earth and originally it was a neutral place – neither good nor bad.

We saw that the ancient Mesopotamians had a pessimistic view of death and the underworld. In one of their myths, they claimed that the gods created death in order to control humans and control the population of the earth. In *Irkalla*, their "land of no return," the dead suffered in agony, eating clay, and were eternally thirsty. Because they did exist, the unhappy dead could find ways to return to earth as demons. Therefore the dead spirits had to be placated with food and drink offerings. All the dead went to *Irkalla*, including kings and heroes. But the difference between kings and heroes and the common dead was that the former did not suffer like everyone else due to the plentitude of offerings that continued long after they were dead. These offerings demonstrated that the dead were *remembered* and it was the memory of the name that gave one a sense of eternal life.

The best way to seek honor and fame was on the battlefield; death in battle guaranteed remembrance. Kings did not necessarily have to die in battle, but their funeral rites were more elaborate than those of commoners. The king's funeral included long lists of genealogies, connecting him to dead ancestors. According to the Sumerians, even the honored dead did not go to a heavenly resting place. Heaven (the sky, or a paradise known as *Dilmun*) remained the abode of the gods. Many of these ideas concerning the afterlife influenced the subsequent empires in Mesopotamia as well as neighboring cultures.

In Egypt, death was viewed more optimistically as another phase of the life cycle of birth, death, and rebirth. In the Old Kingdom (2600–2100 BCE) only the Pharaoh had access to an afterlife due to his nature as a living manifestation of divinity. By the Middle Kingdom (c. 2000–1700 BCE) an afterlife was available to anyone who could afford the process (with mummification, funeral rites, and ritual texts). This period also saw an increase in the popularity of the Osiris cult, particularly in his role as Lord and Judge of the Dead.

The emphasis on Osiris as Judge of the Dead is directly related to a new type of literature in the Middle Kingdom known collectively as Admonition Texts. Immediately preceding the Middle Kingdom, Egypt suffered a series of catastrophes, which may have included foreign invasion, plague, famine, and civil wars. Admonition texts are most often addressed by a father to a son and upheld the moral values of society. The child is admonished to lead a good and pious life and to avoid the pitfalls of evil deeds. Connected now to the Negative Confessions in Osiris's Hall of Judgment, one's deeds (and sins) in this life determined the type of existence in the next life. In these texts, we have some of the earliest indications that views of the afterlife reflect a social and historical context with elements of social justice.

Although the traditions are older, by the New Kingdom (1500–1000 BCE) those who could afford it could obtain a copy of the *Book of Going Forth into Life* (popularly known as the *Book of the Dead*). It provided the spells and passwords needed to get through the 42 gates of Duat, the underworld. Each gate was guarded by a dangerous force, "flesh-eater," or "slayer."

Once they passed through all the gates, the dead reached the Hall of Judgment. Osiris sat in judgment as the person's heart was weighed on a scale against the feather of Ma'at. The person recited the Negative Confessions, a long list of evil things the dead person did *not* do: "I have not committed robbery with violence," "I have not stolen," etc. Scholars speculate that the Negative Confessions may have been a source for the later Ten Commandments of the Hebrew Scriptures.

If the scales were perfectly balanced, the person was rewarded with a new existence in the Field of Reeds, an Eden-like Egypt. If the scales tipped, he or she was eaten by Ammit, a hybrid monster (lion, hippopotamus, and crocodile), and thus annihilated by a second death. The person and his name ceased to exist, which was the worst thing that could happen to an Egyptian. The idea that one's deeds in life would be judged after death eventually became an essential part of beliefs about the afterlife in neighboring cultures, including Greece and Rome.

To help them enjoy a second life, Egyptians were famous for filling their tombs with everything they would need or want. As death was merely another phase of life, the contents of Egyptian tombs contained everything that would be necessary in the next life: furniture, clothing (including underwear), shoes, bathrooms, jewelry, jars of lotions and oil, toys and games, hunting and sporting equipment, chariots, scrolls to read, and model boats. The walls of the tombs were also painted with scenes from daily life: harvesting grain, beer-making, boat-building, temple-building, religious festivals, dancing and singing, and funeral processions. Tombs contained statues of the dead, which were insurance against something happening to the mummy. Pictures of offering tables piled high with food and menus painted on the walls, as in a restaurant, assured that the dead were still served long after funeral duties were forgotten by their relatives.

Other Mediterranean civilizations recognized that often justice in this world remained elusive. Good, god-fearing citizens sometimes suffered disasters, while others achieved fame and fortune through their crimes. Assigning these situations to the will of the gods or the Fates was acceptable in theory, but often came to be resented as arbitrariness on the part of the divine. It appears that there was a human need to believe that one's life matters, either now or later, and that the imbalances of justice in this life would eventually be reconciled in the next one. Codes of acceptable social behavior and social justice went hand in hand with the evolution of detailed elements of the afterlife. This idea that good people are rewarded and evil people are punished after death remains ingrained in the Western tradition.

In the late Bronze and early Iron Ages we have a monistic view of the human person. Monistic or monism refers to the understanding that a person is one entity, a physical body, with an animating principle. In the Archaic period in Greece, *psyche* (soul) was most likely derived from a verb meaning "to cool, to blow," and referred to the vital breath that enlivened the *soma* or body. Thus, in Homer and other early narratives about heroes, the body and soul remain together, at least visibly, in the afterlife.

Through the poetry of Pindar (522–443 BCE) and the emergence of the philosophical schools, monism evolved to dualism, or the belief that the human person consists of two distinct entities, the physical body and the non-physical ethereal soul. The immaterial soul was now understood by many philosophers to be immortal because it originated beyond material existence. This idea was most fully articulated by the Greek philosopher Plato (*Phaedo, Timaeus, The Republic*), where the immortal soul is associated with mind or consciousness.

The philosophical concept of the immortal soul insisted that the body had no place in the afterlife; the soul was released at the moment of death and the body was cremated or buried and decomposed because it consisted of matter. It was only the soul that existed in the afterlife in either good or bad conditions. At the same time, however, Plato's description of Hades appears confusing; the dead *do* things. It may appear illogical to us that a disembodied soul could experience either joy or pain, but it was understood that the soul could sense and experience all the emotions. We do not know how much of the philosophical view influenced average people, if at all. Eventually it would become important in the concept that the soul could be redeemed in the afterlife. In the popular literary tradition, the dead were imagined as spending their time gossiping, moralizing, or in self-indulgent regret, while participating in board games and gymnastics.

With few exceptions, the concept of literally returning from the dead was not possible in ancient Greece or Rome. There were stories of dying and rising gods (Dionysus), but of course, they were already part of the divine realm. Heroes were granted immortality after their deaths, but they remained in Elysium, and a few became gods in their own right (Asclepios). We find an exception in the development of Second Temple Judaism (450 BCE to 70 CE) in which a sect of Jews known as the Pharisees advocated resurrection of all the dead, who were then judged in the "final days" when god would rule on earth. This view was eventually absorbed as a central tenet of Christianity.

The Afterlife in Ancient Greece

Greek ideas about the afterlife emerged in the Archaic period and were established as part of tradition through the works of Homer. By the Classical period, social and cultural conditions had changed. Greece had been exposed to other cultures through trade contacts and colonization. The development of the *polis* brought social legislation of all kinds, including funeral legislation. What emerged was a cult of the dead that did not exist in Homer (although Homeric traditions remained popular). The world of the dead was used to validate the social order and defuse contemporary tension. These ideas spread through the diffusion of Greek culture throughout the Mediterranean region and were combined with local beliefs.

Greek views of the dead appear contradictory to us. On the one hand, the dead are portrayed as weak and powerless and therefore unable to affect anyone. On the other hand, proper burial rituals were required to appease the dead and keep them from harming the living. One way to reconcile both beliefs is to recognize that the dead per se could not act, but they were in the underworld where chthonic powers could be urged to seek revenge and punishment in the upper world. Curse tablets were inserted in graves and tombs, not to curse the dead, but to have the dead convey the message to the chthonic powers (Figure X.1).

In *The Odyssey*, Homer describes the dead as ghosts who lack strength, similar to characters in dreams. They appear frozen in time, with warriors still covered with the blood of battle. The souls must drink the blood of sacrifices to reanimate themselves before they can speak. The dead Achilles relates that although the souls have form or an image, nevertheless they lack wits. Achilles is fairly miserable in the afterlife, claiming that he would rather be a slave in life than a lord of the dead. Odysseus recognizes his mother, so apparently the dead kept their original looks, but he cannot embrace her as she also consists of shadow.

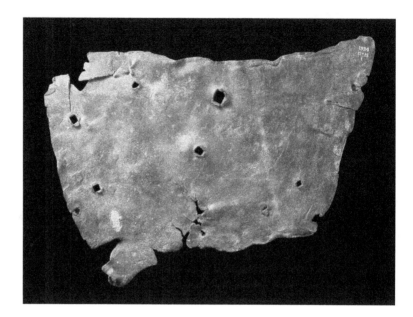

Figure X.1 Curse tablet. *Source:* © The Trustees of the British Museum/Art Resource, NY.

Odysseus sometimes glimpses elements of Hades that will become formalized much later in Greek tradition. He is aware that evil persons suffer eternal punishment, such as Tityus, who tried to seduce Leto (mother of Apollo and Artemis). He is tied down with stakes and has his liver torn out every day by vultures, like Prometheus. Odysseus also glimpses areas of bliss for the heroes. Nevertheless there is no sense of detailed reward and punishment in Homer's concept of Hades. The judge Minos (a king of Crete) occupies his time judging normal cases of the dead within that sphere, unrelated to their former lives. Judgment after death based upon one's behavior and deeds in life (at least for most common people) would become part of the later tradition.

Powerless or not, then as now, once someone was dead he or she was accorded respect and often elevated to reputations beyond reality. In fact, the dead had legal rights. Solon (638–558 BCE) made it a criminal offense to disrespect or speak ill of the dead. If someone told lies about the dead, the heir was legally obliged to defend his forebear in court. The dead person was now among the revered ancestors and therefore was accorded the same level of honor and respect. This respect demonstrated piety (*eusebeia*) and was comparable to the piety shown to the gods. At the same time, piety shown to the dead promoted the status and reputation of the living. A person was judged by society and then in the afterlife on the basis of how well he treated his dead ancestors.

Hades

The Greek underworld, or the place of the dead, was named after the Lord of the Underworld, the god Hades. The son of Cronus and Rhea, Hades was not the god of death (that was Thanatos), nor was he the equivalent of the Devil in the Western tradition. In Greek mythology, Hades referred to both the place of the dead beneath the earth as well as places on the western horizon. Although he was not an evil deity, nevertheless he was feared by humans as they feared the cruel inevitability of death. His attributes were a chariot drawn by four black horses and he was often portrayed with Cerberus at his feet. Cerberus was the three-headed hound that helped to keep anyone from escaping Hades. Throughout the different ages of Greece, details concerning Hades evolved over time. The tradition consisted of elements from Homer, bards, and in the Classical period, philosophers. There were many cult sites in Greece and Italy that served as entrances to the underworld.

Hades was not often represented in art, but when he was, it was usually the story of his abduction of Demeter's daughter Persephone. Once the decision was made that Persephone would stay part of the year in Hades, she became his main consort and Queen of the Underworld.

Hades had five rivers: Styx (river of hatred), Acheron (pain), Lethe (oblivion), Phlegethon (fire), and Cocytus (wailing). Hermes Psychopompos (guider of souls) led the dead to the river Styx, which was the boundary marker for Hades. Hermes handed over the dead to Charon, the Ferryman. He ushered the dead into boats to cross the river, for which he charged a fee. This consisted of a coin (*obolus*) that was placed in the mouth of the dead to ensure that Charon would take them across. If they did not cross (if they did not have the fee), they would remain in the liminal area between death and life, condemned to wander for eternity. Charon also served as a guardian to ensure that no one ever escaped from Hades except gods and heroes.

The dead were consigned to four areas, appropriate to the life of the person. The Asphodel Fields held ordinary souls who did not commit any major crimes, but who also did not achieve fame and glory. The Fields of Punishment contained mythological characters who committed crimes or sacrilege against the gods. Tartarus was reserved for those we would call "the damned." Tartarus appears in some of the oldest mythology and initially was reserved for the Titans after their defeat. It was always understood to be somewhere lower than Hades, and darker than night. Two of the most famous residents of Tartarus were Tantalus and Sisyphus. Tantalus had tricked and humiliated the gods at a banquet (he served them his son in a stew). Food and drink are temptingly nearby, but when he reaches out, the food and drink recede (hence the term "tantalize"). Sisyphus tricked Thanatos, the god of death, and escaped from Hades. He is punished by eternally pushing a large boulder up a hill every day, which then rolls back down.

The Elysian Fields (Elysium) in older mythology was reserved for those humans with a divine parent and legendary heroes. Eventually it was understood as a place for virtuous individuals who contributed great deeds. Homer and Hesiod placed it on the western edge of the earth, bordering Oceanus, and Hesiod also referred to it as the Blessed Isles. It was a utopia where the honored dead led a happy and carefree existence and indulged in their favorite pastimes such as music or athletics. The ruler of Elysium was Rhadamanthus, a son of

Zeus who was famous for his integrity. Rhadamanthus, Aeacus (another wise son of Zeus) and Minos served as judges of the dead in Hades.

The philosopher Plato included a story of the afterlife at the end of *The Republic* (380 BCE) known as "The Myth of Er" that influenced religious and philosophical ideas for centuries. Er was killed in a battle, but when they sorted the bodies it was discovered that his body was not decomposed. He woke up two days later with a strange tale to tell. In Hades, he saw two openings into the sky and two openings into the earth. Judges indicated that good souls were to enter the sky opening while the bad were sent downward. As Er watched, good souls came back from the sky telling of beautiful sights, while the bad related hideous experiences. The souls were then taken to the Spindle of Necessity and were given lottery tokens. As their token was called out, they had to choose a new life. Er noticed that most of the good souls who had been in the sky chose to be dictators or tyrants, because they had no knowledge of how that kind of power could lead to corruption. The souls who had been exposed to punishment always chose a righteous life. After their selections, the souls drank from the River Lethe so that they remembered nothing of their former existence when they were reborn into a new life. (The cult of Orpheus and the followers of Pythagoras also taught this concept of reincarnation.) Er was told to take this tale back to earth so that all men could learn that their deeds in life had repercussions in the afterlife. Socrates highlighted this moral in his comments on the story of Er, warning that the wicked can never fool the gods. Only a life full of goodness, courage, and wisdom led to the soul's proper place in the universe. In Plato's *Phaedo*, however, the souls, after being purified by righteous living, dwell in a heavenly abode.

Other residents of Hades included the earth goddess Hecate, the gorgons, and *Erinyes*. Hecate was associated with ghosts and sorcery because she was a protector of the living against the dead. The early myths had one gorgon who was so monstrous that anyone who looked upon her was turned to stone. In later mythology, there were three gorgons, the most famous of which was Medusa, with snakes for hair. The *Erinyes*, also known as the Furies in Rome, were avenging deities, originally called upon to take vengeance on anyone who violated an oath to the gods and those who committed homicide. In later traditions, they were associated with all forms of vengeance. In order to avert their wrath, Romans often referred to them as "the friendly ones."

All of these details concerning Hades and the afterlife were drawn together from myth, poetry, and drama, with much later philosophical speculation. Contradictory versions coexisted; there was no authoritative body that determined the exact details. For the majority of the ancients, this resulted in the absence of an absolute conviction of what awaited the dead – no one could really be *sure*. It appears that the only thing that everyone agreed upon, however, was the absolute necessity that the dead were honored and rested in peace. The evidence of tombs and descriptions of funeral rites indicates that a proper burial was of first importance in ancient Greece and Rome.

Greek Funerals

In the Mycenaean Age there were rock-cut chamber tombs that often had additional niches and side chambers used for **secondary burial**. Secondary burial was a method in which the skeletons of the original generation were gathered and placed elsewhere to make room for future burials. While **inhumation** (burial) was an early practice, the Greeks later cremated or burned their dead. We find **cremation** as the means of disposal throughout Homer. It appears that the practice of either inhumation or cremation may have followed popular trends in both Greece and Rome, but we do not have enough information to determine the criteria of selecting one form over the other. However, the Homeric cremations made sense for disposal of the dead after a battle in a foreign land.

Once a person died, there was a process involved which the survivors (family) were required to complete through rituals that would stabilize the flux or liminal state caused by death. There were three stages involved: (i) dying itself; (ii) being dead but not yet disposed of; and (iii) completion of the burial rites. Ideally, before dying a person should settle their affairs (by making a will), commit their children (if young) to the care of others, and make the proper prayers for a safe passage to Hades. The soul left the body at the moment of death and sometimes lingered near the body. The son or the next of kin closed the eyes and placed the coin in the mouth for Charon.

The second stage required the laying out of the body (***prothesis***). Women washed the body and dressed it in a shroud or tunic. Soldiers were covered with their military cloak and if the deceased was a young, newly married woman, she was dressed in her wedding clothes. A chin strap was attached to keep the jaw from dropping after rigor mortis had passed off. The dead body was displayed in the house, where family and friends could pay their respects. Greek art displays women in mourning tearing their hair and men holding one hand to their head or chest. Funeral lamentations were sung in both the home and the funeral procession.

The third stage, completion of the burial rites, included the funeral procession (***ekphora***) and the inhumation or cremation. Funeral processions were public events because they were important for the honor and status of the surviving family. They were so important that, from the time of Solon's reforms (sixth century BCE) to the Imperial era, there was consistent legislation to limit the amount of money spent on funerals. Public display and feasts could be interpreted as currying favor with the voters. However, funerals for military heroes and some public figures continued to be lavish affairs in recognition of their service to the community.

The body of the deceased was transported either in a horse-drawn wagon or by pallbearers who were family members. The funeral procession usually wound through the city, with the family and hired mourners and musicians loudly lamenting and attracting attention. The lamentations and demonstrations of grief that accompanied the procession were understood as a catharsis in its meaning of purification or cleansing of the emotions. The funeral oration, or the eulogy (*epitaphios logos*), if for a notable figure, would be given in the public square and was considered the height of Greek oratory. Funeral orations were the pinnacle of the funeral for heroes or soldiers who died in battle or for a cause (such as Pericles's funeral oration during the Peloponnesian War).

In ancient Greece no priests or religious personnel were directly included in the funeral rites. In Athens a council of religious experts (*exegetai*) was available for consultation, particularly when the death was unusual or if there was a question of purification procedures. The idea that corpses were polluting (**corpse contamination**) was shared throughout the ancient Mediterranean, although the degrees of contagion varied from place to place and from group to group. For this reason, almost all cemeteries were located beyond the city walls, although many cities permitted the burial of babies and children inside (usually in pots or amphorae).

Corpses emanated a **miasma**, an oppressive and dangerous atmosphere that was contagious. Gods and goddesses avoided the dead and dying because of this danger. This is why we rarely see a god or goddess invoked in the funeral rites. The purification rituals were done by the family. Bowls of water were placed outside the home for visitors to purify themselves, and relatives took a bath upon returning from the cemetery, cleaned the house with seawater, and made offerings to Hestia (at the hearth). The relatives were considered impure in relation to temples and sacred space until 30 days had elapsed.

At the cemetery, or **necropolis**, the body was placed upon a pyre (cremation) or laid in the grave. Food offerings were brought and burned as a sacrifice in a nearby trench. Libations of wine, honey, milk, and oil were poured on the pyre, and wine was used to quench the ashes after the body was cremated. The bone fragments and ashes were then collected and placed in an urn, which was buried in a grave. This was followed by a funeral feast either at graveside or at the house which was prepared by women.

The family continued to visit the grave on the third, ninth, and thirtieth days. The thirtieth day marked the end of the period of mourning. They would also visit once a year on the anniversary of the death or the dead person's birthday. For the graveside visits the family brought food offerings but we cannot be sure if they ate the food, or just left it for the dead. They also brought wine libations, and a popular gift was a *lekythos* (a vase filled with olive oil). Some graves had tubes inserted into the ground to offer a drink to the dead. Wreaths and ribbons were laid on the graves, also serving as a public demonstration that the family continued to carry out their duties to the dead.

Geometric kraters (large pottery vessels) had been introduced in the Archaic period and served as the funeral monument. Some have scenes of the funeral processions and usually show the life activities of the dead person (such as a military campaign). It was also traditional to erect a *stele* (a stone monument) with a carved relief of the person (Figure X.2). One of the more popular beliefs was that a family reunion took place in the afterlife, and a common art motif on funeral monuments was a picture of the reunion of the husband and wife if

Figure X.2   Greek funerary *stele. Source:* Universal History Archive/UIG via Getty Images.

one had predeceased the other. Unlike tombstones in our modern cemeteries funeral monuments were painted in life-like colors.

Collective *stelae* were erected for the war dead, such as the one at the site of the Battle of Marathon, a custom continued in the war memorials erected in modern towns and cities. Depending upon the circumstances, those who died in a foreign war were either buried in a common trench or cremated in the land where they fell, although individual soldiers could also be shipped home in urns and commemorated in a military cemetery.

Appeasing the Dead

The Anthesteria was an ancient three-day festival in Greece celebrating the maturing of the wine vintages and was one of four festivals in honor of Dionysus. The second day was devoted to celebrating the third birthday of a child, perhaps in recognition that the child had survived the infant stage. If a child died past this stage, there would be a regular funeral outside the city, and the presents received on this holiday were often included in the grave.

On the third day of the festival, the souls of the dead arose from Hades and walked through the cities. Along with other roaming dead, the *Keres* (death spirits) had to be entertained and diverted from seeking out human blood. People chewed buckthorn leaves (a purgative) to symbolically expel the dead spirits and smeared tar on their doors to keep them out. People cooked beans, peas, or lentils, placed them in pots, and offered them to Hermes Chthonios in his function of a god of the underworld, and the dead were ordered to depart. This Nemeseia (or Genesia) was devoted to appeasing Nemesis, the goddess of divine retribution, and to averting the wrath of the dead.

Athens (and other areas settled by Athens) also had a festival devoted to the *tritopatores*, understood as the ancestors of the clans. As progenitors of the group, the focus was on fertility and regeneration, but the festival was also combined with purification sacrifices that were similar to the purification rites for the dead. Plato describes rural religious experts who claimed to be able to instruct people on how to remove pollution from both the living and the dead, although we have few details on how this was accomplished.

Funeral Games

Greece held funeral games, which were athletic competitions in honor of a dead person. Funeral games are dated to the Bronze Age and may have arisen as compensation for the catastrophic loss which death could bring, enabling human skill to achieve a victory over the Fates. Funeral games were held in Mycenaean society and Homer describes the funeral games that were sponsored by Achilles for Patroclus in *The Iliad*. Those games included chariot racing, boxing, wrestling, footraces, archery, and spear-throwing. Homer also mentions the ritual slaughter of youths, dogs, horses, and prisoners of war, although these sacrifices did not remain a standard element of Greek funerals. Funeral games continued to be offered for the war dead throughout Greek history. Many of the athletic skills mentioned in Homer became part of the standard competition at the Olympic Games as well as the other Panhellenic festivals. What we consider pure athletics originated as funeral games, as they celebrated victory over death.

The Afterlife in Ancient Rome

Rome absorbed views of the afterlife and funeral rituals from the indigenous Italian tribes, the Etruscans, and the Greek colonies in Magna Graecia. The Etruscans did not leave a body of literature so we can only piece together their views on the afterlife from their cemeteries. Like the Egyptians, Etruscans included various items for everyday life in their tombs. The murals show people participating in banquets, hunting, swimming, and dancing, and it appears that everyone is having a good time (Figure X.3). It is debatable if these scenes depict the afterlife or the funeral banquet of the survivors. Many tombs had a painted door which represented the entrance to Hades.

The Etruscans had direct contact with Greek culture through both trade and war on the peninsula. Etruscan funeral urns were sculpted with scenes from Greek mythology and stories of heroes associated with glorious deaths. The lids of the funerals urns were unique in this period for their realism. The lid depicts the dead person usually lying on a couch, propped up on one elbow, with a face that is individual and unique, wrinkles, and all (Figure X.4). Etruscans added the figure of Vanth, who was a benevolent chthonic deity and functioned as a *psychopompos*, leading the dead to Hades with her torch.

We can observe the fusion of Etruscan, Greek, and indigenous concepts of the afterlife in Roman views of the underworld. When the Fates decided that someone's life was over, Pluto dispatched Mors (Thanatos, or Death) to bring the dead to his realm. The geography of the Roman Hades was very similar to the Greek, and included the idea of reward and punishment for mythological characters in the afterlife. The poet Vergil (70–19 BCE) provided details of Hades in *The Aeneid*, with different levels associated with various punishments, providing the basis for Dante's Inferno in *The Divine Comedy* (1321 CE). However, we cannot determine the extent of Vergil's influence on average Romans. Among some of the educated elite, the traditional belief in the existence of life after death was often viewed with skepticism. The Epicureans and Stoics had alternative views of the fate of the soul. However, as no one could be sure, it was wise to be aware that one's earthly life *could* influence one's eternal existence.

Citizens of Rome shared the belief that corpses were contaminating, and so with very few exceptions all tombs were located beyond the *pomerium*. The Campus Martius was outside the walls, but this area was reserved for the tombs of military heroes and other famous Romans (it was where Augustus built his family mausoleum). The rest of the dead citizens of Rome were consigned to

Figure X.4   Etruscan funerary urn. *Source:* DEA/G. Nimatallah/ De Agostini/Getty Images.

cemeteries that lined the major roads leading into the city. The proximity to the roads of the larger tombs helped advertise the role of the rich and famous in the history of Rome. The ruins of many of these tombs can still be seen today on the old portions of the Appian Way leading away from the city. In the late Republic and early Empire, the areas of the tombs were notorious for sheltering bandits and the homeless, who often attacked lone travelers.

Roman Funerals

One of the major differences between Greek and Roman funerals is that Rome had what we would call a funeral industry that was subject to state regulation, much like our modern equivalent of funeral homes. In the late Republic and throughout the Empire, a death certificate was required in order to update the census, the grain dole, and tax rolls. The business of death was under the auspices of both the state and the goddess Venus Libitina. Libitina may be Italian or Etruscan in origin, combining the aspects of a fertility and love goddess with a deity of the underworld. This aspect of the goddess Venus made sense to Romans because life and death were part of the never-ending cycle of existence. Venus Libitina symbolized the cessation of the life force.

The temple of Venus Libitina was located on the part of the Esquiline Hill that was outside the city walls (the Campus Esquilinus). All deaths in the city were recorded in this temple and each family paid a death tax here. During the Republic the temple served as the headquarters for the *libitinarii*, who handled all aspects of death and funerals, although *libitinarii* were established in businesses (funeral homes) in other sections of the city. In their role as servants to the goddess Venus Libitina, *libitinarii* were a special order of priests, with no other priestly functions that we are aware of. Romans believed that the soul of the dead stayed near the body for a while immediately following death, which along with the ideas of pollution rendered the corpse dangerous. *Libitinarii* were the first to be summoned to a dead body so that the necessary rituals could be performed to eliminate the danger.

Overseeing the *libitinarii* was a guild (*collegium*) of funeral directors known as **dissignatores** (*domini funeris*). Designators were supervisors of funerals and they were responsible for employing all the necessary performers who were required, procuring the equipment, and organizing the funeral procession. They also made sure that the body was in a presentable state with some embalming methods, depending upon the state of the corpse. This would include makeup and covering up wounds, if any. Designators were the overall liaison with the family in making sure that proper funeral rituals were complete, in the same way that funeral directors organize the process for modern families.

During the Republic one section of the Esquiline Hill was a public cemetery for the lower classes who could afford a proper, cheap burial. The Esquiline also received all the refuse that could not fit down into the sewers. Foreigners with no family, the very poor, and slaves were buried collectively in grave-pits or **puticuli**. Dead animal carcasses from the streets were also dumped into these pits. The *puticuli* were kept open for easy access and public slaves most likely used lime to try to help stench the smell, unsuccessfully. An east wind from the Esquiline affected the northern suburbs so that real estate prices were lower in this area. As part of Augustus's beautification of the city in the early Empire, tons of soil covered the cemetery and it became a public park (the Gardens of Maecenas). Public cemeteries were moved to other areas outside the city.

Roman Funeral Processions

Roman funerals differed in relation to status, wealth, and the circumstances of death. The status of a person (military hero or someone who had given years of public service) could determine if the state would pay for an elaborate funeral. This would include a display of the body in the forum, public orations from the *rostra*, and elaborate feasts for the crowds of Rome. Private funerals could be just as elaborate, depending upon the finances of the family. The lower classes often belonged to *collegia funeratica* or funeral clubs. These were social as well as practical associations; the group would meet once a month for a meal, and the dues of each member were held against the expenses of a funeral upon death.

Criminals who had been executed for the most serious crimes (murder, patricide, treason) would be denied proper funeral rites. If not executed in the arena, they were flung from the Tarpeian Rock, an outcrop on the Capitoline Hill, and their bodies thrown into the Tiber River. Romans believed in eternal punishment, and a denial of funeral rites meant that the deceased criminal never had eternal rest.

Except in cases of sudden death, Romans were obligated to settle their affairs if they thought that death was near. All Romans believed that the making of a will was the right of every citizen from the highest to the lowest, even if you only had a few household items or one slave. It was customary among the rich to set aside funds for a funeral; lacking this detail, the heir assumed the responsibility for the cost. Many Romans also freed their slaves in their will and these freedmen always participated in the funeral procession.

After the washing and anointing of the body, the deceased was laid out on a funeral couch in the atrium of the house, with the feet towards the door. Ordinary citizens were dressed in white, but magistrates were dressed in the appropriate toga and stripe of their office. In an upper-class Roman house, incense was burned because the body was displayed for at least seven days. Cypress branches were hung outside the door to alert the public of a contaminating body inside. On the eighth day, the funeral procession began, organized by the designator, attended by lictors, or bodyguards, dressed in black (if the dead had them in life) (Figure X.5). The musicians led the procession followed by professional mourning women who sang laments, beat their breasts and tore out their hair. The body was carried on a couch or bier, often sitting up.

The nobility of Rome displayed images of ancestors in their home, where there was often a shrine to the dead. Many of these images were death masks sculpted in wax. For the funeral, these images were worn in the procession either by professional actors or by family members. In the late Republic and early Empire, busts of the individual became more popular than funeral masks. This practice

Figure X.5   Roman funeral procession. *Source*: akg-images/Nimatallah.

highlighted the fact that the dead person was now among the ancestors of the family and therefore subject to the same honor and respect.

However, such respect was temporarily delayed. Roman funerals uniquely added *histriones* or actors who appeared as funeral buffoons or clowns to mock the dead. In the days before the funeral, the actor gathered as much information as possible about the deceased, including habits, character traits, personal quirks, and especially scandals. He wore the new death mask, acted as the dead person, and trotted alongside the family and friends as the procession made its way through the streets. He imitated all the person's foibles, favorite expressions, and bad habits. The rationale for this addition to funerals remains theoretical. It was either a Roman way of laughing in the face of death or a way in which to emphasize that all, rich and poor, will eventually end up dead.

If the deceased was noble or a military hero, the funeral oration would be delivered in the forum of the town or city. For everyone else the oration was delivered graveside, usually by a son or the nearest male relative. In earlier times Romans buried their dead, but in the late Republic cremation was more popular until roughly the second and third century CE. Those who were buried were placed in stone coffins (a sarcophagus). For a cremation the pyre resembled an altar with four equal sides. The corpse and couch were both placed on the pyre and the closest relative lit the fire, while others saturated it with incense, perfumes, and oils. The ashes were then soaked with wine and gathered for the urn.

Those remaining at the graveside for the procedure were sprinkled with pure water. As in Greece, a funeral feast was given either at the graveside or at the house, and sometimes both. In the case of the nobility, there was often a distribution of meat to the poor. We have evidence of a *triclinium* or dining room (open-air) built around some burial plots for funeral meals and anniversary meals held at the tomb. Romans visited the tomb and offered sacrifices on the anniversary of the death and on days of festivals for the dead.

The soft tufa-rock around Rome was ideal for easy expansion of cemeteries underground. The earliest form was called a *columbarium* and resembled the holes in a pigeon coop or dovecote. Funerary urns were deposited in carved niches in the walls. The *columbaria* were layered and resembled underground parking lots. By the second century CE, the more popular term for these places was **catacomb**, or "under the tombs." A *columbarium* contained not only many family members, but clients, ex-slaves, and slaves. Most often the *columbarium* was carved out of a piece of land at the family estate. The empress Livia (wife of Augustus) commissioned a *columbarium* on her property that was reserved for clients and ex-slaves who had worked as domestic servants and Imperial bureaucrats in Rome's administration.

The *columbaria* and catacombs both contained wall murals with mythic scenes and symbols of the afterlife. In addition to the standard banqueting scenes, there are praying figures (with their head covered with the toga), vines, flowers, and food offerings. Romans also erected stone monuments with carved reliefs of the dead (Figure X.6). Those who had served in a famous military campaign were dressed in their uniforms, and magistrates in their togas.

Figure X.6 Roman funeral monument. *Source*: akg/Bildarchiv Steffens.

Romans erected more elaborate *stelae* that listed the good deeds and achievements of the individual, their qualities as a family member, their service to the community, and their piety toward the gods. Roman inscriptions tended toward the poetic as well as the philosophical, pointing out that no matter how rich or successful a person is, death is the final victor. Romans were often practical and realistic, as shown in this epitaph found near Padua: "I was not, I was, I am not, I care not" (see the box "Roman Tombstones").

Roman Tombstones

Tombstones are among our best sources for details of the lives of Romans. In addition to the names, they list not only great achievements, but small details of everyday life such as occupations, military rank, marriage partners and children, and status as either free, freedmen, or slave. Paradoxically we learn more about Hades and views of the afterlife from literature than from the tombstones themselves. The references to the underworld are few and when they do appear it is expressed more as hope than as a firm belief in what awaits them. Many tombstones expressed this unknown fate of the dead:

Albia Hargula, freedwoman of Albia: lived fifty-six years. Chaste she was and the soul of honor. If the dead below have any sense at all, may her bones which lie here rest in perfect peace.

The ancient inscriptions are addressed to the living rather than appeals to the gods for a safe passage and a pleasant afterlife. It appears that the most important function of the tombstone was to inform the living of the way you wanted to be remembered:

By my good conduct I heaped virtues on the virtues of my clan; I began a family and sought to equal the exploits of my father. I upheld the praise of my ancestors, so that they are glad that I was created of their line. My honors have ennobled my stock.

Many began by getting the attention of anyone passing by with "Wayfarer, stop here!" Others were more poignant in their appeal:

Young man, though you are in a hurry, this little stone asks you to look at it, and then to read the message with which it is inscribed. Here lie the bones of Lucius Maecius Philotimus the hardware man. I wanted you to know this. Farewell.

Many inscriptions reminded the living that everyone shared the same fate:

Marcus Statius Chilo, freedman of Marcus, lies here. Ah! Weary traveler, you there who are passing by me, though you may walk as long as you like, yet here's the place you must come to.

Memorials for children and those who died young usually included the bitterness of the parents against Fortune or the Fates, with the greatest grief that the young had no chance to leave a legacy:

Great virtues and great wisdom holds this stone with tender age; whose life but not his honor fell short of honors; he that lies here was never outdone in virtue; twenty years of age to burial-places was he entrusted. This, lest you ask why honors none to him were ever entrusted.

Appeasing the Dead

The Roman term for dead ancestors was *di manes*, or spirits of the dead. February 13–21 was the festival of Parentalia which honored dead parents and other relatives. Visitors to tombs brought wreaths, grain, salt, violets, and some bread soaked in wine, and the idea was to reunite the dead and the living. During this festival, the head Vestal conducted a ritual at the tomb of Tarpeia. Tarpeia was the daughter of a Sabine king who was willing to betray Rome for a cache of jewelry. She was later crushed to death and her body thrown from the rock which bore her name. The Tarpeian Rock became the site of execution for all traitors. During this festival, all temples and law courts were closed and marriages were forbidden.

The last night of the Parentalia was called *Feralia*, when the souls of the departed could arise and roam the streets; rituals were required to send them back. (This was similar to the Greek Anthesteria.) We know very little of the public rituals involved in the Feralia, but a legendary story told that the festival originated when an old drunken woman in a circle of young girls used divination rites involving a dead mouse and black beans and impaled the head of a fish with a bronze needle while roasting it in a fire to gag tongues (probably to stop gossip among women as well as to render dead spirits harmless?).

It appears that the Parentalia was concerned with honorable ancestors, while the Feralia addressed the unhappy dead of vengeful spirits. Another festival in the same vein was conducted in May as the Lemuria, a time to propitiate **lemures** or what we can term ghosts. *Lemures* consisted of both those who did not have the proper burial rites as well as ancestors who felt that their cult was being neglected by family members. The roots of this festival are also ancient (and obscure), but related to the black bean story of the Feralia. Black was the color of sacrifices for chthonic deities and Romans believed that *lemures* feasted on black beans. At midnight the *paterfamilias* would throw black beans over his shoulder to appease the spirits and keep them out of the house. If that did not work he banged pots to startle them away.

Rosalia was a festival of roses, or a *rosatio* ("rose adornment"), that sometimes included violets as part of commemorations to the dead. Red and purple represented the color of blood in propitiation sacrifices and thus rejuvenation and rebirth. It was traditional to festoon graves with these flowers and even plant rose bushes at the grave site. In tomb paintings, roses proliferated and they became symbols of the gardens of bliss in the afterlife. Rose petals eventually were included in all major Roman festivals and triumphal processions.

In the fall, Romans celebrated an ancient rite that honored Ceres as the goddess of agriculture as well as underworld deities. Offerings were made at the *mundus cerialis* ("the world of Ceres"), which were pits or underground vaults that were opened to allow the free roaming of underground spirits. The term *mundus* became synonymous with an entrance to the underworld and Roman folklore claimed that witches would gather at a *mundus* to make contact with the dead for their evil purposes. An entrance was located at Cumae near Naples, in the cave of the Sybil (where Vergil has Aeneas enter).

Funeral Games

Although funeral games in Rome celebrated athletic skill, they were quite different from standard athletic competitions. More popularly known as **gladiator games**, these events paired trained fighters against each other ("gladiator" derives from the Roman short sword, *gladius*). Later Roman historians relate that the first gladiator games were sponsored in Campania in 310 BCE and in Rome in 264 BCE, claiming an Etruscan source for the ritual. Originally two slaves of the dead master fought to death at the grave, and the dead slave would continue to serve his master in the afterlife. It may also have been a propitiation rite for the dead through the human blood spilled on the ground. Greek frescoes from the fourth century BCE in southern Italy, however, show paired fighters as part of a funeral and this may have been a cross-cultural element of Etruscan, Greek, and Italian ideas on the peninsula.

Early in the Republic, gladiator bouts were held immediately following the death of an individual, although in later years Romans could offer them several years after a relative's death. We also know that funeral games in the "Etruscan style" were held collectively by the Senate as early as the First Punic War in the third century BCE. They were conducted either to honor those killed in battle and as expiation to the gods, or perhaps to serve as a demonstration of martial skill despite defeats by the Carthaginians. This combination of both private and public (state-sponsored) aspects of gladiator games dominated the late Republic and early Empire.

Figure X.7   Mosaic of gladiators. *Source:* Ann Ronan Pictures/ Print Collector/Getty Images.

The funeral aspect of gladiator games began to change as Rome conquered nearby territories and expanded throughout the Mediterranean; gladiator games began to be incorporated into the national ethos. Gladiators were dressed in armor of the enemies of Rome – Samnites, Thracians, and Gauls. The bouts were moral lessons of the virtues of courage, martial skill, and above all, dying well (Figure X.7). By 105 BCE, individually sponsored gladiator games were combined with the regular *ludi* or religious festivals of the city. Under the Empire they remained individually funded but were also pledged as an offering for the well-being of the emperor.

Gladiator schools were expensive undertakings and several years of training were required to produce skilled fighters. Gladiators were not wasted on fighting common criminals (nor did they fight against Christians in the arenas). Not all gladiators died in the combats and if a fighter survived 25 bouts, he would be granted his freedom. The crowd appreciated their skills and many gladiators became famous sporting figures, although they remained at the lower end of the social scale as all gladiators were slaves. The schools were populated with slaves, prisoners of war, and criminals. However, free men who were in debt often sold themselves into slavery to join a gladiator school. Many retired gladiators signed back up to work as *lanistas* or trainers and in the late Republic hired themselves out as bodyguards or bouncers.

Munus means "duty or obligation" (involving munificence) owed by the nobility in service to the community. In relation to gladiator games, *munus* not only meant the duty of honoring the ancestral dead, but the largesse involved in paying for public games. Eventually, ***munera sine missione*** (fighting without release) came to designate gladiator games where sometimes up to a hundred combatants fought to the death. Given the expense, this kind of largesse was not common. It did impress the crowds so that sponsoring a gladiator *munera* became an element of propaganda for private individuals running for office. Voters would always remember the magnificent games of a man who was working himself up the ladder to eventually obtain the highest office of consul.

A secondary element of gladiator games was the ***venatio*** or the animal hunts. Animals were collected from all the provinces of the Empire (sometimes to extinction) and transported to the cities for arena shows. ***Bestiarii***, or animal men, were trained in gladiator schools to stage elaborate hunt scenes in the arenas with re-creations of their home territory (Figure X.8). Although this element was not the original concept of funeral games, it quickly became a convenient vehicle for the execution of state criminals. Convicts were either part of the hunt, or left to be hunted down by the animals alone. The best examples of *bestiarii* venues are found in the execution of Christians under the Empire. In the more elaborate shows, "fatal charades" were enacted using prisoners, reproducing stories from mythology with living actors who died on stage.

Despite the propaganda and entertainment elements of the gladiator and *bestiarii* games, they remained under the traditional auspices of religion. All of the games began with the necessary sacrifices and prayers to the gods, and images of the gods were paraded in floats around the arena. The executions

Figure X.8 Mosaic of *bestiarii*. *Source:* DEA/G. DAGLI ORTI/De Agostini/ Getty Images.

conveyed the traditional values of Roman tradition, in that law and order was being upheld through the will of the gods. During the execution of prisoners, the statues of the gods surrounding the colonnades of the arena were covered lest they be offended by the convict's crimes. In the regular gladiator bouts, actors wearing the masks of Rhadamanthus and Mercury were part of the show. Rhadamanthus carried a hot branding iron or mallet to verify that the gladiator was not faking his death, and an actor wearing the mask and accruements of Hermes escorted the dead out of the arena and symbolically into Hades.

Summary

- Many concepts of the afterlife were shared by various Mediterranean cultures. Beliefs concerning disposal of the dead and funeral rituals that included processions differed from place to place but the overall value of necessary rituals were important to help the dead rest in peace. The social context of class and status determined the type of funeral in ancient cultures.
- The social context and function of specific beliefs concerning the dead reflected social values, economic class, and projections of delayed social justice.

Suggestions for Further Reading

Garland, R. 2001. *The Greek Way of Death*. Cornell University Press. A detailed outline of Greek funerals from the moment of death to the grave.

Johnston, S. 1999. *Restless Dead: Encounters Between the Living and the Dead in Ancient Greece*. University of California Press. A very detailed study utilizing Greek drama and inscriptions to describe the social changes that took place between the Archaic and Classical Ages in relation to social control of funeral rituals.

Kyle, D. G. 2001. *Spectacles of Death in Ancient Rome*. Routledge. A history of the gladiator games as well as a detailed study of disposal of the dead in ancient Rome.

Toynbee, J. M. C. 1996. *Death and Burial in the Roman World*. Johns Hopkins University Press. An overview of Roman concepts of the afterlife with detailed descriptions of tomb architecture.

RELIGION AND PHILOSOPHY

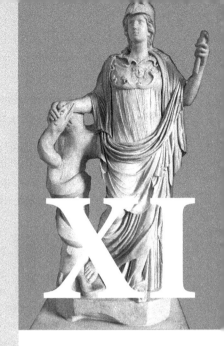

XI

Greek and Roman Religions, First Edition. Rebecca I. Denova.
© 2019 John Wiley & Sons, Inc. Published 2019 by John Wiley & Sons, Inc.

Learning Objectives

After reading this chapter, you will be able to:

- Understand the connections between traditional religious concepts and the schools of philosophy.
- Recognize that schools of philosophy taught different ways of thinking about the divine, which nevertheless validated some conventional beliefs and practices.

According to tradition, a new way of thinking and looking at the world arose in and around the city of Miletus in Anatolia in the seventh century BCE. This new way of thinking was known as philosophy, or "love of wisdom." Philosophy came to stand for an attempt to understand humans and their place in the universe by applying reasoned analysis to a body of observable phenomena which was not based upon the supernatural.

The discipline of philosophy soon spread to other cities along the coast as well as the islands of the Aegean. By the fifth century BCE, however, almost all of the schools were represented in Athens, which became famous for intellectual pursuits of higher knowledge. Such pursuits were most often limited to the upper classes as they required education, money, and leisure-time, assets that the working and lower classes did not possess.

The modern concept of philosophy revolves around a secular pursuit of rationality and metaphysics, or the first principles of being, knowing, cause, time, and space. Modern schools trace their origins to the major philosophers of the ancient world. There is an inherent admiration for these thinkers because of what appears to be their critique of traditional religion and abuses of the political order at times. Philosophers wrote treatises on moral guidelines, ethics, and the role of the conscience.

This concern with ethics is the way in which we distinguish schools of philosophy from popular religion, as the traditional cults did not produce an equivalent type of literature. Because ancient philosophers often criticized the masses for their acceptance of fabulous myths and simple thinking, we tend to identify with these thinkers rather than with those who practiced the native cults. This modern view still dominates the way in which we distinguish ancient philosophy from ancient religion.

It is a mistake to think that the practitioners of native cults had no morals or ethics. They called upon the traditions of their ancestors and the codified laws in Greece and Rome as a guide to their lives and their relationship with the gods. Schools of philosophy did not invent morality or ethics; the ancient philosophers just differed from other religious practitioners in their exploration of the matter of existence, the nature of the gods, the role of the divine in human societies, and the nature and role of the soul in humans.

Almost all of the ancient philosophers discussed the soul – its origin, its nature, its relation to the divine – and how best to nurture the soul without the distraction that physical existence brought with it. Such discussions understandably included morality and ethics, and the writings concerning the soul have contributed to the modern emphasis on philosophy as an ancient enterprise that mirrors our own concerns.

Schools of Philosophy

Philosophy was categorized by "schools of thought" (*haeresis*) that formed communities of disciples (students) around a revered master and his teachings. Each had its distinctive way of life, practices, and worldview. As schools proliferated, rivalries and competition developed. Many aspiring philosophers depended upon fees (tuition) for their livelihood, fees that fathers were expected to pay for an education for their sons. Philosophers hawked their skills and the benefits of their teaching in the *agoras* and forums of cities and towns.

The aim of a school of philosophy was to teach people how to live the best life and, often, to prepare one's soul for the afterlife. In this sense, native cults and schools of philosophy shared many of the same goals. One important difference, however, was that the schools taught a detachment (in varying degrees) from the cares and concerns of the world, in order to develop self-sufficiency without externals (asceticism, from *ascesis*, or "discipline"). Sometimes this involved dietary restrictions, abstinence from normal elements of life such as sexual indulgence or drinking to excess, and a disdain for material possessions.

Some of the elements shared by the various schools included:

- the concept of a "high god," the One, as the unique source of all being and usually expressed in the abstract;
- multiple, lesser powers in the universe that originated in the One;
- compiling and passing on the teachings of their founder (either orally or through writing);
- an emphasis on fellowship (for humankind as well as within the group);
- teachings on morality and piety;
- communal meals (sometimes in memory of the founder);
- rules for admission, retaining membership, and advancement of the members.

The idea of the One, variously named "the highest good," "the ultimate," or "the most perfect," defined god as an abstract consisting of pure essence and removed from the rest of the universe that consisted of matter. In other words, the One did not manifest itself in human form on earth, walk around visiting people or places, and certainly did not mate with humans.

A few of the schools criticized popular religion and practices by pointing out such misunderstandings concerning the divine. Some disdained the traditional myths altogether by mocking the more absurd elements in the stories, such as fantastic monsters. Philosophers particularly attacked the anthropomorphism of the gods and their immoral behavior, their anger, jealousy, and acts of vengeance. At the same time, however, they also discussed what should be proper attitudes during the necessary cultic sacrifices and urged poets and writers to describe more worthy conceptions of the gods.

In other words, most philosophers were not atheists (disbelieving in the gods) as we understand the concept today. It is more appropriate to understand them as redefining and re-imaging the divine, rather than doing away with these powers altogether. Modern descriptions of ancient philosophers often portray them as rejecting traditional beliefs, but it is important to remember that there was no set creeds or dogma (an agreed-upon body of doctrine) for them to officially reject. However, if we accept that Homer and Hesiod enjoyed the status of a canon (an accepted body of belief), many of the philosophers did criticize the stories of the gods found in this literature.

The method by which ancient philosophers often described the universe as well as traditional myths was that of allegory. Allegory is a literary device that posits hidden meanings through symbolic figures, actions, images, and events, usually to provide a spiritual, moral, or political interpretation. The device of allegory offers a way in which a text can be open to more interpretations than traditionally understood.

Teaching how to live the best life included how to understand one's place in the universe and in the natural world. Philosophical schools included the study of mathematics, physics, biology (ancient doctors studied in the schools that focused on medicine), cosmology (the origin and development of the universe), astronomy, geography, and some of the natural sciences. Their teachings on the nature of the divine and the gods nevertheless shared many of the same elements found in the native cults. Importantly, those philosophers who also participated in public life (holding political or civic status) condoned and practiced traditional worship.

We will briefly summarize some of the more influential schools of philosophy in Greece and the Greek colonies, followed by similar schools in Rome. Many philosophers were prolific in their writing but we cannot examine all of their views. For our purposes, the basic ideas of philosophers and their schools are presented in relation to religion and religious concepts. Their views on religion and politics follow in Chapter XII.

Egypt, Babylon, and Persia

Although ancient Greece is most often associated with the rise of philosophical thinking, this did not emerge in a vacuum. The ancient civilizations of Egypt and Mesopotamia developed philosophical speculation. In Egypt, the abstract concept of *ma'at* controlled order and justice in the universe. Ancient Egypt had created the concepts of the *ba* and *ka*, two of the various elements that made up the human person. *Ba* was the equivalent of what we would term the personality, while *ka* was an invisible life force, a twin of the person that was released from the physical body at death. The two are often translated as soul and it may be one of the earliest sources we have for a concept of a portion of our existence that is not physical.

From the Middle Kingdom of Egypt (c. 2000 BCE) we have the wisdom literature that set out proper ethical and moral behavior. Babylonian philosophy promoted the idea of evolution, with the human intellect being at the peak of existence. Regional ideas that became codified in Persian Zoroastrianism are sometimes referred to as Indo-Iranian philosophy, reflecting ancient ideas of Indo-Aryan sources that were also prevalent in India.

In general, all of these older ideas most likely contributed to various schools of Greek philosophy, either through trade, cultural contact, or conquests. We know there was cultural contact even farther afield, as many of the ancient sources claim that various philosophers traveled as far away as India and China and were influenced by the sages in those countries. Or, such a claim could have been merely a device to promote the extensive experience and knowledge of a particular master. Nevertheless many modern scholars identify ancient eastern traditions in some of the schools.

Philosophy in Ancient Greece

Miletus and the Pre-Socratics

As the source of the earliest philosophical schools, the philosophers from Miletus were later categorized as "the Milesian School" and listed together under the category "Pre-Socratics," a nineteenth-century term to distinguish philosophical thinkers prior to the age of Classical Greece. One of the early writers from Miletus was Thales (624–546 BCE), who is considered one of the founders of philosophy. His work only survives in fragments that are quoted by later philosophers.

Thales was one of the first to challenge the idea that the traditional supernatural forces created and controlled the universe and natural phenomena, where water was the basis of all creation. What makes things move and act? Aristotle attributed to Thales the idea that "all things were full of gods." He was most likely not referring to the traditional gods, but to an animating force in the universe. He claimed all things had this force, or soul, even stones. This original animating force became understood as "mind." In some circles, Zeus had been understood as a personification of this mind, with all other powers subordinate to him. Beginning with the Milesian school of thought, many philosophers began to remove personal or physical attributes of Zeus from this concept, leaving only the essence. In this period, mind and god became synonymous.

According to the later Roman excerpts, Thales had stated that of all the things that exist, the most ancient is god, for he is uncreated, and that the universe is beautiful because it is the workmanship of god. We can recognize that Thales maintained the existence of a divine realm but with an innovative definition of what constituted that realm as different from traditional myth.

Xenophanes of Colophon (570–475 BCE)

A poet as well as a philosopher, Xenophanes is said by tradition to have traveled throughout the Mediterranean basin, spending time in exile in Sicily. Only fragments of his poetry survive, together with quotes from later writers. His poetry satirized Hesiod and Homer and other religious views of his time, as well as society. The gods, he said, were simply human projections:

> Homer and Hesiod have attributed to the gods all sorts of things that are matters of reproach and censure among men: theft, adultery, and mutual deceptions … But if cattle and horses and lions had hands or could paint with their hands and create works such as men do, horses like horses and cattle like cattle also would depict the gods' shapes and make their bodies of such a sort as the form they themselves have.
>
> (cited in Clement of Alexandria, *Miscellanies*)

For Xenophanes, god is absolute mind, whose intelligence stimulates all things, including other powers of the universe subordinate to god. Xenophanes also wrote on the subject of the human limitations on knowing everything in its full sense. He believed there is a truth or reality that is beyond human understanding. His critique of society included negative comments on the exaggerated athletic and military victories of the Greeks, where higher learning was the better virtue.

Pythagoras of Samos (582–496 BCE)

Pythagoras of Samos (c. 570–c. 495 BCE) was a philosopher and mathematician who founded the school or movement known as Pythagoreanism. Almost everything we know about him and his teachings comes from much later sources that also contradict each other. Rather than citing Pythagoras directly, the majority of the later sources cite "the Pythagoreans." Born on the island of Samos, he settled in Magna Graecia (southern Italy) in the city of Croton.

He is credited with the Pythagorean theory in Euclidean geometry: in a right triangle, the square of the hypotenuse is equal to the sum of the squares of the other two sides. Besides mathematics, he was also known as an expert in the fields of music, astronomy, and medicine. Music and mathematics combined in his theory of the origin and arrangement of the universe and the nature of numbers, which he called "the essence and source of all things." He expanded this idea to reach the conclusion that the universe operated on a "harmony of the spheres," with stars and planets in sync with mathematical equations corresponding to musical notes. This production depended upon the rates of motion of the planetary bodies. Pythagoras taught that the sun is in the center of the universe.

The followers of Pythagoras created a brotherhood to establish the teachings and lifestyle they inherited from the master, consisting of esoteric knowledge that was confined to members. Much of this involved science and mathematics as well as religious views. We do not have enough information to classify this as a Mystery cult, but members took oaths and presented offerings to his memory.

Pythagoras believed in the idea of transmigration of souls, or reincarnation. A well-known story related that as proof of this belief, he stopped a man beating a dog when he recognized the voice of a deceased friend in the dog's bark. In the concept of reincarnation, the soul goes through several different existences based upon its prior life. A sinner could end up as an animal. The escape from the cycle of reincarnation depended upon pure living and philosophical study.

The teachings on reincarnation may have led to his followers' dietary restrictions, where meat was forbidden. Men should not eat from any being that had life, nor should they cruelly sacrifice these animals to the gods. The casual slaughter of animals could lead to the slaughter of men, and Pythagoras preached a doctrine of peace. Nor could they drink wine, as it led away from pure living and good health. An oddity that was often reported of the Pythagoreans was the ban on eating beans, with various rationales. One story claimed that Pythagoras believed that a part of the soul was lost when humans passed gas, the result of eating beans. The later movement advocated sexual abstinence, although tradition says that Pythagoras was married.

Heraclitus of Ephesus (535–475 BCE)

Heraclitus saw all of nature in perpetual flux. What structured and ordered this flux was rationality, the principle of reason, known as the *logos*. In Greek, *logos* had several different meanings as word, speech, or reason. For Heraclitus, it was the divine principle of order and knowledge. This concept became standard in philosophical views of the universe, with *logos* as the invisible connecting link between god as pure essence and the structuring and behavior of physical matter.

The Sophists (Fifth Century BCE)

The Sophists were eclectic itinerant teachers found in all the Greek cities and beyond by the second half of the fifth century BCE. For a fee, they would train young men in the art of rhetoric or persuasion. They claimed that their educational skills were necessary for the young who would inherit the political duties of the city-state, so they should learn how to address and sway the Assembly. Sophists often suffered negative slurs from society. The word sophistry became a modern term to describe someone who uses clever but fallacious arguments to deceive.

Many Sophists focused on the distinction between nature and law. Law in this case referred to the traditional social conventions and concepts of justice at the time. For Sophists, what most people considered to be just was in direct conflict with nature and hence did not demonstrate true justice. Some of them argued that society's laws and social conventions were created to redirect the natural pursuit of pleasure.

One of the more famous of the sophists was Protagoras (490–420 BCE), who is credited with the philosophical concept of relativism. This derives from his comment, "Man is the measure of all things," and became the basis of his school. Each person subjectively perceives reality in his or her own way. Absolute truth cannot be obtained, for everything is relative because of the many layers between the *logos* and our perception of the universal where reality becomes distorted.

Protagoras is also credited with being an agnostic. In modern usage, an agnostic is a person who believes that nothing can be really known with assurance beyond material phenomena:

> concerning the gods I am not in a position to know either that (or how) they are or that (or how) they are not, or what they are like in appearance; for there are many things that prevent knowledge, the obscurity of the matter and the brevity of human life.
>
> (*On the Gods*)

Later traditions claimed that Protagoras was convicted of impiety for such teaching, was exiled from Athens and drowned at sea.

Democritus (460–370 BCE)

Democritus of Abdera (Thrace) was more famous for his science and mathematics (which he may have learned in Babylon or Egypt) than for a philosophical school per se, but his ideas did influence other philosophers. He taught that everything is composed entirely of imperishable, invisible elements called atoms. This was a practical view of the world which did not rely upon the traditional belief in divine powers as the cause of everything. He became known as "the laughing philosopher," because he laughed at human foolishness and beliefs. Later writers credited him with establishing the science of aesthetics, or critical analysis of poetry and art.

Cynics

The Cynics are difficult to categorize into a school because most of their teachings focused on lifestyle and attitudes to life rather than theoretical treatises. The origin of the name itself stems from different sources. One common story relates that the word *cynon*, which means dog, may originally have been applied here because of a story that a dog once grabbed the sacrifice at an offering to Hercules, who was patron in one of their meeting places.

Another story attaches the term to Diogenes of Sinope (412–323 BCE), considered one of the founders of this philosophy. Either as an insult or a description of the lifestyle of Diogenes, calling someone a dog reflected the shamelessness of Cynic behavior because they openly rejected social conventions. A famous story claimed Diogenes traveled the world looking for "an honest man."

The Cynics mocked the traditional views of the gods as well as their worship, pronouncing all of it thievery. The Olympians steal from humans by asking for material sacrifices, and humans steal those offerings back from the gods. All of this is done in order to achieve fame and fortune, as demonstrated by the obsession of prayers to the gods. Diogenes criticized humans for asking for the wrong things from the gods, things that would not lead to serenity.

The Cynic was to live according to nature through reason, with freedom as the catchword. This freedom meant not only liberty, but the freedom found in self-sufficiency. Society, through its human misunderstanding of the gods, social conventions or codes of behavior, deprives an individual of his true freedom. Diogenes was famous for his neglected appearance and his general public demonstrations that he was no longer bound by the laws of society. He ate and drank without manners in the marketplaces and even defecated and masturbated in public. His sense of freedom could also be understood as political and social rebellion. These ideas upended the traditional understanding of the role of the citizen and his duties to the *polis*.

The Cynic way of life was to help one's soul lose the desire for material aspects of society through learning how to accept hardship and suffering. Cynics gave up possessions and often "took to the road," living an itinerant life and existing on occasional handouts from others. Diogenes was said to have walked barefoot in snow and rolled around in hot, burning sand. The Cynics can often be viewed as the first "hippies," relishing their social shock value.

Plato, Socrates and Platonism (428–348 BCE)

Founder of the Academy in Athens, Plato is one of the most important philosophers in Western history (Figure XI.1). He was a pupil of Socrates, whose teachings were conveyed through the writings of Plato. Socrates was known for the dialectic method of reasoning. This was a dialogue with arguments and counter-arguments to arrive at the truth of a proposition or known belief. These works not only influenced the Greek world, but they continued to influence learning throughout the Roman Empire, including Christian philosophy.

According to Plato, the material world was not the real world but a copy of the forms which existed in the abstract. For example, if you are sitting at a desk in a classroom, you can see and feel the desk with all of its physical properties. If there were no desks in the room and you were asked to go and find a desk,

Figure XI.1   Bust of
Plato. *Source*: DEA/G.
DAGLI ORTI/De
Agostini/Getty
Images.

you would know exactly what it was. "Desk" or the idea of desk exists independently of the physical form. This positing of two different realms later led to debates on whether the realms work in harmony or are opposed to each other.

God, the "highest good," "the ultimate reality," for Plato, did not create the physical universe of matter. To think so would be to admit that god was imperfect because the physical world was imperfect. God is immutable, not subject to change, and change was inherent in creation. God is the highest power, but there were other levels of divinity. Rather than being created by god, these other powers emanated from god. Today we understand light as part of an electromagnetic spectrum that occurs in wavelengths. For ancient philosophers, the idea of emanation from the mind of god was analogous to the light from a candle or the sun. You could see it, but it was not physical. One of the emanations from god was termed the *demiurge*, a subordinate power that became responsible for physical creation.

While god did not directly create the material universe, nevertheless Plato keeps god connected to the physical world through the idea of the *logos*, or the principle of reason. The *logos* imbued the physical universe with rationality. This rationality was present in the soul. Like everything else, the soul was an ideal which existed first on the divine level but was then manifest in the body. Plato has Socrates claim that the soul was trapped in a body until reason helped it to escape. The soul took on rewards and punishments in the afterlife.

One of the more classic cases of the connection between philosophy and religion was found in the trial and conviction of Socrates in 399 BCE. He was charged with impiety (against the traditional gods) and with corrupting the youth of Athens (through teaching against the gods and introducing new deities). We can still debate if the charges were a screen for his unpopularity concerning his critiques of the politics of Athens. He was convicted by the city and ordered to be executed. Even though his friends made plans for his escape, Socrates chose to drink hemlock, demonstrating that he was in charge of his destiny, not the state. This became one of the most famous "noble deaths" in the ancient world. However, Socrates (through Plato) was said to have claimed that before any such act, one must have received a divine call of *ananke*, "necessity." Plato did not elaborate on the nature of this call, other than it derived from "the gods."

Aristotle (384–322 BCE)

Aristotle was a disciple of Plato who founded the school known as the *Lyceum* in Athens (Figure XI.2). Pacing back and forth while they taught in the *peripatoi* (colonnades of buildings), his followers were known as Peripatetics. Aristotle explored mathematics, physics, biology, botany, agriculture, medicine, theater, geography, ethics, and politics. He established the standard approach to logic with his syllogisms. Aristotle was one of the first philosophers to categorize knowledge into areas of discipline. He was the tutor of Alexander the Great.

Aristotle's contribution to the study of the universe, the divine, and the soul are found in his work on metaphysics. Metaphysics examines existence or the

Figure XI.2 Bust of Aristotle. *Source:* DEA/G. DAGLI ORTI/De Agostini/ Getty Images.

first principles of things in abstract concepts, or being itself. Aristotle famously rejected Plato's concept of the forms. He claimed that the theory did not answer enough questions. How does the theory explain the first cause of all things? How does it explain change? Where Plato saw the forms as independent of an object, Aristotle taught that ideas were intrinsic to objects and did not exist separately. The essence of an object led to understanding the true nature of an object.

In accordance with other philosophers, Aristotle dismissed the traditional understanding of the gods by assigning it to an older age before the rise of philosophy (see the box "Aristotle on the Gods of Myth"). To Aristotle, god is the first of all substances, the necessary first source of movement who is himself unmoved. This "unmoved mover" is a being with everlasting life and perfect blessedness, engaged in never-ending contemplation. God causes the motion of the planetary spheres. All nature demonstrates a rational plan which had to originate somewhere. According to Aristotle, in disagreement with other philosophers, the soul, or the rational mind, did not exist independently from the body. Like various body parts, the soul had faculties related to its function in the biological development of the body. It makes more sense to understand Aristotle's conception of the soul as "life force."

In relation to special virtues and ethics, Aristotle taught many of the same concepts of leading a rational life, which by its nature would be a good life. He advocated "the mean" as the ultimate goal, never giving in to extreme behavior either positively or negatively. In social relations, both the family and the state were organizations that had a moral duty to enhance society for the good. His famous line, "man is a political animal," reflects his belief in the rationality of humans over animals in nature. Man is the only life form endowed with the gift of speech, which can be put to use for the benefit of the *polis*.

Aristotle on the Gods of Myth

Like others before him, Aristotle pointed out some of the absurdities of myth, especially found in Hesiod. Hesiod claimed that the gods ate nectar and drank ambrosia, but if they were immortal, why the need to eat or drink? He did acknowledge the role of tradition in society, in that myths had a historical function:

> From old – and indeed extremely ancient – times there has been handed down to our later age intimations of a mythical character to the effect that the stars are gods and that the divine embraces the whole of nature. The further details were subsequently added in the manner of myth. Their purpose was the persuasion of the masses and general legislative and political expediency. For instance, the myths tell us that these gods are anthropomorphic or resemble some of the other animals and give us other, comparable extrapolations of the basic picture.

The myths presented material that made thinkers curious and ultimately led to the enlightenment of philosophy. Aristotle applied the term "*mythos*" in his work on the arts and poetry, using *mythos* the way we understand plot.

Skepticism

The word skeptic is derived from the various movements in Greek philosophy, beginning with the Pre-Socratics and continuing into the Hellenistic and Roman periods. *Skeptomai* meant "to think, to consider," and referred to an attitude of doubt or questioning of what we think we can know and how we can know it.

Under the influence of many of the Pre-Socratics (such as Xenophanes), according to this philosophy, nothing can be known for certain. Humans could be engaged in seeking knowledge, but should suspend judgment. We cannot rely upon sense impressions because our senses can be fooled and reason is often dictated by our own desires. To claim that one knows something will always remain just an opinion. Rather than a school per se, skeptical ideas influenced individual philosophers throughout the period.

Stoicism

Zeno of Citium (334–262 BCE) is credited with founding the school of Stoic philosophy, named after the *stoa* (an open colonnade) where he taught in Athens. For Stoics, deeds and behavior were what mattered, not particularly thoughts, and all behavior had to be in harmony with reason and nature. Because the universe was subject to natural laws, one had to accept everything that happens with equanimity.

All existence in the universe is material; Stoics rejected the idea that things exist in the abstract independently. This material universe is known as god or nature, through which reason is active upon passive matter. All creation has substance, qualities, and exists in relation to other objects (space and time). The universe is one that is energized by divine reason, known as the *logos spermatikos*, which orders things according to laws (cause and effect). This "world-soul" is found in all objects, humans, animals, and plants. Souls are immortal by nature, and at death can unify with the world-soul. The world-soul has a goal in that eventually all creation will cease to exist in a fiery inferno and begin again.

Humans have access to divine reason through their intellect, recognizing that there is a divine plan, often deemed Fate, which the good Stoic learns to accept; it cannot be changed by anything that we think or do. This acceptance is accomplished through a disciplined lifestyle of never letting the emotions rule one's life, or *apatheia*. In modern jargon, a Stoic was to "grin and bear it," being impervious to both pain and pleasure. One exercised one's freedom of will in relation to nature or fate. A Stoic sought wisdom (understanding the true nature of the universe), courage, patience, and justice. Evil arises from human ignorance. Following in the wake of the Hellenistic period, Stoicism became one of the most popular schools of philosophy in the Roman Empire.

Epicurus and Epicureanism

Epicurus (341–270 BCE) founded a school of philosophy that unfortunately has lent its thoughts and name to a way of life that has often been misunderstood. Today we use the word "epicure" for someone with discriminating taste in food and drink, but it is also used to imply someone who is devoted to sensual pleasure of any kind.

Epicurus claimed that philosophy should teach humans how to obtain a happy, serene life in both *ataraxia* (freedom from fear) and *agonia* (the absence of pain). Good and evil are manifest in the world as pleasure and pain. Death sees the end of both the body and the soul, and therefore it should not be feared. Epicurus's house was the center of his school, with "The Garden" the reference for the meeting place. Allegedly, the inscription on the gate read, "Stranger, here you will do well to tarry; here our highest good is pleasure." This school of philosophy was the first officially to admit and welcome women and slaves. Sounding like a club of friends, nevertheless the school had a hierarchy of levels, and disciples swore oaths to the teachings.

Epicurus was an atomist in his belief of how the universe worked. His idea of freedom from fear included any fear of the gods. The gods did exist as powers, but they took no interest in human affairs. There was no concept of reward or punishment in this world or the next. However, traditional beliefs concerning the gods were useful in their positive elements, in demonstrating how to enjoy the pleasurable things in life. Epicurus most likely participated in the native cults. At least, he did not preach against traditional rituals.

Epicurus did not advocate pleasure at any price because any overindulgence led to pain and suffering. Anger and destruction against one's neighbor did not bring a tranquil life; in the end, suffering from such behavior would enter the cycle again. Seeking the absence of pain would lead to tranquility. Epicureans advocated the avoidance of participating in politics, as politics was full of corruption and the abuse of power. However, laws and behavioral codes are necessary for society to live in harmony.

Although Epicurus had insisted on the existence of the gods, the mode of existence was rather like an ethereal substance which enters our minds in visions, imagination, and dreams. When he said, think of god as a blessed and immortal being, he may have meant that humans are able to construct ideals in their minds. This leads to morality, which will help us to lead a blissful life.

Philosophy in Ancient Rome

Although southern Italy and Sicily had been colonized by Greece, philosophy as an object of study did not begin to become important to Romans until after the conquests of Macedonia and Greece (140s BCE). Philosophy then became an important part of upper-class education in Rome, reflecting the Roman admiration of Greek civilization. Educated Romans were fluent in both Greek and Latin. Rather than independent schools, we have the writings of Roman thinkers who continued the basic teachings of the Greek schools and applied them to Roman life and traditions. Some of the Roman philosophers can be categorized under specific schools, but the majority, while maintaining the same basic overviews, also combined elements from many points of view. We use the term "polymath," or a person of wide-ranging knowledge, as a more appropriate descriptor of some of their teachings and lifestyle.

Antiochus of Ascalon (125–68 BCE)

Antiochus of Ascalon taught at the Academy in Athens and in Alexandria, and influenced philosophical thought at Rome (one of his pupils was Cicero). He could be described as eclectic, combining Platonism with Stoicism and the Peripatetics. This period begins what is categorized as Middle Platonism. Antiochus was known for his discourses on skepticism, or how far we can ever fully know the truth of anything. The emotions and senses were not trustworthy tools for this ability, but Antiochus argued that humans could use the tool of reason.

Marcus Terentius Varro (116–27 BC)

Varro personified the Roman concept of service to the community by rising up through the *cursus honorum* and also participating in his military duties during the Civil War between Caesar and Pompey. He sided with Pompey, but Caesar gave him amnesty and appointed him as the director of the public library in Rome. He later ran afoul of Mark Antony, but Augustus provided him with amnesty as well.

Varro studied under Antiochus of Ascalon in Athens. He was one of the most prolific writers in antiquity on a variety of topics, including calendars and agricultural issues. He classified areas of discipline for study that were later incorporated into what became the "liberal arts" of the schools in the Middle Ages. In his *Antiquitates rerum humanarum et divinarum*, he discussed "human affairs" and *res divinae*, "divine affairs." Much of this work only survives in later Christian literature, where it was used polemically against native traditions.

"Divine affairs" were divided by Varro into three kinds: (i) the myths and religious references of the poets; (ii) what he termed the natural theorizing on divinity by philosophers, which should be restricted to the educated elite (common people might be led into doubt concerning the sacred if exposed to these ideas); and (iii) the importance of the civic cults in upholding the state.

Lucretius (99 BCE–c. 45 BCE)

A poet and philosopher, Titus Lucretius Carus influenced the study of Epicureanism in Rome. He is known to us mainly through his only surviving work, *De rerum natura* (*On the Nature of Things*). The traditional gods do not intervene on earth; chance or fate is what motivates events in the world. He criticized contemporary morality in Rome (particularly the absence of moral behavior) as a misunderstanding of traditional beliefs, citing Epicurean principles as the best guide to moral behavior.

But there appear to be elements in the writings of Lucretius that reflect traditional concepts. In his praise for Epicurus, he presented him in a similar fashion to the hero cults, where great deeds lead to divine rewards. In this sense, Epicurus is shown to be a great benefactor to humans and, in fact, outshines Ceres or Bacchus in terms of gifts to humanity. He also used the gods as metaphors to denote elements of human life: Venus for love, Neptune for sea, etc. At one point he prayed to Venus (love) for her help in restraining Mars (war). This may not indicate that Lucretius believed in the traditional gods, but rather that he was appealing to metaphors that his audience would understand.

Lucretius taught that we should never fear death, as we will no longer be able to experience anything after we die. He compared it to sleep in that we do not participate in things while we sleep. Death will be like life before we were born, which we cannot remember. Death happens to us all, so it would be irrational to fear it. Nature demands that the old must make way for the new.

The philosophy of Lucretius most likely influenced the work of two later philosopher-poets, Publius Vergilius Maro (70–19 BCE), known as Vergil, and Quintus Horatius Flaccus (65–8 BCE), known as Horace. They both received patronage from the emperor Augustus, and their works promoted and upheld the values of the early Empire. Vergil's most famous work was the *Aeneid*, the epic poem of the founding of Rome, and Horace produced epodes, or lyric poetry. One of Horace's most famous lines, *carpe diem* ("seize the day"), remains a popular attitude toward life. Another poet of the Augustan age, Publius Ovidius Naso (43 BCE to 17 CE), or Ovid, exhibits much Epicurean thought in his works, although he did not write specifically on philosophy. One would have to survey his major works, such as *Metamorphoses* (on the myths) to cull various pieces of philosophical thinking from them. It is from Ovid's incomplete *Fasti* that we learn the details of the major religious festivals in Rome for half a year.

Epicures

Rather than through literature, it was in the lifestyle of some upper-class Romans that the term "epicure" became associated with the views of Epicurean thought, on the mistaken assumption that Epicurus taught indulgence. Individual upper-class Romans became famous for their excessiveness in exotic food and drink, which became an element of this legacy. One of the most important ways in which to establish contacts (for business, politics, etc.) was through dinner invitations. Dinner became the height of socialization, with traditional structures (who got to sit where) and menus. As Rome expanded through conquest, new food and drink was introduced for those who could afford them, with exotic ingredients and spices culled from all the provinces.

This extravagant lifestyle remains the image we have of ancient Rome through art, novels, movies, and television series. It should be emphasized that only the very rich could afford such luxuries. At the same time, the indulgences of the rich do not necessarily reveal the absence of traditional religious and philosophical views or beliefs.

Cicero (106–43 BCE)

Marcus Tullius Cicero is one of the most famous and popular thinkers of ancient Rome (Figure XI.3). Through his treatises, trial transcripts, and letters during the late Republic, we probably know more about Cicero than others at the time. He followed the Stoic school of thought when it came to ideas concerning the universe and reason, but he also incorporated traditional ideas concerning the gods and their significance in the world. He believed that the Stoic concept of a brotherhood of humans had become personified in the ideal of the Roman way of life.

Cicero was an advocate (lawyer) from a small town outside of Rome (Arpinum) who worked his way up the *cursus honorum* ("course of offices") to become a Consul of Rome. His fame as an advocate began early when he defended a famous case of patricide (that of Sextus Roscius) and won. In another famous case he successfully prosecuted Gaius Verres (c. 120–43 BCE) on corruption charges when Verres governed Sicily. Because his family did not have famous

Figure XI.3 Bust of Cicero. *Source*: Araldo de Luca/Corbis via Getty Images.

ancestors, Cicero was considered a "new man," a pejorative term for a parvenu. He suffered from this insecurity all of his life. His consulship was plagued by what became known as the "Catiline conspiracy," an attempt by the patrician Lucius Sergius Catilina to overthrow the government. Cicero's rooting out of the conspiracy became his claim to fame as the savior of traditional Roman values and governance. He is often cited as the most important contributor to the "science of politics," or as we now deem such experts, politicians.

In relation to religion, perhaps his most famous work is *De natura deorum* (*On the Nature of the Gods*, 45 BCE). It consists of three books in the form of a dialogue discussing the ideas of different schools of philosophy concerning the gods in Stoicism, Epicureanism, and Skepticism. The work is important for the preservation of teachings that have been lost in their original form. Whether or not the gods exist, the nature of the universe, and how we can know and reason about such issues were considered vitally important by Cicero.

At the same time, Cicero recognized the universality of the divine in the customs of ethnic cultures: "Come now: Do we really think that the gods are everywhere called by the same names by which they are addressed by us? But the gods have as many names as there are languages among humans" (*De natura deorum*, Book I, 84). However, he applied the term, *superstitio* ("to stand in terror of the deity") to many of these ethnic cultures, pointing out their excesses in worship as "baseless fear of the gods" (Book II, 28). He was comparing these foreign cults to the traditional forms of worship at Rome.

It is important to point out that as a Consul of Rome, Cicero's duties included the standard rituals and sacrifices to the gods, which he carried out and upheld as ancestral traditions. He also served as a priest in some of the cults, a job that was included with the higher positions of the magistrates. There is no evidence that he found these traditions outmoded or unnecessary. In fact, he was very proud of having been elected as an *augur*. Even if the existence of the gods could not be proved, he found it wise to honor them through the traditional rituals. Through his everyday correspondence as various events unfolded, Cicero consistently made references to "the gods." In an advisory letter to Brutus (one of Caesar's assassins), he reminded him to pray to the gods for strength and resolve.

Seneca the Younger (4 BCE to 65 CE)

Lucius Annaeus Seneca, whose family was originally from Cordoba, Spain, became another famous Stoic philosopher in the first century. He wrote treatises, letters, tragedies, and satire and was singularly placed as the tutor of the emperor Nero. He shared influence on the young emperor with the Praetorian Prefect Sextus Burrus, who, along with Seneca, later received much criticism for not guiding Nero properly. Being in the center of Imperial life, he endured some years of exile and had to juggle his philosophical views with the politics of his day. Seneca is noteworthy for promoting Stoic thought that became standard for later generations.

Seneca wrote on *voluntas* (the "will") in relation to Stoic ideas of assent. Once we receive sense impressions, then we voluntarily will ourselves to the right action. Human emotions can be involuntary (reactions) or voluntary (requiring assent). What makes one foolish or wise is the ability to assent or not to assent to impressions. This is particularly relevant when he discusses the excess of emotion involved in anger. He suggests that readers do as he does every evening, reflect upon his actions that day. This results in the care for one's soul, which for Seneca is the reason we should turn to god out of love (and ultimately become like him). This study (which includes turning to nature) helps us to overcome our fear of death and the subsequent excessive emotions involved in grief and mourning.

Seneca's personal life was not ideal; he had many affairs (he was accused of sleeping with Caligula's sister), he abused his powers when it came to treasury finances in Britain, and he was accused of extreme forms of usury in his personal finances. His treatise on *clementia* (mercy) is advice for how to treat weaknesses in others. The contradiction here is in the fact that this treatise emphasized and highlighted the *clementia* of Nero, which was basically non-existent. The name of Nero became a byword for cruelty. It is easy to see that most have concluded that this was written for sheer flattery of the emperor.

In 65 CE, Seneca was implicated in the Pisonian conspiracy (an attempt to assassinate Nero) and ordered by the emperor to commit suicide. According to later stories, he invited his friends to dinner, where he and his wife, Pompeia Paulina, slit their wrists. He was apparently a slow bleeder, so he took poison as well. He had time to dictate his last words to a scribe, and then sat in a bath until he died. Nero ordered that his wife be bound up and saved. Seneca added a note to his will that he be cremated but without the usual funeral rites.

Epictetus (55–135 CE)

A Greek former slave from Phrygia, Epictetus was another influential Stoic philosopher through the writings of his disciple Arrian. Epictetus was owned and then freed by a secretary to Nero. When the emperor Domitian banished all philosophers from Rome in 95 CE, he moved to Nicopolis, Greece, where the later emperor Hadrian may have visited him.

In the teachings of Epictetus, there is no distinction among "god," "the gods," or Zeus. God is the giver to whom we should be thankful and Epictetus utilized many metaphors for understanding the relationship between the divine and humans. God is the captain of the ship as we voyage to the afterlife; life is a game where it is not objects that matter, but how we play the game. Life should also be enjoyed as a festival. In discussing misfortune, however, he appeals not to the abstractions of philosophy, but to the traditional concepts of the gods and Fate:

> Will you be angry and discontented with the ordinances of Zeus, which he, with the Fates who spun in his presence the thread of your destiny at the time of your birth, ordained and appointed?
>
> (*Discourses*, 1.12.25)

For adversity, Epictetus also utilized metaphors relating to athletes. Why does god order the difficulties that beset humans? These should be understood as challenges presented to an Olympic athlete. Adversity will make him discipline himself and ultimately make him stronger. Troubles ultimately act as a means by which to show the world the character of a person. The concept of god as goodness has been shared with all humans. Included in this gift from the gods are soul and reason. Applying reason can help us attain the level of the gods. We should never become slaves to our desires.

Marcus Aurelius (121–180 CE)

Emperor from 161 to 180 CE, Marcus Aurelius became one of the most important Stoics of the Roman Empire and beyond through his work *The Meditations* (see the box "Excerpts from *The Meditations* by Marcus Aurelius" and Figure XI.4). Beset by problems at the borders (Parthia, Germany), he spent much of his life on campaign with the legions. Apparently he had time to reflect upon how to preserve equanimity in life by living in accord with nature. With no official title to the work, *The Meditations* is appropriate because a major theme is an analysis of one's judgment. This judgment begins with knowing that everything comes from nature and everything will return to nature (ordered by the *logos*).

Figure XI.4 Bust of Marcus Aurelius. *Source*: DEA/De Agostini/Getty Images.

Excerpts from The Meditations *by Marcus Aurelius*

Marcus Aurelius noted that adversity comes to all humans, from the lowly to the emperor. His meditations on life promoted the idea that humans cannot control or change externals, so that wasting one's life through anxiety and remorse would not alter the way things were. Life is full of ups and downs so that at times a person is caught up in this cycle and then let down. In the modern jargon of psychiatry, he sometimes expresses his thoughts in what we term a manic-depressive state. A few later thinkers considered him a prototype for our modern concept of an atheist. However, he consistently referenced "the gods" throughout his work.

Constantly regard the universe as one living being, having one substance and one soul; and observe how all things have reference to one perception, the perception of this one living being.

You see how few things you have to do to live a satisfying and reverent life? If you can manage this, that's all even the gods can ask of you.

Yet living and dying, honor and dishonor, pain and pleasure, riches and poverty, and so forth are equally the lot of good men and bad. Things like these neither elevate nor degrade; and therefore they are no more good than they are evil.

Observe always that everything is the result of a change, and get used to thinking that there is nothing Nature loves so well as to change existing forms and to make new ones like them.

There is a limit to the time assigned you, and if you don't use it to free yourself it will be gone and never return.

When you wake up in the morning, tell yourself: The people I deal with today will be meddling, ungrateful, arrogant, dishonest, jealous, and surly. They are like this because they can't tell good from evil.

Now departure from the world of men is nothing to fear, if gods exist: because they would not involve you in any harm. If they do not exist, or if they have no care for humankind, then what is life to me in a world devoid of gods, or devoid of providence? But they do exist, and they do care for humankind: and they have put it absolutely in man's power to avoid falling into the true kinds of harm.

Plotinus (204–270 CE)

Later scholars have deemed Plotinus to be one of the founders of what is known as Neo-Platonism because he expanded Plato's original ideas. Most of his work is found in the writings of his disciple, Porphyry. According to Porphyry, Plotinus went to Alexandria to study philosophy because he was unhappy with many of the systems. He then traveled to Parthia to study Persian philosophy (which included elements of Indian philosophy at the time). He enlisted for the invasion of Parthia (under Gordian III), but when the invasion failed, he eventually moved to Rome. He attempted to establish a city in Campania along the lines of an ideal city based upon *The Republic*, but he never gained Imperial funds to pay for it.

For Plotinus, "the One" has no division or distinction and cannot even be described as an object that exists in the way we understand existence. Rather, we should understand the One in its potential and dynamic way, in the way it causes the existence of all creation. The One is not a usual creator, but should be understood as light and mind which wills good. Activity and immutability cannot coexist. Rather, existence begins as an emanation from the most perfect to the lesser perfection of subordinate powers and finally materiality (where matter is the least perfect). The emanation never diminishes or takes away anything from the One.

There is a world soul, divided into upper and lower, where the lower is found in nature and human souls. Because all derives from the One, humans can participate in the cosmos through the contemplation of beauty, recognized in the Forms, and finally through an ecstatic union with the One (mysticism). Porphyry claimed that Plotinus achieved this state four times in his life. The most important issue for Plotinus was *eudaimonia* (happiness) in life. Happiness is beyond anything in this material world and can only be achieved within one's consciousness of the true reality of the universe. This way of thinking also follows Stoic thought, where the adversity of life cannot affect the person. Plotinus greatly influenced the philosophy and theology of the later Christian Church Fathers.

Porphyry (232–304 CE)

Porphyry not only gave us the teachings of Plotinus, but wrote many works himself. One of them, *Introduction*, became a standard text on logic in the Middle Ages, where he defined the concept of substance as having five components: genus, species, difference, property, and accident. He also wrote *Against the Christians* and *Philosophy from Oracles* as polemics against the Christian denigration of paganism.

His writings against the Christians only survive in quotations by Christian writers. Apparently he defended the tradition of oracles, which had revealed proper sacrificial rites, and defended the role of astrology in understanding fate. He also defended being a vegetarian (*On Abstinence from Animal Food*, along Pythagorean concepts), which may appear contrary to a defense of animal sacrifice. He acknowledged Jesus as a philosopher but attacked Christian methods concerning prophecy. As almost a forerunner of modern biblical scholars, Porphyry argued that the Book of Daniel was not an early book of prophecy, but written during the time of Antiochus Epiphanes (165 BCE) by a Jew during the Maccabee Revolt. Daniel contained false prophecies concerning future kingdoms, so that any Christian reliance upon them was also false. (Christians had used Jesus's apocalyptic sayings such as Matthew 24:15 as a fulfillment of Daniel.)

Iamblichus (242–327 CE)

Representing the continuation of the teachings of Pythagoras, Iamblichus was a student of Porphyry, originally from Syria, and may have been of local, royal descent. He established a school at Apameia, Syria, where he was known for his austere life and charity and credited with miraculous powers. He wrote *A Collection of Pythagorean Doctrines*, which also contained other philosophical views. He added Pythagorean number theory to Platonic concepts, but also argued that the soul, embodied in the physical person, endows the body with the same divinity.

Between the One and the physical universe, there is a host of intermediate divinities – gods, angels, demons, heroes, and other heavenly beings, who act as guardians of individuals and nations. The numbers of these divinities are in proportion to mathematical principles and these powers influence natural events. They can predict the future and humans can access them through prayers and offerings. The teachings of Iamblichus contained very complicated abstractions and theories. Nevertheless, in late antiquity we still have an appeal that includes a traditional concept of divinities and traditional practices.

Iamblichus taught and practiced theurgy ("divine-working") as the means by which to unify with the One. This consisted of mental exercises that would help the person unveil the layers between the mundane world and that of the divine. Theurgy was an important element of Neo-Platonism in some circles.

The legacy of ancient teachings of philosophers on the concept of a higher god as one is deemed philosophical monotheism by scholars. Beginning in the second century, Christian leaders absorbed this idea in conjunction with their views of god in the Jewish Scriptures. The works of ancient philosophers were thus esteemed and copied, and admired for being prototypes for the belief in one god. However, these philosophers do not meet the modern concept of monotheism in that they nevertheless maintained many of the traditions and practices of native cults. They recognized many other powers in the universe that were manifestations of the one.

Religion, Philosophy, and the Common People

How much of the views of philosophers on the gods and religion influenced the views of common Greeks and Romans? Scholars estimate the level of literacy in the ancient world anywhere from 1 to 5% and it was restricted to the upper classes. However, it might be better to calculate this statistic by positing the term "educated," rather than literate. In what we would now consider "the middle classes," the businessmen and professional craftsmen, some level of literacy in both letters and numbers would have been essential simply to do business. The more intense level of education is termed *paideia*, or the classical education of antiquity, which included philosophy and required money and leisure-time.

However, much of ancient life was experienced through the interaction of social connections and the public venues of villages, towns, and cities. The moral tone set by philosophers could be experienced simply by strolling through the *agora* or forum on any given day. Philosophers could be heard hawking their talents in competition with others. There were frequent speeches by magistrates and candidates for office who had been trained in philosophical schools. Law courts were open to the public and were an additional source of both education and entertainment. Many philosophical views were on display in the theaters, where playwrights integrated views on the gods, philosophy, politics, and moral conduct. There was also the most common form of communication, gossip, where ideas perhaps heard in the streets could be bandied about. Without a body of literature we simply do not have enough information to judge the impact of philosophical attitudes on the religious views of average people.

Summary

- Schools of philosophy arose in an effort to understand the human relationship to the universe and to the divine through the application of reason and observation. They shared elements with religious traditions in that the schools taught the way to live the best possible life.
- Most schools of philosophy attempted to present a different understanding of the universe that nevertheless upheld the traditional morality and social conventions.

Suggestions for Further Reading

Fieser, J. and B. Dowden, eds. 2018. *Internet Encyclopedia of Philosophy*. http://www.iep.utm.edu. An online-only source with peer-reviewed articles on each ancient philosopher.

Herrmann, F.-G. 2010. "Greek religion and philosophy: the god of the philosopher," in *A Companion to Greek Religion*, ed. D. Ogden, pp. 385–397. Wiley-Blackwell. This chapter highlights the essentials of Platonic worldviews.

Mitchell, S. and P. Van Nuffelen. 2010. *One God: Pagan Monotheism in the Roman Empire*. Cambridge University Press. This is a sourcebook for the concept of philosophical monotheism.

Price, S. 1999. *Religions of the Ancient Greeks*. Cambridge University Press. This contains an overview of philosophy and religion.

Warrior, V. M. ed. 2001. "Skepticism of traditional religion: Epicureanism and Stoicism," in *Roman Religion: A Sourcebook*, pp. 151–162. Focus. This has excerpts from Roman philosophy.

Warrior, V. M. ed. 2009. "Challenges to traditional religion," in *Greek Religion: A Sourceboook*, pp. 205–228. Focus. This book contains excerpts from the writings of ancient Greek philosophers and also includes the details on the trial of Socrates.

RELIGION AND THE STATE

XII

**Law and Government
in the Ancient World**

Greece

**Roman Religion
and the State**

**Religion and the State
for the Masses**

Greek and Roman Religions, First Edition. Rebecca I. Denova.
© 2019 John Wiley & Sons, Inc. Published 2019 by John Wiley & Sons, Inc.

Learning Objectives

After reading this chapter, you will be able to:

- Gain an overview of the development of laws in ancient Greece and Rome.
- Understand the relationship among laws, morality, and the divine.

Law and Government in the Ancient World

 It is difficult to ascertain exactly when humans developed formalized laws and law codes, but when they did, they were framed within the worldview and understanding of religious concepts. The earliest attempts to structure society were validated upon the will of the gods, variously interpreted. Whatever this early material consisted of, it was handed down through the generations and became part of the lore of the ancestors and was therefore considered sacred.

One of the functions of a code of laws was first and foremost to regulate society and to establish the parameters of accepted behavior. Essentially this included morality and ethics, which were elements of established law codes. Morality refers to proper behavior (actions) for a society, while ethics is a way in which to define the parameters of moral behavior (definitions of good and evil, what constitutes virtue, justice, etc.). The law codes were also important for the creation of gender and gender roles, as well as distinctions of social class. Many of the ideas behind laws and law codes incorporated the concepts of social justice, which included levels of punishment for specific violations of the codes.

While we can consider some of the laws as protecting individual rights, in the ancient view the most important element behind established laws was the consideration of the good of the community (family, clan, tribe, city-state, empire). Communal prosperity was fully integrated into the relationship with the gods that would reward or punish a society based upon divine dictates.

The two most ancient civilizations, Egypt and Mesopotamia, had systems of law in place very early and we have recorded evidence through the survival of papyrus fragments, inscriptions, hieroglyphs, and cuneiform tablets. We have not discovered an official law code per se from ancient Egypt, although we have court records and references to the laws that were centralized under the pharaoh. In Mesopotamia, Hammurabi (1810–1750 BCE) is credited with the first formalized law code, which structured behavior as well as business relations. It was claimed that the laws were revealed to Hammurabi by the sun god Shemesh (Figure XII.1).

How many of these ideas directly influenced ancient Greece and Rome is sometimes hard to determine. There is evidence of early trade exchanges among all the cultures of the Mediterranean basin, so that many of the concepts behind these laws could have been incorporated into what eventually became the Greek and Roman systems. The Greek historian Herodotus traveled widely and recorded many local laws and customs (fifth century BCE). Allegedly Solon of Athens visited Egypt and was greatly impressed by their system of law and order.

Figure XII.I
Hammurabi *stele*
with Shemesh. *Source*:
DEA/De Agostini/
Getty Images.

Greece

We do not have a complete collection of what constituted a systematic set of laws for archaic Greece; various city-states had their own ancient traditions and some concepts were shared by other communities and neighboring areas. The oldest material can be found in certain references from Homer, but most of our knowledge derives from the Classical period of Athens, in the speeches of orators, decrees, trials, plays, and inscriptions.

By the fifth century BCE, the city-states began to codify and write down their laws, which included legal procedures for the administration of justice. Many of these laws originated in the earlier traditions of relations between city-states and individuals, known generally as "exchanges," which had dictated relations in peace and war and the obligations of benefactors and rulers. These law codes were upheld by sworn oaths to the gods.

Various city-states developed different types of governance, often changing with historical circumstances. You could find power in the hands of a single person (a monarchy) or, usually during a crisis, a tyrant (and absolute ruler). Many city-states were ruled by the aristocracy (rule by the nobility, which often involved bloodlines and lineages) or by an oligarchy (rule by a few powerful men). Athens had a history of all three, but eventually settled on rule by free male citizens, or democracy.

Sparta

The earliest attempt to codify Greek laws was credited to Lycurgus, a lawgiver of Sparta, c. 800 BCE. Many of the laws concerned military matters and military discipline, helping to create the city of Sparta as renowned for its excellence in war and the social conventions that stood behind the ideal of Spartan society: equality among citizens, military excellence, and an austere lifestyle.

According to the later stories in Plutarch, Lycurgus traveled to Crete and Ionia to compare their systems and to gather elements that would be appropriate for Sparta. He also visited the oracle at Delphi. Lycurgus claimed that Apollo told him that the city that followed his laws would become the most famous in the world. With this blessing, he created a *gerousia* of 28 men who shared power with two royal houses of Sparta. This was a council of elders who were over the age of 60 and who were elected by acclamation (shouting) to serve for life. The *gerousia* considered motions that were put to the citizen assembly (*ekklesia*), which held the power of veto and had the responsibility of trying citizens.

Lycurgus instituted the practice of men eating together in companies of 15, who all had to contribute a bushel of meal, gallons of wine, cheese, figs, and some funds with which to buy meat or fish each month. Individual meat sacrifices to the gods were also shared among the company. The wives of these men ate together at home with only younger children; sons over the age of seven lived with the men. Lycurgus reorganized land ownership by distributing the lots in equal shares. The *helots*, the war captives from neighboring Laconia, were owned by the state, not individuals, and were assigned work on common properties. Lycurgus also created laws against luxury by limiting cash to Spartan currency, which could not be traded elsewhere, and discouraged the accumulation of lavish home decorations and articles.

Athens

The first official lawgiver of Athens was Draco (seventh century BCE), who is credited with replacing oral laws and blood feuds with a written code. Draco's laws were published on tablets so that all could be aware of them. The laws covered both major and minor crimes because all crime was wrong. These laws applied to everyone regardless of wealth, gender, or social class.

Although the Athenians initially welcomed his changes, in hindsight many of Draco's laws were judged to be harsh. The modern term "Draconian" refers to unbending rules or laws. If a man owed money to someone of a higher social class and couldn't repay the loan, the debtor became a slave. (The penalty was avoided if the reverse of the classes was true.) Draco freely assigned the death penalty to even minor crimes, such as the theft of food. According to Plutarch, such a harsh penalty for virtually every crime was instituted by Draco both as a deterrent against crime and the fact that the criminal deserved it. He distinguished between murder (homicide) and involuntary homicide, and it was the duty of the relatives of the victim to prosecute the offender.

Draco created the Council of Four Hundred, which was separate from the males who met on the Areopagus ("the hill of Ares"), a traditional site for assemblies. This Council was chosen by lot from the leading citizens who could show a certain level of property, and contained the generals and commanders of cavalry. These men had to have sons born in wedlock over the age of 10, who could then inherit if their fathers were killed in battle. The Council was responsible for keeping the budgets, while the Council of Areopagus guarded the laws and kept watch over the Council of Four Hundred. Under the Athenian constitution, citizenship was conferred on free men who could provide the necessary military equipment in times of war.

Classical Athens

Many of the Greek city-states had individuals known as archons, and sometimes *eponymous archons*. This was equivalent to "lord" or "ruler" as the title of a public office, and eponymous referred to their year of office (much like the Roman system of associating consuls with their term of office, see below). There were nine archons in Athens and three of them were responsible for civic (*archon basileus*, "king ruler"), military (*polemarch*, "war ruler"), and religious affairs, often delegated to the *archon basileus* at times. In 501 BCE, the *polemarch* was replaced by 10 *strategoi* or generals. The archons were originally elected every 10 years, later reduced to one, and served as an executive body. The head of the archons, the *archon eponymous*, presided over meetings of the *ekklesia*.

The assembly consisted of free male citizens, who were the only ones who were permitted to speak, regardless of social or economic status. This is consistent with the origins of democracy, where one's ancestral heritage did not restrict participation. The age of enrollment was 18, but full membership was conferred only after a youth had done his military and civic duty as an *ephebe*.

Solon's Reforms

Solon (638–558 BCE) is credited with reforming Draco's laws and legislating against what was considered a period of political, social, economic, and moral crisis in Athens at the time (Figure XII.2). He was famous for structuring the rules of a democratic society. There are stories of his travels, which included Egypt, and in one later story he visited King Croesus in Lydia. Croesus was one of the wealthiest people in the world and believed himself the happiest because of it. Solon advised him, "Count no man happy until he is dead," meaning that disaster could strike at any moment. Croesus ignored him but realized too late

Figure XII.2 Bust of Solon. *Source:* Azoor Photo/Alamy Stock Photo.

what Solon meant when his kingdom was destroyed by Cyrus the Persian. The traveler Pausanias related that Solon was among the "seven sages" who were listed on Apollo's temple at Delphi.

Solon was elected the *eponymous archon* in 594 BCE, for his wisdom in a period of Greek history that had seen the rise of tyrants. Tyrant was the term for someone who unconstitutionally seized power and was often deemed cruel and oppressive (and thus our modern definition of the term). Athens was torn by economic, regional, and ideological rivalry between tribes. Solon's reforms canceled Draco's legislation (with the exception of the homicide law) and addressed constitutional, economic, moral, and social conventions.

Over the years, the Areopagus had become dominated by the higher classes, excluding any participation by the lower or poorer classes. Solon legislated for all levels of citizens to be admitted to the *ekklesia* and created a court (Heliaia) made up of all citizens. He lowered the requirements of financial or social standing for candidates for public office, although he divided the populace into four political classes according to property. The financial requirements for the highest offices, however, were maintained.

Economically Solon encouraged more subsistence farming (the common way to exist) by banning the export of farm produce to neighboring lands. The exception to the export ban was olive oil, which became a large, profitable industry for Greece. He encouraged fathers to train their sons in trades and crafts. It was at this time that black-figure pottery began to be exported throughout the region. He recruited foreign tradesmen, who were granted citizenship to settle in Athens.

Solon claimed that the earth itself (Gaia) had been enslaved. A boundary marker known as a *horos* was a symbol that the farmer was in debt, and they dotted the landscape. A small farmer's only recourse was offering himself and his family as slave labor, with all of his produce going to the lender. In his reforms, Solon abolished all contracts indicated by the *horoi*, prohibited a person being used as collateral, and released Athenians who had been enslaved through debt.

Other reforms that had simultaneous economic and social goals included a ban on excessive dowries in marriage contracts; limitations on money spent on public sacrifices and funerals (understood to serve as propaganda in elections); reforms on inheritance laws in relation to a female who had no brothers (who had previously been required to marry the nearest relative); and the removal of citizenship status from anyone who refused his military duty. According to tradition, Solon regulated pederasty in Athens, or the custom of male mentors having sexual relationships with young boys. His reforms were designed to control abuses of freeborn boys, and slaves were forbidden to participate in the practice with freeborn sons of the owners.

Solon's reforms were supposed to last at least 10 years (sworn by the citizens in an oath to the gods), but after he retired and left the country, the old divisions arose and resulted in a period of tyrants begun by Peisistratos. Solon died in Cyprus shortly before Peisistratos became the tyrant of Athens.

Peisistratos (ruled 561–527 BCE)

Peisistratos, a distant relative of Solon, was a tyrant of Athens who had two sons, Hipparchus and Hippias, who also became tyrants. At the time, Athens was torn by political strife, with factions competing for power with the aristocrats. One of these factions, the poor (*hyperakrioi*), still had little access to power. Peisistratos championed their cause. He seized the Acropolis and took over the city. He was exiled twice but always returned. On one trip back to the city, he drove in accompanied by a woman dressed as Athena in his chariot. This event convinced many that he had the protection of the goddess.

Peisistratos belies our concept of tyranny because of his popular reforms. Herodotus claimed that he did not change the constitution and left the other archons in power. He attempted to ease tensions between the economic classes by taking land from the aristocrats and distributing it to the poor. He also cut taxes for the lower classes and established circuit judges. He minted coins with Athena's owl on them and attempted to beautify the city. Peisistratos is credited with establishing the Panathenaia, which became one of the largest and best known of the religious festivals. He had the works of Homer copied and placed in the archives. He established trade routes to France, Italy, and the Black Sea, and built the first aqueduct in Athens.

Cleisthenes (b. 570? BCE)

Cleisthenes, who had previously been in exile, was recalled to Athens after the Athenians defeated his rival, Isadoras. He earned the title of "the father of Athenian democracy" for his reforms in 507 BCE. In an attempt to avoid conflict among the clans (which had led to tyranny), he restructured the clans from four (connected by family lineage) to 10 (based upon residence, *demes*). He established the process of sortition, or the random selection of citizens by lot (eliminating kinship in the choice). Cleisthenes increased the *boule* (which had the responsibility of proposing legislation to the assembly) from 400 to 500, with 50 from each tribe, and for the courts an average of 500 jurors were selected each day from an annual panel of several thousand citizens. He may have been responsible for the practice of ostracism, or banishment from the city through the vote of 6000 citizens. This was applied mainly to anyone perceived as a threat to democracy or other elements of society. Under his regime, the religious calendar was also reformed, although most of the festivals remained intact.

Under Cleisthenes, some of the *demes* adjacent to Athens, the rural countryside producers, were integrated into the city-state. This entailed integrating their family and local religious rituals into the overall traditions of the city. For instance, Demeter and Heracles became important deities. At the same time, Athenian deities and rituals were extended to the countryside. This helped to create what we could consider a national identity, built upon common religious practices. But in the subsequent history of Athens, such attempts at integration also stimulated religious conflict at times – did a person's first loyalty belong to their local cult or to Athens?

In highlighting the lawgivers of ancient Greece, we can see that first and foremost their concerns were with regulating society for the good of the community. However, within the law codes themselves, we have very little indication of a direct link between the gods and the codes per se. We have to assume that the basic worldviews of ancient Greece were nevertheless incorporated into their dictates for society. We do have consistent references to the gods in speeches, and such references would have had meaning to their audiences. When Peisistratos established the Panathenaia in honor of the protector of the city, this would have elevated his status above his rivals.

The Athenian Assembly dealt with day-to-day supervision of the city-state. Every meeting of the assembly began with sacrifices and ritual lustrations. This was where the public officials were elected (the *archai*). There were limited terms for officials, which was a method to ensure that officials did not seek power beyond their station. The 10 elected generals (*strategoi*) were subject to votes of confidence by the assembly. Each time these organizations met, the first thing they did was sacrifice to the gods.

Another element connecting religion and the state in the ancient Greek city-states was the trust they placed in oracles, particularly the oracles at Delphi, Dodona, and Didyma. We have hundreds of fragments of inscriptions testifying to the delegations sent to these oracles from various city-states. The delegations consisted of the leading citizens and were often accompanied by choirs made up of young boys and girls, whose job it was to sing the praises of the city at the sacred sites. The subject of the questions concerned major decisions taken by rulers and the assemblies. If the delegation believed they had received a positive answer, they inscribed their gratitude on a public plaque for others to learn the benefits of the oracle.

Beginning approximately at the same time as the rise of schools of philosophy, the evidence that we have for understanding the connection between the divine and law codes is found mainly in the writings of the historians. For the Greeks we have Herodotus, Thucydides, and Xenophon.

The Historians: Herodotus, Thucydides, and Xenophon

Herodotus (484–425 BCE) was able to observe many different constitutions and forms of government in his travels (Figure XII.3). However, writing during the period of the Persian Wars, he consistently compared the democracy of Athens to other systems, pointing out the abuses of a monarch or a tyrant, particularly in relation to war. Throughout his work, he upheld Athenian democracy as the best form of government.

Thucydides (460–400 BCE) wrote the *History of the Peloponnesian War*, which took place between Athens and Sparta in the fifth century BCE. The war brought

Figure XII.3   Bust of Herodotus. *Source:* DEA/G. Nimatallah/ De Agostini/Getty Images.

death and destruction (massacres by both sides), and plague struck Athens at the time. Thucydides's account highlighted the suffering that humans bring upon one another, caused by fear and self-interest. This fear was fear of the gods. Thucydides claimed that such fear was the result of ignorance because the gods do not intervene in human affairs. The self-interest derived from human greed and immorality.

The *Anabasis* by Xenophon (430–354 BCE) is the story of a Greek mercenary army stuck "behind the lines" in Persia and other regions, which had to battle its way home to Greece. The story is important for the narration of local customs and rituals. While Herodotus upheld democracy, Xenophon often warned of the abuses of the mob inherent in such a system. His work *Cyropaedia*, on the rise and life of Cyrus the Great, often emphasizes the good elements of monarchy.

Athenian Courts

Scholars often point out that jurisprudence, or the theory and analysis of law, was absent in ancient Greece (as compared to ancient Rome). In other words, we don't have as much literature analyzing the legal system or the theory of how law functions in society. For most, laws existed to harmonize humans living with each other according to what would benefit the greatest good. With the institution of democracy in ancient Athens, every citizen had the right to a fair and public trial.

In ancient Greece there were no professional court officials. A litigant, someone charging someone else with a crime or personal harm, relied upon the art of persuasion or rhetoric, as did the respondent. This was usually a minor court case, settled within one day. The jury decided the outcome of the case, as well as the punishment, which was most often monetary compensation. Juries were citizens over the age of 30 and were paid a small fee. All jurors had to swear oaths to Zeus, Apollo, and Demeter:

> I will cast my vote in agreement with the laws and decrees passed by the Assembly and by the Council, but, if there is no law, in agreement with my sense of what is most just, without favor or enmity. I will vote only on the matters raised in the charge, and I will listen impartially to the accusers and defenders alike.

It is interesting to note that most of the trial procedures did not rest upon the concept of forensic evidence as we understand it. An advocate could employ someone to investigate the details of a case (or the ancient counterpart to our detectives) but such evidence was not tested in a scientific method. The speeches in the law courts were deemed the most important and they would often utilize the concept of divine intervention in a case. In other words, an advocate would typically cite either direct speech from a god or a god acting through an intermediary. The purpose of these references to the gods was to convince the jury of the pious character of the defendant.

All testimony was sworn upon the gods, which was sufficient for belief that an individual would not lie in such situations or risk angering the gods. In the modern West, although we no longer require court witnesses to swear on a Bible, nevertheless they still "swear to tell the truth." The older version included "to tell the truth so help me God," which is now removed, but everyone understands what witnesses are swearing to.

The enforcement of the punishment was handled by the public at large; social norms and conventions determined that the offender would accept the punishment if he valued his social standing. The more notable public trials (usually against a ruling official) had juries of 500 and, depending upon the circumstances, often drew a wider audience. Famous orators made their mark in public trials.

Political Philosophy and Justice

Philosophers also commented on laws and law codes. This literature focused on the relation between ethics and the nature of politics, and delineated the organized structure of politics with analyses of the best constitutions or forms of government. Philosophers focused on the importance of justice and equality of the classes, and the way in which behavior affects the afterlife (the future of one's soul).

The emergence of politics (who should rule the city-state and why) went hand in hand with concepts of justice. Justice was expressed through poets, philosophers, and lawgivers as the system in which the community should work to benefit all, rich and poor alike. From the very beginning, this equality (among citizens only) was understood to please the gods, so that civic identity was fully integrated with religion. While praised in theory, debates continued as to what equality actually meant when it came to rule. Should the aristocrats have more power because they were educated (wiser) and had more at stake? With the legacy of epic poetry, did city-states with famous hero cults have an edge?

Justice related to the cosmic order of things – as in heaven, so on earth. Yet in the Classical period, Sophists began to question whether human laws reflected nature, or were they man-made, arbitrary decisions imposed by the powerful? The response to these questions created what became a new genre, that of political philosophy. How does one manifest the virtue of the One and the unity of the universe in a city-state? Should philosophers get involved in politics, or should they simply live contemplative lives?

As we saw in the Chapter XI, much of ancient Greek philosophy considered morality and ethics (from the Greek, *ethos*), or the customs and habits of peoples, and opined on what was the best way of life. In this respect, philosophers wrote about the political situation of their communities at the time.

Among the Pre-Socratics we find the Sophist Protagoras (490–420 BCE), whose teachings were described by Plato. When it came to politics, he believed the range of human phenomena and experience could make the best contribution to the city-state. In determining the best contribution, could virtue be taught? Or was it something that existed above and beyond human experience, at the level of divinity? If all truth is relative, did that mean that there is no external influence on human thinking and behavior? According to Plato, Protagoras believed that all humans had been given the gifts of honor and shame and justice from the gods, and this was what should dominate the running of the city-state.

Plato (424–348 BCE)

The two most famous philosophers from Classical Greece who discoursed on politics were Plato and Aristotle. In Plato's writing on politics, he often relates Socrates's analysis of the meaning behind concepts, which should be followed by evaluation of the most correct lifestyle and behavior. War and peace and deciding the best political order are the most important elements for the city-states. Above all is the concept of justice, discussed by the characters in *The Republic*. One individual, Thrasymachus, claims that justice is relative to the dominant group, or "the interests of the stronger." The strong maintain order through their position of power. In that sense, justice would not be seen as universal, but relative to whichever group dominated at any one time, which could often result in the oppression of those without power.

Socrates's response is to describe the best political order that is modeled in heaven, where justice is related to goodness and virtue and always upholds the best interests of the community. Justice is not the privilege of the dominant factions, but something that should be applied to everyone in the city-states, which consist of social diversity. The avoidance of civil strife is even more important than the avoidance of war with external states. However, Plato advocated not democracy, which could lead to anarchy, but the rule of "philosopher-kings," those educated to lead the community. Plato's ideal state would not exist without this transcendent connection to the perfect god. He criticized the Athenians who attributed vice and corrupt behavior to the gods and heroes because they were ignorant of the true attributes of divinity. Learning the true virtue and perfect unity of god was what should instruct the best political order.

In the discussion of justice in *The Republic*, justice should rely upon an understanding of true goodness. This goodness is analogous to the soul, which has a tripartite structure when manifest in a body, a structure which is shared by the city. The rational part or class should rule (wisdom); the spiritual part should act to the support the rule (courage); and the appetitive part (producers) should accept being ruled. Justice in this sense is what brings all three parts into an effective whole with no one factor dominating.

Aristotle (384–322 BCE)

Aristotle was a student of Plato and shared many of the same ideas concerning the best form of government for the city-state, although he disagreed on the conclusions found in *The Republic*. The city-state was at the center of his opinions because he saw this as containing the summation of all other associations (families, trade, crafts). His famous line that "man is a political animal" originally meant that the highest good for society could only be achieved if humans lived as good citizens (of the *polis*). It was the duty of all men to hold public office and administer justice.

The identity of any city-state is determined by its constitution. There are just and unjust constitutions, judged by which ones serve the good of the entire community. When a constitution serves only the powerful, it is unjust, just as a ruler can be just or unjust in the administration of his duties. For Aristotle, a just constitution is one in which benefits are distributed to the citizenry depending upon their contribution to society.

In relation to the different classes in society, Aristotle saw what we would term "the middle class" as maintaining a balance against the domination and corruption by the rich, upper classes. In an early version of what would become fundamental to Western democracy, he distinguished three branches of government: the deliberative, making legislative decisions; the executive, running the actual business of the state; and the judicial, overseeing the legal details. As in Aristotle's teaching elsewhere, all government should be determined by moderation – nothing done in excess by either the ruling powers or the citizenry.

Aristotle advocated public education which would teach everyone the higher virtues, living in accordance with nature. Education in the nature of all objects was a fundamental theme throughout his writings. Of course, education belonged only to free men; women and slaves had a role to play in their labor and that was how they contributed to the state. Being made up of educated citizens, one of the roles of the state was to teach morality and virtue to the community. Thus, ethics, morals, and politics are intimately connected. The perfect government should achieve happiness for its citizens.

Epicureans and the State

Epicureans believed that society existed to protect the community from harm. Justice therefore was functional in that it arose from this need for protection; laws that do not meet this need of social relationships are no longer just. However, some laws are necessary to enforce the common good of the community. The function of the city-state is to provide security and harmony for its citizens. Epicureans did not advocate getting involved in politics, as the wealth and glory accumulated in leadership roles often led to corruption and thus a disharmony of the soul and person. It was best to place one's energies in a community of friends.

Stoicism and the State

According to the Stoic Zeno, Stoics could engage in politics unless a higher need or concept prevented them. For instance, a Stoic should reflect first whether killing a tyrant was a good act. Political participation could be part of the natural order, if based on reasons for the communal good. Humans are social creatures who become political creatures through the establishment of laws, which must be virtuous. The Stoic belief in fate meant that if you were elected to public office, this was your destiny and it had to be accepted. We will consider more Stoic ideas when we cover Rome, below.

Roman Religion and the State

The experience of tyrannical Etruscan kings in the early history of Rome led to the idea of overthrowing a tyrant as the touchstone of Roman political concepts, embedded in the Roman concept of freedom. Monarchy was replaced by two elected consuls, and the body of kings' advisers became the Senate (501 BCE). The Roman form of government with the Senate and the Plebeian Assembly became idealized as the best form of a mixed constitution. Most elected magistrates held *imperium*, or the sacred power and authority inherent in their duties.

We have much more information concerning ancient Rome than ancient Greece on the relationship between the state and religion, from the many speeches that have survived, inscriptions, and particularly the historians Polybius (200–118 BCE), Livy (59 BCE to 17 CE), and Dionysius of Halicarnassus (60–7 BCE).

Polybius, in his *Histories*, detailed the Second Punic War, demonstrating the way in which Rome evolved into greatness largely through its religious precepts and values. In what for us would appear a negative connotation, it was Rome's manipulation of the "fear of the gods" that was able to unify its people for ultimate victory:

> For I conceive that what in other nations is looked upon as a reproach, I mean a scrupulous fear of the gods, is the very thing which keeps the Roman commonwealth together. To such an extraordinary height is this carried among them, both in private and public business, that nothing could exceed it. Many people might think this unaccountable, but in my opinion, their object is to use it as a check upon the common people.
>
> (*Histories*, 6.56.6-15)

Titus Livius, or Livy, writing his history of Rome (*Ab urbe condita libri*) at the end of the Roman Republic, stressed that corruption of an individual could bring down the wrath of the gods against the state. Dionysius of Halicarnassus (in his *Roman Antiquities)* wrote to reconcile Roman rule over the Greeks and everyone else. The latter two writers narrated stories of ancient Rome that demonstrated the piety and great moral character of Romans (although both also claimed that morals had declined at the end of the Republic).

Examples from the Twelve Tables

"If anyone summons a man before the magistrate, he must go. If the man summoned does not go, let the one summoning him call the bystanders to witness and then take him by force."

"One who has confessed a debt, or against whom judgment has been pronounced, shall have 30 days to pay it in. After that, forcible seizure of his person is allowed. The creditor shall bring him before the magistrate."

"As a man has provided in his will in regard to his money and the care of his property, so let it be binding. If he has no heir and dies intestate, let the nearest paternal kinsman have the inheritance. If there is no paternal kinsman, let the members of his *gens* have the inheritance."

"Females should remain in guardianship even when they have attained their majority."

"Should a tree on a neighbor's farm be bent crooked by the wind and lean over your farm, you may take legal action for removal of that tree."

"If one is slain while committing theft by night, he is rightly slain."

"Any person who destroys by burning any building or heap of corn deposited alongside a house shall be bound, scourged, and put to death by burning at the stake provided that he has committed the said misdeed with malice aforethought; but if he shall have committed it by accident, that is, by negligence, it is ordained that he repair the damage or, if he be too poor to be competent for such punishment, he shall receive a lighter punishment."

"A person who had been found guilty of giving false witness shall be hurled down from the Tarpeian Rock."

"The penalty shall be capital for a judge or arbiter legally appointed who has been found guilty of receiving a bribe for giving a decision."

"The women shall not tear their faces nor wail on account of a funeral."

Law in Rome consisted of what was known as the *mos maiorum*, or the body of oral tradition that was passed down from the ancestors, much of which was eventually codified in the Twelve Tables. Apparently the Twelve Tables took written form around the mid-fifth century BCE, at the suggestion of a Plebeian tribune who believed that a written law would stem arbitrary decisions by magistrates. According to tradition, Rome sent a delegation to Athens for a copy of the laws of Solon. Ten Roman citizens were selected to record the known laws on 10 tablets (later increased to 12). These laws included private law and specific legal procedures (see the box "Examples from the Twelve Tables").

The Twelve Tables also addressed social conventions and rules, which then held the same sense of being legally binding. Whether or not they were all written down at one time in Rome's history, they were subject to change as events dictated. For instance, the original tablets forbade marriage between the patrician and plebeian classes. After the plebeians gained the right of filling the position of governing magistrates alongside the patricians, this law was no longer valid.

Some elements not found in the Tables were introduced by special legislation, such as the *Lex Canuleia* (permitting the classes to marry), the *Leges Licinae Sextiae*, which created the *ager publicus* or public lands owned by the state, the *Lex Ogulnia*, which permitted plebeians to hold priesthoods, and the *Lex Hortensia*, which established the validity of the plebiscite or plebeian assemblies.

We know little about the historical origins of Roman law. In all likelihood it was influenced by Etruscan principles, neighboring Italian tribes, and Greek systems in the colonies in Magna Graecia. According to the later foundation stories of Rome, almost of the institutions of the city were established by Romulus himself, followed by the additions of the earliest good kings. King Numa was credited with formalizing the religious and governing traditions introduced by Romulus.

Elected praetors supervised the laws, *praetores urbani* for citizens and *praetores peregrini* for non-citizens living in the city. There were both written and unwritten laws ("custom"). The written laws were those statutes created by both the Senate and the Plebeian Assembly. The unwritten laws were considered sacred, stemming from the ancestors and the gods. There was a distinction between *ius publicum* (public law) and *ius privatum* (private law). Public laws protected the state and private laws protected the individual.

As in Greece, Roman rule was dominated by the upper classes or patricians. While all male citizens had the right to vote, this actually consisted of only about a quarter of the population of Rome (the rest were non-citizens and slaves). While the famous phrase, "the Senate and the People of Rome" (SPQR – *Senatus Populusque Romanus*) appears to demonstrate equality, the Senate always claimed to be the protectors of the city's relationship with the divine, thus having the more important element of rule.

In reality, the Senate could only propose legislation, while the Plebeian Assembly and the Centuriate Assembly were responsible for voting on it. Ten tribunes of the Plebeian Assembly were elected each year to act as a check upon the Senate and they had the right to sit in the Senate and exercise their veto on any legislation. From this combined system we have inherited the idea of checks and balances, a separation of powers, filibusters, term limits, impeachments, and regular elections.

Care and appeasement of the gods were integral elements of Roman government; incorrect rituals or neglectful actions could anger the gods and therefore bring harm to the state. Rituals that particularly involved the entire community would bring benefits to all of Roman society (the **res publica**), continuing the customs that originated with the ancestors. Coexisting with the myriad cults and temples throughout Rome were the state-sponsored cults, centered on the Capitoline triad of Jupiter, Minerva, and Juno. All elected magistrates made sacrifices and vows to the gods upon taking up their office.

The integration of religion and state in Rome was further enhanced by the fact that almost all of the elected magistrates were also priests and *augurs*, either elected or appointed. Thus, elected magistrates did not have to be run through a quick seminar on how to do sacrifices or rituals. They would already know the basics, although they could also consult *haruspices*, *augurs*, and religious professionals at the temples for more knowledge.

For Romans, the gods worked in tandem with the magistrates in a partnership that benefited all. The gods were the official patrons of the city, although most of the time they were silent partners. In other words, they did not directly tell magistrates what to do; they simply agreed or disagreed. All official acts conducted by the government (the Senate as well as the assemblies) were carried out with the assistance of the *augurs* and the *haruspices*. Then as now, religion could be used to either validate or negate proposed legislation or voting, and there were charges of "faked" auspices and readings of entrails on occasion. Every session of the Senate began with a sacrifice (a tradition followed by the United States Congress today when they open each session with a prayer). Most priest-hoods were for life and resulted in public influence, privileges, and immunity (meaning they could not be indicted for lesser crimes while in office).

The Imperial State

When Octavian became "the first citizen" of Rome (acclaimed "Augustus" in 27 BCE), he reformed religion as well as the relationship between religion and the state. In this sense, reform meant simply undertaking a restoration of the tradi-tional concepts and worship that he believed had fallen into disuse and neglect.

Augustus utilized the traditional concept of the ancient Lares (protectors of the home) and the celebrations of the Compitalia to expand upon the idea by using his own family Lares as symbolic of protection throughout the Empire. He and his wife Livia became the father and mother of all and symbolized prosperity. At the same time, he refurbished older temples and built new ones throughout the city and provinces, funding their daily activities.

When Julius Caesar was declared to be among the gods by the Senate after his death, the Imperial cult was instituted as both a means to honor Caesar and a unifying element between Rome and the provinces. Temples to the divine Julius (and later to successive emperors) were established throughout Italy and beyond. For provincial leaders, an appointment as an Imperial priest, along with citizenship, offered a means to participate in the religious elements of Rome as well as enhancing their role in local government. In Rome, Augus-tus reorganized the ancient Arval Brotherhood, which traditionally celebrated ancient fertility deities, to include prayers for the celebration and protection of the Imperial family.

The family, in this case, had divine origins. The Julian clan had always claimed literal descent from the goddess Venus; once in power, Julius Caesar erected a temple to Venus in thanksgiving for his many conquests. Augustus, legally having the same lineage through adoption by Caesar, promoted this divine element to validate his rule. He took the office of *pontifex maximus* for himself, combining religious and political rule in the person of the *princeps* or emperor. These divine roots (and divine blessings) were embellished by the court poet Vergil in his *Aeneid*. Augustus claimed to have restored the *pax deorum*, the "peace of the gods."

Outside of Rome, local cults and deities were respected as long as they did not contradict the religious beliefs of Rome (or promote rebellion). Roman temples and institutions were established alongside older cult temples and altars. The ancient sites remained important to Rome, as Rome had absorbed many of these sacred areas into their own mythology, connecting their history to ancient civili-zations. For instance, not only did Rome refurbish temples to Apollo throughout the Empire, but Augustus had a temple to Apollo built on the Palatine Hill, right next to his house. In other words, the glory that was Rome had been part of the divine plan from the beginning of time.

Roman Courts

As in Greece, Roman courts utilized advocates and a jury system, but added judges who supervised the procedures. The early form of legal procedures involved what was termed the *legis actiones*. The plaintiff approached a defendant in public and demanded that he appear before a magistrate, who decided the merits of the case. If a case was determined, both parties selected a judge. Sureties were set, or an amount of money as insurance if either party did not show up and as a guarantee of compensation if one or the other lost the case. Advocates spoke for each party and witnesses were called. The judge then made a decision. If the losing party could not pay, his property was seized or he became the property of the winner. This evolved into the formulary system, meaning that charges were formally written down.

As cases became more complex, juries were utilized to render verdicts after a summing up of the case by the judge. Juries varied in size depending upon the particular court or the case, anywhere from 51 to 301. The odd number was to avoid a tie, or a "hung jury." Verdicts were rendered on waxed tablets, "A" for *absolvo* or "I acquit," "C" for *condemno*, "I condemn," and "N L," "It is not clear to me." By the late Republic, there were separate courts for embezzlement, property disputes, and murder. Treason cases were heard by the Senate. We should note that Roman literature in the late Republic is replete with accusations of jury bribing.

Beginning c. 200 BCE, praetors began setting legal precedents. Praetors were elected officials who served as judges in the several distinct courts of Rome (murder, embezzlement, property disputes, etc.). Praetors were given an opportunity to set out the rules or legal rationales for the way in which they would govern during their year in office. Many of these edicts either validated existing law or sometimes created new laws or at least new interpretations. In this way, Roman law also consisted of the accumulation of legal precedents over the centuries, a system which is still practiced in Western law courts.

Rome established professional jurists (*prudentes*), who studied the law; the science of law derives its name from this element of Roman history, jurisprudence. Applying Greek philosophical traditions to the understanding of Roman law, Gnaeus Falvius is credited with publishing the formal legal terms to be used in court c. 300 BCE. These terms were previously known only to priests. The jargon and format were then available for study by advocates or lawyers. These jurists were available for consultation by the magistrates and they were often called upon to draft legislation for the Senate. The terminology they created became standard for legal contracts.

All Roman citizens had the right to a fair and public trial, regardless of their social standing. This "protection under the law" for citizens was highly prized. Conquered peoples in the provinces, for the most part, did not attain the same privilege. Slaves, of course, had no legal rights but as they were the property of their owners, the owners were responsible for their behavior. The *paterfamilias* in certain matters was above the standard laws in the management of his own family.

With the exception of murder, arson, and treason, most crimes were punished with a fine or the payment of compensation to the victim. However, Rome also delegated punishment according to class. For the more severe crimes, the upper classes were given "time to depart," which meant that they had a set number of days to get their affairs in order before being sent into exile – no one could offer them "fire or water" within 500 miles of Rome. For the lower classes, convictions for some of the same crimes resulted in execution in the amphitheaters.

There was no such thing as a "life sentence" in ancient Rome, as Rome did not have the facilities to house prisoners for life. The very idea of a lifelong prison sentence was considered anathema to the Roman concept of freedom and was considered as undue cruelty. Roman jails were essentially holding cells which were used to temporarily house prisoners until their date of execution in the amphitheaters, usually during a religious festival. At that time, veils would be hung over the statues of the gods so that they would not have to be exposed to the prisoners. Convicted criminals were denied funeral rituals so that they would suffer even after death.

Roman Political Philosophy

When it comes to political philosophy in ancient Rome, Cicero (106–43 BCE) is one of our best sources. He was a famous advocate, an orator, a consul, a priest, and a philosopher, who is credited with political theory. Although not descended from the traditional elite of Rome, nevertheless Cicero received an education in both Greek and Latin, studying the writings of ancient Greek philosophers and translating their works, particularly the works of Plato.

Cicero lived through great civil strife in the last days of the Roman Republic, which experienced the Social Wars as well as the civil wars under Sulla the dictator and Caesar and Pompey. Throughout, Cicero took the side of the Optimates, or "the best people" (the traditional patrician class of the Senate). In his speeches, he consistently called for the traditional values of the Republic and for holding to Rome's traditional constitution under which no one man alone should consolidate power.

After a period of indecision, Cicero took the side of Pompey and the Republicans during the civil war with Caesar. After Pompey's defeat and death, he accepted Caesar's offer of amnesty. Nevertheless, he supported the assassins of Caesar in their cause for "liberty," providing political advice for both Brutus and Cassius, who often ignored it. (His defense of the assassination is found in *De officiis*.) With the rise of Octavian, Cicero again equivocated and after the defeat of Brutus and Cassius at Philippi, and a famous series of speeches against Anthony in the Senate, Octavian and Anthony agreed that Cicero should be proscribed, or put to death. He stoically accepted his fate and died in 43 BCE. His head and hands were displayed in the forum (with his hands symbolic of the instruments of the insults he wrote about Anthony).

We have already sampled some of Cicero's writings on the gods, so we will focus on his main writings on politics and the state, found in *De re publica* (*On the Republic*, or *Commonwealth*) and *De legibus* (*On the Laws*).

Like much of Plato's work, *De re publica* is a dialogue concerning Roman politics. The setting highlights the wisdom of Scipio Aemilianus (185–129 BCE). Aemilianus was famous for his victories in the Third Punic War (149–146 BCE), which included the final destruction of Carthage. By the first century BCE he was considered a role model and a patron of philosophers. By placing the dialogue in an older age, Cicero could have the characters demonstrate his own opinions without the risk of offending his contemporaries. There are 10 speakers in all and Aemilianus's role became famous in what became known as "Scipio's Dream." Looking down from high above in the stars, he realizes that Rome, like the ruins of Carthage, will ultimately be only an insignificant element in the long history of the world (an element of Stoic influence on Cicero).

The dialogue begins with a discussion on the origins of society. Epicureans believed that humans are not inherently social, but come together for mutual protection and self-interest. This could lead to despotism, or the dominance of the most powerful individuals. Stoics, on the other hand, believed humans had an inherent avoidance of being alone, making them interconnected through family and the larger community.

Some individuals are virtuous, which will lead to their dominance in the *res publica*. Great leaders must demonstrate courage, wisdom, self-control and eloquence (learned from studying Greek philosophy). A decision to go to war must be taken only for just reasons (such as defense); an unjust war is one done for reasons of wrath and greed: "Unjust wars are those begun without a reason. For there is no just reason for war outside of just vengeance or self-defense." A just war has to be announced ahead of time, and reparation demanded first. (Many of the same elements were later expounded by the Church Father Augustine in his Just War theories and remain an important element in modern political science theory.)

What constitutes the ideal citizen (and thus the ideal society)? This consists of three "loves": (i) a love of war (for just reasons), because a totally neutral state will fall victim to conquest; (ii) a love of peace and quiet (to avoid the over-expansion of the state that leads to destruction); and (iii) a love for the state religion. This love (and devotion) to the gods will not only keep the balance between war and peace, but will ensure that the gods are never angry.

The *De legibus* consists of a dialogue not in the past, but among Cicero, his brother Quintus, and Cicero's close friend, Titus Pomponius Atticus. While talking a leisurely stroll on one of his estates, the three friends discuss the nature of law. Much of this dialogue reflects Cicero's views on what he claimed to be the abuses and decay of the Roman constitution in his day.

Cicero argues that laws are not simply written regulations, but something inherent in humans. Humans were created by a higher power which endowed humans with divine elements and resulted in the powers of speech, reason, and ideas. Divinity was benevolent and so humans contained this potential for benevolence on earth by applying their reason. Reason promotes law, which condones good and forbids evil. The fact that this doesn't always work is because of human flaws such as lust, greed, and obsession with status.

Cicero distinguished between legalism (written laws) and natural law (universal right and wrong and morality). Written laws are to be evaluated on their agreement with natural law. Written laws must be enforced by society, whereas natural law needs no enforcement because it is universally agreed upon as the moral thing to do. Laws enacted for the wrong intention or because of greed do not deserve the title of law.

Cicero insists that human laws must be created in conjunction with religious belief because it is both practical and spiritual. He cites King Numa's law against burials within the *pomerium* as an example. Not only would it tempt the Fates to have the dead cohabit with the living, but the fire risk from cremation would be impractical in the crowded city. He then presented his ideas for reforming the constitution of Rome. Reflecting his conservative nature, he proposed that the Senate not just propose legislation, but that it be responsible for approving legislation as well, which in his view would stem the populist ideas of the people. The Senate would be supervised by more virtuous Censors who would eject the more greedy and corrupt so that those remaining could serve as ideal models of Roman virtue. The basic structure of the constitution was left in place (with the traditional offices of the magistrates), but with ideas to avoid voter fraud and laws passed against individuals or groups for simple vengeance purposes.

Cicero did not incorporate any of Plato's ideas of common ownership, maintaining the traditional view that society consists of classes that are not necessarily equal in terms of rights or privileges. Again, natural law created the natural order of things, which should not be changed. In what was most likely his last written treatise (to his son), *De officiis*, Cicero discussed morality in human relationships and the state. Justice must be practiced for all classes, and the function of justice is to do no wrong to anyone.

Seneca (4 BCE to 65 CE)

Seneca's work titled *De beneficiis* considered that the best way for society to live according to natural law was to uphold the benefits to each other (giving and receiving) that would result in a binding together of the moral good of the community. This was particularly relevant to political leadership and the relations among aristocrats, or *amicitia*, the Latin term for friendship.

In traditional Roman culture, aristocrats, being in a position to provide benefits (favors), had a duty as good citizens to do so and to look after the welfare of less-endowed citizens (those on the receiving end). At the same time, this implied ethical behavior on their part and the treatise also served as a guideline on ethics.

Seneca reflects the Stoic belief that virtue is the highest good, and thus leadership that lives by virtue will ultimately lead to a good society. Examples of virtuous benefits are financial assistance, influence to help someone get ahead, and the teaching of virtuous behavior. This creates obligations from those who are helped, and therefore the system helps bind the community together. Even slaves can benefit from these exchanges. Through kind treatment they will be more productive.

In *Natural Questions*, after a long discourse on nature and meteorology, Seneca discussed how individuals became depraved and corrupted by going against nature. Only from the perspective of nature (outside ourselves) can we truly come to see that everyday stresses and concerns are insignificant. What is going to happen will happen and is dictated by nature (Zeus) from the very beginning, including the mortality of humans.

Seneca wrote about whether or not one should live the life of a philosopher or a politician. Both, he said, are beneficial to humankind, in that philosophy can help a politician achieve a social good. According to Stoic teaching, all humans are part of the whole; god has endowed humans with an innate fellowship or feeling for each other. It was pointless to study philosophy if one did not live it. Again, Seneca's thoughts on nature, morality, and justice appear incompatible with the behavior of his patron and pupil, Nero.

Plutarch (46–120 CE)

In his *Parallel Lives*, Plutarch believed that ideal leaders should be grounded in philosophy, which would help them connect to the universal oneness of divinity. He presented ideals for statesmen as opposed to demagogues. Against Plato, philosophers should not rule but should be consultants to leaders, teaching them about the disasters that could result from greed, immoderate behavior, and uncontrolled (emotional) decrees. For Plutarch, the ideal form of government was monarchy, but a monarchy where democratic institutions could help restrain the tendencies of a monarch to be tempted by power.

Epicurus and Epicureanism

Epicurus (341–270 BCE) had advocated the avoidance of participating in politics, as politics was full of corruption and the abuse of power. However, laws and behavioral codes are necessary for society to live in harmony. Thus, all citizens should adhere to the laws laid down by the constitution.

Epicurean philosophers had traveled to Rome to introduce their ideas and a school was established in the Naples area, where Siro and Philodemus were the leading teachers with some influence on the poets Horace, Vergil, and Lucretius. However, conservative Romans such as Cato and Cicero fought against Epicurean philosophy. Calpernius Piso was one of their patrons who came under attack by Cicero, not only for Epicurean ideals, but because of his marriage connections to Julius Caesar. This resulted in very few Epicurean politicians in the late Republic.

Marcus Terentius Varro (116–27 BC)

Having completed the *cursus honorum*, Varro was personally involved in the politics of the late Republic. He allegedly was the author of a political pamphlet entitled, "The Three-Headed Monster," which harshly criticized the triumvirate of Caesar, Pompey, and Crassus. Much of the criticism was based upon his Epicurean ideals that good leadership should be for the benefit of the community. Nevertheless, he was a member of a commission of 20 senators who were charged with implementing Pompey and Caesar's land allotment to veterans in Campania. He later sided with Pompey in the Civil War, working as a legate in Spain. Varro accepted amnesty from Caesar and the two worked together on collecting material for the public library in Rome. Scholars continue to debate "The Three-Headed Monster" as the criticism belies his later behavior. However, Varro was not unlike many other men in this period who changed allegiances depending upon the circumstances.

Epictetus (55–135 CE)

With his Stoic background, Epictetus viewed men as members of a system that includes both gods and humans. This great commonwealth was the ideal goal, but contemporary political cities did not measure up because they were not regulated according to the divine will which was inherent in men. This will was rejected through self-interest and survival. He emphasized that men can only overcome their own self-interest by contributing good to the community.

Marcus Aurelius (121–180 CE)

In his *Meditations*, Marcus Aurelius applauded Roman opponents of kingship and extolled the equality of all citizens under the law. All rulers should act justly, upholding the Stoic ideal as members of a cosmic city. He often warned against the corruption of the temptation to dictatorship; the communal interest surpassed the individual. The rational element inherent in humans can be perfected in justice by the state, as men are capable of creating a perfect political constitution.

Religion and the State for the Masses

While many statesmen and philosophers wrote concerning the ideal state or deliberated upon the best constitutions and laws, we do not know how much of this filtered down to the common citizens of the Greek city-states or Rome. What we do know is that for the most part these writers did not advocate a reversal of the traditional religious concepts. A common theme among the educated was to reinterpret or to eliminate the anthropomorphic elements of myth, but very few actually condoned the elimination of the traditional cults. On the contrary, the writers elevated law codes and justice by ultimately connecting them to the divine, variously interpreted. At the same time, all members of the community would have been witnesses to their rulers and magistrates continuing to perform religious rituals as an essential element of their mandate.

Summary

- Ancient law codes and constitutions were created and enacted on the understanding that they were in accordance with the will of the gods. The law codes established the conventions of society and social roles and thus were understood as validated by the divine.
- Statesmen who set up the laws and philosophers who wrote about them maintained an integral relationship among laws, morality, justice, and the divine. In this sense, there was no separation of "church and state."

Suggestions for Further Reading

Beard, M. 2015. SPQR: *A History of Ancient Rome*. Profile. This readable but scholarly account casts a new look at a thousand years of the city's history.

De Coulanges, N. D. 1980. *The Ancient City: A Study on the Religion, Laws, and Institutions of Greece and Rome*. Johns Hopkins University Press. This is an all-inclusive work that includes laws pertinent to the family and gender roles.

Gagarin, M. 2011. *Writing Greek Law*. Cambridge University Press. This survey traces the evolution from oral to written law in Greece and highlights the importance of communicating the law to all.

Zetgel, J., ed. and trans. 1999. *Cicero: On the Commonwealth and On the Laws*. Cambridge University Press. This translation of the major political works of Cicero also places them in their historical context.

THE LEGACY OF GRECO-ROMAN RELIGIONS IN WESTERN CULTURE

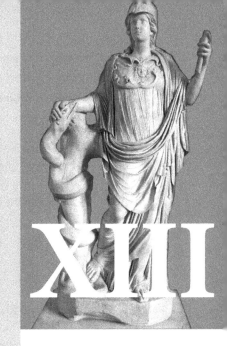

XIII

Second Temple Judaism in the First Century

The Spread of Christianity

Greek and Roman Religions, First Edition. Rebecca I. Denova.
© 2019 John Wiley & Sons, Inc. Published 2019 by John Wiley & Sons, Inc.

Learning Objectives

After reading this chapter, you will be able to:

- Trace the history of the rise of Christianity and distinguish the innovations of this new religious movement.
- Appreciate the continuity of several ancient concepts in the relationship between the divine and humans.

 If you ever have the opportunity to tour the great museums of Rome, Florence, Paris, Berlin, Moscow, London, Washington, DC, Los Angeles, or New York, you will see thousands of paintings and sculptures detailing most of the myths and stories of ancient Greece and Rome. Much of this art originated in the Renaissance, or the period of Western history (fourteenth to sixteenth centuries) when ancient cultures were rediscovered. Western literature became infused with the subjects of the ancient world through poetry, drama, and philosophy.

Through the stories of Homer, the treatises of various schools of philosophy and the poetry of Vergil and Horace, ideas from the ancient world were expressed through the poems of Dante and Milton, the works of theologians, and the plays of Shakespeare. Renaissance art is replete with paintings and statues of the nativity of Jesus, events during his ministry, his crucifixion, and his resurrection. In late antiquity, art and literature recalled the lives and martyrdoms of Christian saints (see below).

Traditionally, late antiquity saw what is proclaimed as "the triumph of Christianity" (381 CE), when Christianity was declared to be the only religion of the Roman Empire. This was understood to be the triumph of the "truth" over the false beliefs and practices of both Judaism and all the traditional cults in the ancient world. However, it is important to understand that Christianity did not emerge in a vacuum. From a small sect within ancient Judaism, Christianity fully absorbed many of the religious and cultural traditions of its mother religion, as well as those of the Greco-Roman world.

This chapter will briefly explore the ways in which religious and cultural elements were adapted by Christians and the Christian leadership as it emerged in the first five centuries. We will highlight the shared concepts that were retained, as well as Christian innovations in a system of beliefs. The structure of this chapter follows the specific elements of ancient concepts and practices that we have outlined in the previous chapters.

Second Temple Judaism in the First Century

Jews in the ancient world followed traditions that were written down in various books by 600 BCE, relating their history as a unique ethnic group and extolling the oracles of their prophets. Central to this tradition was a law code traditionally claimed to have been given by their god to Moses, a redeemer figure who led them from slavery in Egypt to Canaan. This land was promised to them in an ancient covenant between god and Abraham, the founder or patriarch of their community. This Law of Moses detailed how to worship, how to live, and how to maintain a Jewish identity in the midst of their neighbors. Prominent in the prophetic material as well as the Law of Moses was the commandment to worship the god of Israel alone. In this sense, worship meant sacrifices and cult rather than the modern concept of "belief."

Over the centuries, Israel had suffered major disasters, both internal and external. The land had been conquered by the Assyrians in 722 BCE, the Babylonians in 600 BCE, the Greeks in 330 BCE, and the Romans in 63 BCE. Throughout these tumultuous times, Jews had argued among themselves over their relationship to their god, to their neighbors, and to each other. For several hundred years the prophets had castigated the Jews for what they claimed were violations of god's commandments. As a rationale behind the suffering of Israel, they claimed that god had used the powers of conquering cultures to discipline and punish Israel for its sins, particularly the sin of idolatry. At the same time, these prophets issued a message of hope. They claimed that god would intervene in history one more time at a future date and usher in "the kingdom of god." This would mean that after a final battle, all the sinners and enemies of the Jews would receive their just punishment, and that the righteous would be rewarded with a utopia on earth – the original plan of god in the Garden of Eden.

By the first century CE, Roman rule in the Galilee and the province of Judea (where Jerusalem was located) had created tensions among the various groups of Jews. Throughout this period, several men were proclaimed the "messiah" (anointed one), a traditional figure from the line of King David, who would lead the armies of Israel in the final battle against its enemies. Rome had a policy of sending in the legions if any of these claimants had a large following that could lead to riots. They usually killed the leader and rounded up his followers. By 66 CE the Zealots (a group who believed in the sole rule of their god) rallied enough Jews to their side and led the country in open revolt against Rome. The Zealots believed that god would defeat the conquerors. Instead, Rome defeated the rebels and destroyed the temple in Jerusalem in 70 CE.

We have no contemporary eyewitness testimony for the life of Jesus of Nazareth. He does not appear in either the Jewish or the Roman records at the time. The first historical references to Jesus are found in the letters of Paul, a Pharisee who became a believer and wrote letters in the 50s and 60s to the communities he established in the eastern Mediterranean. The next references come from the four canonical gospels (the only ones that the later church would accept). Mark is our earliest gospel (70 CE), followed traditionally by Matthew (c. 85), Luke (c. 95) and John (c. 100). See the box "The Basic Story of Jesus of Nazareth" for an overview of the major events that became foundational for the history of Christianity.

The Basic Story of Jesus of Nazareth

Sometime during the 20s of the Common Era, an itinerant preacher, in the style of the prophets of ancient Israel, began addressing crowds in his native area, mainly the Galilee region of northern Israel. He may have been in the circle attached to a character known as John the Baptist, and it appears that he took up the same message after John's death. His basic message was, "Repent, for the kingdom of god is at hand!" What he meant by this was that the "final days" as foretold by the prophets were approaching when god would rule on earth. It appears from the first three gospels that his favorite method of instruction was a parable, or a short, pithy story containing simple elements, as well as higher abstract concepts in some cases.

Jesus was portrayed as a wonder-worker: healing, raising people from the dead, exorcizing demons (removing them), and performing food miracles (such as the multiplying of the loaves and fishes). He gathered disciples around him, in the symbolic number of "twelve" (reflecting the 12 tribes of Israel). While drawing the countryside to his message, the gospels report a constant harassment and persecution by specific groups of Jews, namely the Pharisees and the scribes, and eventually the Sadducees. This last group was largely responsible for the operating and upkeep of the *cultus* surrounding the temple in Jerusalem. The Pharisees consistently accused Jesus of violating the Law of Moses, while the gospel reports deny that he challenged the customs of the Jews. He offered what was understood as the true interpretation of this Law and the traditions associated with it.

When Jesus entered the city at Passover, the crowds used palm branches to welcome him and proclaimed him the messiah and the "king of the Jews." Jesus then disrupted the services in the temple. His disciples celebrated a Passover meal on Thursday evening (accounts of Mark, Matthew, Luke), or a simple meal on Wednesday evening (John), where the tradition of the ritual known as the "Last Supper" took place. One of the disciples, Judas, betrayed Jesus by telling the priests/temple captains/a Roman cohort (depending upon which gospel you are reading) where he would be that evening and Jesus was arrested. He was condemned by the Sanhedrin (the Jewish city council) and turned over to Pontius Pilate (the Roman procurator) for trial. According to the gospels, Pilate was swayed by the Jewish crowds and condemned Jesus to death. He was tortured and then crucified.

After the death of Jesus, his followers claimed that he had risen from the dead, appeared to some of them, and was bodily ascended into Heaven. His disciples then took the message of the approaching kingdom of god to the cities of the Eastern Empire and beyond.

The Spread of Christianity

Scholars have attempted to reconstruct the movement centered on Jesus, beginning in Jerusalem and spreading throughout the Roman Empire. The best theory is that early missionaries visited Jewish synagogues to spread the "good news" (the eventual Anglo-Saxon term of "gospel") that the "kingdom of God" was coming. In the cities and countryside of the Eastern Empire, the common designation for Jesus of Nazareth became "the Christ." "Christ" was the Greek for "anointed one" (translated from the Hebrew, "messiah").

When most Jews did not respond favorably to the message, Christian missionaries were surprised to find that non-Jews (in the texts, "Gentiles") wanted to join the movement. Greeks and Romans had often been attracted to elements of Judaism and many participated in synagogue activities. This necessitated an early debate – should these people become Jews first (be circumcised) in order to join? Various Christian groups met in Jerusalem to discuss this issue and decided that non-Jews should only do the following: refrain from eating meat with the blood in it, follow Jewish incest laws, and cease all idolatry. Very quickly over the next few decades, the non-Jews became the majority in the movement.

Along with the mother religion of Judaism, many elements of Greco-Roman religions were absorbed into Christianity, although Christians often took the basic precepts and added innovations.

The Divine

Early Christians adopted the general view of the divine from both Judaism and native cults, maintaining the idea that powers existed above in the heavens and in the underworld. Humans dwelled on earth while the underworld remained as the place of the dead, but now designated as hell (see below). In addition to the existence of the gods of Olympus (and others), Christians maintained the Jewish belief that Heaven was nevertheless ruled by the god of Israel and his angels, in their various hierarchies and functions. The archangels Gabriel and Michael became important actors in Christianity. A late Jewish angel, the Devil, was deemed responsible for evil and became embedded in Christian tradition.

The Traditions of the Ancestors

For millennia, ancient cultures had claimed a direct line from their ancestors to their contemporary religious customs. Hence, traditional cults were simultaneously ethnic. Christianity introduced the idea that ancestry and bloodlines were irrelevant to membership in the assemblies. As Paul explained in his letters, it was faith (*pistis*, "loyalty") that was necessary for salvation. In Paul's context, this loyalty was solely to the god of Israel and his "lord," Jesus (who was now divine). In practical terms this meant that Christianity was not confined to a people or a geographic area; Christianity became a portable religion as assemblies were found in every city. This aspect of the new religion was one of the elements that contributed to its rapid spread throughout the Mediterranean.

Class and Status

The elimination of ethnic and geographic criteria also meant that the traditional elements of class and status were not relevant to the new religion. There is a myth that Christianity was dominated by the poor and slaves. This idea arose because of several non-Christian critics who made that charge in their polemical writings against the system. In reality, Christianity appealed to all economic classes. One's status in society was not a criterion for membership.

Jesus as God

Very early after the death of Jesus, his followers claimed that he now sat at the "right hand of god." In some ways this mirrored the ancient Greek concept of *apotheosis*. Paul, and then other Christian leaders, added another element by claiming that Jesus had preexisted in Heaven from time immemorial. He descended to earth and became human in order to proclaim the message of the kingdom and then ascended after his death. As he was now part of the divine, he could be worshipped. This was one of the great obstacles between traditional Jews and the followers of Jesus.

Myths and Sacred Stories

For Christians, the myths and stories of the Jewish Scriptures were incorporated as the basis for understanding the actions of god and his prophets. When the gospel writers and earliest Christians referred to "the scriptures," they meant the Jewish books which had been translated into Greek in the second century BCE.

By the year 200 CE, some rabbis, led by Judah the Prince, determined which books would be considered sacred (either authored by god or through his dictates) and which would not. This concept of a canon, or an authorized set of writings, was adopted by Christians, who were well on their way to canonizing their own sacred texts by the end of the second century. While still important for Christians, eventually the Jewish Scriptures would be designated the Old Testament (or covenant) and the Christian scriptures, the New Testament. The adjectives were the result of deeming the Jewish Scriptures to be superseded by the new understanding of god and his commandments as found in the gospels and church teaching.

Beginning in the second century, new Christian texts emerged known as Apocrypha and Pseudepigrapha. Apochrypha, from the Greek for "hidden things," contained additional teachings of Jesus and his immediate followers. Pseudepigrapha means "false writing" and refers to the ancient practice of writing a treatise or a letter in the name of a famous past figure in order to give it authority. Many of the writings addressed controversial issues in the second and third centuries and served as an authoritative solution for some community disagreement. The most popular stories filled in the gaps in the life of Jesus and his apostles. "The Infancy Gospel of Thomas" and the "Protoevangelicum of James" presented the backstory of Jesus as a child and the earlier life of Mary and Joseph. Several texts of "Acts" ("deeds") of the Apostles chronicled their adventures and miracles. Most of these stories followed the template of Greek romance novels and contained elements of classic myths and stories of heroes.

Sacrifice

We know very little of how Christians understood or redefined sacrifices in the first generation. The temple in Jerusalem had been the only place where Jews could offer animal and vegetable sacrifices. The way in which the dictates of the Scriptures were carried out by Jews who lived in other cities remains unknown as we have few descriptions of this. Philo, a Jewish philosopher of the first century who lived in Alexandria, mentions some "water sprinklings," but our knowledge of this practice remains vague.

For Jews (and the Jewish followers of Jesus), sacrifices were nullified when the temple was destroyed in 70 CE. What we do know is that, very early, the concept of sacrifice for Christians was transformed. Traditional sacrifices were rejected when former participants of traditional cults were urged to cease their idolatry. In Paul's letter to the Romans (written in the 60s?), he utilized the analogy of "first man, last man." The first man, Adam, sinned and his punishment brought death to humans (the loss of his original immortality). The "last man," Christ, brought life through his death. Paul declared him the Paschal sacrifice, or a substitution for the lamb that was slaughtered in the Passover ritual.

This idea of Jesus's sacrificial death became the doctrine of atonement and helped to explain why Jesus had to die. Often shortened to "Jesus died for our sins," or "Jesus took on the sins of the world," the claim did not mean that sin had been eliminated. More fully understood, it meant that Jesus voluntarily took on the *punishment* for our sins – death. The first Christians understood this literally. Paul fully expected to be alive when Jesus returned to earth. Later, as the first and second generation of Christians died and Jesus did not return, this idea was readjusted to claim that Christians would still undergo death, but when Jesus returned he would "judge the living and the dead," raising them up from death at that time. Good Christians would then reside with god and Jesus in Heaven.

With the dominant population consisting of ex-pagans, the Jewish Law of Moses and its commandments for Jewish traditions and practices became irrelevant to Christians by the second century. Through their exegesis of scripture, Christians claimed that god had originally only intended that only the first Ten Commandments should be followed. These commandments were deemed universal (meant for non-Jews as well) and ethical. The rest involved Jewish customs and were no longer applicable to the church.

Hymns and Prayers

In Paul's letters we have early evidence that Christians addressed both god and Jesus in typical prayers and hymns to the divine. Christians borrowed heavily from the Jewish Scriptures, from the books of the Prophets as well as the Psalms.

Psalms were prayers traditionally put to music and became the basis of the lyrics for hundreds of Christian hymns. In a letter written c. 110 CE by Pliny the Younger, we have evidence that Christians met at dawn on the first day of the week and sang hymns to their lord, "as if to a god."

Christian Liturgy and Ritual

Liturgy (from the Greek for "service of the people") was traditionally the concept of promoting benefactions from the aristocracy to the community good. It has come to denote the formalized means of conducting the public worship of any religious group. Many of the early elements of standard Christian liturgy can be reconstructed from some of the New Testament writings of the first century, particularly the letters of Paul and the Acts of the Apostles (the first Christian history by the author of the third gospel).

When Christians met they borrowed the Jewish synagogue practice of reading from the books of Moses and the prophets. Eventually a gospel reading was added. Christians did not convert overnight. There was a three-year initiation period during which new members studied the basics of the system. Scholars debate whether or not a system of initiation was borrowed from the various Mystery cults, as well as the focus on a dying and rising god. During the weekly assemblies, initiates were only permitted to stay for the introductory material. The phrase *ite missa est*, "you are dismissed," meant that they had to leave before the central part of the ceremony began. One theory claims that this may have been the origin of calling the assembly a "mass."

After the completion of the initiation period, members underwent the ritual of baptism ("dunking"). This is an element of Judaism, although we know very little about it. In the surviving Jewish literature, it is mentioned as a ceremony specifically for pagan women who converted to Judaism, as a purifying water ritual. However, the very earliest evidence we have (Paul's letters) indicates that this ritual was adopted by the immediate followers, and tradition holds that Jesus received baptism at the hands of John the Baptist.

Believers stripped naked, were dunked in water, and then given a new white robe that indicated their status of being "reborn." Initially baptism was only administered to adults. After the invention of the concept of Original Sin by Augustine in the fifth century, baptism was understood to wash away the sin of Adam and Eve. By the fifth century, Christians began to baptize infants due to high mortality rates to ensure their place in Heaven.

Another early ritual was the Eucharistic ceremony, or a repetition of the Last Supper of Jesus. In Paul's first letter to the Corinthian community, he repeats an early formula for the words of the Last Supper which matches what we have in the later gospels. Most likely, Christians began meeting weekly on Sunday (the day of the resurrection) as a means by which to honor the words, "do this in memory of me" (Eucharist is from the Greek for "thanksgiving"). What may have begun as a funeral memorial or feast evolved into a central ritual for Christians.

However, it was not until the thirteenth century that the Catholic Church declared the doctrine of transubstantiation to be part of the canon of teachings. For Catholics, transubstantiation takes place when the words of the priest literally transform the bread and wine into the body and blood of Jesus. Protestants maintain that this transformation is symbolic only.

The church developed other rituals over the centuries. Some of these were distinguished as a separate category, known as sacraments. Sacraments were rituals that were literally endowed with the presence of "the Spirit." Initially this was the spirit of god (or Christ) that Christians believed was present in their assemblies. Paul wrote about special "gifts of the spirit" which included speaking in tongues, prophesying, teaching, healing, raising people from the dead, and miracle-working. After the creation of the doctrine of the Trinity (see below), this became the Holy Spirit, or the third element of the Trinity. The sacraments of the Catholic tradition are baptism, ordination, marriage, penance (confession), first communion, confirmation, and the anointing of the sick (usually at death). The sacraments conform to rites of passage found in all cultures.

The Priesthood

By the end of the first century, Christian leadership consisted of bishops, elders, and deacons. The office of bishop (Greek, "overseer") was directly taken from the administrative structure of the Empire. A section of a province was called a diocese and a diocese eventually became the geographic area of a bishop's responsibilities. Bishops were elected by public acclamation of the congregation (shouting). Elders were older men of standing in the Christian communities (borrowed from synagogues). Deacons were organized to help with the distribution of charity (food and clothing), and were responsible for organizing the activities of the congregation. Deacons eventually became priests.

The rules for electing bishops and deacons were written in approximately 80 CE, in the letters of 1 Timothy and Titus. Like their counterparts in native cults, they were to be men of good reputation and able to properly manage their own households. We have very little literature on the early expansion of the hierarchy of the churches, but by the second century Christians had created an innovation for their priesthood. Bishops (and later priests) were now endowed with the ability to forgive sins on earth. For Judaism and the native cults, priests had a role in helping to facilitate forgiveness from god and the gods, but the idea that absolution could be manifest by a mortal is not found in either Judaism or Greco-Roman cults. Christian literature traced this element back to Jesus's commission to Peter in Matthew's Gospel.

Sacred Space

The English translation of the Greek word for assembly, *ekklesia*, as "church" is somewhat misleading. The Christian gathering was modeled on the city-state assembly, and not on a particular building. Believers met in each other's houses. We know of several early Christians leaders (including some women) who were probably wealthy enough to own large villas that accommodated the groups. Gathering together, the assembly stood, while the bishop was seated. The bishop spoke with authority, and thus "from the chair" became a later concept for the official residence of a bishop (ex cathedra, or cathedral).

When Christianity became a legal religion, Christians began building churches. In the 390s, when native cults were forbidden, Christians also had access to former temples, shrines, and public buildings. The standard architectural style for public buildings was the *basilica*. These buildings contained the law courts and places for assembly. Christian basilicas consisted of lines of columns which intersected in the nave, in the form of a cross. Various half-circle niches known as apses contained Christian statues (see below). With the elimination of blood offerings and burnt sacrifices, altars were now moved indoors and became the center of the service. As in traditional cults, bishops and priests served at the altar.

Divination

Maintaining a similar idea from the traditions of the traditional cults, Christians believed that there could be communication between humans and the divine. However, alterations to some of the concepts became necessary because of the background in Judaism as well as rejection by Christians of some of the cultic elements of their former life. Jews had a commandment against "graven images" of the divine in any form. This meant that there was no body of art which could influence or predetermine their dreams and visions.

In the older sources of the Jewish Scriptures, god and/or his angels (messengers) appeared to humans. The Book of Genesis claimed that humans were made in the "image of god," but without details. Nevertheless, characteristic phrases associated god in the form of a body: "the hand of god," "the face of god," etc. With the influence of Hellenism, the idea of god actually coming down to earth was rejected in favor of an abstract being that was not generally manifest on earth. His angels functioned as intermediaries and appeared in dreams and everyday experiences.

Jews communicated with god and his angels through prayers and hymns. God's presence was manifest as "the spirit of god," literally "the breath of god." This spirit was present in the temple and possessed the Hebrew prophets, suspending their normal selves and allowing the spirit to direct their speech and actions. Prophets functioned in the same way as the oracles of Greco-Roman tradition (e.g. as when Apollo possessed the *Pythia* at Delphi).

In the nativity stories of Jesus in the gospels of Matthew and Luke, angels appear to Joseph in dreams and the angel Gabriel appears to Mary with an annunciation hymn of the birth and future career of Jesus. Luke also includes an angelic visitation to Zechariah, the father of John the Baptist. Angels are important in the discovery of the empty tomb, where they announce that Jesus has risen from the dead.

Hirophanies, or appearances of Jesus, were manifest after his resurrection in the gospels of Matthew, Luke, and John. (There is no resurrection appearance in the earliest gospel, Mark.) However, the resurrection appearances are somewhat confusing. Both Luke and John narrate that when Jesus appeared to the disciples, he ate with them. In other words, Jesus was not a ghost, but appeared in a physical body that needed food. At the same time, however, Mary Magdalene has trouble physically grasping the body of Jesus, as he is not quite transformed back into flesh. Jesus also has the ability to walk through walls and locked doors. The gospel of Luke is the only one with a story of a bodily ascension of Jesus which exalts him to Heaven.

Over the next few centuries, appearances of Jesus diminished. A few of the later tales of the apostles include appearances to either clarify or extend teachings not found in the earlier gospels. In the Gnostic gospel of Mary Magdalene, Mary receives a vision of Jesus where he instructs her in additional knowledge. In the "Acts of Thomas," a text that promotes Christian concepts of asceticism and celibacy, Jesus appears in the room of a couple on their wedding night to caution against the urges of the body. It is much later that communication between Christians and the divine arise from the Cult of the Saints (see below). With increased devotion to Mary in the Middle Ages and beyond, she appeared to many individuals and continues to do so in the modern world. As in the ancient world, such visitations result in promoting pilgrimage.

Philosophy

Beginning c. 140 CE, a group of Christian leaders in retrospect became known as the "Church Fathers." When the emperor Constantine converted to Christianity in 312 he selected their version of Christianity. These men emerged from the educated elite of Greek and Roman communities and no longer had direct ties to Judaism. They wrote *apologias*, or explanations of Christianity, against their non-Christian critics, treatises on beliefs and practices in opposition to other Christians, and letters to the emperor and other Roman officials requesting a cessation of the persecution of believers.

Many of these writers were Platonists as well as participants in other schools of philosophy. They applied shared philosophical concepts to Christian teaching, arguing that Christians also believed in one god, "the highest good," who was responsible for everything in the universe. They disagreed on the concept of the demi-urge, but in everything else the systems were the same. They claimed that the idea of the *logos*, the essence of rationality, was in fact Christ in a preexistent form. One of the Church Fathers, Clement of Alexandria, declared that philosophy was the handmaiden of Christianity. This meant that Christianity was in agreement with philosophical concepts and the jargon of philosophy was the best way to describe Christian beliefs. Simultaneously, these writings were the first attempts to systematize Christianity and would become the basis of Christian dogma in later centuries (or what became the official teaching).

Orthodoxy and Heresy

The twin concepts of **orthodoxy** and heresy were an innovation in Christian thinking and teaching. All traditional cults claimed that their ancestral traditions were the proper ones, but they also respected the gods and traditions of their neighbors. We saw that the correct application of ritual was vitally important in the relationship between humans and the divine. Christian leaders developed the idea that a ritual was meaningless without the correct *belief* behind it. Orthodoxy meant "correct belief." "Heresy" was taken from the Greek *airesis*, which meant "choice," or the choice of a particular school of philosophy.

The concept of orthodoxy was created as a means to argue what one particular group considered the absolute truth, in opposition to other beliefs, particularly in Gnostic thought. Arising in the second century, scholars apply an umbrella term of **Gnostics** for the men who proposed some alternative interpretations of the nature of Jesus. Gnostic Christians claimed to have been enlightened with revealed knowledge of the universe and the role of Christ in salvation.

Gnostics utilized the same view of the universe as the philosophers, especially the views of Plato. The higher god of pure essence was not involved in creation; that was the role of Plato's demi-urge. The demi-urge in his jealousy had created matter, and thus all matter, including physical bodies, was considered evil. For many Gnostic systems, the demi-urge was the equivalent of the god of Israel. Gnostics claimed that humans contained a divine spark of the highest god that was now trapped in an evil body. The goal of a Gnostic was to be awakened from the state of having forgotten his true source and nature. Upon death, his soul would traverse the various layers of the upper heavens and be reunited with the god.

Most Gnostic Christian schools taught that as a manifestation of the *logos* on earth, Christ did not literally take on a human body. This was the concept of Docetism (appearance), or the idea that Christ only appeared in human form so that he could teach us the way to salvation. Therefore, many groups dismissed the stories of the crucifixion and bodily resurrection. Writing against such views, the Church Fathers addressed these groups as false "schools of thought" (*haeresis*/**heresy**) and thus the term "heretic" became an important element of Christianity. Orthodoxy and heresy are essentially two sides of one coin; the polarity is determined by which side is accusing the other.

Adversos Literature

A specific type of Christian literature, *adversos*, or "against an adversary," began to emerge in the second century CE. This literature was directed against Jews and Judaism with the goal of achieving the Roman government's recognition of

Christian ethnic identity and customs. Jews had obtained an exemption from participation in the state cults under Julius Caesar. Caesar rewarded the Jews with this decree because Jewish armies and mercenaries helped him in Egypt and the East. When state persecution of Christians began to pick up in the second century, Christian writers addressed letters to the emperors and other leading citizens, claiming the same privileges.

At the same time, Christian addressed another problem inherent in Christianity, that of being deemed a new religion. Conservative Rome often criticized "oriental cults" coming to the city. Christians claimed that they were not a new movement but the culmination of the original covenant between god and Israel, or "*verus Israel*" ("true Israel"). They argued that the Jews had lost their original chosen status with god because they failed to recognize Jesus as god's son. The proof for this claim was in the fact that god let Rome destroy their temple as a punishment for killing Jesus.

In order to prove ancient roots, Justin Martyr read the Jewish Scriptures allegorically. By doing so he claimed that all references to god in the Scriptures were really to preexistent forms of Christ. In this sense, the books of the prophets all pointed to the coming of Christ in their prophecies. Jews could no longer claim their own Scriptures because they did not know how to interpret them. This incorporation of the Jewish Scriptures was an attempt to achieve two ends: (i) it could provide an element of antiquity to Christianity so that it was not considered a new religion; and (ii) Christians hoped that the Roman government would exempt them from persecution (and the state cults) if they were considered to be the real Jews.

The *adversos* literature was highly polemical, malicious, and full of the standard rhetoric directed against an opponent at the time. Unfortunately, much of this literature became the basis for the later polemical charges against Jews in the Middle Ages and beyond. In other words, it established the template for what would become modern anti-Semitism.

Persecution and Martyrdom

Christian refusal to worship the traditional gods emerged as a problem by the end of the first century. This was most likely the time when official Rome realized that there was a group that was similar to Jews, but did not follow Jewish customs. Christians were persecuted with the charge of atheism, or non-participation in the traditional rituals. In a world where religion and politics were never separate, their refusal could endanger the prosperity of the Empire by angering the gods. Atheism in this sense was equivalent to treason; Christians were punished in the arenas because treason carried a death penalty.

Despite traditional Christian history and Hollywood, there were not thousands and thousands of Christians who died for their faith. Magistrates required Christians to toss a handful of incense to statues of the gods (and sometimes the bust of the emperor). Some refused and died, but we also have evidence of some who acquiesced. In 300 years, there were very few periods of persecution (perhaps seven or eight). A pattern was established where Christians were persecuted in times of crises in the Empire – foreign invasions, plague, famine, etc. In those times, Christians became scapegoats for angering the gods. When times returned to normal, no action was taken against Christians.

Inherent in the experience of persecution was the concept of martyrdom. This concept was promoted during the time of the Maccabee Revolt of the Jews against Greek occupation (167 BCE). The Syrian king Antiochus Epiphanes IV had taken the unprecedented step of forbidding the traditional customs of the Jews. He forbade circumcision, set up a statue of Zeus in the temple, and slaughtered pigs on the altar. Throughout the countryside he forced Jews to worship the gods of Greece.

Led by Mattathias and his son Judah Maccabeus, zealous Jews revolted and succeeded in expelling the Greeks. The books of 1 and 2 Maccabees tell this story, with the second book highlighting the suffering of the Jews under the tyrant. In this book, several people were tortured because they refused to commit idolatry. We learn of Hannah and her seven sons; Hannah was forced to watch as one by one, her sons died. Before each son expired, however, he made a speech which included elements that became religiously important in Christian culture.

None of the sons were upset at dying "for their customs," as obviously the nation must have sinned or god would not have permitted Antiochus to oppress them. They were willing to vicariously die for the nation as atonement for such sins. They didn't mind dying because they knew that their god "would raise them up." This phrase came to be translated as "resurrection," in this case, resurrection of the body after death. As they testified, the Greek word for "witness," **martyr**, became an important factor not only in Judaism, but in Christianity and in Islam.

Anyone who died for their customs (belief) became elevated to the status of martyr and was rewarded with instantly being taken to the presence of god after death. This idea mirrored the Greco-Roman concept of "the noble death" and heroes who were rewarded with the Elysian Fields in the afterlife. Christianity completely absorbed these ideas for the Christians who had suffered and died in the arenas. Over the centuries, the concept had to be adjusted in order to separate martyrs from other Christians. If every Christian who died was immediately translated into the presence of god, then the martyr's act would be diminished. This problem necessitated the concept of purgatory ("purging") as an intermediate stage to repent for lesser sins while waiting to be taken into the presence of god.

Persecution for Christians ceased when Constantine became the first Christian emperor and issued an edict making Christianity a legal or recognized religion of the Empire. He funded the building of Christian churches, exempted Christian clergy from taxes, and mediated Christian debates over dogma and beliefs. In his role as mediator, Constantine positioned himself as the head of the church. This meant that anyone who went against his concept of Christianity was now guilty of disbelief (atheism) and the same concept of treason and the death penalty. It is estimated that more Christians, as heretics, died in the arenas *after* Constantine's conversion than before. The torturing and burning of heretics had a long legacy in the Middle Ages.

Constantine's grandson, Theodosius I, issued an edict in 381 which made all other forms of worship illegal in the Empire, promoting Christianity as the only proper and true belief (see the box "The Edict of Theodosius I"). It was at this time that the Olympic Games ceased and temples were either destroyed or taken over by the church.

The Edict of Theodosius I (381)

"It is Our Will that all the peoples We rule shall practice that religion which the divine Peter the Apostle transmitted to the Romans. We shall believe in the single Deity of the Father, the Son, and the Holy Spirit, under the concept of equal majesty and of the Holy Trinity. We command that those persons who follow this rule shall embrace the name of Catholic Christians. The rest, however, whom We adjudge demented and insane, shall sustain the infamy of heretical dogmas, their meeting places shall not receive the name of churches, and they shall be smitten first by divine vengeance and secondly by the retribution of Our own initiative, which We shall assume in accordance with divine judgment."

The Rise of the Cult of the Saints

Christians borrowed three elements from pagan culture in relation to their martyrs: hero cults, pilgrimage, and the concept of patron/client in relation to the divine. Christians considered the tomb of a martyr as a sacred area where Heaven and Earth intersected. Martyrs' tombs became the object of pilgrimage and Christians petitioned the dead martyr through hymns and prayers. This was a direct borrowing of the concept of patron/client, whereas local gods and goddesses had been called upon to provide protection for the local community. Because martyrs were now in Heaven with god, they could be called upon for the kind of mediation and protection that Greek and Roman gods and goddesses traditionally granted. The dead martyrs were now patron saints, and towns and cities that had a martyr's grave became famous sites of pilgrimage.

For non-Catholics, the importance of the saints can be confusing because it appears that believers are praying to other divinities in addition to god and Jesus. Historically the Catholic Church has explained that this is not "worship" but "veneration" – a nuance that remains vague.

A fundamental problem existed in the recycled buildings that Christians were now using, as well as the new churches. The pagan temples and shrines were understood to be tainted because of the prior presence of the pagan gods. Public basilicas were also tainted because meetings of the city councils, law cases, and public assemblies always opened with sacrifices. How could Christians cleanse such buildings from this idolatry? How could the old and new ones become sacred space?

The problem was solved by Ambrose, the bishop of Milan (340–397 CE), when he was building his new church in Milan. He had a dream in which two earlier Christian soldier martyrs, Gervasius and Protasius, appeared to him and revealed where they were buried. He had their bones dug up and brought to the cathedral, where they were interred in the walls. This presence of the holy martyrs infused the building with sacredness and became a standard element in all Catholic Church buildings.

Christians came to believe that the bodies of dead martyrs had a divine power. Such **relics** consisted of the exhumation of body parts of earlier martyrs – bones, hair, teeth, etc. There were also contingent relics, meaning items that had touched dead martyrs, such as clothing or items associated with their martyrdom. It should be noted that Jews and non-Christians found this practice rather revolting. Ancient concepts of corpse contamination still held for these groups, and touching or venerating body parts of the dead was considered an outright reversal of ancient custom.

Relics were placed within a reliquary, or an ornate receptacle often covered with gold and jewels. Beginning in late antiquity and throughout the Middle Ages, the production of relics and traffic in them was big business. Christian communities with famous relics benefited from the pilgrims and tourists by providing housing, food, and selling items associated with the saint. At the same time, there were many fake relics; seven churches in Asia Province claimed to have the head of John the Baptist. The traffic in relics became one of the elements in Martin Luther's criticism of the Catholic Church and the practice was rejected by Protestant Christianity.

The Devil

In the ancient world the existence of evil was often assigned to demons (Greek, *daimónion*). We find references to demons in Mesopotamian literature and neighboring cultures. In the Jewish Scriptures, the Devil, or Satan, had a very limited role as one of god's angels whose job it was to present humans with obstacles and force them to make a choice. "Ha-Satan" in Hebrew means "adversary" or "obstacle," and thus the source of his name. During the Persian period Zoroastrian ideas of the polarity between good and evil led Jews to adopt these ideas as a way to explain evil without assigning disasters to god himself. By the first century BCE, the Devil (Greek, *diabolos*) had become a power that opposed all of god's creation and was responsible for disasters, diseases, and demonic possession through his demons.

The second century Church Fathers gave the Devil his due. Through a process of the personification of evil (assigning people or groups as agents of the Devil), these men began to demonize elements of ancient culture.

In trying to recruit people, it was not good practice to totally denigrate the traditional cults. Instead the Church Fathers claimed that people could not be held accountable for their false beliefs, as they had been tricked by the Devil into ignorance. They did not realize that the ancient gods were in fact demonic agents. Christians had the duty to open their eyes to the truth. Christians imbued all traditional cults and native beliefs, temples, and shrines with evil. This led to an association of paganism with the Devil and still contributes to modern views of ancient religions.

When we began to get Christian art, the church borrowed the elements of the god Pan in the portrayal of the Devil. Pan was half-man, half-goat and so the Devil was portrayed with horns and hooves. As a fertility god, Pan was often shown with a large, erect penis and this also became an aspect of the Devil, representing what the church thought of as evil in the traditional cults with their focus on fertility.

The second century saw the growth of a Christian obsession of relating personal sin to the Devil and his agents. This was particularly highlighted in church concepts of sexual intercourse. With their background in philosophy, the Church Fathers deemed human sexuality as a weakness of giving in to the urges of the physical body and a lack of self-control. While the first commandment of the Jewish Scriptures told humans to "be fruitful and multiply," nevertheless they saw "the flesh" as part of the degradation of the fall in Eden. The church proclaimed that all sexual intercourse was to be restricted solely to the procreation of children.

The medical knowledge at the time claimed that a woman could only get pregnant while lying on her back, receiving the semen in her womb as a receptacle. The church deemed this position as the only legitimate one for intercourse; any other position was deemed "lust," as the goal was not procreation. During the colonial period, missionaries from Europe encountered natives who had different habits and began teaching the correct position. Hence we have the origins of the term "the missionary position," with the man on top of the woman. This was a significant innovation with Christianity. Ancient cultures did not consider human sexuality a sin per se.

Celibacy and Virginity

The Gnostics were the first Christians to advocate **celibacy**, or not entering into a marriage contract. Celibacy was a legal issue, while chastity meant never having sexual intercourse. For Gnostics, celibacy was a way to stop more divine sparks from being trapped in physical bodies. The Church Fathers entwined both concepts, particularly for church leaders. Celibacy for church officials accomplished two goals: (i) In a system that promoted equality, celibacy elevated bishops above the masses and gave them a sense of sacredness in that they did not indulge "in the flesh"; (ii) in an era of increasing persecution, bishops who did not have an opportunity to die in the arenas were viewed as nevertheless having sacrificed a normal life for their beliefs.

However, the church recognized that growth was necessary. Other Christians should marry and have children. The Fathers copied the social conventions and morals of the dominant society, where the family remained the basic social unit for the church. The early communities had women leaders, apostles, prophets, teachers, and healers in their belief that all institutions would no longer be valid when the "kingdom" came. By the second century, and with the diminishing of an imminent return of Jesus, Christian women lost their leadership roles. Instead, women were confined to the ancient gender roles of wife and mother with no voice in the Christian assemblies.

This is also the period of the demonization of women by Christian writers, who claimed that because of their weaker and inferior status, women were consistently used by the Devil to lure men into sin. The view that women tried to control men through their sexuality was a concept of Greco-Roman culture. For Christians, the enormous phallus of the Devil was what attracted women to him to do his bidding. Women were also considered the most likely candidates to fall into heresy for this reason. The way in which a Christian woman could escape this evil was to remain a lifelong virgin. In other words, women had to renounce their gender roles and devote their life to the church. These ideas emerged in the later witch trials and executions of women in the Middle Ages.

Monasticism

The heights of celibacy and asceticism were reached by a movement that was begun by Anthony in Egypt (251–356 CE). He was a rich Christian who accepted the gospel admonition of Jesus to a young man "to go and sell all you own," and went to live in one of the caves in the Egyptian desert. He became famous for wrestling with the Devil every night. Others soon followed and they became known as "the Desert Fathers." One of them, Pachomias, decided to build housing which consisted of cell-like rooms. This became cenobite monasticism, which contained rules for living, working, and prayer. In late antiquity, Augustine and Benedict both visited the monasteries of Egypt and developed their own in North Africa and Italy.

Unlike Gnostics, the monastics did not consider the body evil (it was a gift from god), but recognized that it needed severe discipline so that it could not be tempted into sin. The daily schedule was to help the monks by keeping them busy at work and at prayer. By the middle of the fourth century, after persecution had ceased, a monk's vocation was considered "the new martyrdom." Monks had turned their backs on conventional society and sacrificed a normal life (a wife and children) in order to pray for others. It became an automatic assumption that when a monk died he would be exalted to Heaven among the saints.

Religious Calendar/Festivals

Christianity established a calendar that included annual religious festivals along the lines of the Greek and Roman systems. For the first three centuries the most important religious holiday was Easter. The emperor Constantine established the holiday of Christmas. We cannot historically pinpoint the time of Jesus's birth, but Constantine reworked the Roman Saturnalia as the festival time to celebrate the nativity. December 25 was also the traditional date of the birth of Mithras and was important in sun cults, so he combined many of these elements. It was from the Saturnalia that traditional customs such as family reunions, gift-giving, the hanging of evergreens, and expressions of goodwill became standard in Christmas celebrations.

By late antiquity either the birth date or the martyrdom date of saints was acknowledged in church calendars. With the exception of the sacrifices, the saint's day appears very similar to the religious festivals in antiquity. People gathered in churches and often carried the statue of the saint through the city streets. Food vendors and relic sellers took part, and businesses and courts were closed for the day. Saints are still honored in this way in Mediterranean countries and in Western culture. The summer church festivals in the United States continue this practice, but now add carnival rides and bingo.

By following the recognition of "the days of the dead," eventually November 1 became "All Saints' Day" and November 2 was remembered as "All Souls' Day," when Christians were to pray for the dead.

The Afterlife

The Christian concept of the afterlife derives from both ancient Jewish and Greco-Roman cultural traditions. The Jewish Scriptures rendered all the dead to an area known as *She'ol*. By at least 600 BCE, if not earlier, this idea was replaced by the concept of *Gehenna*. This word derived from the Valley of Himnon in western Jerusalem. It was reported that one of the Jewish kings, Manassah, built a temple to the Moabite god Molech on the western ridge above the valley. Molech was known for requiring child sacrifice. Allegedly, the statue had arms that would bend and lower the victim to fires that were kept constantly burning in the valley below. When this king was deposed, the Jews indicated their scorn for this foreign god by making the Valley of Himnon the city dump. City dumps are noted for their spontaneous fires. Hence, *Gehenna* became the place of the dead for all the wicked, where they would burn in eternal flames.

By the first century, the Hellenization of Jewish communities had exposed them to Greek views of Hades and the afterlife, and Hades is the general term for the place of the dead in the New Testament. The cultural Hellenization of the area also introduced dualism of the person, or the existence of a separate entity from the physical body known as the soul.

One of the sects of Judaism, the Pharisees, had taken the elements of the prophets concerning the final days and developed their own idea of what would happen at that time. After the final battle, they claimed, all the dead, both righteous and wicked, would be physically raised and judged. The wicked would suffer eternal damnation in *Gehanna* and the righteous would be given a utopian existence, a new Eden on earth. For the Pharisees, in order to either enjoy the delights of Eden or to physically suffer the torments of *Gehenna*, one needed a physical body. In the teachings of Jesus in the gospels, it appears that he shared this view of the Pharisees. Thus, Christianity adopted the Jewish idea of physical resurrection of the body and soul together.

The details of what eventually became the Christian hell were derived from some ancient Mesopotamian and Persian ideas of the underworld (where "the punishment fits the crime") and details from Vergil's descriptions in the *Aeneid*. A second-century text known as the *Apocalypse of Peter* is considered one of the first "tours of hell." It describes in graphic detail the punishment for each sin. For instance, liars are hung up by their tongues for eternity. Adulterers were castrated nightly, only to be fully formed the next day so that their ordeal could be repeated. This parallel between sin and punishment culminated in Dante's *Inferno* (1307), where he specified multiple layers of hell for each sin, moving downward to the center. The center of Hell was the area for what Dante considered the worst sin of all, betrayal, and thus the center of hell is shared with Satan by Brutus, Cassius, and Judas.

With the rise of Hellenism and Greek ideas of dualism of the person, ideas concerning Heaven began to change. With a soul that was not subject to decay, this was the part of a human that had the potential to enter the upper echelons of the universe. Christians adopted this idea of Heaven as the reward for the righteous.

Art

The first Christians were former Jews, and Judaism has a commandment against the proliferation of images of the divine (god and the angels). After the first and second generations, however, the dominant population of Christians consisted of former Greeks and Romans. It was only natural that the art of Christians followed the traditions of the dominant culture by assigning anthropomorphic elements and by celebrating the divine in frescos and statues.

Our earliest Christian art is found in the tombs and catacombs located outside the city walls. The catacombs reflect both images of Jesus as well as images of the traditional afterlife elements of Greco-Roman culture. With the Jewish background of Christianity, some tombs combined Jewish aniconic art such as animals, flowers, arks, etc. Jews also buried their dead in catacombs and therefore many of the art forms may have reflected shared culture between Jews and Christians. The tombs demonstrated the Christian predilection for stories from the Jewish Scriptures. A popular reference was the parallel to the story of Jonah and the whale and the resurrection of Jesus.

Catacomb art has several pictures of Jesus, sometimes shown as a clean-shaven young man and sometimes shown with a beard. The most common depiction is Jesus in his role as a wonder-worker, with the story of the raising of Lazarus highlighted (Figure XIII.1). The earliest known depiction shows Lazarus wrapped in Egyptian mummy wrappings, with Jesus holding the typical wonder-worker's wand as he touches the body.

Figure XIII.1   Jesus raising the dead with his wand. *Source*: akg-images/Pirozzi.

Another popular depiction was of a group of believers sitting at a table. When the catacombs were discovered in the modern period, it was assumed that this art depicted the Last Supper of Christian tradition. However, the frescoes do not show the requisite 12 men at the table, which was popular in later medieval art and sculpture. Most likely, these are pictures of men at the funeral feast of the dead Christian

A figure known as "the good shepherd" has traditionally been associated with Jesus and was taken from the metaphor in the gospel of John, "I am the good shepherd." The image depicts a young man with a lamb carried across his shoulders. However, the image is much older in Greek art, as *kriophoros*, or "the ram-bearer." This depiction was associated with Hermes, as Hermes Kriophoros, where the ram represented a proper sacrifice. With the gospel association, this image was borrowed by Christians in their interpretation of the true good shepherd (Figure XIII.2).

Until the fourth century, Christian art was limited to the catacombs. With the legalization of Christianity and the state funding of the building of churches, Constantine opened the door to patronage of Christian art, which now included statues and paintings. In his new capital of Constantinople, church buildings were infused with mosaic art. In the sixth and seventh centuries, the Italian city of Ravenna became the Western capital and the churches copied the mosaic art of Constantinople. These mosaics often depicted the Christian emperor with a halo surrounding his head (the halo of Helios, the sun god). The emperor stands in the center of 12 of his bishops, symbolically representing the emperor as standing in for Christ on earth until Jesus returns.

Figure XIII.2   The "good shepherd." *Source*: De Agostini/ Getty Images.

A significant mosaic from Ravenna demonstrates how far Christianity progressed from a small Jewish sect, to a persecuted minority, to triumph as the dominant religion of the Roman Empire. Jesus is dressed as a Roman legionary, holding a staff with a banner that reads in Latin, "I am the way, the truth and the life" (from John 14.6). In this portrait, we have the ancient fusion of church and state which continued until the period of the Enlightenment in the eighteenth century (Figure XIII.3).

The Council of Nicea and the Trinity

When the followers of Jesus began worshipping him as a god, Christians struggled with a problem that was related to their claim that they inherited the Jewish concept of only one god who was worthy of worship. At the same time, there was no clear understanding of the relationship between god and Jesus, as Christians claimed that Jesus was preexistent and present at creation.

Early in the fourth century, an elder in the church at Alexandria by the name of Arius proposed what became a controversial doctrine. Using simple logic,

Figure XIII.3   Ravenna mosaic of Christ dressed as Roman soldier. *Source:* CM Dixon/Print Collector/Getty Images.

he said that if you believe that god created everything in the universe (which Christians believed), then at some point he created Christ. This meant that Christ was subordinate to god. Riots arose over this in Alexandria and in other cities of the Empire.

In 325, Constantine called for a major conference to settle this issue and invited bishops to the city of Nicea (near Constantinople, which was not finished yet). Roughly 217 bishops attended, along with their entourages. Constantine's goal was church unity. How was the oneness of god (monotheism) to be maintained and yet his various aspects or personas (Christ and the Holy Spirit) accounted for?

The debate boiled down to two choices: was Christ *homoiousios*, an essence *like* the father's, or was he *homoousios*, of one substance *identical* to the father's? The Council opted for the second choice in that god and Christ were identical in substance and that Christ was a manifestation of god himself on earth. The creed was revised several times over the centuries, with a shortened version becoming popular with the Protestant Reformation and commonly known as the Apostles' Creed. See the box "The Nicene Creed (The Short Form)."

The creed was another innovation in Christian thinking. In the ancient world the concept of a creed did not exist. There was no central authority to dictate what everyone should believe. The Nicene Creed is rather long because the Council simultaneously declared specific items in contradistinction to Gnostic teaching. For instance, the Creed emphasizes that Jesus was born of a woman, suffered, died and was buried, against the Gnostic claim of Docetism. For Christians, the concept of the Trinity maintains their view of a monotheistic religion, although non-Christians find it confusing.

The Nicene Creed (The Short Form)

We believe in one God, the Father, the Almighty, maker of heaven and earth, of all that is seen and unseen.

We believe in one Lord, Jesus Christ, the only Son of God, eternally begotten of the Father, God from God, Light from Light, true God from true God, begotten, not made, one in Being with the Father.

Through him all things were made. For us men and for our salvation he came down from heaven: by the power of the Holy Spirit he was born of the Virgin Mary, and became man.

For our sake he was crucified under Pontius Pilate; he suffered, died, and was buried. On the third day he rose again in fulfillment of the Scriptures; he ascended into heaven and is seated at the right hand of the Father.

He will come again in glory to judge the living and the dead, and his kingdom will have no end.

We believe in the Holy Spirit, the Lord, the giver of life, who proceeds from the Father and the Son. With the Father and the Son he is worshipped and glorified. He has spoken through the prophets.

We believe in one holy, catholic and apostolic Church. We acknowledge one baptism for the forgiveness of sins. We look forward to the resurrection of the dead, and the life of the world to come. Amen.

The creed became the basis for the Catholic Church. "Catholic" was the Greek term for "universal," indicating that it was the system required of all Christians. The Catholic Church remained the only legal form of Christianity after 381 CE, until the Protestant Reformation of the sixteenth century under Martin Luther.

For modern Western Christianity, where a growing number of people no longer attend church services, many of the details of the faith remain fixed in formulaic repetitions, with little understanding of the historical roots of the concepts. Even without actual participation, our culture nevertheless maintains many of these elements as metaphors, particularly "sacrifice," "martyrdom," and "salvation." For those not participating, the concept of reward and punishment in the afterlife (variously construed in the modern world) remains embedded in our culture. In elements of shared religious concepts we can find ways in which to connect to our ancient ancestors.

Summary

- As a product of its culture, Christianity both maintained and altered the cultural and religious elements of ancient Greece and Rome. Convincing pagans to join the new movement entailed providing them with similar concepts and in some cases, similar practices.
- While centuries have passed, Christianity has nevertheless imbued Western culture with ancient elements that still find resonance in the human quest for meaning.

Suggestions for Further Reading

Brown, P. 2008. *The Body and Society: Men, Women, and Sexual Renunciation in Early Christianity*. Columbia University Press. An expert in late antiquity, Brown analyzes Christian views of the body and society in relation to Greco-Roman traditions and explains the turn to asceticism and monasticism.

Ehrman, B. 2014. *After the New Testament: 100–300 CE: A Reader in Early Christianity*, 2nd ed. Oxford University Press. This is an anthology of excerpts of the major Church Fathers with introductory essays on the various types of literature.

van Henten, J. W.. and Avemarie, F. 2002. *Martyrdom and Noble Death: Selected Texts from Graeco-Roman, Jewish and Christian Antiquity*. Routledge. This is an anthology of the literature of Judaism, Greece, Rome and Christianity on dying for one's beliefs.

Moss, C. 2013. *The Myth of Persecution: How Early Christians Invented a Story of Martyrdom*. HarperOne. While there are hundreds of surveys on Christian martyrdom, this book includes the evidence of how numbers and actions became the stuff of legends over time.

Pagels, E. 1989. *The Gnostic Gospels*. Vintage. This is a very readable introduction to Gnostic Christianity and the differences between those thinkers and the proto-orthodox communities.

Pagels, E. 1996. *The Origin of Satan: How Christians Demonized Jews, Pagans, and Heretics*. Vintage. This book traces the Persian and Hellenistic concepts of evil to the Devil of the early Church and discusses the process of demonization.

Stark, R. 1997. *The Rise of Christianity: How the Obscure, Marginal Jesus Movement Became the Dominant Religious Force in the Western World in a Few Centuries*. HarperCollins. This book has become a standard survey on the history of Christianity in the Roman Empire.

GLOSSARY

ablutions   ritual washings.

aedile   a magistrate in Rome responsible for the maintenance of temples, road contracts, commercial weights and measures, brothel and tavern regulations, and organizing games for religious festivals.

afterlife   the ancient belief that humans continue to exist in some form after death; the term also refers to a physical place.

agora   the central square of a Greek city; usually the center of religious festivals, government activities, and marketplaces.

allegory   a literary device of attributing symbolic or hidden meanings to a story or poem, usually resulting in new interpretations.

altar   the focus of worship where sacrificial offerings were placed or burned; altars were outside the temple.

amulet   an object that is believed to protect the user/wearer.

ancestor cult   an ancient belief that the dead ancestors retain the power to do good or harm to the descendants, which necessitated rituals of appeasement.

apatheia   unemotional, not showing passion; an ascetic principle of philosophers.

apotheosis   the exaltation of a mortal to the level of the divine.

apotropaic magic   "to turn away," rituals and prayers used to turn away the anger of the gods or bad luck.

archon   "ruler," often used collectively as the divine rulers of the universe.

asclepions   healing temples and medical complexes of the god Asclepios.

Greek and Roman Religions, First Edition. Rebecca I. Denova.
© 2019 John Wiley & Sons, Inc. Published 2019 by John Wiley & Sons, Inc.

askesis   "discipline," usually relating to the discipline of mind and body taught by the schools of philosophy; later adapted for Christian views of behavior and attitudes toward the body.

auctoritas   a Roman's "authority," or the level at which a man held enough sway to attract followers and influence; a Roman's "clout."

***augur*/augury**   the interpretation of omens and signs, particularly lightning and the flights of birds. An *augur* was a ritual expert in the knowledge and practice of the rituals.

augustales   Imperial priests of the state Lares cults instituted by Augustus.

bellonarii   the special priests of Bellona.

bestiarii   specially trained fighters for the animal hunts of the Venatio Games.

bulla*/*bullae   the amulets worn by young boys to protect them in childhood.

catacomb   "under the tombs," layered underground tombs.

catharsis   the releasing of suppressed emotions.

celibacy   the choice to not enter into a marriage contract.

cella   the inner area of temples that held the statue of the deity.

centuriate   an assembly organized in military centuries ("hundreds") and categories from which to recruit the army.

chthonic   relating to underneath the earth; the underworld land of the dead.

client   the recipient of a patron's favors and connections who was obligated to serve the needs of his benefactor.

collegia   "joined together," the term for associations of priestly officials, brotherhoods, and sometimes trade and craft guilds.

corpse contamination   the belief that dead bodies emit a noxious substance that contaminates the living; it requires rituals of ablution and prayers to remove.

cremation   the process of disposing of a dead body by burning it.

cult   from *cultus*, all the elements involved in the care and maintenance of the gods.

curia/curiae   a "gathering of men," in Rome the designation of various assemblies and voting blocs: the centuriate (organized in military "hundreds" from which to recruit the army), the Tribal Assembly (organized by ancestral tribes), and the Plebeian Assembly (organized by Roman citizens below the aristocracy).

cursus honorum   the "course of honor" in Rome for the regulated series of magistrate positions to eventually reach that of consul and then censor.

daemon   originally beneficial divinity or power sometimes associated with the spirits of the heroes, the term came to be associated with evil or disruptive intent in the word "demon."

dignitas   a Roman's public and private reputation, a sum of all his attributes and charisma; dignity.

di manes   the dead ancestors of Rome.

dissignatores   Roman funeral directors and organizers.

ekklesia   assembly, the Greek term for the ruling body in democratic Athens; the form adopted by early Christians for the structure of their communities and translated as "church."

ekphora   the Greek funeral procession.

ekstasis   "ecstasy," referring to the elation of being possessed by divinity.

ephebe   a Greek youth.

epiphany   a manifestation of divinity on earth.

epulones   priests of Jupiter in charge of the festivals and games for Jupiter.

equites   the knight class of Rome.

evocatio   the Roman calling on the god or goddess of an enemy or enemy city to desert them and come over to the Roman side; Rome promised to build a temple to the deity if he or she complied.

fetiales   special priests of Jupiter who advised the Senate on foreign affairs, approved treaties and declared war at the temple of Bellona.

flamen   priest or high-priest of Rome.

freedman/woman   a former slave who has been manumitted (freed).

funeral games   athletic games dedicated to the dead.

galli   the Roman name for the castrated priests of Magna Mater.

games   the common term applied to the combination of dramatic and athletic competition as part of the community religious festivals.

gift-exchange   in the earlier period of Greece, mutual benefactions between city-states; evolved to personal exchanges as part of hospitality.

gladiator games   the funeral games of Rome where trained fighters fought usually in pairs.

Gnostics   from the Greek, "gnosis"; Christians (and others) who claimed to have special knowledge of god and the universe that had been revealed to them; many elements were shared with the concepts of Greek philosophy.

gorgons   "horrifying" female powers, usually with snakes of hair, who terrorized humans.

haeresis/**heresy**   the term for a general philosophical school of thought; Christians later adopted "heresy" as a general term for all philosophical schools that disagreed with mainstream Christian teachings.

haruspex/*haruspices*   an expert ritual priest who could read and analyze the entrails of sacrificial animals.

Hellenism/Hellenistic   from Hellen, the traditional founder of Greece, the term is used as a descriptor of the concepts and ideas spread through the conquests of Alexander the Great.

helot   Spartan state slave, captured from neighboring territories.

hermai   boundary statues with a bust of Hermes and a phallus as a protector.

hieroglyphs   Greek for "sacred writings," the term used by Herodotus to describe the language of ancient Egypt.

hierophany   an experience of an encounter with the divine.

hieros gamos   either a symbolic or literal sexual ritual reenacted between two deities or a god or goddess and a human; rituals that were used to validate kingship in ancient Mesopotamia.

hieroskopia   the art of divination in ancient Greece that included seers, *augurs* and *haruspices*.

honor and shame   the sociological understanding of one's personal status, worth, and public reputation. Traditional and conventional behavior brought honor to you and your extended family, while acts of dishonor or shame went against your legacy.

hymn   a prayer of praise to a deity often set to music.

icon   "image," most often referring to an image of gods or goddesses in carvings, statues, paintings, frescoes, and votives.

idolatry   the worships of idols; a collective term for the worship of gods not your own.

immolatio   the burning of the proper parts of a sacrifice.

imperium   the power and authority granted to levels of magistrates in Rome; the source derived from the center located in the middle of the *pomerium*, and so considered sacred.

impiety   lacking respect or reverence for the gods.

incubation   a ritual procedure of sleeping at the temple of a god, hoping for a visitation.

inhumation   the burying of a dead body.

initiation   special rituals and ceremonies for membership; most often required in the Mysteries.

invocation   calling upon a god or goddess by name.

katabasis   a descent, most often a descent into Hades.

kykeon   the vessel or the special drink at Eleusis that may or may not have produced hallucinogenic experiences

lararium   the household shrine containing the family Lares.

Lares   Roman guardian deities of the family and home.

lectisternium   a propitiatory feast offered to the gods of Rome in which statues of the deities were placed on couches and served.

lemures   Roman shades of the dead; ghosts.

libation   a liquid offering, usually wine, milk or honey.

liknon   a sacred basket that usually carries hidden things; most often associated with the Mysteries.

lituus   an *augur*'s wand for pointing to the sky.

ludi   collectively, "games," most often referring to the athletic games and drama festivals of religious festivals.

luperci   members of the priests who organized and participated in the feast of the Lupercalia; *luperci quintilii* represented Romulus and the *luperci fabii* represented Remus.

lustratio   a purification ritual of the land, usually done on farms.

maenad   the female follower of Dionysus.

magoi/magus   "wisemen," most often translated as "magician."

manumission   the freeing of slaves.

martyr   from the Greek for "witness," or "testifier"; someone who was willing to die rather than compromise their beliefs or practices.

miasma   the noxious substance that emanates from a dead body.

mithraea   temples to the god Mithra.

mola salsa   the Roman ritual cakes used in sacrifices.

monotheism   in modern usage, the belief in the existence of only one god.

mos maiorum   "the way of the ancestors (elders)"; the way things have always been done in Rome, particularly relating to religious rituals, social conventions and mores.

munera/munera sine missione   a gladiatorial funeral game where fighters fight to the death.

mysterion   "things unknown," the source of the word "mystery"; the descriptor for cults with initiation rituals and membership that required never sharing the secrets of the cult.

myth   for our purposes, a traditional story about the gods, heroes, ethnic groups, and foundations of cities and towns.

necromancy   the attempt to communicate with or call up the dead for purposes of revenge, predicting the future, or appealing to the dead to stop haunting.

necropolis   "city of the dead"; a cemetery.

numen/numina   the ancient Roman concept of invisible divine powers that invade the minds and world of humans; *numina* had no form.

omen   usually a phenomenon of nature understood as a sign from a god or goddess.

oracle   a vehicle for the words of a deity through possession; also the site where an oracle operated.

orgia   generally, Greek for "ritual," but often associated with the ecstatic state and ecstatic rituals of Mystery cults; our modern word "orgy" derives from this.

orthodoxy   "correct belief"; a Christian innovation that claimed that there were absolute truths in their system and that having correct beliefs was an essential element of Christian salvation.

pagan   derived from *paganoi*, a later derogatory term coined by Christians to refer to those not yet converted to Christianity; the term came to represent all people who were not Jews or Christians.

paideia   a descriptor of the education of the higher classes; higher culture.

paterfamilias   "head of the family," in ancient Rome. The *paterfamilias* had control over all members of the extended family.

patria potestas   "the power of the father," which refers to the father's standing in the family unit in ancient Rome. The "power" refers to the potential of the semen.

patricians   the aristocracy of Rome, by tradition descended from the first families to settle in Rome.

patron/client   this was the way in which "things got done." According to tradition, the upper classes worked with the lower classes in a mutual exchange of benefits for all.

patron deity   usually an older, local god or goddess who provided protection (as a *patronus*) and benefits for a community that was obligated to provide worship and maintenance of the cult.

pax deorum   "the peace of the gods," generally understood to be the goal of the state or governing magistrates of Rome.

pax romana   "the peace of Rome," the period of peace proclaimed by Augustus after the civil wars.

pederasty   the socially accepted Greek relationship between an older mentor and a younger male.

Penates   the invisible guardian spirits that guarded all the cupboards and storerooms of the house and farm.

phratry   "brotherhood" in Greece; social group connected by tribe or clan; association of beneficial connections.

pilgrimage   a religious journey of achieving a benefit from a deity at a shrine or temple, which also includes spiritual rejuvenation.

Plebeian Assembly   the non-aristocratic, citizen body of Rome which had the power to enact laws and veto the Senate.

plebeians   the non-aristocratic class of Rome; eventually they shared priest-hoods and magistrate positions with the patricians.

polytheism   the belief in the existence of many gods.

pomerium   the boundary drawn by Romulus around the hills of Rome; everything within the boundary was deemed sacred.

pontifex maximus   the high-priest of Rome, holding supervision over all the priestly colleges and rituals; originally appointed by the patricians but elected in the late Republic.

pontifices   the highest of the various priesthoods in Rome; the College of *Pontifices* was responsible for the oversight of all other priests and rituals.

prodigy   abnormal phenomenon of nature that was understood as an omen, as well as an unusual occurrence (a statue sweating); collections of prodigies were kept and interpreted in times of war or crisis.

prophet   a spokesperson for a deity; most commonly referring to the god of Israel; vehicles for the words of the deity.

propitiation sacrifices   sacrifices offered to appease a god, usually from anger.

prothesis   the laying out of the body in a Greek funeral.

psychopompos   a guide of souls to the place of the dead.

purification rituals   specific rituals to restore ritual purity of a person or place.

puticuli   the public burial pits for the poor and slaves on the Esquiline Hill in Rome.

Quirites   another name for Romans.

reincarnation   the belief that dead souls are reborn into another form.

relics   the body parts and artifacts of dead Christian martyrs that became the object of worship in Christianity.

religio licta   "legal religion," coined by the Church Father Tertullian in the second century; it is used to refer to the fact that religious brotherhoods and clubs needed permission from the Senate to assemble.

res publica   perhaps meaning "public matter," the term entails all the elements in the governance of Rome; the Roman Republic describes the elements as well as this period in Rome's history.

rex sacrorum   a vestige of ancient Roman religion, the "king of sacred rites" that was traditionally assigned by King Numa and retained during the Republic.

ritus graecus   ritual "in the Greek manner," usually referring to rituals with the head uncovered.

sacred space   any area understood to be touched by divinity, such as mountaintops, woods, caves, rivers, as well as temples and shrines.

sacrifice   the offering up of something of value; in the ancient world most sacrifices consisted of animals, crops, oil, wheat, and wine.

sacrilege   doing harm or damage to anything considered sacred.

salii   the "leaping" priests of the cult of Mars.

satyr   fertility character, half-man, half-goat; associated with Dionysus.

secondary burial   the practice of collecting bones and moving them to make room for future burials.

seers   a collective term for religious experts who served as *augurs*, *haruspices*, or others who claimed to read and interpret omens; also a term for those who claimed to predict the future.

senatus consulta   the official decrees of the Senate housed in the temple of Ceres.

serapeum   a temple to the god Serapis which also included worship to Osiris and Isis.

sibyl   a female seer or prophetess who was possessed by the divine.

sodales   associations of priests organized by the state to organize festivals and games dedicated to one particular god or goddess.

sorceress   sometimes semidivine, a woman who generally used her powers for evil intent; often translated as witch.

sortition   the ancient system of "casting lots" to determine the selection of some priesthoods and juries.

stele   a stone marker, usually found at boundaries and as a funeral monument.

suovetaurilia   a sacrifice of a pig, sheep, and a bull.

syncretism   the combining of two or more religious concepts and practices resulting in either renewed interpretations or a new religious system.

taurobolium   the ritual of standing beneath a bull when its throat is cut and being soaked in blood.

tauroctony   the image of Mithras slaying a bull.

theurgy   "divine working," usually for unification with the divine with out-of-body experiences.

thyrsos   ritual wand used in the festivals for Dionysus.

toga virilis   the toga of manhood donned as a puberty rite of passage in Rome.

traditional cults   the preferred term for the ancestral customs of peoples, rather than "pagan."

tutelary god   guardian patron of a particular place, geographic region, ethnic group, and individual.

venatio   the animal hunts of the amphitheaters.

Vestal Virgins   the priestesses of the cult of Vesta responsible for keeping the eternal flame and other ritual duties in the state cults.

votive/votive offering   any object that was offered as a sacrifice or dedicated to the gods; an inscription in stone thanking a god for a benefaction.

wonder-workers   *magoi* who claimed to do miracles.

ziggurats   the main temple and temple complexes of ancient Sumer and Mesopotamia; stepped pyramid structures.

INDEX

Greek and Roman Religions, First Edition. Rebecca I. Denova.
© 2019 John Wiley & Sons, Inc. Published 2019 by John Wiley & Sons, Inc.